D1737246

The Shtetl

ELIE WIESEL CENTER FOR JUDAIC STUDIES SERIES

General Editor: Steven T. Katz

The Shtetl: New Evaluations
Edited by Steven T. Katz

The Shtetl

New Evaluations

EDITED BY

Steven T. Katz

NEW YORK UNIVERSITY PRESS

NEW YORK AND LONDON

NEW YORK UNIVERSITY PRESS
New York and London
www.nyupress.org
© 2007 by New York University
All rights reserved

Library of Congress Cataloging-in-Publication Data
Katz, Steven T., 1944-
The shtetl : new evaluations / edited by Steven T. Katz.
p. cm. — (Elie Wiesel Center for Judaic Studies series)
Includes bibliographical references and index.
ISBN-13: 978-0-8147-4801-5 (cloth : alk. paper)
ISBN-10: 0-8147-4801-5 (cloth : alk. paper)
1. Jews—Europe, Eastern—Social conditions. 2. Jews—Europe, Central—
Social conditions. 3. Shtetls. 4. Europe, Eastern—Ethnic relations. 5.
Europe, Central—Ethnic relations. I. Title.
DS135.E8K38   2006
305.892'4043709041—dc22   2006022419

New York University Press books are printed on acid-free paper,
and their binding materials are chosen for strength and durability.
Manufactured in the United States of America
10 9 8 7 6 5 4 3 2 1

Contents

Editor's Note

Steven T. Katz

The Shtetl: New Evaluations is the first volume in a new series sponsored by the Elie Wiesel Center for Judaic Studies at Boston University. Its subject reflects the deep concern of the Elie Wiesel Center to promote and foster the study and analysis of the central aspects of the Jewish past and present in all their richness and diversity.

As the Director of the Center and the editor of this volume, I have the pleasure of thanking a number of individuals whose help and hard work made this publication a reality. First, I want to publicly acknowledge the financial support of Mr. Mike Grossman, who created an endowment through the Marilyn and Mike Grossman Foundation to support the activities of the Center. His recent death is a great loss—as we remember him, we are sure that "his memory will be for a blessing." Second, the active and continuous interest in, and support of, the conference that preceded this volume by Elie Wiesel was very important to its success. Professor Wiesel participated in the vigorous discussions that led to the choice of subject, was active in thinking about the actual form that the proceedings should take, and agreed to provide a paper based, in large part, on his own life experience. Third, I want to thank all the scholars who participated and whose work appears in this collection. Each and everyone was a pleasure to work with. Fourth, I am especially indebted to Professor Samuel Kassow, a distinguished historian of Eastern European Jewry, for undertaking the task of writing the Introduction to the volume. His erudition, displayed both in his Introduction and his chapter on Interwar Poland, is abundantly evident. His willingness to share his knowledge so freely is very much appreciated. Fifth, a special thank you must be extended to Professor Yehuda Bauer of the Hebrew University. Professor

Bauer, whose current research is centered on the fate of the Jews in the shtetls of Eastern Europe during the Holocaust, agreed to contribute a chapter to the volume describing the horrific "end of this story." His long personal friendship and scholarly cooperation on this, and many other projects, is much appreciated.

I also wish to acknowledge the help of Ms. Pagiel Czoka, the Administrative Assistant at the Elie Wiesel Center. Without her dedicated and unflagging commitment, the conference and this book project would not have happened. All the practical aspects of these undertakings—which worked flawlessly—were planned and overseen by her. In addition, she did considerable work on the index of this volume. I am very much in her debt.

Lastly, a public expression of gratitude goes to my wife, Rebecca, who helped in this as in all my scholarly undertakings.

Introduction

Samuel Kassow

During the past thirty years the shtetl has attracted a growing amount of serious scholarly attention. Gross generalizations and romanticized nostalgia still affect discussions of the subject; indeed few terms conjure up as many stereotypes as "the shtetl." Nonetheless, serious students of history, anthropology, architecture, and literature have begun to apply their multidisciplinary insights to describing and understanding this most important facet of East European Jewish life. This volume is just one example of this new scholarship on the shtetl. Included within it, however, are chapters that encompass a variety of approaches—political history, religious history, demographic and literary studies—as well as substantial contributions to many traditional areas of research.

In Yiddish *shtetl* (plural: *shtetlekh*) means a "small town." There were hundreds of them, and no two were alike. The term "shtetl" connoted a Jewish settlement with a large and compact Jewish population who differed from their gentile, mostly peasant, neighbors in religion, occupation, language, and culture. Although strictly speaking the shtetl grew out of the private market towns of the Polish nobility in the old Commonwealth, over time "shtetl" became a common term for any small town in Eastern Europe with a large Jewish population: These included non-noble towns in Poland, as well as towns in Ukraine, Hungary, Bessarabia, Bukovina and the Sub-Carpathian region that attracted sizeable Jewish immigration during the course of the eighteenth and nineteenth centuries.

Underlying the social framework of the shtetl were interlocking networks of economic and social relationships: the interaction of Jews and peasants in the market, the coming together of Jews for essential communal and religious functions, and, in the twentieth century, the increasingly vital relationship between the shtetl and its emigrants (organized in *lands-manshaftn*). No shtetl stood alone. Each was part of a local and regional economic system that embraced other shtetlekh, provincial towns, and cities.

For all their diversity, shtetlekh differed in many important respects from previous forms of Jewish Diaspora communities in Babylonia, France, Spain, or Germany. In these other countries Jews rarely formed a majority of the town. This was not true of the shtetl, where Jews sometimes comprised 80 percent or more of the population.

Two aspects of the shtetl experience, besides religion, were especially important in shaping the character of East European Jewry. One was demographic concentration, the impact of living in a community where Jews often formed a majority. The other was the language of the shtetl, Yiddish. In Germany or Spain, Jews basically spoke the same language as their neighbors, albeit with Hebrew expressions and idiomatic and syntactical peculiarities. But in Eastern Europe, the Yiddish speech of the shtetl was markedly different from the languages used by the mostly Slavic peasantry. (Obviously in some regions, such as Lithuania, Rumania, and Hungary, peasants were also non-Slavs.) To see the shtetl as an entirely Jewish world is wrong, and many of the chapters in this book stress that point. Nonetheless, Yiddish strengthened the Jews' conviction that they were profoundly different from their neighbors.

Occupational diversity also set off the shtetl off from previous forms of Diaspora settlement. While in other lands, Jews often clustered in a few occupations, often determined by legal constraints, in the shtetl, Jewish occupations ran the gamut from wealthy contractors and entrepreneurs to shopkeepers, carpenters, shoemakers, tailors, teamsters, and water carriers. Scattered in the surrounding countryside were Jewish farmers and villagers. Much of the vitality of shtetl society stemmed from this striking occupational diversity, which also helped nurture a rich folk culture—and sharpened social tensions.

The Origins of the Shtetl

Shtetlekh originated in the lands of the old Polish-Lithuanian Commonwealth, where the nobility, having become quite powerful by the middle of the sixteenth century, invited Jews to settle their estates and stimulate economic development. After the union of Poland and Lithuania in 1569, the

Commonwealth expanded eastward just as export markets flourished for timber, grain, amber, furs, and honey. Eager for economic gain and anxious to raise cash to buy foreign luxury goods, the Polish nobles needed competent managers and entrepreneurs—as well as regular markets and fairs on their estates. They found that the Jews were ideal partners, especially because their pariah status in Christian Europe ensured that they could never become dangerous political rivals. This symbiosis of nobles and Jews produced the *arenda* (leasing) system, wherein landlords leased key economic functions to a Jewish agent (*arendar*), who in turn engaged other Jews in a varied and complicated network of sub-leases.[1]

One particularly important aspect of the *arenda* system was the sale and manufacture of alcoholic beverages. Largely in Jewish hands, the liquor trade generated much needed cash and gave landlords an important hedge against falling grain prices in export markets. In time, the Jewish tavern keeper would became a stock figure of the East European countryside, a link between the Jewish world and the local peasantry, a source of news and rumors, someone whom the peasants would regard— depending on the circumstances—both as a familiar confidant and as a despised exploiter. In the Ukraine, especially, the Jews would find themselves resented as the agents of the hated Polish nobility.

In order to persuade Jews to settle on their estates, the nobility established private market towns, called *miasteczko* in Polish and *shtetlekh* in Yiddish. Faced with growing competition from Christian guilds in the cities and towns of western Poland, many Jews preferred to go to these new towns that were sprouting in the eastern regions of the Polish-Lithuanian Commonwealth (today's eastern Poland, Ukraine, Belarus, and Lithuania). As Gershon David Hundert shows in his contribution to this volume, by the mid-eighteenth century, more than 70 percent of the Polish Jewish population lived in the eastern half of the Commonwealth.

These shtetlekh—all built around a central market square—reflected an emerging socio-economic microsphere that brought together nobles, Jews, and the surrounding peasantry. One important contribution of Israel Bartal's chapter, "Imagined Geography: The Shtetl, Myth, and Reality," is to remind us that both in terms of physical space and in terms of population, the shtetl was far from the exclusive Jewish world portrayed by many important Yiddish writers. Usually one side of the market square would feature a Catholic church, built by the local landlord as a symbol of primacy and ownership. Once a week, the bustling market day would bring together Jews and peasants in a web of ties that were both economic and personal. As the Jews settled in these new towns, they received charters from the landlords that promised them protection and that precluded markets on the Sabbath or on Jewish holidays. With their synagogues, Jewish schools, *mikvaot* (ritual baths), cemeteries, and inns, the shtetlekh also became bases for the numerous Jews who would fan out to the surrounding villages as carpenters, shoemakers, and agents. Many Jews who lived lonely lives in the countryside as tavern keepers or leaseholders could come to the shtetl for major holidays and important family occasions.

While many shtetlekh date from the sixteenth century, recent scholarship (the work of Adam Teller, for example) has shown that their establishment in the Polish-Lithuanian Commonwealth became especially marked in the second half of the seventeenth century, following the ravages of the Cossack insurrection and the Swedish invasion.[2] Battered by these economic and political shocks, the Polish nobles tried to regain their standing through even greater economic cooperation with the Jews. The new shtetlekh indeed helped the Polish economy recover from the shocks of the mid-seventeenth century—even though in the nineteenth and twentieth centuries some anti-Semitic Polish historians would argue that the extensive network of shtetlekh retarded the growth of Polish cities and acted as a brake on the overall economy.[3]

Significantly enough, this new upsurge of shtetl development took place just as Polish Jewry experienced a marked increase in numbers, from 175,000 in the late sixteenth century to more than 750,000 by the mid-1700s. In his chapter on "The Importance of Demography and Patterns of Settlement for an Understanding of the Jewish Experience in East–Central Europe," Professor Gershon David Hundert properly stresses the political and psychological implications of this impressive numerical increase. It was hardly accurate, Hundert contends, to see Jews as a tiny minority when they comprised such a large percentage of the settlements in which they lived. Furthermore, Hundert argues, the Jewish population was expanding faster than the Christian. Hundert believes that multiple causes explained this: better systems of social support in the Jewish community; the relative stability of the Jewish family; lower rates of alcoholism and sexually transmitted diseases; and the custom of early marriage.

After the partitions of Poland between 1772 and 1795, Russia, Hapsburg Austria, and Prussia took over the world's largest Jewish community. Created and nurtured in the specific socio-economic and political realities of the Polish-Lithuanian Commonwealth, the Jewish shtetl now faced entirely new challenges. With the Polish nobility severely weakened by the unsuccessful anti-Russian uprisings of 1830–31 and 1863, their Jewish part-ners—a mainstay of the shtetl economy—also suffered. A further blow to the economic power of the Polish nobility was the abolition of serfdom. Railroads and urban development fostered new regional and national markets that undercut the economic base of many shtetlekh. As peasants became more politically conscious and assertive, they often created coop-erative movements that damaged the shtetlekh economy. A salient feature in many shtetlekh was the steady growth of the non-Jewish population; in many towns Jews lost their majority status.

Prussian Poland had had few shtetlekh to begin with, and over time, most Jews there emigrated westward. In Hapsburg Galicia, Jews suffered from a harsh economy but benefited from the relatively liberal political regime established after 1867.

In the Russian Empire, on the other hand, Jews suffered from severe political restrictions. A creature of the old Polish-Lithuanian Common-wealth, the shtetl was foreign to Russian experience and to Russian law. After all, the Jews did not come to Russia: Russia came to the Jews when it took over much of Poland.[4] In Russia proper, smaller towns had been pri-marily administrative centers rather than market towns, which many Russian officials regarded as a sinister bridgehead of Jewish corruption in the countryside.

The policy of the Russian government toward the Jews alternated between a desire to assimilate them on the one hand and to limit their contact with the non-Jewish population on the other. The Tsarist govern-ment was especially determined to keep Jews away from the Great Russian peasantry. In 1791 the Empress Catherine decided to limit Russia's Jewish population largely to the former Polish provinces, and in April of 1835 the Pale of Settlement was formalized by a decree of Tsar Nicholas I. (Con-gress Poland would have a separate legal status.) While certain categories of Jews would eventually receive permission to live in the Russian interior, the earlier Russian residence laws remained in force until 1917. Therefore, on the eve of World War I, well over 90 percent of Russian Jewry was still living in the Pale.

While many observers stressed the ongoing decline of the shtetl during the course of the nineteenth century, residence restrictions and population growth both ensured that in absolute terms, the shtetl population increased. This happened even in the face of massive migration to new urban centers (Odessa, Warsaw, Lodz, Vienna) and emigration to the United States and other countries. Many shtetlekh even showed surprising economic resilience. The shtetl suffered terribly during World War I and during the waves of pogroms that swept the Ukraine in 1905 and in 1918–1921. Nevertheless, it was only the Holocaust that finally destroyed it.

Defining the Shtetl

What was a shtetl? Yiddish distinguishes between a *shtetl* (a small town), a *shtetele* (a tiny town), a *shtot* (a city), a *dorf* (a village), and a *yishev* (a tiny rural settlement). But these terms are obviously quite vague.

Scholars have been hard pressed to agree on an acceptable definition. John Klier compared the task of defining a shtetl to Hamlet's discussion with Polonius on the shape of a cloud in the sky: now a camel, now a weasel, now a whale.[5] In his essay in this volume on "Agnon's Synthetic Shtetl," Arnold Band regards the shtetl as a "problematic term, open to a host of interpretations":

> More often than not, the "shtetl" is an imagined construct based on literary description either in Hebrew or in Yiddish, and even when treated by historians, it is the product of historiographic reconstruction, by no means free of imagining. As such, the "shtetl" is less a specific place than a shorthand way of referring to the life of Jews in Eastern Europe in the late-nineteenth and early twentieth centuries. In this sense the "shtetl" is always a synthesis of facts, memory, and imagination.

For Elie Wiesel the problem of definition is only slightly less troublesome. In his essay "The World of the Shtetl," he asks:

> What makes a place inhabited by Jews . . . a shtetl? Literally the word means "a small city." So it may be accurate to call a city of ten or fifteen thousand Jews a shtetl. But what about a locality of only two thousand? Or a village numbering no more than 120?

In my chapter in this volume, I offer my own, admittedly imprecise definition, which differs somewhat from Wiesel's:

> In defining a shtetl, the following clumsy rule probably holds true: a shtetl was big enough to support the basic network of institutions that was essential to Jewish communal life—at least one synagogue, a *mikveh* [a ritual

bath], a cemetery, schools, and a framework of voluntary associations that performed basic religious and communal functions. This was a key difference between the shtetl and even smaller villages, and the perceived cultural gap between shtetl Jews and village Jews (*yishuvniks*) was a prominent staple of folk humor. On the other hand, what made a shtetl different from a provincial city was that the shtetl was a face-to-face community. It was small enough for almost everyone to be known by name and nickname. Nicknames could be brutal and perpetuated a system that one observer called the "power of the shtetl" to assign everyone a role and a place in the communal universe.

That the shtetl was a face to face community also underscored how it differed from a provincial city.[6] In Yisroel Oksenfeld's cutting satire of shtetl life, *The Headband* (*Shterntikhl*),[7] a city is distinguished from a shtetl by the fact that "everyone boasts that he greeted someone from the next street because he mistook him for an out-of-towner." Of course a new railroad could quickly turn a sleepy shtetl into a bustling provincial city— while a major city like Berdichev could become "an overgrown shtetl" (to quote the Yiddish writer Mendele Moykher Sforim), largely because the rail network bypassed it.

Legally and politically, there was no such thing as a shtetl. Jews had no say in establishing the legal status of localities, and the term "shtetl" meant nothing to non-Jews. What Jews called a shtetl might be a city, a town, a settlement, or a village in Polish, Russian, or Austrian law. In the Commonwealth, Polish law defined a *miasteczko* (small town), but not every *miasteczko* had enough Jews to earn the unofficial sobriquet of a shtetl.[8] In Tsarist Russia, the ruling senate established the "small town" (*mestechko*) as a legal category in 1875. A *mestechko* lacked the legal status of a city but also differed from a village in that it had a legal body of small-town dwellers (*meshchanskoe obshchestvo*). Such legal distinctions assumed vital importance for Russian Jewry after the 1882 May Laws forbade Jews to settle in villages, even in the Pale of Settlement. The Jews' right to stay in the shtetlekh where they had lived for generations depended on whether their home was classified as a town or as a village.[9] Handsome bribes often influenced the outcome, and lawsuits that contested these legal classifications flooded the Russian senate. According to the 1897 Russian census, 33.5 percent of the Jewish population lived in these "small towns," but the shtetl population was probably much higher since many legal cities were actually shtetlekh.

Even when Jews formed a majority of the population, they hardly ever controlled local government. In the Commonwealth the nobles were usually the local masters, although Jews had many ways to protect their interests. The Tsars were never prepared to tolerate Jewish control of either urban or town government, unlike the post-1867 Hapsburg Empire, where many Galician towns were headed by Jewish mayors (who often did the bidding of the local Polish nobility). In interwar Poland it was often the case that even where Jews formed a majority of the voting population, the local authorities found ways to guarantee—by annexing surrounding areas or by subtle pressure—a Jewish minority in the local town councils.

In the period of the Polish-Lithuanian Commonwealth, internal Jewish government was in the hands of the *kehilla*, a legally recognized local Jewish community with its own *kahal* (community board) ruled by an oligarchy based on wealth and learning. A *kehilla*, which collected taxes, supervised basic communal responsibilities; linked to a wider network of Jewish institutions, it was not necessarily a shtetl. For financial reasons a *kehilla* might include several shtetlekh; conversely, new shtetlekh would try to end their subordinate status and set up their own local *kehilla*. A key mark of independence became the right to establish a separate cemetery, which ensured that burial fees stayed within the shtetl.

Whatever the legal status of the *kehilles* under Russian and Hapsburg rule happened to be (and this is a complicated question), some type of internal Jewish communal government remained—even after the formal abolition of the *kahal* in Russia in 1844—and these bodies, whatever they were called, continued to perform important communal functions.[10] In interwar Poland, a 1928 law established popularly elected *kehilles* in both small towns and larger cities. These elections, however, often led to bitter disagreements and outside interference by the Polish authorities.

The World of the Shtetl

One common stereotype of the shtetl—especially popular with those who never lived there—was that it was a warm and cozy community, steeped in a common tradition that linked rich and poor. Stereotypes often possess a grain of truth but this one ignores many negative features of shtetl life. The shtetl could be a cruel place, especially to those who lacked status: the poor, those with little education, and those who performed menial jobs. Those at the bottom of the pecking order—shoemakers, water carriers, or girls from very poor families—were constantly reminded of their humble position. Sanitary standards were low, and living conditions could be dirty and squalid. Foreign travelers who toured the Pale in the nineteenth century pointed out the ugly and wretched physical appearance of the shtetlekh they passed. Spring and fall were the seasons when the rains turned the unpaved streets into seas of *blote* (mud). A hot summer's day in the shtetl would bring a rich admixture of fragrances from raw sewage, outhouses, and the leavings of hundreds of horses that graced the central square on market days. Educational facilities, especially for poorer children, could be shockingly bad. The whole system of nicknames served as a reminder that the shtetl was a community quick to judge and often harsh and merciless in its collective humor.

In both travelers' accounts and in Yiddish literature, descriptions of the physical layout of the shtetl stressed how houses seemed neglected and crowded together, perhaps a reflection of the fact that in many shtetlekh, gentile farms constricted the space available for possible expansion. Building codes were often non-existent and at any rate could be easily bypassed through bribes, especially in the Russian Empire. Shtetl buildings were usually wooden, although the local *gvir* (rich man) might occupy a *moyer* (brick building) on the market square.[11] Fires were common and became a major theme of shtetl folklore and Yiddish literature. Perhaps, as Israel Bartal's provocative chapter implies, many shtetlekh belied this stereotype of the ugly jumble and were in fact well planned and well laid out by their Polish founders. But it could also be that the physical deterioration of many shtetlekh, noted by travelers, reflected the declining power of the Polish nobility in the last half of the nineteenth century.

During the course of the nineteenth and twentieth centuries a whole array of disparate critics—*maskilim* (proponents of the Jewish Enlightenment), Zionists, Bundists, Soviet Jewish Communists—all subjected the shtetl to scathing criticism and predicted its demise.[12] The shtetl, they charged, was a dying community, trapped in the grip of stultifying tradition and doomed to economic collapse. These criticisms, while not entirely untrue, revealed as much about the ideology of their authors as they did about the reality of the shtetl. The reality was more complex, and to understand it one has to consider both historical context and critical regional variations.

When one looks at the shtetl without sentimental nostalgia or ideological prejudice, it is clear that for all its weaknesses, the shtetl also had many strengths—as Elie Wiesel reminds us in "The World of the Shtetl." Even on the eve of World War II, after a century of economic and cultural change, religious tradition remained the single most important factor that determined the culture of the shtetl. (The Soviet Union is a separate case.)[13] To be sure, religious culture reflected important regional variations. Shtetlekh with a strong Hasidic presence were quite different from shtetlekh in Lithuania with few if any Hasidim. Shtetlekh with a major yeshiva— Volozhin (in the nineteenth century), Mir, or Kleck—were far better situated to resist secularization than those that did not attract rabbis and students from far and wide.

During the course of the eighteenth and nineteenth centuries the religious world of East European Jewry was affected by two major revolutionary developments: the Hasidic movement, commonly associated with the Baal Shem Tov, and the rise of a new ethos of learning, linked to the legacy of the Vilna Gaon and his disciple Khaim Volozhiner. It was Khaim Volozhiner who founded the Volozhin yeshiva, a prototype for a new kind of Lithuanian yeshiva.[14]

Despite its major impact on Jewish life, the history and development of the Hasidic movement raises many issues that still await further scholarly research. One of the most significant findings of recent scholarship has been a revision of the view that had regarded early Hasidism as a protest movement linked largely to the poorer strata of Jewish society.[15] Another major development has been the intersection of research into the history of the shtetl and of the Hasidic movement to demonstrate the organizational and the socio-political as well as the ideological reasons for the movement's success.[16]

The rise of the two movements, Hasidism and the new ethos of Lithuanian Jewish learning, heightened regional differences between Lithuanian Jewry, where Hasidism was weak, and the Jews of Galicia, Podolia, Volhynia, and Congress Poland, where Hasidism established a strong base. While it is beyond the purview of this introduction to discuss the actual nature of Hasidism or the world of the Lithuanian yeshivas, it should be noted that both movements served to integrate shtetl Jews into the wider Jewish community. Hasidic Jews in the shtetl would leave their families on major holidays and journey to distant towns to be with their rebbe. There, they would pass their time with other Hasidism from different regions and establish personal bonds that would result in marriages and business deals.

By the same token, the establishment of yeshivas in a small shtetl would bring in new influences, a new ethos, and, often, marked tensions. In his chapter on "A Shtetl with a Yeshiva: The Case of Volozhin," Immanuel Etkes examines the "town-gown" tensions between the shtetl Jews of Volozhin and the outside students who came to study at this elite yeshiva. The Volozhin yeshiva differed from previous yeshivas in that it enjoyed financial independence from the local community, did not answer to local leaders, and had a great deal more prestige. (In short, it was a national "Ivy-league" university rather than a local community college.) Etkes shows that on the whole, during the heyday of the Volozhin yeshiva, the yeshiva students regarded the shtetl Jews with arrogance and condescension. Etkes uses the example of Volozhin to argue that the new Lithuanian Jewish scholarly elite, unlike other Jewish elites that developed during the course of the nineteenth century (maskilim, Zionists, socialists), was much more inward looking and less interested in reaching out to and affecting the wider Jewish community. Nevertheless, the townspeople seem to have accepted the slights as an unavoidable price of hosting such a prestigious center of learning.

The rise of new political parties and ideologies also promoted the integration of the shtetl with the wider Jewish world. In his chapter on "Two Jews, Three Opinions: Politics in the Shtetl at the Turn of the Twentieth Century," Henry Abramson traces the course of Jewish political mobilization in Tsarist Russia, a process that began after the pogroms of 1881 and reached a peak in the years of the 1905 Revolution. Abramson sees five major responses of shtetl Jews to a perceived crisis of East European Jewry: emigrationism, Zionism, Jewish Socialism, Autonomism, and Renewed Traditionalism. Russian Jews did not only look to new ideologies of salvation that promised national renewal, either *do* (here, in Eastern Europe) or *dortn* (there, in Palestine). Millions of Jews also voted with their feet and searched for personal rather than collective solutions: a better life in the United States and other countries. Jews emigrated from the Russian Empire in proportionally greater numbers than non-Jews, and theirs was more an emigration of entire families that were less likely to return. The wave of emigration would have a profound effect on the shtetl psychology, as more and more families now had relatives abroad. Remittances from other lands would play a steadily increasing role in the shtetl economy, especially in the interwar period, and buttress its ability to withstand economic setbacks.

Yet, as Elie Wiesel reminds us in his chapter, even in the face of the secularization and mobilization described by Abramson and other authors, the sense of time and space, as well as the moral culture of shtetl life, were still heavily influenced by a Jewish religion which in Eastern Europe was inseparable from a distinct sense of Jewish peoplehood. Whatever shtetl a religious Jew happened to live in, he prayed to return to Jerusalem and studied a Talmud that had originated in Palestine and Babylonia. He was "here" and "there" at the same time.

In the shtetl it was the religion—the holidays and the weekly Bible portions—that marked off the resonance of the different seasons. The Jewish New Year and Yom Kippur would give way to the rainy weeks of autumn, of Sukkot and the Bible readings of Genesis. The winter snows were associated with Hannukah and the Bible readings of Exodus. Spring was the time of Purim and Passover. Shavuot marked the beginning of the summer. Late in the summer, during the month of Elul, the blast of the *shofar* at morning services would confirm the message of the shorter days and the cooler nights—that a new year was coming. Each holiday had its own customs, and many shtetlekh would observe individual fast days or memorial days to commemorate a past massacre or a miraculous deliverance.

The Jewish religion dictated certain communal obligations that in turn helped determine the public space and public life of the shtetl. The *chevre kadisha*, the burial society, exerted major power and helped enforce the community's code of mutual responsibility. If a rich person shirked his obligations, then the *chevre* might well redress the balance through a hefty funeral bill presented to his heirs. Other *chevres* (associations) also served to meet the community's religious obligations: helping poor girls marry; providing all Jews with a basic minimum to keep the Sabbath and celebrate Passover; caring for the sick; educating children; receiving guests and strangers; providing interest-free loans. Every community had *chevres* that studied holy texts and that catered to the different levels of ability and learning in the Jewish community. *Tsedaka*, or charity, was a basic obligation. In interwar Poland, more than one critical outsider remarked on the greater readiness of shtetl Jews to give to charity and to help each other.

Until the advent of growing secularization, and even beyond, the *chevres* formed the basis of the shtetl's communal life. As the historian Jacob Katz has pointed out, traditional Jewish society frowned on social activities, parties, or banquets that were not connected to an ostensible religious purpose.[17] So each *chevre* would often have a traditional banquet that was linked to the week when a particular portion of the Bible was read. In one Jewish town, as David Roskies reminds us in his *Shtetl Book*, the water carriers would meet on Saturday afternoons to study Talmudic legends (*Eyn Yaakov*). Their yearly banquet took place during the week when the Bible portion of *Emor* was read. This was because *Emor* resembled *emer*, the Yiddish word for "water pail." This pun might have seemed forced. But it reflected the determination to anchor life in religious tradition.

While religious tradition dictated a strict code of public and private behavior, the shtetl Jews also knew how to amuse themselves. Purim, which usually fell in February and March, not only commemorated the deliverance of the Jews in Persia but also provided many opportunities for fun. Purim took place in a carnival atmosphere, with drinking and singing. Adults and children would dress up in costumes, and wandering troupes of amateur actors would go from house to house playing out Purim *shpils*, or skits and parodies loosely based on the story of the holiday. As in other carnivals, the merriment and the relaxation of rules also served as a subtle reminder that the rules, in fact, remained very much in force.[18]

Gender roles in the shtetl were, at first sight, fairly straightforward. Men held the positions of power. They controlled the *kehilla* and, of course, the synagogue, where women sat separately and could not be counted towards a prayer quorum. Nonetheless, any generalizations about the place of women in the shtetl require caution.[19] Girls from poor families indeed faced bleak prospects, especially if they could not find a husband. But women were not totally powerless and helpless.

Behind the scenes, women—especially from well-off families—often played key roles in the communal and economic life of the shtetl. As Nehemia Polen reminds us, women could even wield major influence in the Hasidic movement, a milieu not known for its feminist ethos. His chapter on "Rebbetzins, Wonder-Children, and the Emergence of the Dynastic Principle in Hasidism" discusses a key question that has long intrigued scholars: the origins of the dynastic principle in Hasidism. Of all the important innovations of the Hasidic movement, perhaps the most revolutionary was the rise of a new model of leadership based on the *tsaddik*, whose spiritual powers could bring the ordinary Jew closer to God. Not only could the *tsaddik* make spiritual experiences more accessible to the ordinary Jew, but he could also serve as a new kind of leader, an alternative to communal rabbis or oligarchs. What Polen suggests is that in the development of the dynastic principle to determine succession, women played a key role by furthering the interests of the *yenukah*, the young son or "wonder child" of the departed *tsaddik*. Polen's article notwithstanding, however, many scholars would argue that by and large, it is still hard to made a general case that Hasidism raised the status of women in Jewish society.[20]

Women clearly had opportunities to learn how to read and write.[21] A popular culture that developed alongside the high culture of Talmud study reflected the resourcefulness and the curiosity of generations of Jewish women. A religious and secular literature in Yiddish for women (and poorer, less educated men) included such mainstays as the *Tzenerene* (adapted translations of and legends based on the Five Books of Moses), the *Bove Bukh* (adapted from a medieval romance), and private, individual prayers called *tkhines*.[22] A best selling Jewish writer in nineteenth-century Eastern Europe was Isaac Meyer Dik, who wrote popular Yiddish novels that were largely read by women—and uneducated men.[23]

The rhythms of shtetl life reflected the interplay of the sacred and the profane, of the Sabbath and the week, of the marketplace and the synagogue. On the market day peasants would start streaming into the shtetl early in the morning. Hundreds of wagons would arrive, and the Jews would surround them and buy the products that the peasants had to sell. With money in their pockets, the peasants then went into the Jewish shops. The market day was a noisy cacophony of shouting, bargaining, and hustling.[24] Often, after the sale of a horse or a cow, peasants and Jews would do a version of a "high five" and share a drink. Sometimes fights would break out, and everyone would run for cover. Especially on a hot summer day, the presence of hundreds of horses standing around would lend the shtetl an unforgettable odor. But the market day was the lifeblood of the shtetl.

The market day further underscored the complex nature of relations between Jews and gentiles. In these hundreds of small Jewish communities surrounded by a Slavic rural hinterland, many customs—cooking, clothing, proverbs—reflected the impact of the non-Jewish world. While Jews and gentiles belonged to different religious and cultural universes, they were also drawn together by personal bonds that were often lacking in the big cities. Even as each side held many negative stereotypes about the other, these stereotypes were tempered by the reality of concrete neighborly ties.[25]

If the market day was noise and bustle, the Sabbath (*Shabes*) was the holy time when the Jews in the traditional shtetl would drop all work and turn to God. The exhausted carpenters and tailors who had spent the previous week walking around the countryside, sleeping in barns, and doing odd jobs for the peasants, now returned home. A Jew, they believed, received a *neshome yeseire*, an extra soul, with the coming of the Sabbath. The Sabbath was the only real leisure time that the shtetl Jew had.

In the interwar years in Poland, the shtetl Sabbath began to reflect the major changes coming in from the outside world, and synagogue attendance began to slip. A visiting Yiddish writer from a big city might lecture to a large audience at the fireman's hall. Young people from Zionist or Bundist youth movements would go on hikes or perform amateur theater—much to the dismay of their religious parents who saw this as a desecration of the holy day. Yet these secular Sabbaths continued the concept of a special day as a break in time and as a period dedicated to the spirit.

The Transformation of the Shtetl: Poland and the Soviet Union

World War I marked a major turning point in the history of East European Jewry and in the history of the shtetl. As Konrad Zieliński shows us, the war had a profound impact on the shtetl, a bloody reminder that the shtetlekh were not half-real, half-imagined Jewish worlds but actual towns that were exposed to the assaults of history and the hideous violence of rampaging armies. Congress Poland, Galicia, and the Pale—the core of East European Jewish settlement—saw the fiercest fighting. The Russian army brutally expelled more than half a million Jews from their homes. Shtetl Jews preferred the Austrians and the Germans to the Russians. For the Jews who had been under Russian rule, the Germans and the Austrians brought a modicum of liberty; the war years saw an unprecedented surge of political organization and cultural mobilization, of new schools and libraries. On the other hand, the Germans proved to be experts in economic exploitation. As they requisitioned food supplies and raw materials, shtetl Jews had to turn into smugglers in order to live. In his 1920 novel *Smugglers*, Oyzer Varshavsky coldly dissected what he saw as the social and moral collapse of the wartime shtetl, as long-held ethical norms gave way to greed and ruthless egotism. The lawless clawed their way to the top of the social scale and even the *sheyne Yidn*, the "fine Jews" who had been the shtetl elite, demonstrated that they had few moral scruples.[26]

The breakup of the Hapsburg and the Russian empires after World War I divided the bulk of the Jewish shtetl population between the new Soviet Union and several successor states, the largest being the reborn Polish Republic.

As I show in my chapter in this volume, "The Shtetl in Interwar Poland," the Jewish experience in the Polish Second Republic saw a continuation and an acceleration of a many trends that had begun before World War I. While the cities—especially Warsaw—became the center of political and cultural life, the shtetlekh did not disappear. In 1939 about half of all Polish Jews were still living in these small towns whose Jewish communities were also undergoing far-reaching changes.

The interwar shtetl was influenced as never before by outside cultural influences coming from the city. During the course of the nineteenth century many factors had linked the shtetl to the wider world: yeshivas, Hasidism, the press, and emigration. These contacts now intensified. Dances, sporting events, movies, and even beauty contests all became common features of shtetl life. As road and railroad transport improved, many shtetlekh were on their way to becoming suburbs of larger cities. But in the shtetl, outside forces and modern influences were often filtered and modified through the impact of traditional institutions and established values. A major feature of the interwar shtetl was an intensive development of new organizations that embraced an ever greater proportion of the Jewish community. The 1930s saw a sharp deterioration in Polish-Jewish relations that affected shtetlekh and cities alike. Nonetheless, in some ways, mutual relations were better in the shtetlekh. Relationships that went back for decades were not easily sundered, and many peasants ignored economic boycotts and continued to patronize their familiar Jewish merchants.

The shtetl in the interwar Soviet Union underwent a very different experience from its Polish counterpart. In the early years of Soviet power the Communist Party's policy towards Jews and towards the Jewish shtetl was a work in progress. Since most Communists had inherited a hostile view of the shtetl, the new Soviet state explored various options to provide alternatives to it and to solve the Jewish problem. But while emigration to the big cities, agricultural colonies, and a Jewish Autonomous Region in Birobidzhan all provided new possibilities, a large proportion of Soviet Jewry still remained in the shtetlekh, and the regime could not ignore it.

Although hundreds of shtetlekh in Poland had suffered severe war damage, relatively few had to endure the savage pogroms that ravaged the Ukraine in 1919–1921 and that killed more than 60,000 Jews. The Civil War and the introduction of War Communism dealt a major blow to the traditional role of the shtetl as a market town. While some recovery occurred between 1921–1928, heavy taxation and political discrimination weighed heavily on the shtetl. A large percentage of shtetl Jews suffered from Soviet legislation that deprived former members of the "bourgeoisie," petty shop keepers, and religious functionaries of many legal rights. The advent of collectivization in 1928–1929 ended what was left of the traditional market relationship between the shtetl and the surrounding countryside.

The Soviet state gave its Jews very little liberty, and the Soviet shtetl knew none of the rich political and associational life that developed in interwar Poland or in the Baltic states. But despite persecution, many shtetlekh still preserved a large measure of their Jewish character. In the Ukraine and Belarus local Communist authorities supported the Evsektsiia's policy of promoting Yiddish schools for Jewish children, and right through the mid-1930s Jewish children in these small towns were not only speaking Yiddish at home but also receiving their primary education in that language.[27] Whatever the shortcomings of the Communist Yiddish schools, they did provide some reinforcement against assimilation. On the other hand Jewish parents understood all too well that the path to higher education and advancement favored graduates of Russian schools. There were no Yiddish universities.

By the mid-1930s many former shtetlekh had begun to adapt to the new socio-economic reality created by collectivization and the Five Year Plans. They became centers for local artisan production, or they served nearby collective farms. Despite the momentous changes that transformed these shtetlekh, their Jewish population exhibited strikingly different characteristics from their brethren in the big cities. They were, for example, more likely to speak Yiddish and much less likely to intermarry than their urban counterparts.[28] It was only the Holocaust that finally destroyed the Soviet shtetl. Unlike Jews in the big cities of the Russian Republic, shtetl Jews in the Ukraine and Belarus had a very difficult time escaping the *Wehrmacht*. Their destruction changed the entire character of Soviet Jewry by eliminating its most nationally conscious and least assimilated elements.

The "Imagined Shtetl"

During the course of the nineteenth century the shtetl also became a cultural and a literary construct. This "imagined shtetl," unlike the real shtetl, was often exclusively Jewish, a face-to-face community that lived in Jewish space and that preserved a traditional Jewish life. In literature and in political and cultural discourse the "imagined shtetl" evoked many different reactions that ranged from parody and contempt to praise for a supposed bastion of pure *Yidishkayt* (Jewishness). As a shorthand symbol, the "imagined shtetl" provoked reactions that were a revealing litmus test of the Jewish encounter with the dilemmas and traumas of modernity, revolution, and catastrophe. After the annihilation of East European Jewry, the shtetl also became a frequent, if inaccurate, metonym for the entire lost world of East European Jewry.[29]

As a new Yiddish and Hebrew literature developed in the nineteenth century, the portrayal of the shtetl closely followed the *Haskalah* (Jewish Enlightenment) and its critique of Jewish traditional society. While writers such as Isaac Meyer Dik, Yisroel Aksenfeld, and Yitshok Yoel Linetsky became extremely popular with their parodies and criticisms of shtetl life, it was Shalom Abramovitch (Mendele Moykher Sforim) who developed a literary shtetl—especially in *The Magic Ring, Fishke the Lame, The Nag,* and *The Journeys of Benjamin the Third*—that would have enormous influence on future writers. Abramovitch had been a maskil, and the names he assigned his fictional shtetlekh and towns—Tuniyadevka-Betalon (Donothingburg), Kaptsansk-Kabtsiel (Beggartown), and Glupsk-Kesalon (Stupidville)—speak for themselves.

In a well-known essay, the literary critic David Frischmann wrote that if some day the shtetl were to entirely disappear, future historians would only have to consult Mendele's stories to reconstruct a reliable and accurate picture of shtetl life. Yet as Dan Miron, a prominent Israeli literary critic and also on the faculty of Columbia University, pointed out, Frishman completely missed the significant discrepancies between the literary shtetl, as constructed in the works of Mendele and Sholom Aleichem, and the actual shtetlekh that these giants of Yiddish literature knew first hand. Insofar as these works were realistic, their mimetic realism was only a part of a complex aesthetic structure that many critics erroneously mistook for an accurate ethnographic description of the shtetl. Miron pointed out that the shtetl of the classical Yiddish writers was shaped by a system of metaphors and motifs that turned the shtetl into Jewish space and linked it to recurring themes of Jewish history: the destruction of Jerusalem, exodus, and exile, as well as final redemption. Myths of shtetl origin, fires, and the appearance of mysterious strangers created a rich overarching metaphor that tied the shtetl to the wider destinies of the Jewish people.

Through this structure, a Judaized shtetl served as a Jerusalem *shel mata*, an earthly Jerusalem set down in Eastern Europe. In this "imagined shtetl," myths of origin, legends, and customs could be parodied and satirized—but nonetheless fused to a collective consciousness shaped by Jewish tradition and messianic hopes.[30]

Israel Bartal shows that in this literary construct, the "imagined shtetl" was described in such a way as to emphasize the differences between the Jewish and the Christian spheres:

> The literary map deliberately obliterates the presence of the Christian urban population from the Jewish heart of the shtetl. It identifies the non-Jewish world with the countryside, thereby intensifying the distinctly urban identity of Eastern European Jewry. This representation of urban experience, the legacy of hundreds of years of colonization in the heart of a foreign and hostile population, did not reflect the demographic and geographic truth. It did, however, express the profound internal truth of alienation from the countryside outside the town. This alienation was very familiar to Mendele and Sholom Aleichem. They gave it expression in the imaginary geography of Kabtzansk and Kasrilevke.

Through the mediation of a brilliant character, Mendele the Bookseller, Abramovitch transcended well-worn *Haskalah* criticism of the shtetl and fashioned a persona to negotiate the space that separated the Jewish intelligentsia (including the author himself) from the ordinary shtetl Jews. Torn between his pungent criticism of Jewish society and his deep attachment to the Jewish masses, quicker to discern problems than to suggest solutions, Abramovitch let Mendele pass through the shtetl, an outsider and insider at the same time. He could thus skewer the common Jews and the Jewish intelligentsia with equal finesse.

Sholem Aleichem created one of the most important literary shtetlekh, Kasrilevke, which serves as a partial corrective to Mendele's Stupidvilles and Beggartowns. The "Little Jews" (*Kleyne Menshelekh*) who live in Kasrilevke meet misfortune with dignity, humor, and an inner strength imparted by their folk culture and their language. As the Kasrilevke Jews hear the ominous tidings of an encroaching outside world—tidings of pogroms and anti-Semitism—they nonetheless stubbornly refuse to give up their faith in the eventual triumph of *yoysher* (justice). An even more positive treatment of the shtetl appeared in Sholem Asch's 1904 novella, *A Shtetl*. Asch portrayed a shtetl deeply rooted in the age-old Polish landscape. It has its share of squabbles and natural calamities, such as fires. Nonetheless, Asch's shtetl is an organic community, where natural leaders enjoy moral authority and where the economy is based on a natural order undisturbed by railroads and industrialization.[31]

The chapters of Naomi Seidman, Jeremy Dauber, and Michael Krutikov demonstrate, as did Miron, just how rich and complex a topic the "imagined shtetl" is and how changing strategies of representation and aesthetic presentation of the shtetl theme served as key markers of cultural evolution. While the scholarly consensus has located the beginning of the shtetl theme in Yiddish and Hebrew literature in the *Haskalah*, Dauber's chapter—while discussing the *Haskalah*—actually begins with the earlier literature of Hasidism, the *Haskalah*'s major polemical target. In his discussion of such seminal Hasidic works as *Shivkhei HaBesht* (*Tales in Praise of the Ba'al Shem Tov*), Dauber stresses the lack of concrete, mimetic representation, the absence of description of the physical or social aspects of the shtetl. This eschewal of mimetic representation was closely bound up with the ethos and ideology of the emerging Hasidic movement. The *Shivkhei HaBesht*, Dauber argues, attempts to replace traditional representation with a new kind of "seeing" that focuses on the *tsaddik* rather than on one's own observations.

> Indeed, if the *Shivkhei* is seen as a foundational text for the Zaddikist movement, such marginalization serves an even deeper polemic purpose: it suggests that representation, description at a distance, mediated texts, is no substitute for direct contact with the Zaddik (the mystical master), who is able to perceive "the real truth."

But in their polemics against the Hasidim, maskilic ("enlightened") opponents like Joseph Perl and Yisroel Aksenfeld had to confront their own ambivalence, not only with regard to Yiddish but also with regard to the very strategies of literary representation that they employed to discredit their opponents. Dauber sees Aksenfeld's *Headband* as a "seminal maskilic text not in its certainty but in its doubt: about itself and about its methods." Dauber examines the same marginalization of direct representation in Mendele's *Fishke the Lame* (*Fishke der Krumer*). The complex negotiations among Fishke, Mendele, and Shalom Abramovich reflected the uncertainties and anxieties of a maskilic author at once a part of and yet distanced from the society he is trying to describe.

Naomi Seidman's "Gender and the Disintegration of the Shtetl in Modern Hebrew and Yiddish Literature" not only provides new analyses that complement Miron's examination of the image of the shtetl in Yiddish literature but also serves as a case study of how the insights and tools of gender studies can enrich and enhance our understanding of Jewish culture. Focusing on the image of the *agunah*, the abandoned woman who cannot remarry, Seidman notes that the *agunah* "functions *both* as a metonym for nineteenth-century social upheaval *and* as a metaphor in a national-religious epic." Surveying the themes of exile and abandonment in Yiddish literature, Seidman argues that "in the *literature* that describes the departure from the shtetl, what is left behind is gendered as feminine and emblematized by the figure of a woman." But as Seidman also perceptively points out through the example of the writer Dvora Baron, Jewish women could in fact subvert established cultural tropes and metaphors. Baron's short story "Fedka" describes a shtetl inhabited by women whose men have all emigrated. But the shtetl women find comfort with the gentile mailman Fedka.

> In "Fedka," Baron reverses the perspective, near universal, that privileges the masculine journey over the experiences of the women left behind, uncovering a store of hidden pleasures in a shtetl emptied of Jewish men. "Fedka" both mobilizes and undoes the metaphorical structure that, in the classic shtetl literature, views the shtetl as a fallen Jerusalem.

As revolutions and total war ravaged Jewish Eastern Europe, the treatment of the shtetl in Yiddish literature increasingly diverged from the models of Mendele, Sholom Aleichem, or Asch. Paraphrasing Miron, Michael Krutikov, in his chapter on "Rediscovering the Shtetl as a New Reality: David Bergelson and Itsik Kipnis," notes that new writers abandoned the metaphorical vision of the shtetl crafted by the classical writers and forged a new "metonymic deflation" of the shtetl myth. Itche Meier Weissenberg's 1906 masterpiece, also entitled *A Shtetl*, had portrayed a community torn apart by an internal Jewish class conflict. Yet, Weissenberg asked, what was the ultimate importance of these internecine Jewish struggles in a fragile shtetl, a negligible dot in an enormous gentile world lying just beyond its muddy streets? In his 1913 classic *Nokh Alemen* (the title essentially means "when all is said and done") and in many shorter stories, the gifted writer Dovid Bergelson presented a picture of a shtetl marked by banality and emptiness. Like Weissenberg, Bergelson too denied the shtetl any redemptive meaning.

Krutikov's chapter, in showing how two major Soviet Yiddish writers dealt with the theme of the shtetl in war and revolution, offers a suggestive and illuminating look at the complex attitudes of shtetl Jews towards the Bolshevik Revolution. The revolution shattered the market economy that had been the shtetl's lifeblood, stifled traditional Jewish culture, and sparked pogroms that took tens of thousands of Jewish lives. But the Bolsheviks also emerged as protectors against anti-Semitism, and they promised a new world that would replace the old shtetl with wider vistas, education, and social mobility.

Kipnis and Bergelson were only two of the many important Yiddish writers who believed that the Soviet system, while far from perfect, nonetheless represented the best hope for Yiddish mass culture.[32] Krutikov's incisive analysis of how these writers dealt with the shtetl theme also complements and to some degree modifies Miron's thesis. Miron saw the metonymic countervision of the shtetl in the works of Weissenberg, Bergelson, and others as a "mere foil, a contrasting backdrop against which the contours of the richer and more complex vision of the *klassiker* stands out." What Krutikov argues is that the best of the post-classical writers such as Bergelson and Kipnis achieved

> a new metaphorization of the shtetl based not on its special position as Jerusalem in exile, but on its relationships with the real world around it. For Bergelson the underlying metaphor is *midas-hadin* (stern justice), a world devoid of *midas-harakhamim* (mercy). Kipnis, drawing upon Sholom Aleichem's archetype of Jewish character, creates a new figure of a *folks-mentsh* (an ordinary Jew), an eternal and indestructible hero capable of overcoming obstacles and surviving disasters without losing his Jewish soul.

Apart from the "imagined shtetl," the real world of the shtetl ended only with the Holocaust. But the subject of the shtetl in the Holocaust has received relatively little attention from scholars; the memorial books (*yizker bikher*) compiled by survivors after the war have remained the single most important source on the final days of hundreds of shtetlekh.[33] Yet as historical sources, these books have their obvious limitations. Yehuda Bauer's chapter, "Sarny and Rokitno in the Holocaust: A Case Study of Two Townships in Wolyn," goes beyond the memorial books and uncovers little used archival sources and testimonies in Yad Vashem to chart the experiences of two shtetlekh during the war. Bauer traces the impact of the Soviet occupation on inter-ethnic relations and on the Jewish community, and he examines basic differences between Jewish responses in big ghettos like Warsaw and in smaller towns.

What has elsewhere been called *amidah* (standing up against German policies, armed and unarmed) took a completely different form from what we have learnt in large centers such as Warsaw, Lodz, Bialystok, Vilna, etc. If one considers hiding and/or escaping into the forest as an active Jewish reaction—and this is what is proposed here—then the individual initiatives to do so were an expression of the refusal to surrender. Such initiatives were fairly massive in both communities [of Sarny and Rokitno].

Bauer adds that the proximity of dense forests, the presence of a Soviet partisan movement, and the willingness of a few gentiles—Polish peasants, Baptists, Old Believers, and some Ukrainians—enabled a small minority of Jews to survive.

After the Holocaust

For an American Jewry just beginning to come to terms with the Holocaust, the shtetl—reviled and forgotten before the war—came to represent a lost world that was brutally destroyed. It became a symbol of the integral Jewishness and the supportive community that many American Jews—economically secure in their new suburban homes—now began to miss.[34] In 1952 the publication of Mark Zborowski's and Elizabeth Herzog's *Life Is with People* presented American readers with a composite portrait of a Jewish shtetl that was the quintessential "home": culturally self-sufficient, isolated from gentiles, and timeless. The 1964 Broadway production of *Fiddler on the Roof* transformed Sholom Aleichem's village Jew, Tevye, into a shtetl dweller. Tevye's genuine conflicts with his wife and daughters—expressions of the growing religious, class, and inter-ethnic tensions of Jewish society—found a resolution on the Broadway stage that harmonized Jewish and American values. The shtetl had become a way station to America.[35]

In Poland, as we read in Katarzyna Więcławska's chapter on "The Image of the Shtetl in Contemporary Polish Fiction," a small but important number of Polish writers tried to describe a community that had been brutally exterminated and about which they had little first-hand knowledge. Yet, aware that they were dealing with a critical part of their nation's history, they began the difficult and artistically risky project of constructing a literary shtetl. In Piotr Szewc's 1993 novel *Zagłada* (*Annihilation*), the story focuses on one boring summer day in 1934 in his home town of Zamosc. It is precisely this portrayal of quotidian routine that underscored the sheer horror of the destruction that was to come. Andrzej Kuniewicz's *Nawrócenie* (*Turning Back*, 1987) takes another tack, laying out how the traces and impressions of the shtetl affect his imagination and memory—the memory of a Pole who realizes that he will never be able to penetrate the Jewish world that he can only observe as an outsider. "Too late" is how Więcławska describes this attempt by gifted Polish authors to engage with the Jewish world that at one time had been so much a part of the Polish landscape.

If Poles could still imagine the former shtetlekh in the streets and squares of their provincial towns, in Israel in the 1950s and 1960s, the shtetl mainly served as a negative symbol, a reminder of the narrow, doomed world that Zionism had transcended. For Israelis the "shtetl mentality" represented everything that the new state had to avoid.[36] By the 1970s, however, there were some signs of a renewed interest in Yiddish culture and in the shtetl, and prominent Israeli scholars published much valuable material. It was mainly in Israel that survivors joined with older emigrants to publish hundreds of *yizker bikher*, or memorial books. These *yizker bikher* often contained hundreds of pages with pictures and personal reminiscences. For understandable reasons, many of these books were largely eulogies and elegies, and the committees that compiled them avoided including unflattering details on the shtetl and its inhabitants. Some, however, were edited by professional historians and have great historical value.

As Arnold J. Band reminds us in "Agnon's Synthetic Shtetl," one of the greatest *yizker* projects of all—the large number of stories that Shai Agnon wrote about his shtetl, Buczacz—went largely unnoticed. Both before and after the Holocaust, Agnon crafted an "imagined shtetl" that differed significantly from both the classical image described by Miron and the deflation of the shtetl myth that marked the writings of Weissenberg, Bergelson, and others. Band describes Agnon as an author who "negotiated" with Jewish history. Unlike Mendele, whose portrayal of shtetl life was mainly satiric and whose style, Band believes, was fundamentally European, Agnon engaged with traditional Jewish sources in ways that both recognized their authority and subverted them. Above all, Agnon made great demands of his readers: like him, they had to know the tradition in order to understand its ongoing confrontation with the Jewish present. Band compares Agnon's literary shtetl with *Fiddler on the Roof*, which, in contrast, required very little of the audience:

[Agnon] challenges the reader, requires both erudition and work, and thus operates in the intellectual milieu of the "shtetl," as he conceives it, a world of dense Jewish life, where even his simplest characters have significant Jewish literacy. If, as we have argued, what we call the "shtetl" today is primarily the product of literary representations of all sorts and levels, these sources determine the image of the "shtetl" we present and, indeed, cherish. And to the extent that they are memorials, they, like all memorials, generate and shape memory. The differences we have cited are not merely academic, but ultimately existential and fateful. And the stakes are high.

Vulnerable as it was, the shtetl for many Jews continued to symbolize the distinct Jewish peoplehood in Eastern Europe that had evolved over the course of centuries. It long influenced the contours of Jewish collective memory, and its spaces, streets, and wooden buildings remained etched in the collective imagination. Both the real shtetl and the "imagined shtetl" are an integral part of East European Jewish history and of the Jewish cultural heritage. But it is far from certain that the shtetl will be studied for what it was. This volume is certainly a start.

Notes

1. Among the many good studies of the *arenda* system and of relations between Jews and nobles are Murray J. Rosman, *The Lord's Jews* (Cambridge, MA, 1990); and Gershon D. Hundert, *The Jews in a Polish Private Town* (Baltimore, 1992).

2. Adam Teller, "The Shtetl as an Arena for Polish-Jewish Integration in the Eighteenth Century," *Polin, The Shtetl: Myth and Reality*, Vol. 17 (Oxford, 2004), pp. 25–40.

3. See for example Roman Rybarski, *Handel i polityka handlowa Polski w XVI stuleciu* (Poznań, 1928).

4. See for example John Klier, "Polish Shtetls under Russian Rule," *Polin*, Vol. 17 (Oxford, 2004), pp. 109–119.

5. John Klier, "What Exactly Was a Shtetl?" in Gennady Estraikh and Mikhail Krutikov, eds., *The Shtetl: Image and Reality*. Papers of the Second Annual Mendel Friedman International Conference on Yiddish (Oxford, 2000), p. 27.

6. This "face-to-face community" engendered a different sense of belonging to a place than one found in a big city. As Annamaria Orla-Bukowska points out, "a strongly emotional and psychological bond with a specific place (something eliminated by modern mobility) is founded upon the significance with which a

specific natural landscape is endowed, the edifices built by its residents or their forefathers, and, above all, the people who are born, live, work and die there and all the extraordinary and ordinary events they experience individually and together. Of such a connection is made a *Heimat a mała oyczyzna* (small homeland) or *ojczyzna prywatna* (private fatherland)." See Annamaria Orla-Bukowska, "Maintaining Borders, Crossing Borders: Social Relationships in the Shtetl," *Polin*, Vol. 1 (Oxford, 2004), pp. 173–174.

7. *The Headband* was published in an English translation in *Shtetl: The Creative Anthology of Jewish Life in Eastern Europe*, edited and translated by Joachim Neugroschel (Woodstock, NY, 1979), pp. 49–173.

8. For Adam Teller, the working definition of a shtetl was a Jewish population of at least 40 percent in a settlement defined by Polish law as a *miasteczko*: a place that engaged in agriculture and that possessed under "300 chimneys" or a population of under 2,000 inhabitants. See his "The Shtetl as an Arena for Polish-Jewish Integration in the Eighteenth Century," pp. 28–29.

9. More on this in Klier, "Polish Shtetls under Russian Rule"; and Ben-Cion Pinchuk, "The Shtetl: An Ethnic Town in the Russian Empire," *Cahiers du Monde Russe*, Vol. 41 (2000), p. 498.

10. Eli Lederhendler, "The Decline of the Polish-Lithuanian Kahal," *Polin*, Vol. 2 (1987), pp. 150–162.

11. For some good discussions of shtetl architecture and spatial layout see Thomas Hubka, "The Shtetl in Context: The Spatial and Social Organization of Jewish Communities from the Small Towns of Eighteenth-Century Poland," www.earlymodernorg/workshops/summer2005/presenters/hubka/01/intor.php; and Alla Sokolova, "The Podolian Shtetl as an Architectural Phenomenon," in Gennady Estraikh and Mikhail Krutikov, eds., *The Shtetl: Image and Reality*.

12. The Bundists were members of the Jewish Labor Bund, the leading Jewish socialist organization in Eastern Europe. It was anti-Communist and anti-Zionist. There is a large literature on the subject of the severe criticism of the shtetl. See for example Dan Miron, *The Image of the Shtetl and Other Studies of Modern Jewish Literary Imagination* (Syracuse, NY, 2000); Dan Miron, *A Traveler Disguised* (New York, 1973); Mikhail Krutikov, "Imagining the Image: Interpretations of the Shtetl in Soviet Literary Criticism," *Polin*, Vol. 17 (Oxford, 2004), pp. 243–258; and David Roskies, "The Shtetl in Jewish Collective Memory," in his *The Jewish Search for a Usable Past* (Bloomington, 1999), pp. 41–46.

13. As Gennady Estraikh has shown, however, religious tradition still kept its hold over many Jews in the interwar Soviet shtetl. See his "The Soviet Shtetl in the 1920s," *Polin*, Vol. 17. On this subject see also Anna Shternshis, "Soviet and Kosher in the Ukrainian Shtetl" in Gennady Estraikh and Mikhail Krutikov, eds., *The Shtetl: Image and Reality*, pp. 134–135.

14. The best work on the Lithuanian yeshivas is Shaul Stampfer, *Ha-yeshiva ha-litait be'hithayuta* (Jerusalem, 1995).

15. Moshe Rosman has shown, for instance, that far from being a marginal figure, the Ba'al Shem Tov was a respected pillar of the Miedzyboz community. See his *Founder of Hasidism: A Quest for the Historical Ba'al Shem Tov* (Berkeley, 1996).

16. Glenn Dymmer has studied the interplay of the new hasidic movement and shtetl politics in the late eighteenth and early nineteenth centuries in *Men of Silk: The Hasidic Conquest of Polish Jewish Society* (Oxford, 2006). For an important study of the important early Hasidic leader Levi Yitshak of Berdichev in the socio-political context of his surroundings, see Yohanan Petrovsky-Shtern, "The Drama of Berdichev: Levi Yitshak and His Town," *Polin*, Vol. 17 (Oxford, 2004), pp. 83–95.

17. Jacob Katz, *Tradition and Crisis: Jewish Society at the End of the Middle Ages* (New York, 1971), pp. 162–163.

18. A good discussion of the transgressional aspects of the Purim *shpil* can be found in Ahuva Belkin, "The 'Low' Culture of the Purim Shpil," in Joel Berkowitz, ed., *Yiddish Theater: New Approaches* (Oxford, 2003), especially pp. 31–34.

19. A good example of the growing scholarship on the social history of Jewish women in Eastern Europe is Chae-ran Freeze, *Jewish Marriage and Divorce in Imperial Russia* (Hanover, 2002). See also Paula Hyman, "East European Jewish Women in an Age of Transition," in Judith Baskin, ed., *Jewish Women in Historical Perspective* (Detroit, 1998), pp. 270–286.

20. For example, see Ada Rapoport-Albert, "On Women in Hasidism: S. A. Horodecky and the Maid of Ludmir Tradition," in Ada Rapoport-Albert and Steven Zipperstein, eds., *Jewish History: Essays in Honor of Chimen Abramsky* (London, 1988), pp. 495–525.

21. See Iris Parush, *Reading Jewish Women: Marginality and Modernization in Nineteenth-Century Eastern European Jewish Society* (Hanover, 2004); and Shaul Stampfer, "Gender Differentiation and Education of Jewish Women in Nineteenth-Century Eastern Europe," *Polin*, Vol. 7 (Oxford, 1992), pp. 187–211.

22. On these women's prayers, see the excellent study by Chava Weissler, *Voices of the Matriarchs: Listening to the Prayers of Early Modern Jewish Women* (Boston, 1998).

23. An excellent treatment of the reception of Dik's work can be found in David Roskies, *A Bridge of Longing* (Cambridge, MA, 1995), pp. 56–99.

24. A vivid description of a market day can be found in Yaffa Eliach's *There Was Once a World: A 900-Year Chronicle of the Shtetl of Eishyshok* (Boston, 1998), pp. 313–331.

25. There is a growing literature on the subject of Jewish-gentile relations in the shtetl. Good introductions are Anna-Maria Orla-Bukowska, "Maintaining Borders, Crossing Borders: Social Relationships in the Shtetl," *Polin*, Vol. 17 (Oxford, 2004), pp. 171–195; Rosa Lehmann, *Symbiosis and Ambivalence: Poles and Jews in a Small Galician Town* (New York, 2001); and Eva Hoffman, *Shtetl: The Life and Death of a Small Town and the World of Polish Jews* (Boston, 1997).

26. See the illuminating discussion of this novel in David Roskies, *Against the Apocalypse* (Cambridge, MA, 1984), pp. 118–121.

27. Evsektsiia were the Jewish sections of the Communist Party, established in Soviet Russia in 1918 and disbanded in 1930. Their main function was to conduct Communist propaganda in Yiddish, to fight religion, and to promote Soviet Yiddish culture.

28. On this see Mordecai Altshuler, *Soviet Jewry on the Eve of the Holocaust: A Social and Demographic Profile* (Jerusalem, 1998); and also Gennady Estraikh, "The Soviet Shtetl in the 1920s," *Polin*, Vol. 17 (Oxford, 2004), pp. 197–212.

29. See Dan Miron, "The Literary Image of the Shtetl," *Jewish Social Studies*, Vol. 1 (Spring 1995), pp. 1–43.

30. In addition to Miron, see also David Roskies' article, "The Shtetl in Jewish Collective Memory," in his *The Jewish Search for a Usable Past* (Bloomington, 1999), pp. 41–67.

31. See Mikhail Krutikov, *Yiddish Culture and the Crisis of Modernity* (Stanford, 2001), as well as his previously cited article "Imagining the Image: Interpretations of the Shtetl in Soviet Literary Criticism."

32. On this, see also Gennady Estraikh, *In Harness: Yiddish Writers' Romance with Communism* (Syracuse, 2005).

33. On these memorial books, see *From a Ruined Garden: The Memorial Books of Polish Jewry*, edited and translated by Jack Kugelmass and Jonathan Boyarin; with geographical index and bibliography by Zachary M. Baker (Bloomington, 1999).

34. Steven Zipperstein, "Shtetls There and Here: Imagining Russia in America," in his *Imagining Russian Jewry: Memory, History and Identity* (Seattle, 1999), pp. 37–38.

35. See Seth Wolitz, "The Americanization of Tevye, or Boarding the Jewish 'Mayflower,'" *American Quarterly*, Vol. 4 (1988), pp. 514–536.

36. Mordekhai Zalkin, "From the Armchair to the Archives: Transformations in the Image of the 'Shtetl' during Fifty Years of Collective Memory in the State of Israel," *Studia Judaica*, Vol. 8 (1999), pp. 255–266.

1

The Importance of Demography and Patterns of Settlement for an Understanding of the Jewish Experience in East–Central Europe

Gershon David Hundert

If we could travel back to eighteenth-century Eastern Europe, what would we see? One way to attempt to discover the answer to this counterfactual question is to travel there with eighteenth-century tourists from Western Europe and America, who were as foreign to that region as we would be. In their descriptions, the most recurrent observation about Jews in Poland-Lithuania is how numerous Jews were. Nathaniel William Wraxall (1751–1831), an English diplomat and Member of Parliament, visited Warsaw in the late 1770s at a time when Jews constituted no more than 5 percent of the population. Yet he was impressed with the size of the Jewish population and found that "Warsaw is . . . crowded with Jews, who form a considerable portion of the inhabitants." Archdeacon William Coxe (1747–1828), perhaps the best known of the English travelers of this period, as well as the most scholarly, asserted that the Jews in Lithuania were even more numerous than those of Poland. Indeed, they

seem to have fixed their headquarters in this duchy. If you ask for an interpreter, they bring you a Jew; if you come to an inn, the landlord is a Jew; if you want post-horses, a Jew procures them, and a Jew drives them; if you wish to purchase, a Jew is your agent: and this is perhaps the only country in Europe where Jews cultivate the ground: in passing through Lithuania, we frequently saw them engaged in sowing, reaping, mowing and other works of Husbandry.[1]

John Thomas James (1786–1828), an English academician who took holy orders when he returned from the Continent and eventually became Bishop of Calcutta, offered similar observations but added a plausible explanation:

> We now crossed the frontier of Poland, and passed from the land of the credulous to the habitations of the unbelievers, for every house we saw was in the hands of Jews. They seemed, indeed, the only people who were in a state of activity, exercising almost all professions, and engaged in every branch of trade: millers, whitesmiths, saddlers, drivers, ostlers, innkeepers, and sometimes even as farmers. Their constant bustle makes them appear more abundant in number than they really are; and although the streets of Zytomir [Żytomierz; Zhitomir] seemed full of them, we were informed that out of a population of 6,000, not more than one third were of this sect, . . . we could easily have imagined the contrary to have been the fact.[2]

In emphasizing Jewish numbers, the travelers were not far from wrong in identifying what must be a central element in any description of East European Jewry. Consideration of demographic history is indispensable to an understanding of the Polish Jewish experience. Their large numbers, their residence mainly in urban settlements, their concentration in the eastern half of the Commonwealth, and their continuing intense expansion, all profoundly affected both their relations with the state and their non-Jewish neighbours, as well as the quality of Jewish culture in East–Central Europe. In this brief chapter I will illustrate how important demography and patterns of settlement are to a proper understanding of the Jewish experience in East–Central Europe in the eighteenth century.

We begin with the term "minority." It is used to describe groups outside of an imagined homogeneous citizenry in modern nation-states. But it has a set of connotations that are misleading when applied to Jews in the Polish Commonwealth. First of all, identity in pre-modern European society was characterized by a multiplicity of loyalties and memberships. Indeed, there was no majority as we now understand the term. Local patriotism was the order of the day, and there was little sense of belonging to a nation, let alone a nation-state. Even in the eighteenth century, ethnic Poles were not a majority in Poland-Lithuania. In addition to having autocthonous Lithuanians, Ukrainians, and Belarussians, alongside Tatars and Romany, many of the cities and towns were distinguished by the further ethnic and religious diversity of their residents: Germans, Italians, Scots, Armenians, and Greeks. Therefore, Jews cannot be seen as a minority group when less than 20 percent of the population of the country was urban, and only 40 to 60 percent was ethnically Polish.

More important, however, is the fact that about half of the urban population of Poland-Lithuania in the eighteenth century was Jewish. A significant proportion of Jews lived in towns where there was a Jewish majority, and an even larger proportion can be said to have *experienced* living in towns where there appeared to be a Jewish majority because so many of the Christian town dwellers had turned to agriculture. A substantial majority of Jews lived in communities of 500 or more.[3] Thus, most of the shops and stalls on the marketplace as well as the inns and the taverns would have belonged to Jews. Indeed, as Bishop James observed in Żytomierz, most of the people moving through the streets would have been Jews. In other words, most Jews lived in communities that were quite large enough to support the living of the dailiness of life in a Jewish universe. For all of these reasons, the term "minority group" is utterly inappropriate.

The best estimate of the number of Jews in Poland-Lithuania is the one arrived at by Raphael Mahler based on his analysis of the count carried out in 1764–1765.[4] The actual count was 429,587 for Poland and 157,649 for Lithuania. After correcting for children under one year of age (6.35%) and under-reporting (20%), Mahler concluded that there were 750,000 Jews (549,000 in Poland, 201,000 in Lithuania) in the Polish Commonwealth in 1764–1766.[5] While tax records are not the best place to seek the truth about any population, Mahler's corrected figures are a sound beginning point, and they will be used throughout this chapter.

Mahler's figures can be used to estimate the number of Jews in earlier periods. Assuming a moderate rate of growth of 1.6% per year, there should have been about 150,000 Jews in Poland-Lithuania in 1660, and 375,000 in 1720.[6] The Jewish proportion of the total population of the Commonwealth also rose: whereas Jews formed less than .5% of the Polish population in 1500, by 1672, they made up about 3%, and by 1765, about 5.35%. This shows that the Jewish population was increasing at a rate substantially faster than the general rate of growth.[7] The usual estimate of the Polish population for the last decade before the first partition in 1772 is

14,000,000.[8] This faster rate of growth was due less to higher birth rates than to lower death rates. That is, the incidence of infant mortality was lower among Jews. Zdzisław Budzyński studied 26 sets of data from various years between 1777 and 1799. In 25 of the 26 cases the Jewish death rate was lower, and generally significantly lower, than the rate for Christians.[9]

The Jewish population was expanding more rapidly if compared with the entire Christian population of the country. There can be no single explanation of this phenomenon. The existence of systems of support within the Jewish community undoubtedly helped poorer people in the community to find the shelter and nourishment necessary for nurturing children to a certain extent. The relative stability of the Jewish family, which may well have meant lower incidence of sexually transmitted diseases and relatively lower rates of alcoholism, probably also contributed to lower rates of infant mortality among Jews. Finally, the system of *kest* in which a newly married couple was billeted at the home usually of the parents of the bride also may have played a role in the lowering of rates of infant mortality. The age at marriage of those who expected to be supported by their parents in this way was generally low. Statistics published by Jacob Goldberg show that early marriage and the practice of *kest* was characteristic of about 25% of Jews.[10] These were self-evidently the wealthier stratum. The accommodation of additional "mouths to feed" in the form of the young couple and newborn children as well was possible only for the wealthier. That is, it was in the families best able to provide heat, clothing, and food that the age at first birth was likely to have been the lowest.[11]

The data on the growth in Jewish numbers are incontrovertible. And if this growth was, as we have maintained, largely because of a lower rate of infant mortality, it means that the proportion of young people among Jews was expanding continuously. I have proposed elsewhere that this fact must be integrated into our understanding of the origins and growth of Hasidism.

Keri

More than one scholar has noted that the solution to the problem of how to atone for *keri* (nocturnal seminal emission) attracted almost obsessive attention during the late seventeenth and eighteenth centuries and beyond.[12] Entire books were devoted to the subject, and it is addressed in virtually every work of moral and ethical guidance published in that period. According to the *Zohar*—and this position is repeated in the *Shulhan arukh*—*keri* was a sin for which there was no atonement. Still, sixteenth-century and later authorities generally maintained that forgiveness was possible if extraordinary acts of penitence were undertaken.[13]

The demographic history of Polish-Lithuanian Jewry is one of the ingredients that must be included in any explanation of the eighteenth-century preoccupation with this matter. As the proportion of young people in the population grew, the number of those for whom the traditional solution of early marriage was available would have diminished. That is, the number of young people with families who could not afford the practice of housing, feeding, and supporting the newly married couple for a number of years would have increased. The enormous popularity of the Kabbalistic understanding of the commandments, the preoccupations with the demons of "the other side," and the notion of almost inescapable sinfulness, together with the burgeoning number of young males, combined to make *keri* a central and urgent problem.

Patterns of Settlement

The Jewish population was unevenly distributed. Forty-four percent lived in the southeast (Ruthenia-Ukraine) and 27% in the northeast (Lithuania-Belarus). Seventeen percent lived in the central areas (Małopolska), and only about 12% lived in the west (Wielkopolska). That is, more than 70% of the Jewish population of the Polish Commonwealth was concentrated in the eastern half of the country. Five of the six provinces (*województwos*) with the largest Jewish populations were in the east: Ruś (100,111); Volhynia (50,792); Podolia (38, 384); Troki (33,738); and Wilno (26,977). The sixth was Sandomierz, in the center (42,972). The distribution of larger communities followed the same pattern. Of 44 towns in which more than 1,000 Jews lived, 4 were in the west, 7 in the center, 5 in Lithuania-Belarus, and 27 were in Ruthenia-Ukraine. One, Warsaw, was in Mazovia. That is, the Jewish population became more concentrated as one moved eastward.

Slightly more than two thirds of Jews lived in urban settlements, though many of these were rather small cities. In the second half of the eighteenth century there were just over 2,000 cities in Poland. The remarks of Hubert Vautrin (1742–1822), a Frenchman who resided in Poland for several years, are relevant here.[14] He wrote that he would not use the French term for "city" to designate what the Poles call *miasto* because the Polish term denotes something that is little more than a village. The word *miasto*, Vautrin said, has no analogue in French. In sum, the characteristic form of urban settlement in Poland was the small town. Even at the end of the eighteenth century, not more than twelve Polish cities had populations in excess of 10,000, while more than a thousand had less than 2,000 inhabitants. Despite their small size, though, those settlements were not agricultural villages, at least not with respect to their Jewish populations. Christian city dwellers, by contrast, tended in their majority (60%) actually to be burghers who had turned to farming to support themselves, cultivating plots on the edges of the town, while others pursued both artisanal and agricultural activities.[15] In light of this, it will easily be seen how much urban commerce and production were dominated by Jews, particularly in the eastern half of the Commonwealth. In Great Poland, where there was a substantial ethnic German population, Jews made up about 16.5% of the population of the towns.[16] William Coxe's impression that they had "in a manner engrossed all the commerce of the country" thus becomes easier to comprehend.[17]

In 1765, the cities with the largest Jewish populations were Brody (c. 7000), Lwów (c. 6000), and Leszno (c. 5000). About 3,500 Jews lived in Cracow, in Wilno (Vilna, Vilnius), and in Brześć-Litewski (Brisk, Brest-Litovsk), respectively.

There were significant regional variations in the urban-rural distribution of the Jewish population. In parts of western Poland, 2% or less of Jewish residents lived in villages.[18] In the eastern regions, the rural proportion of the population sometimes exceeded one-third. Overall, almost 27% of Polish Jews resided in villages in 1764–1765. A significant proportion of village Jews, however, was only temporarily rural and either maintained residences in towns, or returned to an urban centre after the expiration of their *arenda* contracts. On average, less than two Jewish families (7.1–9.6 people) would live in a village. Moreover, from the last decades of the eighteenth century, the number and proportion of Jews living in villages constantly diminished. Most Polish villages had no Jewish population. In the Cracow *województwo*, for example, Jews lived in less than one-third of 2,628 villages. In Galicia in 1785, village Jews accounted for less than 3% of the total rural population.[19] The Jewish population, in general, was quite mobile, particularly those who were most prosperous as well as those who were at the opposite side of the economic scale—the vocationless, itinerant poor. It should be stressed not only that the Jewish population was essentially urban, but also that it lived in the midst of a society that was overwhelmingly rural and agricultural. The consequence of this was that half of the urban population—and in large parts of the country, more than half—was Jewish.

How did all this affect the quality of the exchanges between Jews and Christians in the eighteenth century? Perhaps it is best to state from the outset that a simple dichotomous view is not nearly complex enough to reflect the actual situation. Nevertheless, it would appear, at least at first, that the demographic situation just described constitutes a strong argument for Jewish insularity and apartness in the context of Polish-Lithuanian society as a whole. The dramatic contrast between the rate of expansion of the Jewish population and that of the Commonwealth's population as a whole suggests cultural and physical isolation. Culturally, the phenomenon suggests Jewish distinctiveness as regards to practices related to marriage, hygiene, diet, and child rearing. Physically, it constitutes an argument suggesting isolation in terms of infection and the spread of communicable diseases.

This apparently powerful argument, however, is flawed. It takes the population as a whole, which was overwhelmingly agrarian, as its comparison group. Jews, as noted earlier, were mainly urban. Still, it might be answered, urban European populations in this period, including those in Poland, were unable to reproduce themselves. Yet, the upper socio-economic strata of those cities did succeed in increasing their numbers, and it may well be that this is the group with which Jews should be compared. For the moment, unfortunately, there are no such finely tuned studies of Polish urban demography in the eighteenth century.

Moreover, the argument for insularity is vitiated considerably by a review of the patterns of residence of Jews. Except for large crown cities like Poznań and Lwów, there was no residential segregation. The degree of concentration of Jewish homes varied somewhat, but in many, if not most cases, Jews and Christians lived interspersed.[20] The tendency of Jews to live on the marketplace (*rynek*) intensified this phenomenon. For example, Jews occupied more than half the dwellings on the marketplace in Dobromil (68%), Łańcut (84%), Chyrów (59%), and Sieniawa (87%). Overall, of six towns in the Przemyśl-Sanok region studied by Jerzy Motylewicz, Jews occupied 119 of 208 houses on the marketplaces.[21]

It can be seen, then, even from this very brief survey, that demography is indispensable for an understanding of the economic, social, and cultural history of Jews in East–Central Europe.

Notes

1. William Coxe, *Travels into Poland, Russia, Sweden and Denmark Interspersed with Historical Relations and Political Inquiries* (London, 1784), Vol. 1, p. 163. Coxe (1747–1828) was an accomplished biographer and historian. He tutored young men on their grand tours of Europe.

2. John Thomas James, *Journal of a Tour in Germany, Switzerland, Russia, Poland, during the Years 1813 and 1814* (London, 1819), Vol. 2, p. 367.

3. Raphael Mahler, "Di Yidn in amolikn Poyln," in *Yidn in Poyln*, Vol. 1 (New York, 1946), col. 179.

4. The occasion for the count was the abolition of the Council of Four Lands by the Sejm and the decision to collect the capitation tax on the basis of the actual number of Jews.

5. Unless otherwise indicated, all of the figures for 1764–1765 mentioned in this chapter follow the analysis of Raphael Mahler, *Yidn in amolikn Poyln in likht fun tsifern*, 2 vols. (Warsaw, 1958). In general, this section depends heavily on Mahler's work. His data and procedures have been reviewed by Shaul Stampfer, "The 1764 Census of Polish Jewry," *Bar-Ilan: Annual of Bar-Ilan University: Studies in Judaica and the Humanities*, Vol. 24–25 (Ramat Gan, 1989): *Studies in the History and Culture of East European Jewry*, edited by Gershon Bacon and Moshe Rosman, pp. 41–147, who concluded that "Mahler's estimates appear more reasonable than . . . any others." See also Zenon Guldon and Jacek Wijaczka, "Die zahlenmäßige Stärke der Juden in Polen-Litauen im 16.–18. Jahrhundert," *Trumah: Zeitschrift der Hochschule für Jüdische Studien* (Heidelberg, Vol. 4 (1994)), pp. 91–101.

6. Weinryb proposed a rate of growth of 2% per annum of the Jewish population between 1667 and 1765. This, if correct, would reduce the estimate for 1660 to about 100,000. Bernard Dov Weinryb, *The Jews of Poland; A Social and Economic History of the Jewish Community in Poland from 1100 to 1800* (Philadelphia, 1973), p. 320. R. Mahler suggested that the Jewish population did not exceed 190,000 in 1675.

7. Some have suggested a larger proportion. For example, Jerzy Topolski has written that in 1771 Jews made up 9% of the total population and between 40% and 50% of the urban population of the country. "The Role of the Jews on the Polish Home Market in the Early Modern Period," Typescript, pp. 6–7.

8. Although some have put it higher, Emanuel Rostworowski has estimated the proportion of the *szlachta* [gentry] as a whole at this time at between 6% and 6.5%. "Ilu było Rzeczypospolitej obywateli szlachty?" *Kwartalnik Historyczny*, Vol. 94 (1987), p. 31.

9. Zdzisław Budzyński, *Ludność pogranicza polsko-ruskiego w drugiej połowie XVIII wieku: Stan, rozmieszczenie, struktura wyznaniowa i etniczna* (Przemyśl-Rzeszów, 1993) Vol. 1, pp. 102–108.

10. Jacob Goldberg, "Jewish Marriage in Eighteenth-Century Poland," *Polin*, Vol. 10 (1997), pp. 3–39.

11. The data analysed by Raphael Mahler for 1764–65 suggested that the average size of a Jewish family in Poland was 3.4 persons. Mahler, however, on the basis of comparative data from other years and other regions, proposed that the most reasonable overall estimate of the average size of a Jewish Polish family was 5. The more likely figure is probably closer to the one that emerges from the data themselves. Rural Jewish family units were larger than urban ones by about 25%. The number of Jews per dwelling varied in different regions, and no global average is useful.

12. Jacob Katz, *Tradition and Crisis*, 2nd ed., translated by Bernard D. Cooperman. (New York, 1993), pp. 116, 121; A. J. Heschel, "R. Nahman miKosov havero shel haBesht," in *Sefer hayovel likhevod Tsevi Volfson*, edited by Saul Lieberman (New York, 1965), p. 138; Joshua Trachtenberg, *Jewish Magic and Superstition* (New York, 1939), p. 282, n. 16; and David Feldman, *Marital Relations, Birth Control and Abortion in Jewish Law* (New York, 1974), p. 118.

13. See, for example, Isaiah Horowitz, *Shenei luhot haberit hashalem*, edited by Meir Katz (Haifa, 1997), *Sha'ar ha'otiyot*, nos. 342, 343, 349, 350–355, 360.

14. Hubert Vautrin, *La Pologne du XVIIIe siècle vue par un precepteur francais*, edited by Maria Cholewo-Flandrin (Paris, 1966), p. 61. (First published as *L'Observateur en Pologne* [Paris, 1807].)

15. Emanuel Rostworowski, "Miasta i mieszczanie w ustroju Trzeciego Maja," *Sejm Czteroletni i jego tradycje*, edited by Jerzy Kowecki (Warsaw, 1991), pp. 138–151.

16. Jacob Goldberg, "Polacy-Żydzi-Niemcy w Polsce w XVII–XVIII wieku," in *Między Polityką a Kulturą* (Warsaw, 1999), p. 176.

17. Coxe, *Travels into Poland, Russia, Sweden and Denmark*, Vol. 1, p. 193.

18. On the village population in Western Poland, see, for now, Stefan Cackowski, "Wiejscy Żydzi w województwie Chelmińskim w 1772r.," *Acta Universitatis Nicolai Copernici: Historia*, Vol. 28 (1993), pp. 61–72, and the references there. See also Antoni Podraza, "Jews and the Village in the Polish Commonwealth," in *The Jews in Old Poland, 1000–1795*, edited by A. Polonsky, J. Basista, and A. Link-Lenczowski (London, 1993), pp. 299–321.

19. Z. Budzyński, *Ludność pogranicza*, Vol. 1, pp. 324–325.

20. G. Hundert, "Jewish Urban Residence in the Polish Commonwealth in the Early Modern Period," *Jewish Journal of Sociology*, Vol. 36 (1984), pp. 25–34; M. J. Rosman, *The Lords' Jews: Magnate-Jewish Relations in the Polish-Lithuanian Commonwealth during the Eighteenth Century* (Cambridge, MA, 1990), pp. 42–48. In 1764, in the private town of Uła (woj. Połock), there were nine streets. Jews lived or owned real estate on seven of them. *Istoriko-iuridicheskie materialy, izvlechennye iz aktovykh knig gubernii Vitebskoi I Mogilevskoi, khraniaschchikhsia v tsentralnom arkhivie v Vitebskie*, Vol. 22 (Vitebsk, 1891), pp. 420–450. Cf. Jacek Wijaczka,

"Raport Ignacego Husarzewskiego o domach i placach żydowskich w Kozienicach z 1767 roku," *Studia Historyczne*, Vol. 43 (2000), 503–512; and Jerzy Motylewicz, "Ulice etniczne w miastach ziemi przemyskiej i sanockiej w XVII i XVIII wieku," *Kwartalnik Historii Kultury Materialnej*, Vol. 47 (1999), pp. 149–155.

21. Jerzy Motylewicz, "Żydzi w miastach ziemi Przemyskich i Sanockiej w drugiej połowie XVII i w XVIII wieku," *Żydzi w Małopolsce: Studia z dziejów osadnictwa i życia społecznego*, edited by Feliks Kiryk (Przemysl, 1991), p. 121. Sometimes churchmen objected to Jews living on the marketplace which was the scene of church processions. They viewed the presence of Jews and particularly of a synagogue as blasphemous. Adam Kaźmierczyk, *Żydzi Polscy 1648–1772: Źródła* (Cracow, 2001), no. 21, p. 32 (1725).

2

A Shtetl with a Yeshiva
The Case of Volozhin

Immanuel Etkes

The first thing that comes to mind whenever one hears the name "Volozhin" is the yeshiva, which was founded in the early nineteenth century by Rabbi Hayyim of Volozhin. In the course of that century, it became the most important institution of Torah studies in the Jewish world.[1] However, "Volozhin" is also the name of a town, the one where the famous yeshiva was located. This chapter focuses on the questions: What sort of relations were there between the yeshiva and the town, which in many ways was no different from many other shtetls in Lithuania? How was the town seen in the eyes of the yeshiva students? And how were the yeshiva students seen by the people of the town? Were there mutual connections in daily life, and, if so, what were they like?

Information relating to these questions can be found in the memoirs of Rabbi Meir Bar-Ilan, the son of Rabbi Zvi Yehudah Berlin, who was the head of the yeshiva in the second half of the nineteenth century, and who was widely known as *Hanetziv*. Here are Bar-Ilan's words:

Relations between the yeshiva students and the townspeople of Volozhin were not bad, just as they were not good: there simply were no relations between them. For it was a kind of city within a city.[2]

Later on Bar-Ilan shows what the people of the shtetl looked like to the yeshiva students:

> If outwardly there was no contact between the yeshiva students and the townsfolk, inwardly there was a certain attitude of contempt on the part of the former toward the latter. They would look down their noses at them. Not only that, there was a well-known word for the residents of the town: "*stopaks*" [stoppers]. Whenever a yeshiva student was in an angry or jocular mood and said "stopper," the concept was clear. It meant a Jew who had no connection with the yeshiva.[3]

Bar-Ilan portrays the relations between the yeshiva students and the townsfolk as distant, saying that the yeshiva students regarded the residents of the town with contempt. Other accounts present a more balanced and complex picture of the relations between the yeshiva and the shtetl. However, those accounts, too, lead to the inevitable conclusion that the relations were characterized by a gross imbalance, in which the yeshiva students had the upper hand. When we seek to understand the background and the causes of this imbalance, we must first examine the relations between yeshivas and communities in the generations preceding the establishment of the Volozhin Yeshiva.

The type of yeshiva that was common in traditional Ashkenazic society from the sixteenth to the eighteenth centuries may be called the "community yeshiva" because it was, in fact, supported by the community. According to the regulations instituted by the autonomous Jewish national organizations, every community was required to maintain a yeshiva. The number of yeshiva students was determined by the economic power of the community. The rabbi of the community usually served as the head of the yeshiva, and support of the yeshiva students was provided by the members of the community (*ba'alei batim*). They contributed money for the weekly stipend of the students and invited them to eat at their tables, an arrangement that was known as "eating days."[4]

Those who drafted the regulations regarding the maintenance of yeshivas made an effort to create a balance between the community and the yeshiva. In order to compensate for the absolute financial dependence of the yeshiva on the local community, the head of the yeshiva was given complete autonomy with respect to the management of the yeshiva itself. He had the authority to accept students into the yeshiva or to expel them from it. Similarly, the head of the yeshiva was authorized to determine the weekly stipend that each student received. On the other hand, the community determined the number of students who could study in the yeshiva, and they received their allowances directly from the *gabaim* (officials) of the community.[5] Yeshivas of that kind were modest in size, and a few dozen students, at the very most, studied in each of them. Consequently, their public influence usually did not extend beyond the boundaries of the community where they were located and by which they were supported.

The arrangement by which local communities supported yeshivas gradually disappeared during the eighteenth century. The reasons for this appear to have been mainly economic. Nevertheless, it is possible that the decline in the status of Torah study and of Torah scholars, which followed the spread of Hasidism, also influenced this process. In any event, when Rabbi Hayyim of Volozhin wanted to establish a yeshiva in the early nineteenth century, it was clear to him that he could no longer count on the old arrangement for supporting yeshivas. Therefore, instead of turning to the community of Volozhin, where he was serving as the rabbi, he chose to base the funding of the yeshiva on a new system: in a letter that he circulated among the Jews of Lithuania, Rabbi Hayyim called upon the public to support the yeshiva. In effect, he was asking for voluntary support on the part of individuals who identified with the values of the yeshiva. Indeed, many people responded to Rabbi Hayyim's appeal and contributed money. Over time, the circle of contributors spread throughout the Pale of Settlement, to Western Europe, and even to the United States. A team of *meshulahim*, or agents of the yeshiva, raised money and transferred it to the yeshiva.[6]

The new system of funding had far-reaching social consequences. First, the yeshiva was detached from the local community and no longer depended on it. Indeed, within a few years, the Volozhin Yeshiva became a focus of spiritual and religious leadership for the whole country. A large public, including students and graduates of the yeshiva, those who had contributed money to it, and many others who had heard of it and identified with it, viewed the Volozhin Yeshiva as a model and source of authority.

At the same time, a very significant change also took place in the status of yeshiva students in relation to the residents of the shtetl. Many sources report the humiliation that was involved in "eating days" at the tables of *ba'alei batim*. Although support of Torah scholars was regarded as a religious duty, many students from community yeshivas felt as if eating at the tables of householders was like begging. The students of the Volozhin Yeshiva were exempt from that humiliation, for they bought their food with stipends given to them from the yeshiva treasury. The change in the status of the students was expressed, among other things, in the new name given to them. The old name of *yeshiva-bokher*, which had a connotation of misery and poverty, was now replaced by a new name, *yeshive-man*.

Not only was the Volozhin yeshiva no longer dependent on money from the community of Volozhin, but the tables were now turned: the yeshiva became an important source of livelihood for many townspeople. The yeshiva students rented rooms in the homes of townspeople, and they generally ate in those homes. For these services, the students paid in full with the stipends they received from the yeshiva.

We do not possess exact data regarding the role played by the yeshiva in the livelihood of the townspeople. However, it is possible to make a good estimate. According to a census taken in 1897, nearly 2,500 Jews lived in Volozhin, out of a total population of about 4,500 people. As for the number of students in the yeshiva, various sources indicate that in the second half of the nineteenth century they came to 400. One writer argues for a higher number, claiming that in the 1880s and early 1890s, when the yeshiva was at its height, nearly 500 students attended.

The sources of livelihood of the Jews of Volozhin included trade in lumber, grain, flax, and livestock. Four times a year, great fairs were held in the town, in addition to the weekly market days. Thus, many of the town's Jews earned their living from trade on various levels and from handicrafts. Hosting the yeshiva students was also an important source of income. Some families took in two, three, or even four students. However, many students made other arrangements. Usually these were the married students or the wealthier among them. According to the numbers presented above, we may estimate that about 200 families took in one or more yeshiva student. In some cases, taking in the yeshiva students was the family's main source of livelihood, and in some cases, it was a source of extra income. In any event, it may be stated with a high degree of certainty that the livelihood of about half of the Jewish families of Volozhin was based to one degree or another on accommodating yeshiva students.

We can draw some conclusions about the amounts of money received by the Jews of Volozhin for taking in yeshiva students from the budget of the yeshiva in the 1880s.[7] In 1883 the yeshiva allocated 6,000 rubles for that purpose, in 1884 it allocated 7,500 rubles to it, and in 1885 the sum came to 10,769 rubles. To that sum we must add the salary received by the heads of the yeshiva and its workers which, when spent, added to the vitality of the economic activity in the town. Moreover, thanks to the yeshiva, Volozhin became an attraction for visitors from elsewhere. Among them were wealthy merchants and important rabbis who came to the town in order to see the splendid yeshiva there with their own eyes.[8] Naturally those visits also contributed to the town's economy.

Thus, we have found that the Volozhin Yeshiva caused a radical change in the balance of power between the community and the yeshiva. Earlier, in places other than Volozhin, there had been a certain equilibrium between the two bodies: the yeshiva was dependent on the community for its support, and the community received prestige thanks to the yeshiva. The Volozhin Yeshiva, by contrast, did not depend on the support of the townspeople, and there was no longer any institutional connection between it and the local community. Furthermore, the livelihood of many residents of the town now depended on the yeshiva. However radical these changes were, though, the new balance of power between the yeshiva and the town cannot fully explain the distant and supercilious attitude of the yeshiva students, as it is reflected in Bar-Ilan's memoirs. It seems probable that other important factors were at work in this context, including the ethos and values that characterized the Volozhin Yeshiva.

Among the Jews of Lithuania in the nineteenth century, a scholarly elite arose that enjoyed great prestige. The image and character of that elite were greatly influenced by the personal example of the Vilna Gaon and by the ideological doctrines and educational activities of Rabbi Hayyim of Volozhin.[9] The Vilna Gaon established a model of excellence in Torah study. His extraordinary achievements were the result not only of his talents but also of his way of life, mainly his withdrawal from all worldly matters and his unbounded devotion to Torah study. Rabbi Hayyim, who based his doctrine on Kabbalistic ideas, stated that Torah study keeps the world in existence—quite literally. Hence, Torah scholars bore responsibility for the existence of the world. Furthermore, Rabbi Hayyim claimed that Torah study was also the most promising means for spiritual elevation and for bringing the individual close to God.

The primacy of the Volozhin Yeshiva, the fact that it was founded and led by Rabbi Hayyim, the greatest of the Vilna Gaon's disciples, the high level of the yeshiva students, and the ethos of dedication to study that characterized them made the Volozhin Yeshiva a symbol of excellence. In the eyes of many Jews of Lithuania, and certainly in the eyes of its leaders and scholars, the Volozhin Yeshiva was viewed as the marvelous embodiment of the ideal of Torah study. This, of course, had social consequences: the students and graduates of the yeshiva enjoyed extraordinary prestige among the Jews of Lithuania. Among other things, they enjoyed a considerable advantage with respect to matchmaking and obtaining rabbinical posts. It is not surprising that the self-image of these yeshiva students was also extremely high. They regarded themselves as members of a spiritual and religious elite that everyone had to honor. This, then, was the background of the arrogant attitude of the yeshiva students toward the towns-people.

Let us now return to Bar-Ilan's memoirs. To emphasize the distance between the yeshiva and the town, Bar-Ilan points to the fact that the Volozhin Yeshiva collected contributions from every Jewish community with the exception of that of Volozhin, which was never asked to contribute. Bar-Ilan goes on to say that he does not know whether that custom was instituted from the start or whether it developed on its own. In any event, he interprets it to the detriment of the people of Volozhin: the fact that they were not asked to contribute to the yeshiva placed them "to a certain degree below the inhabitants of other towns."[10]

Bar-Ilan finds another expression of the distance between the yeshiva and the town in the fact that the yeshiva students almost never entered the local *bet midrash* (house of study). The exceptions were those who were late to prayers in the yeshiva and hoped to find a *minyan* (prayer quorum) in the *bet midrash*. Conversely, only outstanding individuals from among the townspeople entered the yeshiva building. Moreover, even in the rooms where yeshiva students lived, a distance was maintained between them and the householders: "They were truly two different worlds. When a yeshiva student rented a place to live, or when he settled his account, he dealt with the landlady. The men of the house, the householders, had no part in those matters."[11]

This fact can of course be seen as reflecting the status of women in managing household affairs and the division of functions between wives and husbands. However, Bar-Ilan prefers to see it as another manifestation of the distance between the yeshiva students and the townspeople. Citing an unusual example of solidarity with the townspeople, Bar-Ilan mentions that the yeshiva students rallied to put out fires that broke out from time to time. However, that volunteerism was not without self-interest, for the fires also threatened the yeshiva building, the homes of the head of the yeshiva, and the rooms where the students stayed.

Bar-Ilan devotes a detailed description to a conflict that broke out between the yeshiva students and the community leaders of Volozhin. The conflict focused on the *korobka*, the indirect tax paid by the Jews when they bought kosher meat. During the nineteenth century, the revenue from that indirect tax was the main source of income for the communities. However, the yeshiva students came to the decision that the community should reimburse them for the tax they had paid for eating meat. The background of this demand was the financial distress of the *Biqur Holim* society, which operated among the yeshiva students, helping those who were ill by paying for doctors and medicines. Because many of the students were ill, and the expenses were very high, the members of the society sought new sources of revenue, in addition to the contributions made by the students themselves. Thus, it occurred to them to demand return of the *korobka* from the community leaders. When this demand was refused, the students declared a boycott on meat slaughtered in the town of Volozhin and began to import meat from other towns. This step made the conflict more severe and led to a physical confrontation between the butchers and the yeshiva students. Ultimately a compromise was reached through the intervention of a number of rabbis from other communities. The Netziv, however, took care not to be involved in the conflict between his students and the townspeople.[12]

In describing the incident, Bar-Ilan tends to emphasize the solidarity shown by the yeshiva students toward their sick colleagues. However, his words show no understanding of—to say nothing of identification with—the viewpoint of the community leaders. The most sympathetic remark in Bar-Ilan's memoirs regarding the householders of Volozhin refers to those who led the prayers in the yeshiva on the High Holy Days. Bar-Ilan describes them as marvelous cantors, "unlike any in our generation." At the same time he stresses that to be invited to lead the prayers in the yeshiva was, for them, "a great privilege."

The impression that the attitude of the yeshiva students toward the townspeople was distant and arrogant emerges both from Bar-Ilan's factual accounts and from his interpretations of the facts. While we have no reason to doubt the veracity of his memoirs as an expression of his true personal experience and point of view, they cannot be viewed as a full and balanced representation of the relations between the yeshiva and the town. For it is difficult to imagine that young men in their teens would live for a long period in the homes of townspeople without forming any personal ties with them at all, without ever needing their help, as in cases of illness, and without showing any interest in their daughters. Indeed, as we shall see below, we possess more balanced testimony that modifies the picture painted by Bar-Ilan.

It must also be remembered that Bar-Ilan was the son of the Netziv, and his memoirs naturally reflect the point of view of the leadership of the yeshiva. The extended family of the heads of the Volozhin Yeshiva were known as *Beit Harav* (the Rabbi's House), and they enjoyed a kind of noble status. Another member of this family was Rabbi Baruch Epstein, the author of the well-known book, *Meqor barukh* (The Source of Barukh), who spent several years as a student in the Volozhin Yeshiva. He was the nephew of the Netziv and, after his second marriage, became his brother-in-law.

In his memoirs of the Volozhin Yeshiva, Epstein devotes considerable space to a description of the Netziv's personal virtues. In so doing, he recounts an anecdote from a Purim banquet in which the Netziv was sitting with his students in an atmosphere of closeness and companionship, and one of the students was so bold as to ask:

> Will our Rabbi please explain to us, for we all see and know, that whenever someone comes through Volozhin, there is no limit to the wonderment of his soul and the elation of his spirit because of the splendor of the honor of the Torah that prevails in it. . . . Yet why is it that the people of the town of Volozhin itself, . . . they who see the prestige of the Torah every day and every night, . . . nevertheless remain on the level of ordinary people, of spiritual degradation and obtuseness. Their eyes see and their ears hear this holy sight, yet they seem like people who have never seen the light of Torah in their days.[13]

The Netziv answered this question by telling an anecdote: once, during the *haqafot* (circling round) of Simhat Torah, a girl caught his attention. While all the other boys and girls pushed in on every side to kiss one of the Torah scrolls, the girl stood on the sidelines as though Torah scrolls meant nothing to her. When the Netziv asked the meaning of her behavior, the girl answered that her father was a scribe and that her house contained many Torah scrolls. The girl's answer, continued the Netziv, contains the answer to the question regarding the behavior of the people of Volozhin. Since these people are always near the yeshiva, it is no wonder that they do not express the enthusiasm about it that is expressed by guests who come from far away.

The arrogance of the yeshiva students toward the townspeople, as reflected in the anecdote told by Epstein, is more outspoken than what we found in Bar-Ilan's memoirs. The student who asked the question to the Netziv accused the people of the town of "spiritual degradation and obtuseness," because they did not accord the yeshiva the honor due to it.

For his part, the Netziv defended the people of Volozhin and rejected the charge against them.

Indeed, in contrast to the removed and arrogant tone of the writings of Bar-Ilan and Epstein, other voices can heard in memoirs written by graduates of the Volozhin Yeshiva. We find that at least for some of the yeshiva students, contact with the townspeople was a positive experience that made a favorable impression on them.

Rabbi Isser Unterman, for example, who was to become the Chief Rabbi of Israel, studied in the Volozhin Yeshiva around 1910 when its head was Rabbi Raphael Shapira.[14] According to him, at that time there were several distinguished scholars who lived with their families in the town of Volozhin. They served as a bridge between the yeshiva and the town. He also spoke of the influence of the yeshiva on the townspeople, saying that the householders of Volozhin wished to bring up their sons to be Torah scholars, and they found husbands for their daughters among the yeshiva students. Unterman became aware of the high level of Torah knowledge among the people of Volozhin from the following episode:

> I remember that an important guest came from Lodz, a respected merchant and learned Jew, to visit his sons in the yeshiva, and he told "great things" about the wagon drivers of Volozhin. While he rode from the Polochny station to the city, a three hour journey, he heard the wagon driver quote homilies and verses . . . and he was amazed. He was used to riding in wagons from city to city in Poland, and in ten years, he had never heard so much Torah from wagon drivers as he had heard in that journey to Volozhin.[15]

Unterman's description is idealized, but the wagon driver whom he described was apparently a real person: Rabbi Peretz the teamster, who is also mentioned in the memoirs of Yehudah Hayyim Kotler:

> My happiest days were those when I studied in the *Etz Hayyim Yeshiva* in Volozhin. A figure impressed on my memory from those days is Rabbi Peretz the teamster, a former student at the yeshiva, and a great scholar. After his marriage, he bought a horse and wagon and made his living by taking yeshiva students back and forth from the railroad station. . . . Once I rode to the railroad station with him to make my way to Vilna. I intended to study in a yeshiva there on an independent basis, as a student who did not need a rabbi. . . . Independent students did not eat "days" but received their allowance from the treasury of the yeshiva. On the way I told Rabbi Peretz

about the purpose of my trip. Hearing what I said, he stopped the horse and
called a halt in the journey, saying: "Let me examine your strength in
Gemara, to see whether you have really reached the level of an independent
student." He wanted to test me on Tractate *Nedarim*, for which there is no
commentary by Rashi. Therefore, I asked him to test me on a different tractate. Rabbi Peretz said: "If you can't study a tractate without Rashi's commentary, you show that you haven't reached the level of an independent
student, and you'd be better off eating days."[16]

Unlike Unterman and most of the other authors of memoirs, Kotler was
not only a student in the Volozhin Yeshiva but also came from the town of
Volozhin. Perhaps that is the reason why the first person who comes to
mind when he begins his memoirs is Rabbi Peretz the teamster. Kotler also
tells about a landlady who, during a famine, took care to feed the yeshiva
student who was living in her house with boiled potatoes. That woman
used to listen attentively to her student when he recited the grace after
meals.

Living figures from among the townspeople are also present in the
memoirs of Aharon Zvi Dudman-Dudai.[17] Like Rabbi Unterman and
Kotler, Dudai also studied in Volozhin at the time of Rabbi Raphael
Shapira. According to him, more than three hundred students attended
the yeshiva, and some of them married women from Volozhin. Dudai
even lists them by name, giving details about the families whose daughters
married yeshiva students. Dudai also remembers the name of quite a few
townspeople and mentions them one after the other, indicating their voca-
tions:

> The tailor of the yeshiva was Reb Hayyim. Shoes and boots were sewn by
> the son of Yekutiel. The town physician was Reb. Aharon Tzart and later his
> son Abraham. . . . The warden was Reb David. One of the water-carriers is
> engraved in my memory. His name was "Pinya the water carrier." He owned
> a horse and wagon. He brought the water from *aroftsu* to *aroiftsu* [from the
> lower to the upper part of the town]. Sometimes his horse would balk and
> stand halfway up the hill and refuse to move. Then merciful Jews would
> gather and perform the commandment of "thou shalt surely help" so that
> the wagon wouldn't roll down.[18]

Dudai also remembers the names of the householders in whose homes
he lived while he was studying at the yeshiva. One of them made an espe-

cially strong impression on him: "Then I moved to Vilna Street and stayed in the home of Rabbi Hertz Eskind. He was a model of diligent learning. Every night he would stand and study with a candle in his hand."[19] Such close attention to the townspeople as we find in Dudai's memoirs can be found in no other writing about Volozhin that is known to me. Perhaps the explanation for this is to be found in the lines with which he chose to conclude his memoirs: "Volozhin, the mother of yeshivot in Russia, Lithuania, and Poland—how have you been orphaned? The dreadful Holocaust destroyed you. All our saintly relatives have been burned in fire. May their memory be blessed."

How is it possible to understand the difference between the reserved and arrogant tone of Bar-Ilan's and Epstein's writings and the friendlier position toward the townspeople that emerges from the writings of Unterman, Kotler, Dudai, and others? The first answer is that there were indeed different attitudes among the yeshiva students regarding the townspeople. Another explanation might lie in the periods when the memoir writers stayed in Volozhin. The writers who display a more sympathetic attitude toward the townspeople studied in the yeshiva in the beginning of the twentieth century. By then, the Volozhin Yeshiva had already lost some of the great prestige that it had enjoyed at the time of the Netziv. Moreover, at that time the age of the yeshiva students rose, and for that reason they were probably more sensitive to the human environment in which they lived. Finally, as suggested above, it is most likely that memoirs written after World War II reflect awareness of the terrible loss, and therefore they express affection for all the Jews of the town of Volozhin.

Between the two voices described here—those expressing a reserved and arrogant attitude toward the townspeople and those showing fondness for them—stand the memoirs of graduates of the yeshiva as well as the descriptions of visitors from outside, many of whom simply ignored the townspeople. A typical example is the book of memoirs written by Rabbi Yitzhak Nissenboim, *'Alei heldi* (*About My Youth*). Nissenboim devotes a special chapter to a description of the experience of his studies in Volozhin during the 1880s. He speaks at length about the daily schedule of the yeshiva, about the difference between the lessons of the two heads of the yeshiva, the Netziv and Rabbi Hayyim Soloveichik, about prayer in the yeshiva, and about the various types of students. However, the town of Volozhin and its inhabitants are absent from his memoirs.

When we try to summarize the testimony regarding relations between the Volozhin Yeshiva and the town of Volozhin, the imbalance between them stands out. The Volozhin Yeshiva was seen both by itself and by the public as the leading yeshiva of Lithuania. In a society that venerated the Torah and those who studied it, Volozhin enjoyed extraordinary prestige. The town of Volozhin, in contrast, was one of many shtetls, and the main thing of which it could boast was the famous yeshiva located there.

We posses no testimony written by the townspeople of Volozhin. The only source for their attitude toward the yeshiva students is found in the memoirs of the graduates. From their writing, it appears that the towns-people admired the yeshiva students and treated them with great respect. This fact seems self-evident, for the Jews of Volozhin were part and parcel of the Jewish society of Lithuania, and they shared its values.

The inferiority of the community of Volozhin compared to the yeshiva was expressed, among other things, in the character of the rela-tions with its rabbi. As mentioned earlier, Rabbi Hayyim of Volozhin served as the rabbi of the community of Volozhin before he established the yeshiva. For that reason, there was a tradition in Volozhin that the head of the yeshiva was also the rabbi of the community. From testi-mony about the Netziv's way of life, however, it appears that he devoted most of his time and effort to the yeshiva, whereas his contacts with the townspeople were quite limited. Indeed, the Netziv always prayed in the yeshiva. His visits to the town synagogue were limited to the sermons that he gave on the eve of Yom Kippur, on one of the two days of Rosh Hashanah, on *Shabat Shuvah* ("the Sabbath of repentance" between Rosh Hashanah and Yom Kippur), and on *Shabat Hagadol* ("the great Sab-bath" before Passover). Thus, it appears that the people of Volozhin had to make do with very little direct attention from their rabbi. At the same time, they could console themselves with the great honor that had befallen them, for the rabbi of their community also was the head of the most famous yeshiva in the Jewish world.

The encounter between the Volozhin Yeshiva and the town of Volozhin thus tells us less about the Jews of Volozhin than about the character and self-image of the scholarly elite that grew up in Lithuania during the nine-teenth century. This was a closed elite whose goal was the development of the scholarly excellence of each of its individual members. The members of the scholarly elite believed that their Torah study made a vital contribu-tion to the existence of the Jewish people. Nevertheless, they had no sense of a mission involving direct action in the community. On the contrary, their devotion to Torah study required them to detach themselves as much as possible from daily life and social problems. The tendency of the scholarly elite to shut itself off and concentrate all its efforts on fostering the achievements of its members stands out against the background of the new elites that appeared among the Jews of Eastern Europe during the nineteenth century: the *Haskalah* movement, Zionism, and the socialist movement. All of these produced leaders imbued with a sense of mission on behalf of society and the Jewish people.

Thus, the attitude of the students of the Volozhin Yeshiva toward the townspeople derived from the character of the scholarly elite. Essentially this was a functional attitude: the purpose of the town of Volozhin was to supply lodging and food to the students of Torah and to treat them with respect. In the view of the yeshiva students, the townspeople of Volozhin represented "simple" householders, those who were not learned. If many yeshiva students also displayed a reserved and arrogant attitude toward the townspeople, some students simply ignored them. To be sure, some of the yeshiva students did show fondness for the residents of Volozhin. But that fondness was influenced by scholarly ideals. Thus, it was possible to praise the cantors of Volozhin for making the prayers of the yeshiva students more pleasant; and it was possible to praise householders who wanted their sons to be Torah scholars and who took yeshiva students as husbands for their daughters; and of course it was possible to be amazed by Rabbi Peretz the teamster because he was not simply a wagon driver, but also a learned scholar.

Consequently, we can conclude as we began: the name "Volozhin" stands for a yeshiva with a shtetl, rather than a shtetl with a yeshiva.

NOTES

1. For a comprehensive discussion of the Volozhin Yeshiva, see Saul Stampfer, *The Lithuanian Yeshiva* (Jerusalem, 1995), pp. 217–225 (Hebrew). See also the recent study by Mordechai Breuer, *The Tents of Torah: The Yeshiva, Its Stucture and History* (Jerusalem, 2004) (Hebrew). On the background for the establishment of the Volozhin Yeshiva, see Immanuel Etkes, *The Gaon of Vilna—The Man and His Image* (Berkeley, 2002), pp. 151–208. For memoirs written by former students at the Volozhin Yeshiva in the late nineteenth century, see *Memoirs of the Lithuanian Yeshiva*, edited by Immanuel Etkes and Shlomo Tikochinski (Jerusalem, 2004), pp. 218–259 (Hebrew).

2. Meir Bar-Ilan, *From Volozhin to Jerusalem* (Tel Aviv, 1971), Vol. 1, p. 107.

3. Ibid., p. 108.

4. Jacob Katz, *Tradition and Crisis: Jewish Society at the End of the Middle Ages* (New York, 1993), pp. 164–169. Mordechai Breuer, *Tents of Torah*, pp. 308–314.

5. See, for example, "Regulations of the State in Moravia," in Simchah Assaf, ed., *Sources for the History of Jewish Education* (Tel Aviv, 1954), Vol. 1, pp. 134–137 (Hebrew).

6. See Stampfer, *The Lithuanian Yeshiva*, pp. 31–43.

7. Ibid., p. 187.

8. Baruch Epstein, *Meqor Baruch* (Vilna, 1928), part 4, p. 1814.

9. On the image of the Vilna Gaon as a great Torah scholar and on the doctrinal teachings of Rabbi Hayyim of Volozhin, see Immanuel Etkes, *The Gaon of Vilna*, pp. 10–36 and pp. 151–202, respectively.

10. Meir Bar-Ilan, *From Volozhin to Jerusalem*, p. 81.

11. Ibid., p. 107.

12. Ibid., pp. 109–111; Stampfer, *The Lithuanian Yeshiva*, pp. 143–144.

13. Baruch Epstein, *Meqor Baruch*, part 4, pp. 1816–1817.

14. Rabbi Raphael Shapira (1837–1921), was the head of the Volozhin Yeshiva from 1899 until World War I.

15. Wolozin, *The Book of the City and of Etz Hayyim Yeshiva*, Eliezer Leoni, ed. (Tel Aviv, 1970), pp. 333–335.

16. Ibid.

17. Ibid., pp. 332–333.

18. Ibid., p. 333.

19. Ibid.

3

Rebbetzins, Wonder-Children, and the Emergence of the Dynastic Principle in Hasidism

Nehemia Polen

The Origin of Hasidic Dynasties

The institution of the tsaddik and the lineal inheritance of the position of tsaddik are considered perhaps the most characteristic features of the social structure of Hasidism. Yet while the theology of the tsaddik and his role are discussed at length in Hasidic theoretical literature, the dynastic principle is seldom discussed—or even mentioned—in Hasidic *derashot* (sermons, or discourses). Similarly, while the emergence of the Hasidic dynasties has been duly noted in scholarly studies, the reasons for that emergence have never been fully explained. In a recently republished group of essays, Joseph Dan has underscored the centrality of the institution of the tsaddik for understanding Hasidism; according to Dan, it is the only really new feature of the movement as a whole.[1] After the first few decades of the movement's existence, the tsaddik's charismatic leadership became hereditary, so that "the *tzaddik* is a miracle worker both because of his charismatic relationship with the divine world and because of his being a descendant of great magicians like the Besht or the Maggid."[2] Eventually, the charismatic element dwindled, and entitlement to leadership became "genetic, rather than an intellectual or spiritual."[3] Dan characterizes hereditary leadership as "legitimate, organic, and central"[4] to the movement, yet he cannot entirely hide his puzzlement with this "stupendous phenomenon,"[5] which "introduced into Jewish culture the oxymoron of a hereditary charismatic leader and miracle worker."[6] Dan argues persuasively that the main factor securing the miraculous contemporary rebirth of Hasidic communities in the aftermath of the Holocaust and other recent crises was "adherence to their hereditary *tzaddikim*."[7] But this does not shed light on how the principle took hold originally, well over a century before the challenges of the twentieth century. Following in the footsteps of many earlier researchers, Dan explores the historical and theological roots of the institution of the tsaddik: the relationship to Sabbateanism, the mediation between heaven and earth, the responsibility of the tsaddik to channel blessings to his community, and so on. But nowhere does Dan explain why this theology required "the establishment of hereditary leadership in the people of Israel after almost a millenium of its absence."[8]

In her now-classic essay "Hasidism after 1772: Structural Continuity and Change,"[9] Ada Rapaport-Albert demonstrates that in the earliest period—the era of the Baal Shem Tov (d. 1760) and the Maggid of Mezhirech (d. 1772)—there was no dynastic principle at all. Rather, Hasidism began as a "loose association of autonomous units," and no thought was given to the inheritance of leadership. Indeed, the Maggid of Mezhirech, a charismatic figure of enormous power and stature, actively worked to promulgate Hasidism as a decentralized movement, with no thought of bequeathing a unified body of followers to his own biological heir.[10] Following Shmuel Ettinger's observation that "[The Maggid] set up group after group with a pupil at the head of almost every one," Rapaport-Albert concludes that the Maggid worked actively to establish courts in different centers—led by disciples, not descendents.[11]

So how and why did the principle of dynastic succession take hold? Rapaport-Albert suggests that this mode of organization arose to preserve the distinctive identities of the various schools after the death of the founder.[12] But this suffers from circularity: if, as Rapaport-Albert amply demonstrates, Hasidism began as a fraternity of leaders and followers loosely bound together by a distinctive set of religious practices and theological teachings, why could the movement not have continued on that basis? And if various schools developed as the movement grew and matured, why could not the "distinctive identity" of a school be preserved by a gifted disciple as well or better than by a son? Later in the same essay

Rapaport-Albert suggests that the Polish-Russian pattern of inheritance of noble estates may have served as a model.[13] This is indeed quite plausible, but we would still need to understand what internal forces arose within Hasidism at this time which made the aristocratic model appear attractive and legitimate. Rapaport-Albert poses the problem with admirable clarity: "The matter has not been addressed by scholars, but the institutionalization of the hereditary principle in both tsaddikism and hasidism should not be taken as self-explanatory."[14]

In point of fact, the move to hereditary succession was neither inevitable nor universal. Rabbi Elimelekh of Lyzhansk passed away in 1787, and it was his students such as the Seer of Lublin, the Maggid of Kozienice, and Rabbi Abraham Joshua Heschel of Apta who were seen as his primary successors.[15] In Eretz Israel, after the death of Rabbi Menahem Mendel of Vitebsk in 1788, Rabbi Abraham Kalisker was widely if not universally acknowledged as the former's legitimate successor and the leader of the Hasidic *Yishuv* in the Holy Land. In the Ukraine, R. Levi Yitzhak of Berdichev passed away in 1810, and despite his enormous reputation and influence, he never established a dynasty; his sons were rabbis and scholars, but they never became "Berdichever Rebbes."[16] Bratslav Hasidim rejected the dynastic principle entirely by regarding the death of Rabbi Nahman in 1810 as in some sense not real; the founder continued to lead them as an ongoing living presence.[17] In White Russia, after the death of Rabbi Shneur Zalman in 1813, a struggle for succession developed between one of the rabbi's sons and a gifted disciple, with the result hardly a foregone conclusion.[18] In Polish Hasidism, the hereditary principle never triumphed completely, as time and again a charismatic senior disciple attracted the younger Hasidim of an aging or deceased master. As late as the mid-nineteenth century, the Halakhic authority and tsaddik Rabbi Hayyim Halberstam could write that the office of Hasidic rebbe should not be inherited, since "I do not know how the ability to pray can be inherited."[19]

Stephen Sharot has studied the Hasidic dynasties from a sociological perspective, drawing upon Max Weber's work on the routinization of charisma.[20] While Sharot acknowledges that "[n]o detailed theology was developed to justify the dynastic principle," he makes reference to a Hasidic belief that "the holy thoughts of the tsaddik at the time of conception would bring down an exceptional soul from heaven and that a child conceived and brought up in holiness would himself be holy."[21] He further notes that "it was considered important for not only the tsaddik but also his wife to be of pure lineage. First-cousin marriages strengthened the 'holy seed' of the next tsaddik."[22]

In a similar vein, Louis Jacobs has written that "particularly from the period of the Seer of Lublin, the idea of dynastic succession took hold, in the belief that the *tsaddik*'s holy thoughts when he made love to his wife could succeed in drawing down a specially elevated soul into the child conceived, who was thereby ideally suited to take his father's place when the father departed this life."[23]

The term "holy seed"—*zera kodesh*—occurs frequently in Hasidic discussions of tsaddikim and their families. It appears originally in the Bible (Ezra 9:2; cf. Neh. 9:2), in the context of the post-exilic program of forbidding intermarriage and banishing foreign wives, so that the "holy seed" would no longer "mingle with the people of the land."[24] When applied to Hasidic tsaddikim, it clearly suggests a theology of genealogical sanctity, involving the wife and her *yihus* (distinguished ancestry) no less than the husband.

Yet most studies of Hasidism until now have largely overlooked the significance of women even in matters of genealogy. To take one striking example, the *Encyclopaedia Judaica* has an excellent chart of the relationships of the leading Hasidic dynasties, from the Baal Shem Tov to the present times, containing hundreds of names. With the exception of the Baal Shem Tov's daughter, women are completely absent. The key to the chart lists the following relationships: father, son, grandson, son-in-law, teacher-disciple; but not mother, wife, daughter, or sister-in-law. This near-complete omission confirms an unfortunate pattern to which feminist historians have called attention and which they have attempted to redress. As Joan Wallach Scott has written, "Recent research has shown that women were not inactive or absent from events that made history, but that they have been systematically left out of the official record."[25] We shall argue here that the role of the wives and mothers of tsaddikim was pivotal in the emergence of several key Hasidic dynasties and that the presence of women, when brought to the foreground, will reveal much about Hasidism in its economic, social, genealogical, and spiritual dimensions. The retrieval of this suppressed presence will be the subject of the rest of this essay.[26]

The Crisis of the Interregnum, 1802: Chava, the Mother of Rabbi Israel of Ruzhin, and the Appearance of the Yenuka

Around the year 1800 the distinctive identities of the various Hasidic courts began to emerge into full view.[27] In 1796, for example, Rabbi Shneur Zalman of Liady published his famous work known popularly as *Tanya*, which did so much to forge the special character of Habad Hasidism. In 1802 Rabbi Nathan of Nemirov, a devotee of Hasidism who had previously visited many tsaddikim, became a faithful disciple of Rabbi Nahman of Bratslav, apprenticing himself to this one master exclusively. As the foremost follower and amanuensis of Rabbi Nahman, Rabbi Nathan had a central role in the crystallization of Bratslav Hasidism.[28] And in 1798, after the death of Rabbi Menahem Nahum of Chernobyl, his son Rabbi Mordecai succeeded him; this has been called the first appearance of the dynastic principle in Hasidism.[29] It was due in large measure to Rabbi Mordecai that the House of Chernobyl became the exemplar of what is meant by a Hasidic dynasty. He was among the first tsaddikim to establish an aristocratic court on the grand style; each of his eight sons became a rebbe in his own right, establishing courts in various Ukrainian towns and thereby propelling the geographic diffusion of Chernobyl Hasidism and the movement as a whole.[30]

David Assaf, in his recent biography of the celebrated tsaddik Rabbi Israel of Ruzhin (1796–1850), states that "little is known about Chava," Israel's mother.[31] And indeed, in the over five hundred pages of his meticulously documented and insightfully written study of Rabbi Israel, Chava receives only passing mention. In this, Assaf mirrors the more traditional works of Hasidic hagiography, which, when they speak of Chava or most other women, nearly always do so to highlight and frame the virtues of the male tsaddik. Yet Chava lived to about seventy-five, an unusually long lifespan in those days; she outlived Rabbi Shalom Shakhna, her husband and Rabbi Israel's father, by forty-two years. (Rabbi Shalom Shakhna was the grandson of the Rabbi Dov Ber, the Maggid of Mezhirech, the most famous figure in Hasidism after the Baal Shem Tov and widely considered the actual founder of Hasidism as an organized movement.) She accompanied her son through every stage of his controversial and stormy career and died in Sadgora only six years before he did. It is hard to believe that she was not a significant influence on her famous son, despite the near silence of the sources. In such a circumstance it seems appropriate to carefully examine and reassess the materials we have, bringing neglected information to the foreground and looking for patterns which eluded or were not of interest to earlier writers. What emerges not only will tell us much about women in Hasidism, but will shed new light on the Hasidic movement as a whole.[32]

One unusual phenomenon which appeared early in the Hasidic movement was the *yenuka*, the "wonder-child" who assumes a leadership role at a very young age. As Assaf notes, perhaps the very first *yenuka* in Hasidism was Abraham (1787–1813), Chava's eldest son. When Abraham's father Rabbi Shalom Shakhna died in 1802, the fifteen-year-old Abraham took over the leadership of his father's Hasidim. Rabbi Shalom Shakhna died just before Sukkot that year, and as the Hasidim tell the story, "on the first night of Sukkot [just hours after his father's funeral and burial] Rabbi Abraham entered the sukkah, sat on his father's seat, and began to assume the reins of leadership, in the grand manner, as his father's successor."[33]

The assumption of communal leadership by a fifteen-year-old boy was noted with derision by the maskilim. Joseph Perl mentions Abraham by name in his anti-Hasidic polemic, *Uiber das Wesen der Sekte Chassidim* (On the Nature of the Sect of the Hasidim), completed in 1816.[34] And from that time on, the phenomenon of the *yenuka* became a frequent target of maskilic scorn and satire. We will have more to say about a later instance of this below.

Abraham's behavior is never fully explained in the Hasidic sources. Many of the faithful probably saw it as just one more example of the preternatural powers of the tsaddik, often expressed in patterns of action which cannot be comprehended by lesser mortals. The more learned undoubtedly recalled passages in the Zohar where a *yenuka* makes an appearance, bringing particularly sublime and recondite wisdom.[35] For his part, Assaf sees Abraham's action as "cynical behavior," a power-grab by a youngster who, in his "urgent need for legitimization," rushed to gain the assent of his family to his succession.[36] But how plausible is it that a youngster, barely fifteen years old (as Joseph Perl already pointed out in 1816), is so filled with the urge for power and the attendant burdens and responsibilities of communal leadership, that he grabs the reins just a few hours after his dead father has been interred? It is certainly reasonable to ask whether an adult may have been involved in the decision.

The main account of young Abraham's succession appears in a hagiographic collection of Ruzhin traditions known as *Bet Yisrael* (House of Israel), originally published in 1913 by Reuben Zak.[37] The stories about Rabbi Abraham do not hide the astonishment felt by many, even among the Hasidim, that such a youngster had assumed the reins of his father's community.

It is interesting that nearly all the accounts of this episode make specific mention of Abraham's mother. One such tradition states that

> on that night of Sukkot [Abraham] took his younger brother, the future Ruzhiner Rebbe [who was six years old at the time], and wanted to enter the sukkah. He said, "We must first go to our mother the *zaddeket* and say *Gut Yom Tov* (essentially, Happy Holiday) to her." He told her, "God now has a new guest in heaven; we ought to send Him something in honor of the guest. What should I send? I will say Kiddush in his honor." So he entered the sukkah and made Kiddush.[38]

Chava's response is not recorded, but her silence suggests agreement. And the line "'We must first go to our mother the zaddeket (a saintly individual) . . .'" may be a way of hinting at the obvious: that no family decision—especially at such a time, and of such consequence—could have been made without the mother, and that Chava may have been actively involved from the very beginning. In any event, it is clear that Abraham was concerned to receive his mother's consent, post facto if not ab initio.

Consider the following: Chava was a granddaughter of Rabbi Menahem Nahum of Chernobyl (1730–1797), a foundational personality from Hasidism's early period, a disciple of the Baal Shem Tov and the Maggid of Mezhirech, and the author of the seminal work *Me'or Eynayim* (The Light of the Eyes).[39] Chava's uncle was Rabbi Menahem Nahum's son and successor, Rabbi Mordecai of Chernobyl (1770–1837). As noted above, he was one of the first tsaddikim to live on a grand scale, in the manner of Russian nobility.[40]

Rabbi Shalom Shakhna enjoyed a successful tenure as rebbe in Prohobitch. His popularity extended to the wider region; he was a well-known and respected personality throughout Ukrainian Hasidism.[41] He must have had a sizable following. In light of this, it should come as no surprise that he had already begun living in a princely manner, much unlike his ascetic father, Rabbi Abraham "the Angel." This mirrors the generational trajectory that his wife Chava had experienced in Chernobyl. Her grandfather Rabbi Menahem Nahum had lived a life of extreme self-denial and poverty, while his son Rabbi Mordecai—Chava's uncle—had introduced the aristocratic style of leadership.

At the time of Rabbi Shalom Shakhna's passing in 1802, Chava was confronted with the dissipation of his community and the collapse of her position within it. We recall that at this time dynastic rights were not universally asserted or recognized, and the very notion of an "heir" to the seat of a tsaddik had not fully crystallized. In general the corporate identity of a Hasidic community did not long survive without direct personal contact with a living master.[42] Without the announcement of a successor, the Hasidim of Prohobitch would have naturally dispersed, each looking for a new tsaddik in some other location. But if the Hasidic community of Prohobitch were not to survive with its identity intact, Chava would have been just another widow with most uncertain prospects. And without dynastic succession, her two sons would have been not heirs, but mere orphans in a society which had no dearth of fatherless children.

The force of these concerns is brought into greater relief when seen in light of an earlier episode in the family's history. Rabbi Abraham the Angel—Rabbi Shalom Shakhna's father, son of the Maggid of Mezhirech—had himself died young, in the fall of 1776. His widow, Gitl, left her two young children and went to Eretz Israel, spending the rest of her life there in obscurity. The two orphans were taken in by the tsaddik Rabbi Shlomo of Karlin, who educated them and found appropriate matches when the time came (the older brother married Rabbi Shlomo's own daughter, while Shalom Shakhna was betrothed to the granddaughter of Rabbi Menahem Nahum of Chernobyl—our Chava). Gitl's departure was never explained, and the whole episode is shrouded in obscurity. But the abandonment of the eight-year old Shalom Shakhna by his mother, just after the death of his father, must have profoundly shaken him and left its mark on the entire family. Now, one generation later, Rabbi Shalom Shakhna had himself died, leaving two young children. It must have seemed an eerie echo of the past, with history in danger of repeating itself. The fifteen-year-old Abraham would have had strong motivation to step in and try to fill his father's shoes, for his own sake as well as for his mother's. Nothing would have been more important than the stability of the family, which required the continuity of the community his father had built up.

Abraham and his mother, Chava, had a convergence of interests. The fifteen-year-old still needed his mother, for himself and his six-year-old brother, Israel. And if he was to succeed as a rebbe, he surely needed the guidance and experience his mother could provide. Chava would have known the Hasidim as individuals—not just their personal idiosyncrasies and aspirations, but the role each Hasid played in the constellation of her late husband's community. This detailed information would have been indispensable for an inexperienced youngster trying to lead a group of followers out of a crisis of continuity. For her part, Chava needed her son Abraham, for, being a woman, she could not officially lead the Hasidim. As a Twersky of Chernobyl, she had had first-hand knowledge of the emerging aristocratic leadership style. But whatever her depth of experience and knowledge, only her son Abraham could be the tsaddik. Only he could avert the dissolution of the community her husband had built. In light of this convergence of interests, it is only reasonable to assume that Chava would have assisted her son in his consolidation of leadership, and she may have pointed the way from the very beginning. This supposition receives support from the repeated references to Chava's motherly guidance of Abraham and Israel. (Abraham died in 1811, at which point Israel assumed leadership of the community. Strikingly, Israel was then fifteen years old—the same age his older brother Abraham was in 1802, when *he* first sat in his father's seat!) Hasidic tradition preserves memories reflecting Chava's deep concern for her children's development, even from before birth. There is a notable remark from the Apter Rav, Rabbi Abraham Joshua Heschel, considered Hasidism's most senior and revered figure in the last decade of his life (1815–1825).[43] When Chava was pregnant with her younger son, Israel, the future Ruzhiner Rebbe, the Apter is quoted as calling Chava "the Holy Ark" who was carrying (in her womb) a Torah scroll.[44] It would be a mistake to dismiss this as nothing but typical Hasidic exaggeration, a pious encomium for a future leader. The phrase "Holy Ark" (*Aron ha-Kodesh*) resonates with Kabbalistic meaning, alluding to the *Sefirah* of *Malkhut*, or "sovereignty," and associated with the receptive feminine aspect of the divine realm, also known as *Shekhinah*.[45] To anyone with even a modest familiarity with Kabbalistic symbolism, this would have suggested that the union of Chava with her husband, Rabbi Shalom Shakhna, was a sacred rite destined to produce extraordinary offspring. A related tradition states that during the entire nine months of her pregnancy with Israel, Chava was secluded in her private chamber. No one came into her room other than her maids and ladies-in-waiting, thus protecting the pure and holy soul of the future Ruzhiner Rebbe from wayward glances and influences.[46] These traditions reflect an intense level of agency on Chava's part in the spiritual development of her offspring.

Chava's active involvement in the upbringing of her children continued during their childhood and apparently intensified after the death of her husband. The sources tell of visits to the great tsaddikim of the day to receive their blessing, including the Seer of Lublin[47] and the Apter Rav. Around 1805 (three years after her husband's death) Chava brought the two brothers to Berdichev, home of Rabbi Levi Yitzhak. Rabbi Shneur Zalman of Lyady, the founder of Habad Hasidism, who was visiting in Berdichev at the time, is said to have been greatly impressed with Israel's profound religious insight.[48] The picture which emerges from these stories is that of a mother engaged in the project of introducing her sons to the foremost Hasidic leaders of the era. As a devotee of Hasidism, she was undoubtedly following the pious practice of securing blessings from holy masters; but it also seems evident that she was intent on grooming her sons, orphaned from their father, in the ways of the tsaddikim. In addition, these courtesy calls built support among influential leaders to legitimate her sons' succession.

At times Chava appears as an unspoken but clear presence in her sons' life. An example of this is Israel of Ruzhin's *Tosefet Ketubah*—a codicil of supplementary provisions to the *ketubah*, the traditional marriage contract. In this fascinating document, recently published for the first time,[49] the boilerplate *ketubah* obligation has been augmented by the sum of 1,548 rubles. This substantial commitment indicates that the family already had considerable financial resources. And the date (9 Elul 5569) reveals that Israel was wed in 1809, at age twelve—before his Bar Mitzvah![50] Given that he had no father, it is impossible to suppose that his mother was not involved in the arrangements and negotiations. Significantly, young Israel is repeatedly referred to as *ha-yanik*—a variant form of the word *yenuka* we have already encountered, but here in a legal document. The word bespeaks his youth and precocity. But it also conveys a hint of its etymological origin, from *yanak*—to suckle, nurse, breast-feed—hence pointing to a mother hovering in the background, providing nurturance and guidance, even if not acknowledged.

We have a report from the early years of Israel's marriage that Israel refused to perform his marital duty. He gave pious reasons for his behavior, but it must also be remembered that he was scarcely a teenager at this time. In any event, Chava sought the intervention of Rabbi Abraham Joshua Heschel of Apta, who was able to assure Israel that "engagement in the commandment to be fruitful and multiply" was entirely proper and that he would be blessed with children worthy of his sacred lineage.[51]

Rabbi Abraham Joshua Heschel of Apta was also the source for an extraordinary and widely circulated claim made about the Ruzhiner: that he never forgot what the angel had taught him in his mother's womb.[52] This relates to the old rabbinic *aggadah* (legend) that for the nine months of gestation, babies in the womb are taught Torah by an angel, only to be tapped on the mouth at birth, forgetting everything.[53] A prominent follower of the Ruzhiner, Rabbi Reuven Horenstien of Odessa, was astonished at the thought that his master had retained his prenatal memories, and once ventured to ask the rebbe, "'How can such a thing be?'" The Ruzhiner replied, "'Go ask my mother.'" Rebbetzin Chava answered as follows:

"There is indeed a rabbinic teaching that an angel studies the entire Torah with the baby before he is born into this world. Just as he is about to leave his mother's womb, an angel comes, slaps him on the mouth, and he forgets everything. But these very different tasks—that of teaching, and that of expunging memories—are not performed by the same angel, rather by two different angels. What then, gives rise to the Angel of Forgetting? It is the final thought of intercourse [the self-awareness of orgasm]. Believe me that neither I nor my late husband, Rabbi Shalom of Prohobitch, had such a thought at that time, so no Angel of Forgetting was created. That is why my son remembers everything."[54]

In this extraordinary exchange, Chava is asserting the unique spiritual power of her son; more, she is asserting her co-responsibility—along with her late husband—for engendering that power in an act of conception without sexual lust. By avoiding the indulgence of orgasmic forgetting, Chava and Rabbi Shalom Shakhna were in control of their sexual natures. Having maintained their spiritual awareness at a moment when most couples surrender to passion, they birthed a child continually in contact with God and His pristine Torah. Furthermore, by referring the questioner to his mother, the Ruzhiner was effectively endorsing her reply: his birth was the result of a sacred union, and his charismatic powers derived from his mother as much as his late father. And the narrative frame of the story—in which a prominent follower turns to the great tsaddik's mother for a decades-old truth that only she could know—inscribes Chava's role as matriarch of the family, as the repository of sacred knowledge and history, and as the wise guardian of origins and bedrock of dynastic identity.

Finally, there is an astonishing family tradition that the Ruzhiner attributed his imprisonment in Kiev to his mother, Chava. During the period of incarceration (1838–1840) Chava longed to hear some word from her son. A certain Hasid managed to gain entry to the Ruzhiner's cell and was able to converse with him. As the visit ended, the Hasid asked the tsaddik for a sign, a signal by which he could prove to Chava that he had actually met with her son. Rabbi Israel responded, "'Tell my mother that she is responsible for my entire incarceration.'" When the Hasid reported on his visit to Chava and told her what her son had said, she replied:

> "That's exactly right—It's my fault that my son is in prison. Let me tell you the story. Before he gave birth in holiness to his youngest son [Mordecai Shraga of Husyatin], he came to me and said that he has the opportunity to bring down a very great and lofty soul, such as the world has not seen in the last two thousand years; but as a consequence he would be forced to suffer a painful exile. So he asked me for my advice, and I replied, 'My son, what don't we do for our children's sake?'"[55]

This story once again links the Ruzhiner's mother, Chava, with motifs of holy sexual union and the birth of sacred souls. Here she is depicted as the matriarch of the family, steering it toward a glorious spiritual destiny at whatever cost to her son's physical or material welfare. Whatever we make of the theology implicit in this story, it places Chava in the role of behind-the-scenes guide to her son on a matter of utmost gravity, of vital concern to the lineage and her family's future.

When taken in the aggregate, the sheer number of vignettes and reminiscences which feature Chava is impressive. I cannot think of another early tsaddik who is linked so strongly and consistently in the hagiographic literature with his mother.[56] And these traditions always spotlight Chava's concern for family continuity, a concern whose spiritual and material components are inseparable. Willy-nilly, these memories testify to Chava's ongoing leadership in the Ruzhin dynasty.

So far as I know, we have no correspondence from Chava, but one item which did survive is Chava's ring, extant to this day.[57] On one side are engraved the words "To light the Sabbath lamp," and on the other, "Chava daughter of our master Rabbi Abraham, may God preserve and redeem him." Such a ring, crafted at a time when her father was still living, bespeaks a confident self-awareness of aristocratic position.[58] In all, we catch sight of an influential woman, utilizing her stature to advance the situation of her sons while securing her place at the very core of Hasidism's new aristocracy. While any analysis of her motives must include the factors of economic self-interest and social position, for Chava these considerations would have been totally intermingled with thoughts of her venerable ancestors, on the one hand, and her belief in her sons as tsaddikim, on the other. Chava surely believed that the great legacy of the Maggid of Mezhirech, Rabbi Abraham the Angel, her husband, Rabbi Shalom Shakhna, and her grandfather Rabbi Menahem Nahum of Chernobyl could best be preserved and transmitted by the sacred souls which she had brought into the world.

Let us now return to that first night of Sukkot in 1802, mere hours after the death of Rabbi Shalom Shakhna. We will never know in full what motivated the newly orphaned boy to move (quite literally) into his father's seat, to the chagrin and astonishment of the Hasidim. But it was surely the case that Abraham sought and received his mother's consent, post facto if not ab initio. Rising to the role of filial successor—a role still rare and unexpected in Hasidism—Abraham, with his mother's support, saved the cohesive community built by his father from immediate dissipation. Crystallized around family loyalty and the memory of great predecessors, the community's identity remained intact, much as had already happened in Chava's own family where the Hasidic community of Chernobyl had become a proprietary domain. With his mother as his silent partner, the son laid the foundation for what would soon flower into the great lineage of Mezhirech-Prohobitch-Ruzhin. Abraham of Prohobitch and his younger brother, Israel (later of Ruzhin), were no longer orphans but heirs, dauphins of an emergent dynasty which would influence Hasidism for all time to come.

On the twelfth of Tammuz (midsummer) 1844, Chava passed away. She was the first person to be interred in the family's burial plot in Sadgora; her son the Ruzhiner Rebbe would join her six years later. It is reported that when the burial was concluded, the Ruzhiner took three steps back from her grave and paused. Then he said, "Thus far the border of the Land of Israel."[59] It should not be missed that the given name of the Ruzhiner Rebbe was Israel.

The Crisis of the Interregnum, 1873:
Sarah Devorah Shapiro and the Yenuka of Stolin

In 1875, an article appeared in Peretz Smolenskin's *Ha-Shahar* (The Dawn), published in Vienna, titled "Hitgalut ha-Yenuka mi-Stolin," or "The Debut of the Yenuka of Stolin." Israel Davidson, in *Parody in Jewish Literature*, writes that the "Hitgalut" is a "satire directed against the abuses of the Tsaddikim of the House of Karlin in general, but in particular against the accession of the five year old son of Rabbi Asher of Karlin into the office of Tsaddik."[60] The historical background of the satire is as follows: Rabbi Aaron the Second of Stolin (1802–1872) was a prominent master in White Russia, a grandson of the celebrated Rabbi Aaron the Great of Karlin (1736–1772). His incumbency as leader of the Karlin-Stolin Hasidim lasted forty-five years. When he died in 1872, he was succeeded by his son Rabbi Asher the Second (1827–1873). But Rabbi Asher died only one year after his father, and Karlin-Stolin Hasidism was beset by a crisis of continuity, having sustained in rapid succession the loss of two beloved leaders. The only male heir was Rabbi Asher's son, Israel, who was about four and a half years old at the time of his father's passing. When the child was about five years old, the Stolin elders announced that Israel had been designated his father's successor and would henceforth lead the Hasidic community of Stolin.[61]

When this turn of events became known to the wider community, it provoked astonishment; almost immediately maskilim rushed to satirize what in their view was an absurd example of Hasidic credulousness. The best-known example is "Hitgalut ha-Yenuka mi-Stolin," signed "Had min Havraya," a pseudonym meaning "One of the Fellows." One question which seems not to have been asked by either the maskilim or the subsequent scholarly writers on this topic is, Why did the Stoliner Hasidim do it? That is, even granting their putative naivete, there must have been a compelling reason which led them to the extraordinary step of appointing a five-year-old as their leader. They must surely have anticipated that such a decision would attract ridicule and contempt.

To answer this question, we must take a closer look at the article published in *Ha-shahar*, which Davidson attributed to Yehuda Leib Levin.[62] This attribution is only partially correct. The "Hitgalut" actually has a composite character, with two distinct sections. The article begins and concludes with a "Letter to the Editor," which introduces and frames the core document, a letter from "the Rabbi of Turov, a town near Pinsk." The tone of the two sections differs dramatically. The frame letter is a typical maskilic satire, by turns ludicrously pompous, bathetic, and ribald, with repeated references to the rumored sexual inadequacy of the tsaddikim. By contrast, the core letter is entirely serious. It does herald the advent of the *yenuka*, and portrays him as gifted with an extraordinary intellect, musical ability, and supernatural powers; it also claims for him a messianic soul. But with all this, the tone is quite different from the carnivalesque style of the frame letter, which is typical of anti-Hasidic parodies such Joseph Perl's *Megaleh Temirin*.[63] The core letter is characterized by an earnest and plaintive note of urgency which accurately reflects the Karlin-Stolin crisis of succession and the concern of the elders to hold the group together around the child as titular leader.

"The Rabbi of Turov" is a historical figure: his name is Ya'akov Noson Weisman (c. 1832–1916), who indeed served as rabbi of Turov (a small town east of Pinsk) and later emigrated to Eretz Israel where he was a rabbi in Tiberias; he died in Safed in 1916.[64] Yehuda Leib Levin was shown a copy of Weisman's letter and grasped the opportunity to augment it into a full-scale assault on Karlin-Stolin Hasidism. He wrote the frame letter which enabled him to incorporate other scandalous and embarrassing material. He also festooned Weisman's original letter with mock-serious footnotes, which added to the fun but further obscured the composite character of the whole. The original, authentic letter without Levin's embellishments (but with a side-by-side Yiddish translation) appears in a Yiddish-language journal published in Lemberg, *Jsrulik* (The Israelite), in the issue of October 30, 1875.[65] Levin tells the entire story in the year 1900, in *Hatchiah* (The Renaissance), a Hebrew literary weekly published in Chicago.[66]

For all their differences, Weisman's original letter, Levin's 1875 parody, and Levin's 1900 article agree on one thing: young Israel Perlow's mother had a hand in her son's accession to the leadership of Karlin-Stolin. Levin (1900) writes that the idea to give the Karlin-Stolin dynastic seat to the child came from the mother's circle of supporters (*mekoraveha*); the Rabbi of Turov, who was acting as *gabbai* (administrative assistant) for the mother, wrote and circulated his letter to gather support for the child's accession.

Levin's 1875 satire states that in contrast to tsaddikim who are accused of living in extravagant style, "this lad drinks only a little wine in order to get accustomed to sacred service; he eats little and dresses modestly. He takes no pleasure in all the money he receives from thousands of hasidim, for he gives it all to his mother."[67]

But undoubtedly the most reliable source is Rabbi Weisman's original letter. Weisman mentions steps that were already taken to place the child in charge of Karlin-Stolin institutions in both Russia and the Holy Land. He continues, "His mother the Rebbetzin has the authority to appoint overseers for governance of the sacred institutions, as well as tax collectors (*anshei ma'amad*) of her choice. [This arrangement will hold] until the righteous Shoot will grow to adulthood. . . . And everyone knows about the matter of Jehoash of blessed memory."[68]

The rather cryptic reference to Jehoash requires some elucidation. In 2 Kings 11–12 (cf. 2 Chronicles 22–24) Jehoash, son of Ahaziah, is the only survivor of a bloody purge which attempted to eliminate every legitimate contender for the Davidic throne. He is secreted away as an infant by his aunt Jehoshiba and kept hidden for six years. In his seventh year, Jehoshiba's husband, the high priest Jehoiada, reveals the young lad to the people, and Jehoash is anointed and crowned as king in a ceremony celebrating the renewal of the Davidic dynasty. The salient parallels are clear: Davidic descent and messianic claims were advanced for young Israel Perlow, he was a "child-king," and his cause was being championed by a close woman relative: for Jehoash, his aunt; in the case of Israel Perlow, his mother. The naming of Jehoash at the very end of Weisman's letter is intended to invoke a powerful biblical precedent for the installation of a child-leader, but it also points to the central role that young Israel's mother had in directing the course of events.

Who was Israel Perlow's mother? Born in 1844, her name was Sarah Devorah Shapiro; she was a great-great granddaughter to Rabbi Israel the Maggid of Kozienice (1737–1814), one of the founders of Hasidism in Poland. Her first marriage, to a second cousin who was heir to the Kozienice Hasidic dynasty, ended with her husband's death in 1866. The young widow soon remarried (1867), this time to Rabbi Asher Perlow of Stolin (1827–1873), whose role as tsaddik of the Karlin-Stolin line has already been mentioned.[69] When Sarah Devorah left Congress Poland for White Russia to marry Rabbi Asher, she brought along her two children from her first husband, a boy and a girl. In Stolin, Sarah Devorah presented her husband, Rabbi Asher, with three children, two girls and a boy. The boy, born in 1868, was named Israel. When his father died in 1873, it was he who was brought forward as successor; he is our *yenuka*.

Let us consider Sarah Devorah's situation at the time of Rabbi Asher's death in 1873. She was twenty-nine years old. Within a span of just seven years, she had lost two husbands (she had lived about six years with each one). This was enough to stigmatize her and make it most unlikely that she would ever marry again. But she was the mother of five children, and—of special importance in Hasidic society—she had given birth to two boys, each of whom was heir to a well-known lineage: Kozienice in Poland, then Karlin-Stolin in White Russia. Sarah Devorah would have had an intense personal interest in the deliberations regarding the choice of a successor to her late husband, Rabbi Asher Perlow, and her efforts to see her son installed are fully understandable.[70]

Sarah Devorah figures prominently in a memoir[71] written by her grand-daughter and published in Israel in 1967. The granddaughter, whose name was Malkah Shapiro, writes of her youth in Kozienice, Poland. The memoir is set in 1905, after Sarah Devorah has returned from White Russia to her native Poland, together with her son from her first marriage, Yerahmiel Moshe Hapstein, who assumed the incumbent seat as Rebbe of Kozienice.

In Shapiro's memoir, Sarah Devorah manages the affairs of the court and makes all major decisions. She is appropriately respectful to her son, who is after all the Rebbe, but Yerahmiel Moshe treats his mother with the greatest reverence. She is constantly chastising him for endangering his health with a grueling schedule of study and service, and with extreme asceticism. A major point of contention is the question of building a new mansion to replace the elegant home which was destroyed in a fire about six years earlier. Sarah Devorah, along with a group of loyal and generous Hasidim, conspires to go ahead with plans for new construction, but Yerahmiel Moshe does his best to subvert their intentions. Eventually the new house does begin to rise, due to Sarah Devorah's indefatigable marshalling of architectural, financial, and managerial resources. Speaking Polish, she works with contractors, artisans, and suppliers of raw materials, conducts labor negotiations, and deals with work stoppages and strikes. Everyone is frightened of her: she need only give one look in the direction of a group of chatting workers, and they fall silent and return to work. In addition to managing the household and court in Kozienice, she owns a country estate where the family would often spend summers. Shapiro remembers her grandmother Sarah Devorah as a woman of elegance, culture, and refinement, who prizes education and piety. Her knowledge of German and of delicate embroidery techniques was obtained from a tutor whom she herself had imported from Hungary. She maintains excellent relationships with members of the Polish nobility; they respect her family heritage and cultural sophistication, and share her aristocratic values rooted in an era that was fast disappearing. But along with the ambience of majesty and nobility that Sarah Devorah cultivates, there is also devout piety and the fear of heaven. In between her managerial activities she prays and recites psalms. The Rebbetzin's blessings are sought by Polish peasants as well as by Hasidim.

As depicted in her granddaughter's memoir, Sarah Devorah is a dynamic, enterprising, and courageous individual who confidently travels to the crown city of St. Petersburg for an interview at the Russian imperial palace. With a memory of events going back to the first half of the nineteenth century, she is the repository and transmitter of the family's sacred traditions and foundational stories. Shapiro depicts her sitting at the head of the table, surrounded by family members and Hasidim who listen in rapt attention as she tells mystic stories from her childhood. She is domineering and assertive, but these qualities are essential for her effectiveness in managing the household and court.

Sarah Devorah's fears for her son's health are entirely justified: Yerahmiel Moshe died in 1909. She lived through the Great War, and it was she who made the decision for the family to leave Kozienice for Warsaw when the town became a battlefield. Scion of the Maggid of Kozienice and widow of two major tsaddikim, it was she who nurtured and transmitted the household's sense of itself as a royal dynasty. She died in Warsaw in 1921 at age seventy seven, surviving both her sons.

This portrait of Sarah Devorah is entirely consistent with the image that emerges from the sources we have examined in connection with her son Israel Perlow, the *yenuka*. In particular, Rabbi Weisman's original letter asserting her control of communal institutions and funds testifies to her role as dynastic regent, the actual power behind her son, the "child-king."

David Assaf has written about the enormous financial resources that were necessary to run the large Hasidic courts such as that of Ruzhin, and the techniques that arose to supply the requisite funds. But Assaf and his primary sources say almost nothing about actual administration: who made purchasing decisions and paid the bills; who hired, fired, and supervised the large staff of servants, workers, kitchen help, artisans, and contractors; who oversaw the comings and goings of honored guests, Hasidic pilgrims, and the poor; who decided on renovations, additions, and major construction; who purchased real estate and invested assets, negotiated with local and regional authorities, tracked the distribution of charitable funds and the governance of religious institutions, and so on?[72] Such a major administrative role could only have been filled by a trusted intimate of the tsaddik, most likely a close family member.[73] Malkah Shapiro's memoir makes it clear that at least in one instance it was the family matriarch, Sara Devorah Shapiro, who filled that role.

Nor can such a role be dismissed as marginal to the tsaddik's spiritual focus. The regal Hasidic court as it developed through the nineteenth century expressed an embodied social theology. The tsaddik's role as sacred pivot of his community, as "axis mundi,"[74] was concretized in the court itself, so that the structures of the court create a sacred domain analogous to the sacred space of the biblical Tabernacle and the Jerusalem Temples.[75] The life of the court, in both its material and spiritual culture, displayed the theology of the tsaddik and nurtured the experience of the Hasid who came as pilgrim to see and to be seen.[76]

The Hasidic court was not characterized by sharp delineations between the public and private, between domestic and communal. Hasidim, at least Hasidic intimates, came into the family residence all the time. Rebbetzins interacted with the entire community and could easily exercise control if they so desired. So it should not surprise us that in some cases it was a Rebbetzin such as Sarah Devorah Shapiro Perlow who guided the court's administration. Such a Rebbetzin should be thought of as a regent directing the spiritual and material fortunes of the lineage, bearing the dynasty's vision of itself.[77]

When writing of the Stolin *yenuka*, *Haskalah* (Jewish Enlightenment) writers saw a story of venality, credulity, and superstition. They never bothered to think much about the mother of the wonder-child, other than to accuse her of appropriating the *pidyon* (redemption)-money. The "Hitgalut ha-Yenuka mi-Stolin" parody does not even refer to her by name. From the research presented here, however, a different picture emerges, a narrative of a woman of courage, intelligence, and energy, working to secure the continuity of her tradition and lineage. By struggling for her son's position as dynastic heir, she was assuring her own continued role as queen mother, but she had every right to do so. Not the sovereign but the regent, Sara Devorah Shapiro Perlow, was destined to be forever the power behind the throne, the guardian of dynastic vision.

Our analysis of Chava, mother of Rabbi Israel of Ruzhin, and Sarah Devorah Shapiro Perlow suggests the following: where there is a *yenuka*, there is likely a recently widowed mother, with very legitimate concerns about her lineage, promoting the role of her son and thereby securing her own position as well. After the crisis of the interregnum has passed and her son has successfully taken his place as tsaddik, a woman such as Chava or Sara Devorah would often settle into the role of dynastic elder, prized for first-hand knowledge of the events, traditions, and personalities of bygone days. If she also had the energy and ability, she might emerge as the de facto if unacknowledged leader of the Hasidic community, making key decisions and guiding its destiny as much as or even more than her son the tsaddik.

Hasidic writers would have had no reason to publicize such an arrangement; wherever it existed, the Hasidim would have worked hard to shield it from view. And that is why the large corpus of hagiographic literature contains mere hints of the roles played by women such as Chava and Sara Devorah. This underscores the importance of reexamining that literature, as well as searching for documents and texts previously overlooked or undiscovered.

At one point in Malkah Shapiro's memoir, she mentions that Sarah Devorah Shapiro Perlow carried a pouch tied around her neck. The pouch was for some of her most precious possessions: heirloom jewelry bequeathed by her dynastic predecessors and plans for the family's country estate in Polesia. But the pouch also contained "holy letters she had received from tzakkikim, including appreciations of her son the wonder child."[78] The land documents and approbations of her son which this matriarch carried in her bosom were more than priceless possessions. They were the crown jewels of her Hasidic lineage, embodying its dynastic identity and hopes. There was no safer place for them than on the tablet of Sarah Devorah's heart.

NOTES

1. Joseph Dan, "A Bow to Frumkinian Hasidism," in *Jewish Mysticism, Vol. 4: General Characteristics and Comparative Studies* (Northvale, NJ, 1999) p. 93. The article was originally published in *Modern Judaism*, Vol. 11, No. 2 (1991), pp. 175–193.

2. Dan, "The Contemporary Hasidic *Tzaddik*: Charisma, Heredity, Magic, and Miracle," in *Jewish Mysticism, Vol. 4*, p. 118.

3. Ibid., p. 119.

4. Ibid., p. 120, n. 7.

5. Ibid., p. 119.

6. Ibid., p. 112.

7. Dan, "Hasidism: The Third Century," in *Jewish Mysticism, Vol. 4*, p. 80.

8. Dan, "The Contemporary Hasidic *Tzaddik*," p. 119. But see a more recent publication, *The Heart and the Fountain: An Anthology of Jewish Mystical Experience* (New York, 2002), where Dan writes of Hasidic leadership as "a hereditary power inherent in the families of the founders" (p. 40). This·emphasis on family moves closer to the approach we shall adopt herein.

9. In Ada Rapaport-Albert, ed., *Hasidism Reappraised* (London, 1996).

10. In the event, Rabbi Dov Ber's grandson, Rabbi Shalom Shakhna, successfully established himself as a tsaddik; he and his descendents will play prominent roles in the discussion that follows. But while Rabbi Shalom Shakhna drew on the spiritual power and prestige of the Great Maggid, in no sense did he inherit an established Hasidic community, nor did he ever make the claim that he was the designated successor to his illustrious grandfather. His *Rebistve* (rabbinic office; tenured chair of a recognized tsaddik) in Prohobitch was his own making. Similar remarks pertain to Rabbi Barukh of Medzibozh, grandson of the Baal Shem Tov.

11. Martin Buber begins his chapter on the Maggid of Mezhirech, in "Dov Ber of Mezritch, the Great Maggid" (*Tales of the Hasidim: Early Masters* [New York, 1975]), with a story that depicts the five-year-old Dov Ber consoling his mother on the loss of her family tree, burned in a fire which destroyed their house. The tree traced the family's lineage back to the great talmudic sage Rabbi Yohanan the sandal-maker. The young Dov Ber is quoted as saying, "'And what does that matter! I shall get you a new family tree which begins with me!'" (p. 98). But this story, which appeared first in 1930 and purports to describe an event from around 1710, may be a retrospective projection of the later situation back to the time of the illustrious paterfamilias. The story actually supports the thesis developed herein: the dynastic vision emerges out of a child's assuming responsibility for his mother in the wake of crisis.

On the broader question of the reliability of hagiographic traditions, see below, nn. 37–38. It is obvious that as the time between the ostensible event and its first appearance in print increases, one's confidence in its historicity diminishes proportionally. Here, there is a gap of over two hundred years, much too long to give the story historical credence.

12. Rapaport-Albert, p. 118.

13. Ibid., p. 137. See also Arthur Green, "Typologies of Leadership and the Hasidic Zaddiq," in *Jewish Spirituality*, edited by Arthur Green (New York, 1994), Vol. 2, pp. 127–156. Green observes that "The very notion of inherited dynasty, the right to authority in the Hasidic community by virtue of birth, smacked of royalism" (p. 144). For the earliest examples of leadership in the regal style, Green

mentions Baruch of Medzibozh as well as Mordecai of Chernobyl. But Baruch is not the best example of the pattern under discussion because while he drew on the prestige of the Besht, he did not inherit an ongoing, established Hasidic community; see above, n. 10. There was a gap of nearly thirty years between the Besht's death and Baruch's establishing his court in Medzibozh. And when Baruch died in 1810, his sons-in-law did not inherit his court (he had no sons). Shortly after Baruch's death, Medzibozh became the seat of Abraham Joshua Heschel (formerly of Apta), until the latter's death in 1825. On Mordecai of Chernobyl's assumption of leadership, see below, n. 40.

14. Rapaport-Albert, p. 137, n. 239.

15. Moshe Menahem Walden, *Nifla'ot ha-Rabbi* (Warsaw, 1911; reprinted, Brooklyn, 1985), records the story that before Rabbi Elimelekh passed away, "he placed his hands on his disciples, bestowing aspects of his radiance upon them. He gave the Rabbi of Lublin the light of his eyes; to Rabbi Israel the Maggid of Kozienice he gave the power in his heart; to Rabbi Mendel of Pristik [later of Rymanov] he gave the soul in his mind; and to Rabbi Abraham Joshua Heschel of Apta he gave the power in his mouth" (pp. 24–25, #29). See also Abraham Chaim Simhah Bunem Michaelson, *Ohel Elimelekh* (Przemysl, 1910), p. 78, #186.

16. The apparent lack of interest on the part of Rabbi Levi Yitzhak in establishing a dynasty is conveyed in the following story, told by Rabbi Yitzhak of Neskhizh (d. 1868), son of the famed tsaddik Rabbi Mordecai of Neskhiz (d. 1800). The story involves Rabbi Yitzhak himself and Rabbi Levi Yitzhak of Berdichev. "The Rabbi of Berdichev, in his last year of life (c. 1810) sent for Rabbi Yitzhak of Neskhizh to teach him the esoteric intentions of the *mitzvah* of Lulav and Etrog. The descendents of the Berdichever became jealous of the rabbi of Neskhizh, thinking, Why was the Berdichever teaching him and not them? The Berdichever answered them as follows: 'When old Rabbi Mordecai of blessed memory [who had already died in 1800] will ask me in the World of Truth, What did you teach my son? I will need something to answer him, so that's why I'm teaching him these esoteric intentions of Lulav and Etrog.' Then the Berdichever closed the door to his descendents and transmitted to Rabbi Yitzhak those secret teachings." The story, which appears in the collection *Zikhron La-Rishonim* (reprinted Brooklyn, 1976 [original, Piotrkow, 1910]), pp. 135–136, has the effect of promoting the standing of the teller, Rabbi Yitzhak. But it certainly captures accurately the reality that Rabbi Levi Yitzhak did not groom a successor from his own family.

17. Rapaport-Albert, pp. 118–119; cf. Arthur Green, "Nahman's Final Years," in *Tormented Master: The Life and Spiritual Quest of Rabbi Nahman of Bratslav* (Woodstock, VT, 1992 [original, 1979]), pp. 221–265.

18. See Naftali Loewenthal, *Communicating the Infinite: The Emergence of the Habad School* (Chicago, 1990), pp. 100–138; and Rachel Elior, "The Controversy over the Leadership of the Habad Movement," *Tarbiz*, Vol. 49 (1980), pp. 166–186.

19. Rabbi Hayyim Halberstam, *Divrei Hayyim*, Vol. 2, p. 208, *Hoshen Mishpat* #32, quoted in Shaul Stampfer, "Inheritance of the Rabbinate in Eastern Europe in the Modern Period—Causes, Factors and Development over Time," *Jewish History*, Vol. 13, no. 1 (1999), p. 48. Stampfer argues that in the face of often bitter leadership struggles, the dynastic principle at least "limited the field of potential candidates and gave a justification for an heir's claim" ("Inheritance of the Rabbinate," p. 48). See also David Assaf, *The Regal Way: The Life and Times of Rabbi Israel of Ruzhin*, translated by David Louvish (Stanford, 2002), in particular chapter 2, "'The Main Thing Is One's Own Distinction': The Argument over Succession," pp. 47–65. Assaf adroitly traces the significance of hereditary succession in the Ruzhin dynasty, the claims of Davidic descent, the merit of the Maggid of Mezhirech, and the subdivisions of Ruzhin lineage in later generations. But there is little in the way of theological analysis.

20. Stephen Sharot, *Messianism, Mysticism, and Magic: A Sociological Analysis of Jewish Religious Movements* (Chapel Hill, 1987).

21. Ibid., p. 170.

22. Ibid., p. 172. Joseph Dan approaches this insight in his editor's introduction to *The Heart and the Fountain: An Anthology of Jewish Mystical Experience*, where he writes that the establishment of mystical leadership was seen as "a hereditary power inherent in the families of the founders" (p. 40).

23. Zevi Hirsch Eichenstein, *Turn Aside from Evil and Do Good*, translated by Louis Jacobs (London, 1995), pp. xxii–xxiii.

24. The holy seed rhetoric in Ezra has recently been studied by Christine A. Hayes in her *Gentile Impurities and Jewish Identities: Intermarriage and Conversion from the Bible to the Talmud* (New York, 2002). Hayes is very careful to point out that "Ezra does not say that Gentiles are genealogically impure (i.e., an impure seed, in contrast to Israel's holy seed)." Rather, they are simply profane— that is, common, not distinguished by the gift of holiness, but not tainted or impure (pp. 30–32). The situation in Hasidism is rather similar if not identical: to this day, the families of tsaddikim have a strong preference for endogamous unions or, at a minimum, marriage to another aristocratic line, but there is no actual prohibition against a Hasidic scion marrying a Jewish commoner.

25. Joan Wallach Scott, "The Problem of Invisibility," in *Retrieving Women's History: Changing Perceptions of the Role of Women in Politics and Society*, edited by S. Jay Kleinberg (Oxford, 1988), p. 5; cited in Nathaniel Deutsch, *The Maiden of Ludmir: A Jewish Holy Woman and Her World* (Berkeley, 2003), p. 8.

26. Our discussion here will concentrate on aspects of the key dynasties of Ruzhin, Chernobyl, and Karlin-Stolin. Habad-Lubavitch will not be a major focus here but is a very important part of the topic as a whole; I hope to devote a separate study to dynastic emergence in Habad-Lubavitch. In an earlier article I discussed the question of women as charismatic leaders in Hasidism; see Nehemia Polen, "Miriam's Dance: Radical Egalitarianism in Hasidic Thought," *Modern*

Judaism, Vol. 12, No. 1 (1992), pp. 1–21. Here my focus is not on women as charismatic leaders but as wives and mothers of tsaddikim, and their contributions to dynastic emergence and continuity.

27. Rapaport-Albert, "Hasidism after 1772: Structural Continuity and Change," p. 129, n. 201; p. 136. And cf. Dan, "Hasidism: The Third Century": "the hereditary aspect of the cult of the *tzaddik* did not develop in the Hasidic movement until the early decades of the nineteenth century" (p. 81).

28. Rapaport-Albert, p. 136.

29. Rapaport-Albert, p. 129, n. 201.

30. Arthur Green, *Menahem Nahum of Chernobyl: Upright Practices, The Light of the Eyes* (New York, 1982), notes that eventually this pattern of division and fragmentation was to lead to the impoverishment of the Hasidic courts (p. 21, n. 22). See also Assaf, *Regal Way*, pp. 63–65; 307–309. But at the beginning of the nineteenth century there was ample opportunity in the form of new territory to be conquered for Hasidism. Thus, at this stage, the needs of family members to stake out their own territory dovetailed nicely with the expansionist agenda of the movement as a whole. The situation is reminiscent of the settling of New England in the roughly two centuries before 1800. The goal of every farmer was to clear enough land to set up each of his sons in an economically viable farm. Each succeeding generation cleared and cultivated new areas farther away from earlier settlements. This process continued until they ran out of new territory, and there was no more available land to clear; see Diana Muir, *Reflections in Bullough's Pond: Economy and Ecosystem in New England* (Hanover, 2000). Note, for example, her remark that "For several generations . . . Massachusetts was a land of plenty. [Colonial farmers] lived well, married young if they pleased, and reared large families in the full confidence that their children would enjoy a life as comfortable as their own. . . . [E]arly-settled towns might not have had enough space for every young couple to settle on, but there was land enough elsewhere to allow the surplus young people of each generation to pioneer farms of their own" (pp. 47–48). One can look at the spread of Hasidic territories during the nineteenth century in a similar way, as being largely driven by the ongoing branching of dynastic trees, as successive generations of sons and sons-in-law of famous tsaddikim were motivated to find new towns in which to establish a *rebistve*.

31. David Assaf, *Derekh ha-Malkhut: Rabbi Yisrael mi-Ruzhin* (The Zalman Shazar Center for Jewish History, Jerusalem, 1997), p. 63, n. 21. An English translation of the Hebrew original has appeared under the title *The Regal Way: The Life and Times of Rabbi Israel of Ruzhin* (Stanford, 2002). Since the quality of the translation is very fine, I generally cite the English edition except in places where the Hebrew provides fuller information. The passage now under discussion appears only in the Hebrew text.

32. This approach draws upon feminist methods of historical-theological reconstruction, whose goal is not only the recovery of women's voices as a

domain of interest, but the reconstruction of a movement's history in light of fresh awareness of women's central role. See Elisabeth Schussler Fiorenza, *In Memory of Her* (New York, 1983); note esp. ch. 2, "Toward a Feminist Critical Method," and ch. 3, "Toward a Feminist Model of Historical Reconstruction," pp. 41–95. See also Fiorenza's *Bread Not Stone: The Challenge of Feminist Biblical Interpretation* (Boston, 1984), pp. 15–22. Following Paul Ricoeur, Fiorenza adopts a "hermeneutic of suspicion," by which texts placing women in a marginal role may be interrogated to recover women's central contributions. In my view such a "hermeneutic of suspicion," however useful, must be accompanied and complemented by a hermeneutic of appreciation and gratitude. See below, note 37.

33. Reuben Zak, *Beit Yisrael* (Piotrkow 1913 [Bene-Barak, 1983]), p. 7, #1.

34. Joseph Perl, *Uiber das Wesen der Sekte Chassidim*, edited by Avraham Rubinstein (Jerusalem, 1977), p. 94. Perl also mentions another *yenuka*, "Pinchsel Sohn des Rebi Srul Abraham." The editor of *Uiber das Wesen der Sekte Chassidim* says that he was unable to identify this person, but Perl was evidently referring to Rabbi Pinhas Shapiro of Cherny Ostrov, a grandson of the famed Rabbi Zusia of Hannipol. Pinhas's father, Rabbi Israel Abraham (1772–1814) was the publisher of *No'am Elimelekh* by his uncle Rabbi Elimelekh of Lyzhansk (Yitzhak Alfasi, *Ha-Hasidut mi-Dor le-Dor* (Jerusalem, 1995), Vol. 1, p. 149). Alfasi states that after Rabbi Israel Abraham's death in 1814, "his widow conducted herself as a Rebbe," and also offers the information that in 1834 she emigrated to the Holy Land and was killed in the earthquake of 1837 (ibid.). S. Z. Weinberg, *Nezah she-be-Nezah* (Jerusalem, 1994), records the tradition that her in-law Rabbi Mordecai of Chernobyl once attended her *Se'udah Shelishit* (third Sabbath meal, a sublime event) (p. 33). The phenomenon of a widow leading her late husband's community, together with the appearance of a child-successor, is fully consistent with the thesis of this essay. Rabbi Israel Abraham was the father-in-law of Rabbi David Twersky of Talna; for more on him, see *Nezer Yisrael va-Ateret Avraham*, published in *Torat ha-Hasidim ha-Rishonim*, edited by Menahim Mendel Viznitzer (Bene-Barak: Nahalat Zvi, 1986).

35. See, for example, *Zohar*, Vol. 1, 138b–140b; Vol. 2, 170a; Vol. 3, 186b–192b.

36. *Assaf Derekh ha-Malkhut*, pp. 82–83; *Assaf Regal Way*, p. 34.

37. It is a scholarly commonplace that Hasidic hagiography must be used with great caution as a historical source. Nevertheless, a number of highly regarded studies do rely on this genre, at least to some degree. See for example Arthur Green's *Tormented Master*, which draws extensively on the Bratslav literature on Rabbi Nahman. For Green's discussion of the methodological issues, see pp. 6–14.

Immanuel Etkes makes extensive use of the first Hasidic hagiographical collection, *Shivhei ha-Besht*, for his study of the Baal Shem Tov in *Ba'al Hashem: The Besht—Magic, Mysticism, Leadership* (Jerusalem, 2000), pp. 217–265. In contrast to other scholars who treat *Shivhei ha-Besht* with great suspicion, Etkes, in a lengthy excursus on *Shivhei ha-Besht* as a historical source, concludes that "a significant proportion of the stories brought in this collection can be categorized as testi monies and reliable traditions anchored in the personal experiences of the Besht and his circle" (p. 265).

The entire issue is discussed by David Assaf in his biography of Rabbi Israel of Ruzhin (see above, n. 31). After noting the characteristics typical of hagiography, such as avoidance of problematic topics, apologetic intent, naivete, exaggerations, and imagination (*Regal Way*, pp. 8–28), Assaf nevertheless concludes that the critical scholar cannot disregard this genre but must take advantage of it by "separat[ing] the wheat from the chaff. . . . [I]n any source that is not prima facie unacceptable, there is a core of truth grounded in factual reality" (p. 26). Of special importance for our purposes is Assaf's statement that "Although the pronouncements attributed to Rabbi Israel and stories about him were published many years after his death, it is assumed as a rule that the material is basically authentic, although perhaps not as actually worded" (23).

Assaf and others have pointed out examples where specific hagiographic assertions have received surprising confirmation in newly discovered historical materials. It now seems clear that the very reason that Hasidic hagiographic writing is often so tendentious—namely, the deep esteem and reverence of the writer for the tsaddik—is precisely the impetus for collecting and preserving traditions about the master with great care and zeal. In this paper we will assume that the stories about the Ruzhiner and his family are in large measure genuine traditions transmitted orally or in writing, sometimes for several generations, but that their mode of presentation and contextualization may reflect the interests and perspective of the final editor or anthologist. It is therefore appropriate and necessary to read with attention to anomalies, silences, gaps, and suppressed voices. See above, note 32.

Most important for our purposes is that the editor of the collections from which we will quote often provides a named source for his stories. As Etkes and others have noted, this type of attribution is generally quite reliable; it is not at all the case that the editor is simply making up names or an attribution chain. See the next note.

38. Reuben Zak, *Bei Yisra'el* (Piotrkow, 1913 [Bene-Barak, 1983]), pp. 7–8; cf. Assaf, *Regal Way*, p. 34. Zak says that he heard this story from Rabbi Israel of Medzibozh. Not to be confused with the Besht, this is Israel Shalom Yosef of Medzibodz (1852–1911), a descendent of Rabbi Abraham Joshua Heschel of Apta (who spent his last years in Medzibozh). Israel Shalom Yosef was a son-in-law of Rabbi Abraham Jacob of Sadgora, a child of Rabbi Israel of Ruzhin. It is only reasonable that as a close family member, he would have been privy to stories about the dynasty's origin. For more on Israel Shalom Yosef, see Yitzhak Alfasi, *Ha-Hasidut mi-Dor le-Dor* (Jerusalem, 1995), Vol. 1, pp. 218–219. Alfasi includes a portrait and an autograph.

39. See *Menahem Nahum of Chernobyl: Upright Practices, The Light of the Eyes*. Rabbi Menahem Nahum had served in Prohobitch before arriving in Chernobyl;

thus Chava's family had deep roots there and her husband's tenure was in some sense picking up on family ties from the previous generation.

40. According to Aaron David Twersky, *Sefer ha-Yahas mi-Chernobyl ve-Ruzhin* (Lublin, 1938; reprinted Brooklyn, 1990), Rabbi Mordecai was already living in expansive style during his father's lifetime. During a visit to his son, Rabbi Menahem Nahum observed "gold and silver vessels and many clocks," and asked what need there was for such things (p. 5, #3). Rabbi Mordecai is said to have replied with reference to Rabbi Judah the Patriarch, who according to the Talmud was surrounded by abundance yet maintained a personal asceticism (see B.T. *Ketubot* 104). Whatever the historicity of this family tradition, it sheds light on how Hasidism viewed the opulent lifestyle of the tsaddikim: Rabbi Judah the Patriarch is remembered as the editor of the Mishnah as well as a revered and effective communal leader who related to Roman rulers on equal terms; he embodied "Torah and worldly grandeur in one place." It should also not be overlooked that Davidic descent was claimed for Rabbi Judah the Patriarch.

Twersky also states that Rabbi Mordecai of Chernobyl's tenure as tsaddik lasted "about fifty years" (p. 102, #1). If correct, this suggests that not only Rabbi Mordecai's lifestyle but his aristocratic court system may have originated during his father's lifetime. Rabbi Mordecai died in 1838; fifty years earlier brings us back to 1788, almost ten years before Rabbi Menahem Nahum's death in 1797 (see Arthur Green, *Menahem Nahum of Chernobyl*, pp. 24–25). Other sources, however, say that Rabbi Mordecai led his community for about forty years; this would place the beginning of his tenure about the time of his father's death. See, for example, Moshe Chaim Kleinman, *Mazkeret Shem ha-Gedolim* (Brooklyn, NY, 1976; original 1907); the text has no pagination but the passage appears at the very end of the section devoted to Rabbi Mordecai.

41. Assaf, *Regal Way*, p. 32.

42. Immanuel Etkes has described the attempt of Rabbi Menahem Mendel of Vitebsk and Rabbi Abraham of Kalisk to lead White Russian Hasidism from Eretz Israel in the 1780s. Their efforts were largely unsuccessful because Hasidim simply began traveling to the courts of other tsaddikim in Volynia and elsewhere. Immanuel Etkes, "The Rise of Rabbi Shneur Zalman of Lyady as a Hasidic Leader," *Tarbiz*, Vol. 54, No. 3 (1985), pp. 430–439.

In recent years we have the example of Hasidic communities after the Holocaust. Almost without exception, it was only where a scion of the dynasty survived the war that the community was able to reconstitute itself, generally in Israel or America. The fate of Alexander Hasidism is instructive: before World War II, it was one of the largest groups in Poland. But no dynastic heir survived to rebuild the community, and the remnant of Alexander Hasidim generally affiliated with dynasties that had a living tsaddik, typically Ger.

43. This is because virtually all of the celebrated early masters and dynastic founders had died by 1815; the Apter was viewed as one of the inheritors of the

spiritual legacy of Rabbi Elimelekh of Lyzhansk, along with the Maggid of Kozienice, the Seer of Lublin, and Rabbi Mendel of Rymanov, who had all died around 1815.

44. Reuben Zak, *Bei Yisrael* (Piotrkow 1913 [Bene-Barak, 1983]), p. 9, #6 and #8.

45. See Rabbi Moshe Cordovero, *Pardes Rimmonim* (Jerusalem, 1962), *Sha'ar Erkei ha-Kinnuyim*, ch. 1, p. 7b.

46. Rabbi Joseph Landau, *Kol Nehi* (a eulogy for Rabbi Israel of Ruzhin), cited in *Ner Yisrael*, Vol. 4, p. 17, #34.

47. Walden, *Nifla'ot ha-Rabi*, p. 127; cf. Assaf, *Regal Way*, p. 33. I do not know why Assaf believes that "this trip to Poland never took place."

48. A version of this story is found in *Kerem Yisrael*, which states that the meeting took place in Prohobitch at the time when Rabbi Shneur Zalman "was returning from [St.] Petersburg," presumably after his release from prison in 1801 (p. 58, #4). But if he was returning home to White Russia after his ordeal in St. Petersburg, he would hardly have gone by way of Prohobitz, roughly 1000 miles to the south. The location in Berdichev is mentioned by the grandson of Rabbi Shneur Zalman, Rabbi Menahem Mendel Schneerson ("the Zemah Zedek"), in *Derekh Mitzvotekho* (Brooklyn, NY: Kehot Publication Society, 1991); significantly, the context there is the spiritual symbolism of the union of bride and groom (p. 277). Hayyim Meir Heilman, *Beit Rabbi* (Berdiehev, 1903), says the occasion was "the wedding" (p. 123). Perhaps Heilman is referring to the betrothal of Israel and his wife-to-be, Sarah, which took place in Berdichev in 1803. Some say that the magnificent betrothal celebration was arranged by Rabbi Levi Yitzhak of Berdichev himself, and it is at least plausible that Rabbi Shneur Zalman might have made the journey to attend the reception in honor of the great-grandson of his master the Maggid of Mezhirech. For more on the betrothal and the versions of the story, see Assaf, *Regal Way*, pp. 33–35 and notes.

49. *Tiferet Israel*, Vol. 37 (1996), pp. 38–39; reprinted with corrections in *Iggerot ha-Rav ha-Kadosh mi-Ruzhin u-Vanav* [Letters of the Holy Rabbi of Ruzhin and His Children], edited by Dov Ber Rabinowitz (Jerusalem, 2003), Vol. 1, pp. 61–64; a facsimile reproduction of the original is also provided.

50. In that day it was not uncommon for boys who were not yet Bar Mitzvah to enter into marriage. The legal validity of such arrangements is the subject of a responsum by Rabbi Ezekiel Landau in his *Noda bi-Yehudah* (second series, *Even ha-Ezer*, #54), quoted in *Iggerot ha-Rav ha-Kadosh mi-Ruzhin u-Vanav*, p. 61, n. 11.

51. This episode was told by the famed tsaddik Rabbi Elimelekh Shapiro of Grodzisk; see Meir Wunder, "Teshuvat Rabbi Elimelekh mi-Grodzisk le-Rabi Hayyim mi-Zanz," *Sinai*, Vol. 81 (1977), pp. 164–168.

52. Rabbi Elimelekh of Grodzisk attributes this to the Apter Rav, with the explanation, "What angel would dare hit such a holy mouth?!" See Wunder, "Teshuvat Rabbi Elimelekh mi-Grodzisk le-Rabi Hayyim mi-Zanz," p. 166. See also *Bet Yisrael*, p. 10, #1.

53. See B.T. *Niddah* 30a.

54. *Ner Yisrael,* Vol. 4, p. 58, #15, citing *Kelilat Hen.* Hasidic sources routinely deny that *yihus*—noble ancestry—alone can impart spiritual perfection to progeny. At most, ancestral merit may ease the pathway to spiritual attainment, but only when combined with personal striving; see Rabbi Kalonymos Kalman Epstein of Cracow, *Ma'or va-Shemesh* (Jerusalem, 1992), Vol. 2, p. 412, *Parashat Naso,* s.v. "*Va-Yedaber Ha-Shem el Moshe.*" The same master states that "a talismanic practice (*segualah*) for having good children is to picture in his mind, during sexual intercourse, the image of *tsaddikim.*" Therefore, when a man marries a woman of distinguished lineage (cf. B.T. *Ta'anit* 31a), "during intercourse, he should picture in his mind the image of the tsaddikim of her family whom he has become familiar with." *Ma'or va-Shemesh,* Vol. 2, p. 751, comment on B.T. *Ta'anit* 31a. See also idem, Vol. 1, pp. 42–43, s.v. *Ve-Avraham ve-Sarah zekenim . . .* At the same time, this author, when discussing the tsaddik's power to channel blessing like the prophets of the Bible, notes that "the tsaddik has the power to transmit this to his disciple . . ." and makes no mention of transmission from father to son. *Ma'or va-Shemesh,* Vol. 2, p. 575, *Parashat Re'eh,* s.v. *Od ba-pesukim ha-nizkarim le'el . . .*

The transmission of leadership and charisma from a master to disciple rather than to the master's children is already discussed by the early midrash in relation to the biblical narrative of the succession from Moses to Joshua (Num. 27: 15–23). Commenting on Num. 27: 22, *Midrash Sifrei Zuta,* edited by H. S. Horovitz (Jerusalem, 1992, p. 321), states that Moses appointed Joshua "with joy"; "As he bequeathed his glory to Joshua, Moses was as happy as a man bequeathing his property to his sons." On the broader issue of the role of lineage in the rabbinic world, see Jeffrey L. Rubenstein, *Talmudic Stories: Narrative Art, Composition, and Culture* (Baltimore, 1999), chapter 6, "Torah, Lineage, and the Academic Hierarchy (Horayot 13b–14a)," pp. 176–211. See also Richard Kalmin, "Genealogy and Polemics in Rabbinic Literature of Late Antiquity," *Hebrew Union College Annual,* Vol. 67 (1996), pp. 77–94.

55. Reuben Zak, *Knesset Israel* (Warsaw, 1906; reprinted Bnei Brak, 1983), pp. 142–143.

56. Rabbi Hayyim Meir Yehiel Shapiro, the "Seraph" of Mogielnica, transmitted hagiographic material about his mother Perl, but the sheer volume and variety does not approach that of the Ruzhiner and Chava. See Nehemia Polen, "Miriam's Dance: Radical Egalitarianism in Hasidic Thought," pp. 1–21.

57. Assaf, *Derekh ha-Malkhut,* p. 63, n. 21. Assaf also notes that Chava possessed a stylish, elegant wardrobe, "in the spirit of the house of Ruzhin." But our suggestion here is that Chava and her fashionable taste may have actually helped to create "the spirit of the house of Ruzhin!"

58. Compare my remarks on the seal of Sarah Horowitz Sternfeld of Checiny, the "Chentshiner Rebbetzin," in Nehemia Polen, "Miriam's Dance: Radical Egalitarianism in Hasidic Thought," p. 13.

59. *Ner Yisrael*, Vol. 4, p. 363, quoting *Darash Moshe* of Rabbi Moshe Kohlenberg. Abraham Bromberg claims that Rabbi Israel did not attend the burial, but this is hardly credible. Bromberg is apparently the first author to make this assertion, though he states, without indicating a source, that the story was told to Rabbi Meir of Premishlany. Abraham Isaac Bromberg, *Migdolei ha-Hasidut: Ha-Admor Rabbi Israel Friedman me-Ruzhin* (Jerusalem, 1982), p. 145.

60. Israel Davidson, *Parody in Jewish Literature* (New York, 1907), p. 76.

61. Ya'akov Yisraeli (Kula), *Bei Karlin-Stolin* (Tel Aviv, 1981), p. 257.

62. Yehuda Leib Levin, known by his pen-name Yahalal, was a grandson of the tsaddik Rabbi Moshe of Kobrin. As a child, he showed great promise with impressive knowledge of Talmud and Hasidism; his embrace of the *Haskalah* scandalized the Hasidic community and caused great anguish to his family. See Wolf Zeev Rabinowitsch, *Lithuanian Hasidism* (New York, 1971), pp. 186–187; also p. 119, n. 156.

63. Joseph Perl, *Megaleh Temirin* (Vienna, 1819). The work is now translated into English with an introduction and extensive notes: Dov Taylor, *Joseph Perl's Revealer of Secrets, The First Hebrew Novel* (Boulder, CO, 1997).

64. Among Weisman's published works is *Mahshavot be-Etzah* (Berdichev, 1902; Jerusalem 1967), a Halakhic compendium which bears an approbation from none other than Rabbi Israel Perlow of Stolin, our *yenuka*, who was by then about thirty-four.

65. *Jsrulik*, October 30, 1875, pp. 1–3. My thanks to Dr. Leah Orent of Harvard Widener Library for assistance in locating the microfilm of this journal. In the *Ha-Shahar* article, *Hitgalut ha-Yenukah mi-Stolin* (The Debut of the Yenuka of Stolin) *Ha-Shahar* 6 (1875), pp. 25–44, Weisman's authentic letter appears on pp. 36–42 (the footnotes are not his); Levin's satiric frame letter appears on pp. 25–36, and on pp. 42–44.

66. For the spelling of *Hatchiah*, I follow the transliteration supplied by the journal itself. The masthead provides the following: "*Hatchiah* (*Regeneration*), A Hebrew literary WEEKLY in America for the purpose of promoting the knowledge of the ancient hebrew language and literature, and to regenerate the spirit of the nation. Editor & Publisher, W. Schur." I have followed the orthographic idiosyncrasies of the original. Levin's article appeared in two installments, #23 (March 23, 1900), p. 4; and #24 (March 30, 1900), pp. 3–4.

67. *Ha-Shahar*, p. 44.

68. *Ha-Shahar* 6 (1875), p. 42. For a description of the annual tax and the role of tax collectors in Hasidic courts, see David Assaf, *The Regal Way*, pp. 299–303.

69. At the time of Sarah Devorah's second marriage in 1867, her husband was forty, and she was about twenty-three.

70. Later sources tell an even more complicated story: there were some Stoliner Hasidim who were inclined to follow Sarah Devorah's older son, named Yerahmiel Moshe. He was about fourteen at the time of his stepfather's death and

had recently married. According to these reports, the Stolin elders were fearful that Yerahmiel Moshe might emerge as leader, in effect absorbing the Karlin-Stolin lineage into that of Kozienice. It was to forestall such an outcome that the elders moved to proclaim the five year old Israel Perlow as Rebbe. See Ya'akov Yis-raeli (Kula), *Bei Karlin-Stolin*, pp. 256–257; see also *Stolin: Sefer Zikaron*, edited by A. Avtihai and Y. Ben-Zakai (Tel Aviv, 1952), pp. 151–155. But even if we accept this version, one can hardly doubt Sarah Devorah's central role in the unfolding of events, given that she was mother of both candidates!

71. Malkah Shapiro, *Mi-Din le-Rahamim: Sippurim me-Hatzrot ha-Admorim* (Jerusalem, 1969); English translation: *The Rebbe's Daughter*, translated, edited, and with an introduction and commentary by Nehemia Polen (Philadelphia, 2002).

72. Assaf simply says that "the use of the funds was at the sole discretion of the tsaddik (or of his representative)" (*Regal Way*, p. 287). In some sense this is prob-ably true, but it sheds little light on the actual administrative structure and proce-dures of the household. See also his remark that "Any surplus money was invested by the tsaddikim or their financial advisors" (p. 295). But who were those finan-cial advisors?

73. Stella Tillyard writes about the family estates of aristocrats in England with their "complex command structure," employing up to several hundred peo-ple, including a core of professional artisans and a hierarchical staff of servants who had servants of their own. Tillyard writes about one such estate: "Cumber-some, leaky, and above all expensive, the household at Carton creaked through the years like an ageing man-of-war, industrial in its scale and cost, a centre of employment and production" (*Aristocrats* [New York, 1994], p. 106). Mutatis mutandis, this picture illuminates the situation of the large Hasidic courts in their heyday.

74. See Arthur Green, "The *Zaddiq* as *Axis Mundi* in Later Judaism," *Journal of the American Academy of Religion*, Vol. 45, No. 3 (1977), pp. 327–347.

75. See Nehemia Polen, "Coming of Age in Kozienice: Malkah Shapiro's Mem-oir of Youth in the Sacred Space of a Hasidic Tsaddik," in *Celebrating Elie Wiesel: Stories, Essays, Reflections*, edited by Alan Rosen (Notre Dame, 1998), pp. 123–140.

76. There is a clear parallel here to the lavish country residences of the Russian nobility which, as Priscilla Roosevelt has shown, expressed ideals of culture, fam-ily wealth, and status, and embodied the relationship between land-ownership and political power (*Life on the Russian Country Estate* [New Haven, 1995], p. 3). It is certainly suggestive that, as Roosevelt notes, "[a]lmost all the great houses were built between the mid-eighteenth and mid-nineteenth centuries, and the majority were constructed during the nobility's brief 'golden age'" (p. xii)—the decades just before and just after 1800, a time span remarkably coincident with the period under discussion here, when the great Hasidic lineages arose and flourished. This implies that the Hasidic adoption of aristocratic ways and resi-

dences was more than just a lifestyle choice, but embodied a sense of noble lineage, a heraldry of rank to be transmitted from generation to generation.

77. Compare Tamara Haraven's observations on the close relationship between "family time" and "social time" in women's lives in "The Family as Process: The Historical Study of the Family Cycle," *Journal of Social History*, Vol. 7 (1974), pp. 322–329; quoted in Jane Lewis, "Women, Lost and Found: The Impact of Feminism on History," in *Men's Studies Modified: The Impact of Feminism on the Academic Disciplines*, edited by Dale Spender (Oxford, 1981), pp. 55–72. We would expand this horizon to include sacred time and sacred space as well: the embodied theology of the Hasidic court can be understood only when all these dimensions are viewed as a unity. The adoption of such a perspective would force a reassessment of the role of women in Hasidic life.

78. *The Rebbe's Daughter*, p.137.

4

Two Jews, Three Opinions
Politics in the Shtetl at the Turn of the Twentieth Century

Henry Abramson

Organized mass Jewish politics, despite its pervasive influence in contemporary Israel and the Diaspora, is a relatively new phenomenon, stretching back only to the late nineteenth century. Prior to the watershed pogroms of 1881–1884 in the former Tsarist Empire, Jewish politics were characterized by an institution known as *shtadlones*.[1] Pre-modern in essence, the system of *shtadlones* had an "intercessor" or "lobbyist" in contact with the ruling powers, local or otherwise, to avert or at least delay changes that would have an impact on the Jewish community. This individual would typically have a strong command of the non-Jewish vernacular, a charismatic personality, and personal wealth, all of which would be used to sway the will of the powerful to advance and protect interests dear to the Jewish population. To be sure, functioning through *shtadlones* required great political acuity, but given the system's nature of back-room negotiations and occasional bribery, it was *ipso facto* not a mass movement, involving the Jewish population as a whole.[2]

The pogroms that followed the assassination of Tsar Alexander II in May of 1881 changed the Jewish political landscape dramatically.[3] Unwilling to submit to the behind-the-scenes political maneuvering of the Jewish elite, many argued that the times demanded a more aggressive and proactive policy to deal with the vexing issue known as the "Jewish Question": how to deal with the distinct nature of Jewish identity within a non-Jewish host culture. This question—sometimes referred to as a problem—was a major issue in the late nineteenth century, as Eastern Europeans began to explore political options for expressing their national identities within the multi-national empires of Russia and Austria-Hungary [and Western Germany]. Jewish political mobilization progressed throughout the period of late Tsarism, flourishing after the Revolution of 1905, and eventually coalesced into five fairly distinct political orientations:

1. *Emigrationism*, a popular but politically inchoate movement to abandon Europe and create a new, as yet undefined, Jewish community in the United States and elsewhere.
2. *Zionism*, a movement to create a refuge for Jews in the traditional homeland of Israel. Like emigrationists, however, Zionists also did not come to agreement on just what shape this Jewish country would take.
3. *Jewish Socialism*, a movement to deal with the Jewish Question, not by abandoning Europe, but by radically transforming the general political climate of the entire region.
4. *Autonomism*, a movement to similarly maintain the presence of Jews in Eastern Europe, but without the dramatic change demanded by the Jewish Socialists. Instead, a more moderate, secularized form of the status quo would be the basis of a renewed Jewish shtetl in a democratized all-Russian federation.
5. *Renewed Traditionalism*, a movement originating in the circles closest to the old system of *shtadlones* yet propelled by many of the methods and ideals of mass political mobilization. The last to organize, Renewed Traditionalists used the tools of modern politics to advance the religious platform of the Orthodox population.

Each of these groups will now be described in greater detail.

Emigrationism

Jewish-American popular mythology presents the emigration from the Tsarist Empire as a pell-mell refugee movement, epitomized by the image of Tevye's impoverished family picking up whatever possessions they can muster and leaving the pogrom-ridden Anatevka in *Fiddler on the Roof*. To be sure, a massive number of Jews chose emigration as the solution to their woes—by 1914, almost two million had left the Russian Empire, together with over half a million from the neighboring Austro-Hungarian

Empire and Romania.⁴ Notwithstanding the reality of the pogroms, however, the major impetus for departure was undoubtedly the economic hardship occasioned by the discriminatory Tsarist commercial legislation that imposed unnecessary hardships on the Jews of the Pale of Settlement, which "either deprived the Jewish population of opportunities to enter new regions, new markets, new areas of employment, or made it considerably more costly to overcome the barriers erected by the discriminatory practices."⁵ Moreover, as Arcadius Kahan continues, corrupt local officials extorted Jewish entrepreneurs through various bribes designed to preserve even those limited protections that they were entitled to by law.⁶ Indeed, while America was the land of refuge for many, it was more properly known as *di goldene medine*—the Land of Gold—the land of economic opportunity.

Consider the following passage by Mary Antin, an emigrant who arrived in the United States in 1891:

America was in everybody's mouth. Businessmen talked of it over their accounts; the market women made up their quarrels that they might discuss it from stall to stall; people who had relatives in the famous land went around reading their letters of the enlightenment of the less fortunate folks, the one letter-carrier informed the public how many letters arrived from America, and who were the recipients; children played at emigrating; old folks shook their sage heads over the evening fire, and prophesied no good for those who braved the terrors of the sea and the foreign goal beyond it; all talked of it, but scarcely anybody knew one true fact about this magic land. For book-knowledge was not for them; and a few persons—they were a dressmaker's daughter, and a merchant with his two sons—who happened to be endowed with extraordinary imagination (a faculty closely related to their knowledge of their old countrymen's ignorance), and their descriptions of life across the ocean, given daily, for some months, to eager audiences, surpassed anything in the Arabian nights.⁷

America was seen as some sort of economic Shangri-La, and indeed in comparison with the poverty of much of the Pale of Settlement, it was. I recall my grandmother's stories of Simna, her Lithuanian shtetl, and how, as a child, she resented the daily job of going to the home of *Khaye di Amerikaner* to help her tie her corset. *Khaye di Amerikaner* was so named because she had lived in the United States for a time, returned with prodigious wealth, and as a demonstration of her financial security, built a magnificent home for her herself and her husband (who was known as *Moishe Khayes*—Khaye's Moshe, to distinguish him from the other Moshes in town, further evidence of Khaye's status).[8] This home was notable for the fact that it was one of only a handful of brick buildings in the entire shtetl. In other words, without dismissing the reality of violent anti-Semitism, one can say that the predominant motive for emigration was the desire to achieve greater economic security, something that was increasingly difficult in the Pale of Settlement.

Writing twenty years after arriving in the States, Mary Antin describes more of the particular circumstances that led to her emigration from the Russian Empire in her early teens, after her father lost his job as the manager of a gristmill:

> The next year or so my father spent in a restless and fruitless search for a permanent position. My mother had another serious illness, and his own health remained precarious. What he earned did not more than half pay the bills in the end, though we were living very humbly now. Polotzk seemed to reject him, and no other place invited him.
>
> Just at this time occurred one of the periodic anti-Semitic movements whereby government officials were wont to clear the forbidden cities whom, in the intervals of slack administration of the law, they allowed to maintain an illegal residence in places outside the Pale, on payment of enormous bribes and at the cost of nameless risks and indignities.
>
> It was a little before Passover that the cry of the hunted thrilled the Jewish world with the familiar fear. The wholesale expulsion of Jews from Moscow and its surrounding district at cruelly short notice was the name of this latest disaster. Where would the doom strike next? The Jews who lived illegally without the Pale turned their possessions into cash and slept in their clothes, ready for immediate flight. Those who lived in the comparative security of the Pale trembled for their brothers and sisters without, and opened wide their doors to afford the fugitives refuge. And hundreds of fugitives, preceded by a wail of distress, flocked into the open district, bringing their trouble where trouble was never absent, mingling their tears with the tears that never dried. . . .
>
> Passover was celebrated in tears that year. In the story of the Exodus we would have read a chapter of current history, only for us there was no deliverer and no promised land.
>
> But what said some of us at the end of the long service? Not "May we be next year in Jerusalem," but "Next year—in America!" So there was our

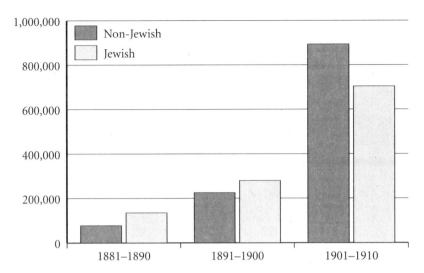

Non-Jewish and Jewish Emigration from the Russian Empire, 1881–1910.

promised land, and many faces were turned towards the West. And if the waters of the Atlantic did not part for them, the wanderers rode its bitter flood by a miracle as great as any the rod of Moses every wrought.[9]

Millions of subjects of the Tsar fled the Russian Empire, but none at a greater rate than the Jews. During the decade after the assassination of Tsar Alexander II in 1881—an era which witnessed a wide-scale pogrom wave sweeping the Empire and harsh anti-Jewish legislation known as the May Laws—over 200,000 emigrants left the Russian Empire, 63 percent of them Jews. During the next decade, Jews continued to dominate emigration, albeit at a slightly lower rate of 55 percent, and it was only in the first decade of the twentieth century that a greatly increased non-Jewish emigration outpaced the flood of Jews from the Russian Empire.[10]

For Jews, emigration was a family affair, as statistics on gender and age clearly indicate. Compared to Slavic emigration from the Russian Empire, for example, Jewish emigration was characterized by its relatively high proportion of females making the journey. While Jewish women and girls never outnumbered male emigrants during the peak years of emigration, they were consistently represented at a greater rate than any non-Jewish group, usually over 40 percent of all Jewish emigrants. This suggests that emigration, for Jews, was more likely to be a permanent decision, with

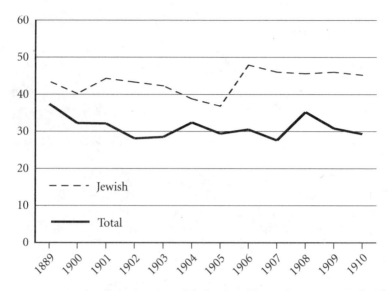

Percent of Female Immigrants to the United States, 1899–1910.

whole families settling at once or following a gender-related chain of emigration, with men arriving first and then sending for their families once they were established. This was the common pattern, evinced not only by Mary Antin's example, but also by that of all of my own grandparents.[11]

Jewish emigration was also characterized by its unusually broad representation of age groups. The overwhelming majority of Slavic emigrants (e.g., Poles, Ukrainians, and Russians) from the Russian Empire was male, traveled without female companions or dependants, and was between the ages of 14 and 44. This profile was basically typical of Jewish emigrants as well, but with significant statistical differences. The Jewish immigrant to the United States was some 50 percent more likely to be female, as shown above, and when age groups are compared, the differences are still more striking. Jewish emigrants over the age of 45 came at twice the rate of Slavic emigrants, and Jewish children under 14 between two-and-a-half and five times the rate of their non-Jewish boatmates. Children under 14 represented less than 5 percent of the Ukrainian emigration, for example, whereas Jewish children numbered nearly a quarter of all Jewish emigrants. Taken together, Jewish emigration was clearly a solution adopted by entire families, young and old, male and female—unlike *Khaye di Amerikaner*.[12]

Emigrationism was the most significant mass Jewish reaction to modernity in the late nineteenth century. It was also the most pre-modern of all of the options developed in the waning years of the Tsarist Empire. Unlike Socialism, it did not radically challenge the fundamental economic structure of society nor did it openly advocate the massive rejection of the traditional religious structure of Judaism and Jewish life. (To be sure, a considerable number of traditions were jettisoned in the American environment, but not with the kind of gusto characteristic of the Soviet "League of Militant Atheists.")[13] Although America was a frontier destination, and its lack of a Jewish infrastructure was legendary, nevertheless emigrationism was ultimately the most traditional of responses: it was a strategy of flight that had characterized Jewish reaction to persecution and hardship for centuries.

Zionism

In its most basic understanding, Zionism—the "soul of the Jew soul yearning . . . to be a free people in our own land, the land of Zion and Jerusalem," in the words of Naphtali Herz Imber's famous 1878 poem "Hatikvah," anthem of the Zionist movement and later the State of Israel—is almost as old as the Jewish people themselves, with expressions of Zionist thought stretching back to the sixth century before the common era, as in the biblical song of Zion by the rivers of Babylon: "if I forget you, O Jerusalem, let my right hand forget, let my tongue cleave to my palate if I do not remember you" (Psalm 137). The Talmudic Rabbi Yohanan teaches that "anyone who walks four cubits in the world to come is assured of a place in the world to come" (*B.T. Ketubot* 111a), and the weekday Orthodox liturgy includes several petitions for a speedy return of the Davidic Messiah and the remnant of the Jewish population to Israel.

The key element of this early form of Zionism, however, was its emphasis on the divine assent given to the project of Jewish statehood. The traditional Orthodox establishment in the shtetl did not, until the turn of the twentieth century at the earliest, envision the creation of a Jewish form of nationalism, with the stated purpose of creating a Jewish state in the land of Israel, complete with all the trappings of sovereignty (flags, armies, borders, and the like). The reason for this opposition was the traditional theological position that the Jewish status in exile—in Yiddish, *goles*—was a consequence of their inappropriate behavior while in the land of Israel.

Ages of Slavic and Jewish Emigrants from the Russian Empire, 1899–1909

	Pol.	Ukr.	Rus.	Jews
45 and older	2.4	2.7	2.5	5.4
14–44	88.1	92.7	90.0	69.8
Under 14	9.5	4.6	7.5	24.8

For centuries, Jews read Leviticus 28:26–28 with a feeling of immediacy that has largely been lost since the creation of the State of Israel in 1948: "You will observe these my decrees and my laws, and not partake of all these abominations . . . that the land not vomit you out for your defilement, as it vomited out the nation that came before you." The lack of Jewish sovereignty, therefore, was seen as divine punishment for the multitude of Jewish sins in the biblical period.

Therefore, the first organized movements of Jews from the shtetl were not bent on creating the infrastructure of eventual statehood, with its concomitant rebellion against the divine decree of *goles*. The earliest movements—BILU (which is a Hebrew acronym for Isaiah 2:5, "House of Jacob—let us rise up and go") and *Hovevei Tsion*, originating in Ukraine during the 1880s—sought only to establish agricultural colonies in the land of Israel, and were basically free of larger political aspirations. Their goal of settling the land of Israel for its own sake received approval in traditionalist Orthodox circles.[14] These proto-Zionist movements remained predictably small, attracting small numbers of Jews to their cause. Given the choice between emigration to the land of opportunity and the then-barren land of Israel, the vast majority chose to cross the Atlantic.

It was during the 1890s that modern Zionism got its major boost, as secular, politically motivated variations on the Zionist theme were articulated in both Eastern and Western Europe. Unlike the earlier forms of proto-Zionism, the new Zionisms either avoided the question of the traditional rabbinic approval or actively sought to undermine the authority of religion altogether. Indeed, the traditional historical connection between the Jews and the land of Israel, reinforced by millennia of religious argument, was not considered an absolute necessity by many Zionists, as is clearly demonstrated by Herzl's argument for Uganda as an alternative homeland for the Jews in place of Palestine, a motion that passed by 295 votes in favor versus 178 votes against at the sixth World Zionist Congress (1903).[15] Although the idea failed to come to fruition, largely because of the opposition of the delegates from the Russian Empire (who, by dint of their unique experience of persecution, had the moral authority to decline the offer), the very fact that the idea could be approved at the congress indicates the level of secularization of the Zionist movement.[16]

In the shtetl, Jews embraced a wide variety of versions of Zionist philosophy. The largest single group was the General Zionists (*Algemayne Tsionisten*), which, as the name implies, was an umbrella group of several varieties of moderate Zionisms, including youth groups. The General Zionists were closest to Herzl's vision of Zion—that is, a secular democratic state that basically duplicated the best qualities of European countries. It is difficult to get accurate statistics to quantify precisely the degree of popularity of the General Zionists, but a look at the chaotic Jewish communal elections of 1918 shows that they took 45 percent of the votes cast for Jewish political movements (35 percent of the popular vote), and thus proved to be the most successful of all platforms in those elections.[17]

Another major group was the *Poalei-Tsion* (Workers of Zion), a hybrid party that emphasized a socialist interpretation of Zionism: in other words, whereas the *Poalei-Tsion* agreed with Herzl's vision of a homeland for the Jews in Palestine, they argued that this homeland should be securely founded on Marxist principles. Their popularity in the shtetl was considerably lower than that of the General Zionists (they only won 6 percent of the popular votes in the elections mentioned above, for example), but they were very effective in translating their small numbers of dedicated followers into actual pioneers in Israel, and they are largely credited with the creation of the kibbutz network there. Ironically, although the *Poalei-Tsion* were closely identified with the Zionist movement historically, during the brief period of Jewish political activity following the fall of the Tsar in 1917, they chose to ally themselves with the Jewish socialist parties rather than the General Zionists.

Before moving on to the Jewish Socialists, it is important to note two more movements that were small in size but had significant influence: Revisionism, a brand of Zionism championed primarily by Vladimir Jabotinsky, and Mizrachi, an Orthodox Zionism associated with Rabbi Avraham Isaac Kook. The former was a secular Zionism that differed from the General Zionism not so much in terms of goals, but in terms of methodology. Herzl spent much of his energies shuttling between one European capital and another, meeting with various dignitaries and lobbying for the Zionist cause. Like a traditional *shtadlan*, he hoped to intercede through force of his personal charm for the benefit of the Jews of Europe. Jabotinsky, on the other hand, had a much more pragmatic and pessimistic view of the outside world, and felt that the Zionists would be better served by direct military action than more and more political negotiations.[18] Although a negligible presence in pre-Revolutionary shtetl politics, Revisionism had a major impact in Israel.

Mizrachi represented the first organized Orthodox response to the growing popularity of modern, secular Zionism. Rather than excoriating the movement as a heresy, several Orthodox thinkers came to embrace it, if for no other reason than the fact that it drew non-observant Jews closer to at least some aspect of Jewish identity. More concretely, they felt that the establishment of a Jewish state in the land of Israel might in fact be part of the divine plan—given an expression of enthusiasm that took the form of concrete action to create a state, God might be moved to reciprocate by sending the long-awaited Messiah.[19] Like Revisionism, the Mizrachi movement had an impact far outweighing its numbers.

Jewish Socialism

Jews were attracted to various forms of socialism in great numbers after the pogroms of 1881. Reliable statistics are hard to come by, but their disproportionate representation in virtually all socialist movements is proverbial. Benjamin Pinkus, for example, estimates that there were nearly a thousand Jews in the Communist Party before the revolutions of 1917, representing about 4 percent of the total membership.[20] This is disproportionate to the population of the Jews in the Russian Empire, but not unreasonable when compared to urban populations alone. More significantly, however, the Jews tended to find greater representation in the leadership of various socialist groups. Considering again the Communist Party, prominent Jewish figures such as Trotsky and Zinoviev, as well as the participation of Jews in the dreaded *Cheka*, lend some credence to the widespread view of the "Judo-Kommuna."[21]

It is important to note the distinction, however, between Jews in purely socialist parties such as the Bolsheviks and the Mensheviks, and Jewish socialist parties. Jews who participated in general socialist parties often jettisoned their Jewish identity completely, essentially subsuming any specifically Jewish aspect of their political views within the overall platform of their party.[22] The Jewish Socialist parties, on the other hand, attempted to reconcile at least some aspect of Jewish identity with socialism, usually irreparably compromising one or the other.

Emigrationism sought to simply relocate the Jews from the Russian Empire to a potentially better location. Zionism identified that location as the Land of Israel. By contrast, Jewish Socialism focused not on the presence of the Jews, but on the Russian Empire itself as the problem. Rather than move the Jews and possibly exchange one set of problems for another, the Jewish Socialists sought to transform the host society altogether, forcing it to adapt to the needs of its multinational population. Rallying around the various interpretations of Marxist ideology, the Jewish Socialists aimed to create a workers' paradise in which all forms of national discrimination would be abolished. The real question, however, was how to reconcile Marxist ideology with Jewish identity.

Marx, baptized at age six by his upwardly-mobile parents, harbored a deep-seated resentment against Jews and Judaism, and treated both with special scorn in his writings.[23] Nevertheless, Jewish Socialists sought to reconcile Marx's vision of a secular utopian future of egalitarianism by arguing that Marx's opposition to the Jews was specifically religious in nature. By divorcing Judaism from Jewish culture, they believed, Jewish peoplehood could be maintained; Jews, like all other fraternal peoples of the Russian Empire, could march together in socialist unity towards a society free of class and national conflict.

The largest single Jewish Socialist group was the General Jewish Worker's League, known commonly as the "Bund." Originally, the Bund took a very doctrinaire stance towards the Jews, defining itself as Jewish only insofar as it was necessary to mobilize their target population, the Bund itself, essentially working as an organ to translate Russian-language propaganda into Yiddish. Within a few years of its founding in 1897—ironically, the same year as the convening of the first World Zionist Congress—the Bund adopted a friendlier attitude to expressions of Jewish identity, under a doctrine defined as "Neutralism" by its most colorful leader, Vladimir Medem. Seeing how Jews resisted efforts to downplay their distinctive identity, Medem argued that the Bund should adopt a "neutral" attitude to those aspects of Jewish culture that must be tolerated as the Jewish population move towards a more revolutionary consciousness. The very size of the Bund, with some 30,000 card-carrying members before the Revolution, meant that Neutralism was defined in very different ways throughout the Empire, with some Bundists adopting a more hostile attitude to Jewish practice, while others embraced even some religious customs.[24]

Autonomism

Less well-known than the previous three responses, Autonomism was nevertheless an extremely competitive ideology among Jews in the Russian Empire, and not only played a very important role in establishing the post-Revolutionary political status of Jews in Ukraine, Poland, and the Baltic States, but also had an impact on the organization of the American Jewish community. The ideology of Autonomism was first developed by the Austrians Otto Bauer and Karl Renner, and independently by the Ukrainian Mykhailo Drahomaniv, as an attempt to deal with the multinational makeup of the Austro-Hungarian and Russian Empires. Later, the historian Shimon Dubnow adapted these ideas to the Jewish population.[25]

Working with the historical precedent of the medieval Council of Four Lands, Dubnow envisioned a national register of all Jews in a posited future democratic Russian republic. Jews on this register, or *kadaster* as it was called, would constitute the voting body and tax base that would create a Jewish parliament, with its Prime Minister acting as a Minister of Jewish Affairs within the overall Russian government. Jewish affairs would be democratically discussed on a state-wide basis, and the tax revenues collected from *kadaster* members would fund a variety of programs such as a Jewish school system. Moreover, the Jews would have a communal voice in the highest levels of national government through the Ministry of Jewish Affairs. Through this arrangement, Jews would preserve their individual democratic rights as citizens of the Russian Federation, but would retain a communal identity through the state-wide Jewish parliament. In other words, Dubnow sought to create a modern, secular version of the medieval Council of Four Lands, a phenomenon from a period of history in which he had invested considerable research energy.

Dubnow's party, the *Folkspartey*, and related parties such as the *Faraynikte*, were never very successful in democratic elections, but they had a few distinct advantages. For example, their centrist position made them a natural link between the larger Socialist and Zionist blocs. Secondly, since they advocated neither the major social upheaval of Socialism nor the mass defection of Jews to Israel, their position was amenable to many non-Jewish nationalist movements, and their relative silence on religious matters might have made them more popular with the traditional Orthodox population. In practice, however, the Autonomist parties tended to form coalitions with the Socialists, ruining many of their chances of a serious *rapprochement* with the Zionist parties and alienating the Orthodox vote in the process.

Renewed Traditionalism

The last ideological option exercised by shtetl Jewry was the political mobilization of the traditional Orthodox establishment, most notably with the formation of the *Agudat Yisroel* party in 1912.[26] Although the traditionalist mentality had originally looked down on the growth of secular Jewish politics, by the first decade of the twentieth century, it had become evident that mass politics had become a major force among Jews—and something that the Tsarist government would also have to reckon with.[27] As a consequence, the *Agudat Yisroel* was formed with the goal of defending the traditional practices of Orthodoxy: the protection of Jewish observance of the Sabbath, the availability of ritual baths, and the preservation of standards in the dietary laws. In other words, the primary foe was the encroachment of socialist ideology among shtetl Jews, but the *Agudat Yisroel* also looked with a skeptical eye at Zionism, even the religious Zionism adopted by the Mizrachi movement.

In many ways, this was a political party without a political platform, but the Renewed Traditionalists proved to be quite adaptable to changing political circumstances. They commanded the loyalty of a significant segment of the population: taking the 1918 results for Ukraine cited above, for example, we find that a Renewed Traditionalist party called *Akhdes* (Unity) took 13% of the vote, the third largest result after the General Zionists (42%; with a youth party 45%) and the Bund (19%), and handily beating the Autonomists (*Faryanikte*, 9%, *Folkspartey*, 3%) and the *Poalei-Tsion* (8%). Given the anti-clerical bent of the Socialist bloc, however, *Akhdes* formed a coalition with the larger Zionist bloc, despite their reservations about the nature of the movement. This is a strategy that the Renewed Traditionalists would use throughout the twentieth century: keeping an eye on the defense of traditional Jewish practice, they could lever support from larger political bodies.

Same Politics, Bigger Shtetl

In this chapter I have tried to categorize the five principal options that shtetl Jews exercised in reaction to the situation in the Russian Empire after the pogroms of 1881: Emigrationism, Zionism, Jewish Socialism, Autonomism, and Renewed Traditionalism. Although the Revolutions of 1917 radically altered the political landscape of the region, and the Holocaust two decades later totally destroyed the centuries-old culture of the shtetl, nevertheless shtetl politics continued in an altered form in the United States and Israel.

In brief, the Emigrationists and the Zionists did very well, each achieving their respective goals: a strong Jewish center in America and the establishment of the State of Israel in 1948. Among the Zionists, the socialist hybrid *Poalei-Tsion* formed the backbone of the Labor Party, and the General Zionists, together with the more radical Revisionists, evolved to make a major contribution to the Likud Party; their respective policies reflect their origins in the shtetl disputes of the turn of the twentieth century.

Jewish Socialists did not do as well—after the success of the Soviet revolution, all of the Jewish Socialist parties split, with their left-leaning halves joining the Communist movement, into which they were all forcibly absorbed in the 1920s. The right-leaning halves found brief popularity in North America, and established a network of Workmen's Circle organs that operated for decades. Unfortunately for these American Jewish Socialists, however, their ideology failed to take root in younger generations, and by the turn of the twenty-first century they were virtually extinct.

Autonomism had its heyday in East-Central Europe during the early interwar period, but was overwhelmed by the tide of integral nationalism that swept Europe in the 1930s. After the rise of successful fascist movements, no country had much patience for the liberal approach to communal politics advocated by the Autonomists. Their ideology, however, did find some expression in the organization of the World Council of Jewish Federations, with their informal *kadaster* of contributors to the United Jewish Fund and the like. Their fundraising abilities are legendary—as the joke goes, the only way to avoid the UJA is to go into the FBI Witness Protection Program—but their coercive powers are a pale shadow of what the Autonomists envisioned, and so too is the range of Jewish services that a fully functioning Autonomist state would have provided.

The Renewed Traditionalists found their niche in modern American and especially Israeli politics. Bolstered by new Sephardic allies such as the Shas Party, the Renewed Traditionalists were able to use the coalition-dependent nature of the fractioned Israeli political system to engineer tremendous successes for the defense of Orthodoxy. This is ironic, given that the traditional Orthodox mentality originally opposed both Emigrationism and secular Zionism, yet it was precisely in America and Israel that parties like *Agudas Yisroel* would eventually have the most power. Yet after the Holocaust, the rich shtetl culture, which once supported this wide variety of Jewish political expression, was no more.

NOTES

1. Many Yiddish terms are of Hebrew derivation; hence the word *shtadlones* would be pronounced *shtadlanut* by a speaker of modern Israeli Hebrew. All such terms in this paper will be transliterated according to the YIVO system of Yiddish transliteration, unless otherwise noted.

2. For a detailed breakdown of the component parts of the Jewish community and the role of *shtadlones*, see the two volumes by Isaac Levitats: *The Jewish Community in Russia, 1772–1844* (New York, 1943), and *The Jewish Community in Russia, 1844–1917* (Jerusalem, 1981).

3. For information on the pogroms and their aftermath, see I. Michael Aronson, *Troubled Waters: The Origin of the 1881 Anti-Jewish Pogroms in Russia* (Pittsburgh, 1990); and Stephen Berk, *Year of Crisis, Year of Hope: Russian Jewry and the Pogroms of 1881–1882* (Westport, CT, 1985).

4. A[rye] Tartakower, *In Search of Home and Freedom* (London, 1958), p. 31.

5. Arcadius Kahan, *Essays in Jewish Social and Economic History*, edited by Roger Weiss (Chicago, 1986), p. 35.

6. Kahan, *Essays*, p. 36.

7. Mary Antin, *From Plotzk to Boston* (Boston, 1898). Cited in Mark Wischnitzer, *To Dwell in Safety: The Story of Jewish Migration Since 1800* (Philadelphia, 1948), p. 70.

8. Actually, my grandmother informs me that Moishe Khayes was so named because his mother's name was also Khaye. I can only speculate how Moishe avoided the customary ban on marrying a woman with the same name as one's mother, but it is nevertheless another interesting detail of shtetl life.

9. Mary Antin, *The Promised Land: The Autobiography of a Russian Immigrant* (Boston, 1940 [f.p. 1911]), pp. 140–141.

10. These statistics are adapted from Samuel Joseph, *Jewish Immigration to the*

United States from the Russian Empire from 1881 to 1910 (New York, 1969 [f.p. as Columbia University Ph.D. dissertation, 1914), table xxx, p. 174.

11. Statistics adapted from Joseph, *Immigration*, table xxxvi, p. 178.

12. Statistics adapted from Joseph, *Immigration*, table xxxix, p. 180. Note that the term "Ruthenian" is used there to describe the people more commonly known today as "Ukrainians," and thus the Ukrainian figure may be skewed by the large number of migrants from Galicia, a province in the neighboring Austo-Hungarian Empire where the term "Ruthenian" was used as a translation of the terms *Rus'* or *Rusyn*.

13. On the Soviet transformation of Jewish life, see Zvi Gitelman, *Jewish Nationality and Soviet Politics: The Jewish Sections of the CPSU, 1917–1930* (Princeton, 1972).

14. Details on the early period of Zionism are discussed in David Vital, *The Origins of Zionism* (Oxford, 1975).

15. Walter Lacqueur, *A History of Zionism* (New York, 1972), p. 129.

16. For an interesting discussion of modern influences on some prominent Zionist figures, see Michael Stanislawski, *Zionism and the Fin de Siècle: Cosmopolitanism and Nationalism from Nordau to Jabotinsky* (Berkeley, 2001).

17. Grosman, M., Y. Grinfeld and E. Tcherikover, eds., *Di idishe avtonomie un der natsionaler secretariat in Ukrayne: materialn un dokumentn* (Kiev, 1920), pp. 210–213. This figure includes youth groups. For the circumstances behind these elections and an interpretation of their results, see my *Prayer for the Government: Ukrainians and Jews in Revolutionary Times, 1917–1920* (Cambridge, MA, 1999), pp. 93–99.

18. See Shmuel Katz, *Lone Wolf: A Biography of Vladimir (Ze'ev) Jabotinsky*, 2 vols. (New York, 1996). Jabotinsky's more aggressive approach to questions of self-determination and his alliance with Ukrainian nationalists have given him a renewed popularity in contemporary Ukrainian circles. His *Vybani statti z natsional'noho pytannia* were published in Kiev by the Republican Association for Ukrainian Studies in 1991, and a recent study of his work was published by the Canadian Institute for Ukrainian Studies: Israel Kleiner, *From Nationalism to Universalism: Vladimir (Ze'ev) Jabotinsky and the Ukrainian Question* (Edmonton, 2000).

19. See for example Lawrence Kaplan, ed., *Rabbi Abraham Isaac Kook and Jewish Spirituality* (New York, 1995).

20. Benjamin Pinkus, *The Jews of the Soviet Union: The History of a National Minority* (Cambridge, 1988), pp. 77–79.

21. I have discussed aspects of the perception of Jews in the Communist Party apparatus in "Lokale Elemente in anisemitischen Ikonographie der NS-Propaganda in ukrainischer Sprache," *Jahrbuch des Fritz Bauer Institut*, Vol. 6 (Frankfurt am Main, forthcoming).

22. See, for example, Joseph Nevada, *Trotsky and the Jews* (Philadelphia, 1972);

Stuart Kahan, *Wolf of the Kremlin: The First Biography of L. M. Kaganovich, the Soviet Union's Architect of Fear* (New York, 1987).

23. See Julius Carlebach, *Karl Marx and the Radical Critique of Judaism* (London, 1978).

24. For the membership of the Bund, see Pinkus, *Jews of the Soviet Union*, p. 43. Studies of the Bund include Henry Tobias, *The Bund in Russia: From its Origins to 1905* (Stanford, 1972); and Y. Sh. Hertz, *Di geshikhte fun Bund*, 5 vols. (New York, 1960).

25. See Shimon Dubnow, *Nationalism and History: Essays on Old and New Judaism*, edited by Koppel Pinson (New York, 1970). See also Oscar Janowsky, *The Jews and Minority Rights (1898–1919)* (New York, 1933). For a discussion of the development of Autonomism in Ukraine, see my *Prayer for the Government*; the Baltic states are discussed on pages 163–167.

26. See Gershon Bacon, *The Politics of Tradition: Agudat Yisrael in Poland, 1916–1939* (Jerusalem, 1996); and Mordechai Altshuler, "Ha-politika shel ha-mahane ha-dati ve-ha-haredi be-Rusyah be-shnat 1917," *Shvut*, Vol. 15 (1992), pp. 195–234.

27. One of the most thorough studies of the Jewish Question and the Russian Imperial government, which pays considerable attention to the Orthodox establishment, is Heinz-Dietrich Löwe, *The Tsars and the Jews: Reform, Reaction and Anti-Semitism in Imperial Russia, 1772–1917* (New York, 1993).

5

The Shtetl in Poland, 1914–1918

Konrad Zieliński

World War I had a serious impact on Jewish life in the Polish shtetlekh. While the first year of the war turned out to be dreadful for Jews, after the Russian evacuation in the summer of 1915, when the whole territory of the Kingdom of Poland came under German and Austrian-Hungarian occupation, this occupation resulted in the predatory exploitation of the country and pauperization of the population. In this essay I examine aspects of Russian politics, drawing attention to the anti-Semitism of the tsarist army. I then consider the problem of the forced migration of Jews and the destruction of their shtetlekh, their economy, and their local markets. Here, I also examine the political and cultural development of the Jewish population, which was connected with the policy of Germans and Austrians. Finally, I offer some remarks on Polish-Jewish relationships.

The Beginning of the War

Near the beginning of World War I, Herman Bernstein, an American journalist, wrote that more than three million Polish Jews "are starving, homeless, driven from place to place, by the armies that are fighting against Russia and by the armies that are fighting for Russia."[1]

Bernstein's words truly describe the beginnings of World War I and its impact on the Jewish population. It turned out quickly to be the case that the tsarist army was a bastion of anti-Semitism,[2] with the Cossack troops especially winning for themselves the worst kind of reputation. There were cases of plunder everywhere. The fact that many Jews trying to avoid conscription escaped from enlistment resulted in accusations of espionage and sabotage.[3] Even warnings against such acts as destroying telephone lines, poisoning wells, or spreading disquieting rumors about the military situation in the war-zone were often directed at the Jews exclusively, as were punishments for such acts.[4] The Russians removed from one place to another soldiers and officers of Jewish and German origin in order to avoid the possibility of their disloyalty and cooperation with the enemy. In the report of the Commander of Staff to the Chief Commissariat of Armies of the southwestern front from June of 1915, one can read both "sensational" and seriously treated information that Jewish organizations in Germany were paying prostitutes to infect Russian officers and soldiers.[5]

Jewish and other organizations in the West tried to intercede on behalf of their compatriots in Russia and Poland. They pointed out that about 400,000 Jews served in the Russian army; that the number of Jews who had been awarded the Cross of St. George was estimated at 400; that many Jews had been promoted to non-commissioned rank; that some 3,000 Jews had been distinguished for their valor on the field; and that many Jews had founded hospitals and supported the army. All these facts did little to change the authorities' attitudes towards the Jews. One of the few Jewish deputies to the Duma, N. M. Friedman, said in July of 1915:

> "Many complimentary speeches have been uttered in the Duma with regard to Poland. This of course is right and just. But you must also remember that on Polish soil and other parts there flows the blood of other nationalities, including Jewish blood, and, unfortunately not at the hands of the enemy alone."[6]

In fact, the treatment of the Jews in Poland was especially severe. While Germans and Austrians hired Jews as interpreters since they could easily communicate in Polish, this was sufficient to start repression by the Russian authorities after the recapture a town or a village. In many places the Russians burned down whole Jewish quarters; thousands of people were accused of espionage and sabotage; and hundreds of them were punished by death or killed by soldiers without any trials. Already at the beginning of the war, it turned out that correspondence in Yiddish and Hebrew between Jewish soldiers and their families was "getting lost." In addition, in July of 1915 all the Jewish newspapers were closed by the Russians military authority.[7] Moreover, it was common practice for the Russians to accuse the Jews of destroying telephone lines and forcing them to pay high compensation and so-called contributions.[8]

I. The number of registered refugees from the Kingdom of Poland
in 1916, according to the Central Citizens' Committee

Gubernya	Number of refugees
Lomza	81,654
Kholm	57,811
Lublin	56,898
Suwalki	25,835
Radom	21,101
Piotrkow	10,834
Plock	11,059
Kalisz	4,348
Kielce	3,603
Warsaw (city)	43,562
Warsaw	28,400
Total	336,105

Source: M. Korzeniowski, *Na wygnańczym szlaku . . . Działalność Centralnego Komitetu Obywatelskiego Królestwa Polskiego na Białorusi w latach 1915–1918* (LTN: Lublin 2001), p. 116.

Jewish women suffered the most bitter fate. In Zarnow in March and April of 1915, the local commander systematically raped women in the presence of their fathers, husbands, and brothers. According to the Anglo-American Jewish Conjoint Committee investigation, during this time thirteen Jewish women were raped; however, we do not know if the commander was punished or not. In Senno, in the Radom province, when the local military authorities imprisoned all the Jews of the village and kept them under arrest for two days, soldiers raped Jewish girls.[9] In a few places in the Kielce *gubernya* (province) "the rapists bit and killed their victims."[10]

Maurice Paléologue, the last ambassador from France to tsarist Russia, wrote in his diary entry of October 28, 1914, that "for the Jews of Poland and Lithuania the war is one of the greatest disasters they have known."[11] In fact, not a day passed in the war-zone without a number of Jews being hanged on a trumped-up charge of spying. Additionally, the local Christian population did not remain passive: very often the Jews were wrongly accused of disloyalty and other crimes by their Polish or Ukrainian neighbors.

Migrations

When ungrounded fears that Jews might en masse collaborate with the Central States' armies arose, the Russian military authorities started mass deportations. According to the memorandum submitted by the Petrograd Relief Committee to the consideration of the governor of Minsk, the Jews usually had to leave their homes within three to twelve hours. They were forced onto the roads with the few possessions they could carry.[12]

Some researchers estimate that during the years 1914 and 1915 about 1,200,000 people were evacuated from the Kingdom of Poland: tsarist officers, teachers, Orthodox clergy, Polish workers from military factories, and railroad workers.[13] But in trying to establish the actual number of citizens forced to leave the Kingdom of Poland, we find many difficulties. Besides Russians, about 1,000,000 people were forced to leave the country in 1914 and 1915; however, this number includes residents of the Galicia territories occupied by the Russians.[14] At the beginning of October of 1916 the Central Citizens' Committee of the Kingdom of Poland announced that 744,319 refugees stayed in Russia.[15] According to the newspaper *Haslo* (Signal), there were 850,000 Poles and about 150,000 officers, railroad workers, Orthodox clergy, workmen, landlords, and factory owners remaining in 1915—hence, about 1,000,000 refugees and evacuated people from Galicia and the Kingdom of Poland (not including Polish POWs and Russian soldiers of Polish nationality). Other Polish sources also note that there were about 850,000 refugees from the Kingdom of Poland. While the Central Citizens' Committee stated that during the Russian evacuation the number of refugees from the Kingdom of Poland came to 400,000, subsequent reports of the committee refer to about 500,000 people from both the Kingdom and Lithuania, and according to the *Dziennik Kijowski* (Kiev Daily), the number of refugees in October of 1915 amounted to about 900,000 from the Kingdom of Poland.[16]Assuming the most often cited number of refugees—1,000,000—and taking into consideration the fact that Polish organizations and rescue committees had no chance to register all of them, we can estimate that about 750,000–850,00 people left the territory of the Kingdom of Poland and about 150,000–250,000 refugees left Galicia and Lithuania.

Since the data above primarily concerns the Polish population, it is difficult to establish the number of Jewish refugees. In addition, the Jews who did not leave the territory of the Kingdom of Poland were often chased from place to place.[17] According to a report from Jewish rescue committees in Petersburg, Moscow, Kiev, and Odessa, dated May 20, 1915, about 160,000 Jews were expelled from the Polish provinces of the Russian Empire.[18] When the Russians were repelled in the summer of 1915, the uprooting intensified.[19] According to Max Warburg, one of the leading

II. Population afflicted by the war and buildings destroyed in
the Kingdom of Poland in towns and cities with a population above 20,000 (1919)

City	Gubernya	Total population	Afflicted people	Afflicted families	Destroyed buildings
Kalisz	Kalisz	60,550	17,848	2,975	333
Konin	Kalisz	11,918	468	78	18
Zdunska Wola	Kalisz	23,808	64	11	2
Warsaw	Warsaw	845,130	6,945	1,157	75
Lodz	Piotrkow	459,353	3,026	504	55
Zgierz	Piotrkow	21,531	281	47	12
Radomsk	Piotrkow	20,627	594	99	20
Kholm	Lublin	22,019	1,487	248	43
Siedlce	Siedlce	29,031	26	4	1
Lomza	Lomza	26,726	150	25	5
Total		1,520,693	30,888	5,148	564

Source: AAN GUL 331, p. 41.

members of *Hilsverein für Deutschen Juden,* about 340,000 Jews were forced to leave the Kingdom of Poland.[20] In documents prepared by the Jewish Conjoint Committee in 1915 relating to the ill-treatment of the Jewish population in the eastern war-zone, we read that all the Jews had been expelled from twenty-one towns.[21] Nonetheless, we have to remember that the data did not cover all the Jews from the country since Jewish committees were not able to register all the refugees, including those who left with other national groups and those who did not reach the registration points. The data of the Jewish communities and branch unions are also inaccurate. In fact, because it was difficult to keep records of refugees and evacuated people during the war, all the statistics, including the most often cited number of Jewish refugees—340,000—should be treated as inaccurate. However, we can say that nearly every Jewish family in the Kingdom of Poland, especially on the right bank of the Vistula River, was afflicted by the forced migration.[22]

The Jews who were persecuted by the Russians also met with threats from the Christian population.[23] For example, in Lopuszno, near Kielce, the Poles and the Jews welcomed the Russians after a short occupation of their village by the Germans. Despite this fact, all the Jews of the village, including women, children, the elderly, and the disabled, were forced to gather together and then were driven by Cossacks over seven miles away from the village. Left there in the middle of the night, they were then allowed to return home. On the way back, the population of one of the villages attempted to prevent them from passing through. The peasants, in turn, were threatened with the burning of their village by the Cossacks, but after a long bargain, the Jews were allowed to sleep in one of the sheds, and the peasants sold some bread to them. After the Jews returned home, they found all their households completely robbed and vandalized.[24] The Jews of Bychawa in the Lublin province, expelled by the Russians, were pelted with stones by the Polish peasants.[25] Such situations took place in many towns and villages of the Kingdom of Poland.

Destruction

Not only rapid displacement but also "scorched-earth" tactics accompanied the Russian evacuation. Within the bigger towns and cities, the most serious destruction was registered in Kalisz, which was bombed by the Germans at the beginning of the war, and, subsequently, in Warsaw, Lodz, and Kholm. However, taking into consideration the territory of all the *gubernyas*, the southeast and northeast parts of the Kingdom experienced the most severe damage.[26] During the first year of the war, 6,530 villages were destroyed. In the Kingdom of Poland, 11.2 percent of all the real estates in the villages were completely destroyed.[27]

Many Jewish houses and communal buildings were among those destroyed. For example, in the small administrative district of Krasnystaw in the Lublin province, the *beit midrash* (house of study) in Zolkiewka and the Jewish bath in Wysokie were destroyed, while the center of Krasnystaw

III. Number of buildings destroyed in gubernyas *of the Kingdom of Poland during the years 1914–1915*

Gubernya	Total number of buildings	Number of destroyed buildings	Percent of total buildings destroyed
Warsaw	147,292	15,024	10.2
Kalisz	109,504	600	0.5
Piotrkow	140,904	6,917	4.9
Kielce	112,106	4,695	4.2
Radom	123,529	16,468	13.3
Lublin	172,658	35,416	20.5
Siedlce	63,313	3,085	4.9
Lomza	70,365	18,178	25.8
Plock	55,232	4,827	8.7
Total	994,903	105,210	10.6

Source: M. Przeniosło, *Chłopi Królestwa Polskiego w latach 1914–1918* (Kielce, 2003), pp. 58-61.

IV. *The number of families afflicted by the war in towns and cities of the Kingdom of Poland according to profession (1919)*

	Town category	
	Towns with a population of less than 20,000	Towns and cities with a population of more than 20,000
Christian tradesmen	2,120	944
Christian artisans	989	440
Christian workmen	1,978	880
Other Christian workmen	1,978	880
Christian families (servants, officers, etc.)	7,065	3,144
Jewish tradesmen	12,487	1,583
Jewish artisans	1,606	204
Jewish workmen	3,746	475
Jewish families	17,839	2,262

Source: AAN GUL 331, p. 43.

and all the buildings in Turobin were burned down. In Pulawy, the whole Jewish quarter was burned; in neighboring Konskowola, the synagogue was destroyed by the withdrawing Russian soldiers.[28] The Russians set fire to Markuszow, and 80 percent of the buildings burned.[29] In Siedliszcze, near Kholm, the synagogue, bath, and community buildings were destroyed when the Jews did not pay the contribution. In some towns the grave stones from Jewish cemeteries were used as material for fortifications.[30]

According to a document entitled "List of Destruction" (April 1918) prepared by a branch organization named the Lublin Contractors' Association, there were in the Kingdom of Poland fifty-one towns where more than 30 percent of buildings were completely destroyed during the war. In the majority of cases, Jews lived in these destroyed towns. In some of them—for example, Sienna near Ilza; Ozarow, Gliniany, and Wasniow near Opatow in the Kielce province; or Sawin, Swierze, and Pawlow near Kholm—more than 90 percent of the buildings were destroyed. In shtetlekh like Gorzkow and Wierzbica, near Krasnystaw, the destruction was 98 and 99 percent.[31] In the spring of 1915, in the Kingdom of Poland there were about one hundred Jewish communities that were completely devastated.[32]

It is difficult to say how many buildings were destroyed by the Russians and how many by the Central States' armies. However, there is no doubt that the "scorched-earth" tactics applied by the Russians were the main factor in producing the war losses. Among the urban population, the Jews were the most afflicted group. According to post-war data on the destruction of real property, 20,686 Jewish families and 9,594 Christian families were afflicted by the war.[33] If we also include contributions and robberies, we find that about 125,000 Jews and about 142,000 Christians from the urban population of the Kingdom of Poland suffered.[34]

When we take into consideration the direct destruction of buildings and of arable acreage, we might suppose that the peasants were the most afflicted group within the population. In spite of a decrease in acreage under cultivation, a decline in productivity per hectare, and a drop in the number of livestock, however, the war damage in agriculture for the country as a whole was less than that in industry.[35] According to Polish sources, 155 industrial plants, including 88 factories, 41 distilleries, 13 sugar-mills, 7 breweries, and 6 printing houses, were taken away. Moreover, the limitation on trade and production introduced by the new authorities in 1915 applied to the Jewish tradesman, artisans, and traveling salesman. The new authority's orders practically deprived many Jewish families of any sources of income.[36]

The first year of the war brought plunder of Jewish property on a large scale. Then, during the German and Austrian occupation, when "normal" trade activity practically vanished, its place was taken by smuggling and speculation. Deprived of their rights to free trade, many Jews who engaged in such practices were punished and imprisoned for them.[37] In addition, those Jews who smuggled and illegally crossed the borders between the Kingdom and Galicia and between occupational zones often fell victims to robbers. The great number of robberies during the war years was, in fact, a problem. In order to defeat it, the occupational authorities used not only the police and gendarmerie, but also soldiers of the front army. The Warsaw General Government even formed the special *Banditenkommissionen.*[38]

From the fall of 1915, the occupants started to organize civil-worker units. While some of them worked in the Kingdom of Poland, the number of those employed in Germany in the last year of the war is estimated at 700,000 to 800,000. Some of them were seasonal workers kept in Germany by force after the outbreak of the war, and some came from recruitment. But from 1916 on, their presence was mainly forced. The 56,000 workers employed by the Germans occupation authorities in workers' battalions (*Arbeiterbataillone*) and by the Austrian authorities in workers' detachment groups (*Zivilarbeiterabteilungen*), because of their heterogeneity, their dispersal, and their regimented way of life, were not characterized by social, political, or organizational activity despite their numbers. The Austro-Hungarian authorities recruited and transported to Hungary and Austria about 20,000 workers.[39] There is no sufficient statistical data to say how many Jews were forced to work in such troops, but we have enough information to say that the percent of Jewish forced laborers was significant.[40]

The living conditions in many shtetlekh and Jewish quarters were terrible. "Lublin's ghetto is a big source of epidemics," alarmed *Kurier Lubelski*, the main Polish newspaper in the city.[41] In Lublin during the years of 1915–1916, the sanitary services recorded 1,960 cases of typhus and other diseases; 79 percent of the victims were Jewish.[42] In many provincial towns the population was afflicted with cholera, typhus, and other epidemics. For example, a report of a Polish charity institution states that "Bilgoraj and Tomaszow were afflicted with cholera recently. In Bilgoraj almost 2,000 victims, the Jews mainly; in Tarnogrod about 1,000 victims (Jewish). No victims in manors and villages."[43] Indeed, undernourished and living in dreadful sanitary conditions in over-populated ghettos, in shtetlekh, and in crowded apartments, the Jews were very susceptible to epidemics.

Food rationing, as well as the lack of consumer and other goods during the war years meant that prices were very inflated. The food supply became particularly sparse in 1917–1918. Rations shrank, and the gulf between the index of the cost living and that of the nominal wages of both workers and white-collar employees rapidly grew. Per capita consumption in the Kingdom of Poland dropped from about 3,097 calories before the war to 891 calories in the spring of 1918, including both rationed and free-market supplies. This was followed by deterioration in health and an increase in the death rate, especially among the poorest people in the big industrial centers of the areas under German occupation as well as in shtetlekh in the eastern part of Poland.[44] Crowds of beggars filled the streets of Polish towns and cities. Because of lack of money, kosher rules were not obeyed. There were times that the people fainted of hunger.[45]

In reports of the Austrian military authority from 1916, we find the opinion that "the Jews are dissatisfied with the new situation, and their attitudes towards the new authorities are negative."[46] This change was significant: we must remember that, given the barbarism of the tsarist army, the Jews had welcomed the seizure of the country by the Central States. But as the war years came to have the most severe impact on the Polish economy, the shtetl Jews were one of the most afflicted groups of inhabitants of the Kingdom of Poland.

Political and Cultural Development

Did this turbulent period bring only disaster? To my mind, this period also yielded experiences of great significance and inspiration for the Polish Jewry. Marked social and political changes occurred in towns where the lifestyle had remained constant for decades or even centuries. What is more, although these changes did not affect the topographic character of the shtetl, they were rapid, taking place in only months. It is obvious that the outbreak of the war, Russian evacuation, and the economic policy of the occupants resulted in a decline in the economy of the population. But, on the other hand, German and Austrian policy was much more liberal toward Jews and differed from the official and non-official tsarist anti-Semitism. Most noteworthy is the fact that during the war the people of the Kingdom managed to release an unprecedented amount of energy into public activities such as social aid, education, and local self-government. To help the people more afflicted by the war, a whole network of committees was established. These committees organized shelters for the homeless, communal kitchens and food distribution centers, orphanages and medical aid stations. Sometimes this work established common links between the Poles and the Jews; more often, it became a source of conflict. But the population of Poland did not remain passive. The development of local autonomous agendas, rescue committees, Polish patriotic manifestoes, and other political activity could be considered as conditions conducive to the above-mentioned changes within the Jewish communities.

The years of the war marked a noticeable rise in the intensity of social and political life of the Polish Jews. It was during the 1914–1918 period and soon after the war when such political movements as the conservative ultra-Orthodox *Aguda,* Zionism, and socialism appeared in the Polish shtetlekh. A development of the non-Orthodox system of education and of cultural and social life accompanied those events. Although war as a rule does not stimulate such processes, a significant revival of the intellectual sphere could be observed. In fact, a considerable disproportion in such reformist activities and aspirations existed between the more urbanized regions, like Lodz and its vicinity, and the tiny shtetlekh in the eastern part of the Kingdom. Although, quite often, those changes were attempted by only a handful of enthusiasts, the significance of this phenomenon was qualitative and consisted in the fact that some Jews were reaching for "new" ideas and views. In the majority of Polish shtetlekh, Zionism turned out to be the most attractive. Such new trends, which won over the youth in a short time, resulted in clashes between them and the older generations, who did not like to accept any "modern" activity or changes.[47] This development in social life after 1915 was as dangerous for the orthodox and the rabbinate as assimilation.

The beginnings of independent and intensive social and educational work could be observed in almost every town under the Central States' occupation. Emancipation tendencies could be noted throughout the whole territory of Poland, especially in places where, as a result of war migration, people from the intelligentsia appeared.[48] In the flow of refugees from territories outside the Kingdom of Poland, Jews coming from Russia and Lithuania during the years 1914–1918 brought views advocated by Litvaks (traditional Lithuanian Jews), which, in turn, became increasingly popular among Polish Jews.[49] Focusing on the shtetl during the war, we have to take into consideration the presence of many Jewish soldiers and officers in the ranks of the Central States' armies and administrations. Among the newcomers there were many Jews, and the confrontation of their lifestyle with the one typical for Polish Jews, used to locking themselves up in ghettos and discriminated against by the gentiles and authorities, constituted a very important experience.[50]

Polish-Jewish Relationships

Returning to the beginning of the war, we find the American journalist Herman Bernstein writing that the Jews in Poland are "boycotted, humiliated, slandered by the Poles, accused of the vilest crimes, of disloyalty, of espionage and treachery—all for the purpose of discrediting them . . . [and robbing] them even of the hope of freedom and justice in the future." Bernstein added that "the pogrom policy, abandoned by the Russian government, was taken up in another form by the Poles." According to him, through various machinations and provocations, the Poles tortured the Jewish people and ruined them upon one pretext or another.[51] Likewise, a memorandum circulated by the Anglo-American Conjoint Committee on the Jews of Poland from March of 1915 notes that "a very painful impression has been created throughout Western Europe and America by the persecutions suffered by the Jews of Poland at the hands of their Polish fellow countrymen during the last 18 months and more particularly since the outbreak of the war."[52] *The New York Times* wrote in October of 1916 that "the anti-Semitic Poles, to whom Jewish competition in business was always distasteful, did everything in their power to fan the flames of suspicion and hatred."[53] In September of 1915, Lucien Wolf, diplomat, journalist, and the president of the Conjoint Committee, who in 1917 became a secretary of the Joint Foreign Committee formed by the Board of Deputies of British Jews and the Anglo-Jewish Association, wrote in a private letter:

> To the normal destructiveness of the military operations have been added the trials resulting from a wicked outburst of Polish anti-Semitism, supplemented by hasty and ill-considered expulsions of the Jewish populations by the Russian military authorities.[54]

And according to yet another source, in Warsaw a pogrom atmosphere prevailed, and in various places Jews were being assaulted in the streets. Many Jews in Kielce and its vicinity also fell victims to Polish denunciations, and "even Jewish children were hanged." (However, at least so far, we do not have any other information from any other sources to verify this claim.) Everywhere shops and workshops were plundered, men were beaten, and women were raped.[55]

Sometimes opinions promulgated by the Jewish media in the West were exaggerated or based on rumor, which in turn alarmed and annoyed the public in Poland. Although there were no civilian pogroms during the first year of the war, and although it is not true that "there are records of Jewish families slain, burned to death, as in the time of the Inquisition,"[56] there are many well-documented accounts that some Poles did indeed take part in denunciation, accusation, and instigation.

For example, in the Radom province, a day before Yom Kippur, peasants accused the local Jews of burning a country house. The military arrested twenty-one Jews and hanged three of them. Three Jewish women, wives of these three men, committed suicide after this tragic accident.[57] In Krasnik, a few Jews, including the rabbis Fisher and Mendelsohn and the wealthy merchants Hirsh and Samuel Goldberg, were wrongly accused by their Polish neighbors. After a quick trial by the war court, the Jews were condemned to death, hanged, and buried in the yard of the prison. Before dying they had written a letter:

> We are not guilty at all, we did not meet the Austrians, we did not enquire of anybody about the positions of the Russian troops, no information was given by us to anybody, no tables with sweets were arranged by the Jews at

the town and by any of us, as you well know. Many Christians of the town
can prove our innocence. . . . The mayor of the town Garbowsky and the
Commander of the District Police know that we are innocent.[58]

The Orthodox priest and a few Russians interceded with military authorities on behalf of the Jews. Unfortunately, help came too late, and they were
hanged. Afterwards, the commander of the local garrison allowed the Jews
to remove the bodies to the Jewish cemetery.[59] We do not know: did the
Jews in Krasnik welcome and help Austrians or not? However, no Pole
rushed to help his Jewish neighbors.

A similar situation took place in Skierniewice: after accusations of espionage by the local Polish community, the Russians chose every tenth Jew
and started to hang them one after another. There, too, an Orthodox
priest and a local agent of the Russian trade company, who testified that
the Poles "welcomed Austrians with salt and bread, and some of them
even made themselves drunk with the enemy," interrupted the execution.
In 1914 Zamosc was for a short time taken by the Austrians. Some Poles
from Galicia, serving in the auxiliary paramilitary units called *Sokoly* (Fal-
cons), accompanied the Austrians. After the Austrian retreat, the Polish
population of Zamosc, wanting to avoid repression, accused the local Jews
of helping the Austrian troops. As a result, fifteen Jews were arrested, and
the executions began the next day. When five Jews were already hanging
on the gallows, an Orthodox priest appeared with a sacred image, testify-
ing on oath to the complete innocence of the Jews.[60]

While the Jewish communities in Poland adopted a wait-and-see attitude, the gentile population, at least at the beginning of the war, favored
the Russians. In the report of Conjoint from September 1915, we read that
"in the early stage of the war, when the Germans were near Warsaw and
occupied many of the outlying towns, the Jews assumed that their advent
was a permanent one, and did not hesitate to welcome the Germans and
in every way make it impossible for the Poles who sympathized with the
Russians." When the Germans retired from Poland in October and the
Russians came back, "the Jews were naturally in a very unpleasant predicament, as the Poles did not lose any time in telling the Russians of how the
Jews had acted when the Germans were there."[61]

Indeed, a series of assaults against the Jews took place under the banner
of Russian patriotism. The reason could be that the fathers, husbands, and
sons of inhabitants of the Kingdom of Poland served in the ranks of the
Russian army and, according to the tsarist propaganda, fought with the

"Jewish supporters"—i.e., Germans. But no doubt, for some Poles, it was an excellent opportunity to seize Jewish property. The pre-war boycott and propaganda of the Polish nationalists, or National Democrats, contributed to ill-treatment by the Poles of the Jews.[62]

In 1915 the Jewish population welcomed the seizure of the whole territory of the Kingdom of Poland by the Central States.[63] The beginnings of the German and Austrian occupation seemed to be promising. One of the first decrees of the Austrian authorities was to grant to the Jews rights equal with the Poles. The Jews also expected to be able expand their trade.[64] Bernstein, after his visit in Warsaw, wrote:

> There is not the slightest doubt in anyone's mind that the fate of the Jews in the occupied provinces is much better than it was under the Russian regime of provocation, of cruelty and of militant anti-Semitism, of plunder and pogroms.[65]

Although ruthless requisitions and forced contributions, special war collections and prohibition on trade strongly affected the whole population and the Jews in particular, some Polish Jews found their way to the occupational administration, often into supply departments where many of their co-religionists worked. And the Jewish merchants obtained the coveted licenses. The decisive factor for the Germans and Austrians was the broader commercial experience and the connections of Jews, as well as their readiness to be content with a smaller profit. The fact that the German and Yiddish languages were closely related to each other could have been helpful, as well. Relative to the whole population, only a small proportion of Jews managed to obtain licenses and contracts for supplying the army, while the rest experienced all the harshness and adversities of life under occupation. However, during the economic crisis links between the occupants and the Jews annoyed many Poles. "The Jews use their language in order to obtain trade licenses and exploit peasants," we read in many reports from the province. Jews were increasingly accused of speculation, too.[66]

No doubt, in shtetlekh and villages the difficult economic situation was the most important and the most direct factor in producing the deterioration of Polish-Jewish relations during that period. The political question, i.e, the issue of revising and liberalizing the status of Jews in Polish political life, rarely thrilled the shtetl population as it did the inhabitants of the big cities. There were considerably fewer opportunities to create a platform of co-operation between the Jews and the Poles in the shtetlekh than in the towns. For example, the shtetl Jews had no opportunity to take part in Polish national holidays and anniversaries. The elections and joint work in the local self-governments also brought intensification in the Polish-Jewish contacts; however, it was a source of conflicts as well.[67]

Conclusions

The years 1914–1918 brought decline and pauperization of the shtetl population, which were connected with the "scorched-earth" tactics applied by the Russians. The events of the first year of the war were marked by great migration movements, which also afflicted the Jewish population to a large extent.

In the summer of 1915, the whole territory of "Russian Poland" was seized by the Germans and the Austrians. The occupants allowed the introduction of Polish and Jewish educational models and of the Polish judicial system, as well as making certain political concessions, especially after 1916, but in industry their policy was predatory and devastating. As Jan Molenda writes, "the impact of the war on the country's economy and living conditions and on the modernization of Poland's social structure was unequivocally negative."[68] Despite the fact that, after the barbarism of the Russian soldiers, the Jewish population welcomed the new rulers of the country, all the inconveniences associated with the occupation made many Jews reluctant to accept the new regime.

Indeed, one feature characterizing the social life and community relations at the time of the German and the Austro-Hungarian occupation was a new parallelism developing between economic disaster and unprecedented political activity and between a decline in a traditional lifestyle according to the Torah and the noticeable development of secular Jewish culture. Despite the fact that the "great policy," involving these religious, cultural and political issues, rarely reached the shtetl population, modern political movements based on nationalist ideology and secular culture appeared in some Polish shtetlekh.

During the years of the war there was a visible worsening in the Polish-Jewish relations in the small towns and village communities, which earlier had been relatively free from the anti-Semitism and chauvinism. The pre-war propaganda of the Polish nationalists, the anti-Semitism of the Russian authorities, the predatory and devastating economic policy of the occupants had a serious impact both on the shtetl economic system and on Polish-Jewish relations.

Notes

1. Institute for Jewish Research in New York (YIVO) Herman Bernstein Papers 1897–1935 (HB) 713 Box 32/69 fo. 766.

2. Piotr Wróbel, "Przed odzyskaniem niepodległości," in Jerzy Tomaszewski, ed., *Najnowsze dzieje Żydów w Polsce* (Warszawa, 1993), pp. 111–115.

3. YIVO Poland: Vilna Archives 1850–1939 (VA) RG 28 Box 1/24.

4. Archiwum Państwowe w Krakowie (APK) Archiwum Naczelnego Komitetu Narodowego 1914–1921 (NKN), 147 pp. 122–125; YIVO WM 109 fo.13345; Gossudarstviennyi Archiv Rossiiskoi Fiederacii, Moscow (GARF) Fond 217 op. 1 d. 1326, pp. 1–3, 15–18.

5. YIVO, Wolf Lucien and Mowschowitch David Papers 1865–1957 (WM) 108 fo. 13013.

6. Polish Institute of Arts and Sciences of America in New York (PIASA), Lednicki Aleksander Papers 1881, 1900–1932, 1962 (LP) 6/19 part I p. 81. See also S. B. Rohold, *The War and the Jew* (Toronto, 1915), pp. 49–52.

7. GARF Fond 9458 op. 1 d. 25, pp. 5–6; GARF Fond 9458 op. 1 d. 168, pp. 4–7.

8. GARF F. 9458 op. 1 d. 159, pp. 4, 12–13.

9. YIVO WM 108 fo. 13257–13260; YIVO, WM 109, fo. 13345.

10. GARF F. 9458 op. 1 d. 164, pp. 71, 312, 315. See also GARF F. 9458 op. 1 d. 159 pp. 78, 119, 131.

11. Maurice Paléologue, *An Ambassador's Memoirs*, Vol. 1 (New York, 1925), p. 173.

12. YIVO, WM 108, fo. 13017. See also YIVO VA 28, Box 16/24. In fear of the prospect of falling into the Russian hands, between 200,000 to 300,000 Galician Jews fled westward at the beginning of the war. Although most of them returned home after the Austrians had broken the Russians and retaken the most of Galicia, a significant number of them found themselves in deep Russia. Michael R. Marrus, *The Unwanted: European Refugees in the Twentieth Century* (New York, 1985), p. 63. See also *Nowiny Wiedeńskie Ilustrowane*, Vol. 16 (1915): 1–2.

13. Edward Kołodziej, *Wychodźstwo zarobkowe z Polski 1918–1939. Studia nad polityką emigracyjną II Rzeczypospolitej* (Warszawa, 1982), p. 35. See also *Archiwum Główne Akt Dawnych w Warszawie (AGAD) K.u.k. Milit(rgeneralgouvernement in Polen/Lublin 1914–1918* (MGGL) Präs. 1790, pp. 15–19; Peter Gatrell, *A Whole Empire Walking: Refugees in Russia during World War I* (Bloomington, 1999), pp. 22–23.

14. Walentyna Najdus, "Uchodźcy polscy w Rosji w latach 1917–1918," *Kwartalnik Historyczny*, Vol. 6 (1957), p. 26.

15. Mariusz Korzeniowski, *Na wygnańczym szlaku . . . Działalność Centralnego Komitetu Obywatelskiego Królestwa Polskiego na Białorusi w latach 1915–1918* (Lublin, 2001), p. 107.

16. Ibid., pp. 108–109. See also Gatrell, *A Whole Empire*, pp. 15, 17–34, 51–52, 57, 79, 88, 129–135, 139, 142, 154–157.

17. APK NKN 90, p. 30.

18. YIVO, WM 59, fo.4854.

19. Marrus, *The Unwanted*, p. 53.

20. Leo Baeck Institute in New York, Kahn Bernard. Memoirs 1914–1921 ME 344, pp. 59–60.

21. YIVO, WM 58, fo. 4738; YIVO, WM 59, fo. 4854; Mieczysław B. Markowski, "Żydzi w życiu gospodarczym województwa kieleckiego w okresie międzywojennym," in *Żydzi w Małopolsce. Studia z dziejów osadnictwa i życia społecznego*, Feliks Kiryk, ed. (Przemyśl, 1991), p. 310.

22. YIVO, WM 58, fo. 4737–4738; YIVO, WM 109, fo. 13339–13340.

23. Paléologue, *An Ambassador's Memoirs*, pp. 308–309.

24. YIVO WM 108, fo. 13318.

25. Konrad Zieliński, *Stosunki polsko-żydowskie na ziemiach Królestwa Polskiego w czasie pierwszej wojny światowej* (Lublin, 2005), p. 148.

26. Archiwum Akt Nowych w Warszawie (AAN) Główny Urząd Likwidacyjny 1918–1919 (GUL), 331, pp. 40–41.

27. Marek Przeniosło, *Chłopi Królestwa Polskiego w latach 1914–1918* (Kielce, 2003), p. 50–53.

28. AAN GUL 900, pp. k. 1, 17, 30, 44, 51, 65, 67; Archiwum Państwowe w Lublinie (APL) Urząd Wojewódzki Lubelski-Wydział Społeczno-Polityczny (UWL WSP) 10, pp. 15–17, APL UWL WSP 730, pp. 78–82; APL UWL WSP 1557, pp. 4–6; APK NKN 84, p. 10.

29. Moshe Nachshon, *Kadimah—ershte zionistishe organizacie*, in David Shtokfish, ed., *Hurbana ugevurata shel ha-ayara markushov* (Tel Aviv, 1955), p. 75.

30. Andrzej Dziubiński, Jerzy Znojek, *Żydzi i synagoga Stara w Pińczowie* (Pińczów, 2002), p. 14.

31. Zieliński, *Stosunki polsko-żydowskie*, p. 141.

32. YIVO WM 67, fo. 7575–7576.

33. AAN GUL 331, pp. 39–40.

34. Ibid.

35. The economic policy of the Austrian authorities in the part of the Kingdom of Poland they occupied was milder than that of the Germans. See Jan Molenda, "Social Changes in Poland during World War I," in Bela K. Király and Nandor F. Dreisziger, eds., *East Central European Society in World War I* (New York 1985), pp. 189–190.

36. Zieliński, *Stosunki polsko-żydowskie*, pp. 219–221.

37. Ibid.

38. Wojciech Szwarc, "Uprawnienia i działalność policyjna niemieckiego zarządu wojskowego w Generalnym Gubernatorstwie Warszawskim (1915–1918)," *Annales Universitatis Mariae Curie-Skłodowska*, Vol. 19, No. 8 (1972), p. 191. See also AGAD MGGL Präs. 11717, pp. 351–352.

39. Molenda, "Social Changes," pp. 193–194.

40. Klaus J. Bade, "Labour, Migration and the State: Germany from the Late 19th Century to the Onset of the Great Depression," in Klaus J. Bade, ed., *Population, Labour and Migration in 19th- and 20th-Century Germany* (Leamington Spa, 1987), pp. 59–85. Zosa Szajkowski, "East European Jewish Workers in Germany during World War I," in Saul Lieberman, ed., *Salo Wittmayer Baron. Jubilee Volume*, Vol. 2 (New York, 1974), p. 896. See also text of a labor contract for Polish-Jewish Workers during World War I concluded by the *Deutsche Arbeiterzentrale* in Warsaw and the deposition of two Jewish workers from the *Stadtsarchiv Dortmund*: Nancy L. Green, *Jewish Workers in the Modern Diaspora* (Berkeley, 1998), pp. 58–61.

41. *Kurier Lubelski*, Vol. 8 (1916), pp. 3–4.

42. Konrad Zieliński, *Żydzi Lubelszczyzny 1914–1918* (Lublin, 1999), p. 67. See also Paul J. Weindling, *Epidemics and Genocide in Eastern Europe, 1890–1945* (New York, 2000), pp. 76, 85, 431.

43. APK NKN 93, p. 55.

44. Molenda, "Social Changes," p. 196.

45. Anna Kahan, "The Diary of Anne Kahan. Siedlce, Poland, 1914–1916," *YIVO Annual*, Vol. 18 (1983), p. 334; and Wróbel, "Przed odzyskaniem niepodległości", p. 132.

46. AGAD MGGL 1013, p. 786.

47. Konrad Zieliński, "The Changing Shtetl in the Kingdom of Poland during the First World War," *Polin*, Vol. 17 (Oxford, 2004), pp. 120–123, 129, 131.

48. Ibid.

49. Ezra Mendelsohn, *Zionism in Poland: The Formative Years, 1915–1926* (New Haven, 1981), pp. 21–22; and Magdalena Opalski and Israel Bartal, *Poles and Jews: A Failed Brotherhood* (Hanover, 1992), pp. 104–105.

50. Erwin A. Schmidl, *Juden in der K. (u) K. Armee 1788–1918* (Eisenstadt, 1989), pp. 122; Zieliński, "The Changing Shtetl," pp. 127–128.

51. YIVO, HB 713 Box 32/69, fo. 766.

52. YIVO, WM 57, fo. 4659.

53. YIVO, WM 21, fo. 1713–1714.

54. Ibid.

55. PIASA LP 6/19 part I p. 81; YIVO, WM 59, fo. 4880, 4887, 4890; YIVO, WM 67, fo. 7575.

56. YIVO, WM 129, fo. 15969

57. YIVO, WM 109, fo. 13346.

58. YIVO, WM 58, fo. 4755.

59. YIVO, WM 58, fo. 4741.

60. YIVO, WM 59, fo. 4884–4885, 4889–4890.

61. YIVO, WM 59, fo. 4822–4824. See also GARF Fond 9458 op. 1 d. 159, p. 25.

62. Jerzy Jedlicki, "The End of the Dialogue: Warsaw 1907–1912," in Sławomir Kapralski, ed., *The Jews in Poland*, Vol. 2 (Cracow, 1999), pp. 111–112; and Roman Wapiński, "The Endecja and the Jewish Question," *Polin*, Vol. 12 (Oxford, 1999), pp. 271–272.

63. Haus-Hof und Staatsarchiv Wien (HHStA), Ministerium des Äußern 1848–1918 (MA), P.A.I 899a, pp. 406–407. HHStA MA P.A.I 522, pp. 774–775; HHStA MA P.A.I 1051, pp. 240–241.

64. Arthur Hausner, *Die Polenpolitik der Mittelmächte und die österreichisch-ungarische Militärverwaltung in Polen während des Weltkrieges* (Wien, 1935), p. 4.

65. YIVO, HB 713 Box 32/69, fo. 766.

66. Markowski, "Żydzi w życiu gospodarczym," p. 309; Zieliński, *Stosunki polsko-żydowskie*, pp. 230–238.

67. Konrad Zieliński, "Stosunki polsko-żydowskie w Królestwie Polskim w czasie I wojny światowej (na przykładzie działalności rad miejskich)," *Kwartalnik Historii Żydów*, Vol. 2 (2003), pp. 164–194.

68. Molenda, pp. 189, 197.

6

The Shtetl in Interwar Poland

Samuel Kassow

In his 1932 introduction to a newly published, handsomely bound history of Polish Jewry, *Zydzi w Polsce Odrodzonej* (The Jews in Reborn Poland), Senator Ojciasz Thon stressed that although Polish Jewry found itself in an economically desperate situation, it still had to recognize its special responsibilities as the cultural leader of world Jewry. American Jewry was richer, Thon implied, Soviet Jewry had more prospects for education and social mobility, but only Polish Jewry possessed the national pride and the cultural resources to guide the Jewish people. All the more important, therefore, was the need for this new history book that would remind Polish Jews of their links to Poland's past and of their contributions to its economy and to its welfare.[1]

The three and one half million Polish Jews were certainly a fractious community, divided by politics, culture, and even by language. (The new history volume that Thon was introducing was aimed at a Jewish middle class that could afford to buy expensive "coffee-table books" and that was increasingly Polish-speaking.) It was a community that was becoming increasingly urbanized. By the eve of World War II one out of four Polish Jews lived in the five largest cities, and 40 percent were living in settlements of over 10,000 Jews. Polish Jewry was also a work in progress, defined by an interplay of centripetal and centrifugal forces. The reborn Polish state had brought together Jewish tribes—Litvaks, Galician Jews, and Jews from Congress Poland—with marked cultural differences that stemmed from history, language, and religious practice. Bridging these differences was not always easy.[2] (Nor, for that matter, was it that simple to bring together Poles who had lived under three different empires for over 120 years.)

Despite internal differences and conflicts, there were also significant centripetal forces that were helping to turn these disparate Jewish communities into a new national entity that could be called Polish Jewry. Warsaw, the new capital, was building a new shared identity not only for Poles but also for Jews. It served as the headquarters of the main Jewish political parties, as the base of a national Jewish press in Yiddish and Polish, and as the most important center of Jewish literature and theater. By the 1930s Warsaw had become the nerve center of Polish Jewry.

Thon's statement about the national mission of Polish Jews serves as a useful caution against viewing the history of interwar Polish Jewry through the prism of the Holocaust. After the war, scholars published books about Polish Jewry with titles like *On the Edge of Destruction* or *On the Brink of an Abyss*.[3] From the perspective of the interwar period, however, it would be wrong to say that Polish Jewry was gripped by terminal despair. Polish Jews may have been beleaguered but they were not demoralized. One way of gauging the true state of Polish Jewry is to study its associational and communal life, not only in the big cities but also in the shtetlekh, the small towns.

Despite ongoing urbanization, about 50 percent of Polish Jews still lived in small towns—shtetlekh—on the eve of World War II. While some observers were writing off the shtetl as an irrelevant vestige of the past, others praised its tenacity and saw it as an important reservoir of a resilient and healthy folk culture. The shtetl was a visible reminder of the longstanding ties that bound the Jews to the Polish lands. This theme of *ayngefundevetkayt* (rootedness)—as well as a growing interest in regional studies—became a major trope of interwar Polish Yiddish literature. It was a key leitmotif of Joseph Opatoshu's *In Poylishe Velder* (*In Polish Woods*), of Shie Perle's *Yidn fun a Gants Yor* (*Ordinary Jews*), and of Michal Bursztyn's *Bay di Taykhn fun Mazovie* (*Along the Rivers of Mazowsze*). Despite Jewish migration to the cities, the shtetl retained its outsized importance as a determinant of the contours of Jewish collective memory. The spaces, streets, and wooden buildings of the shtetl remained etched in the collective imagination.

Most shtetlekh had begun as "company towns" on the lands of Polish nobles anxious to attract Jewish economic know-how. As a form of Jewish settlement in the Diaspora, the shtetl in the old Polish Commonwealth was unique. It was not just a Jewish neighborhood or a Jewish street. It was an entire town with a Jewish majority.

For centuries the shtetl had nourished a distinct folk culture that was shaped by numbers, religion, language, and economics. In most of the Ashkenazi Jewish Diaspora, Jews had been concentrated in rather narrow economic roles: money-lending, trading in livestock, or whatever else a particular prince or king allowed them to do. In Poland, on the other hand, Jews did practically everything. They were farmers and tailors, teamsters and milkmen, beekeepers and merchants, water carriers and penniless teachers. The interplay of this striking economic diversity and common religious values—in a town where Jews usually formed a majority—gave shtetl society a unique vitality.

After the collapse of the Polish Commonwealth, many major changes undermined the shtetl economy and transformed the shtetl community: the economic decline of the Polish nobility after the abortive revolts against Russian rule in 1831 and 1863; the impact of railroads and big cities on the rural economy; the growth of peasant cooperatives that eliminated the Jewish middleman; the blows of wars and revolution; the rapid growth of major Jewish urban centers; the rise of new ideologies and youth movements that changed the face of the shtetl, especially during the period between World War I and World War II.

Despite these changes, the shtetl in interwar Poland remained important for many reasons. First, as we have just seen, many Jews still lived there. Second, the shtetl continued to be an important arena of Jewish-gentile relations. For centuries the shtetl had been a place where Poles and Jews had met in a pattern of what Rosa Lehmann has called "symbiosis and ambivalence."[4] Relations between Poles and Jews in the shtetl were far from idyllic, but there are ample grounds to assume that they were, on the whole, better than in the big cities. Perhaps the shtetl experience did not neutralize growing economic and political anti-Semitism. But it did serve to slow down the process of estrangement and to preserve a social universe where Poles and Jews met as neighbors, as economic partners, and even as friends.

Third, the interwar shtetl offers important insights into the social dynamics of Polish Jewry. Unlike the big cities, the shtetl processed political and cultural change as a face-to-face community that was both preserving traditional institutions and building new ones. On the one hand, the shtetl was influenced as never before by the cultural influences of the city: the newspaper, political parties, youth movements, credit societies, the visiting lecturer, the theater troupe that performed in the fireman's hall. As road and railroad transport improved, many shtetlekh were on their way to becoming suburbs of larger cities. On the other hand, to a far greater degree than the big cities, the shtetl was a community where there was no straight line between tradition and modernity, where outside forces and modern influences were often reflected and refracted through traditional institutions and established values. Unlike the major cities, the shtetl was not a community with a large proportion of migrants from elsewhere. The framework of social interaction and the structure of status and place reflected a complex interplay of memory, tradition, and change that underscored key differences between the shtetl and the major urban centers. Despite ongoing secularization, the interwar shtetl was a place where even non-religious Jews were more likely to go to synagogue on Sabbath and holidays—if only to "keep up appearances" (*haltn shtat*).

How does one define a shtetl? Modern Yiddish literature has given us many different versions and images of a shtetl.[5] But how can we define a real one? In his recently published memoirs, an Israeli Holocaust scholar, Sholem Cholavski, described his early years in Nieswiezh, a shtetl that developed on the Radziwill lands on Lake Narocz—some one hundred miles east of Vilna. Now, most Jews would call Nieswiezh a shtetl. But Cholavski, after he graduated from the Teachers Seminary in Vilna, took his first teaching job in the tiny shtetl of Rakow. After describing his students in Rakow and his love of the school there, he casually added that Rakow had been the first time he had ever lived in a shtetl![6]

What, then, distinguished a shtetl from villages, on the one hand, and growing provincial cities like Rzeszow, on the other? It is important to remember that there is no absolutely objective criterion that distinguished a shtetl from a provincial city. One should rather think of a continuum of factors that was constantly changing the status of the shtetl. Shtetlekh comprised and were defined by interlocking networks of economic and social relationships: the interaction of Jews and peasants in the market, the coming together of Jews for essential communal and religious functions, and the increasingly vital relationship between the shtetl and its emigrants abroad.

While the essential economic function of the shtetl was to serve as a market town, a point of intersection between an agrarian hinterland and a predominantly Jewish settlement, here too there were important variations. Railroads and bus transport were only one of many factors that were determining and changing the precise economic function of the shtetl. While shtetlekh in isolated parts of the Vilna region or Polesie usually conformed to the classic model of a market town, a shtetl like Minsk

Mazowieck or Kaluszyn, linked to the Warsaw metropolis by rail, found itself far less dependent on the market and more oriented towards light industry and specialized handicrafts. Absent a railroad, the shtetl's economic hinterland consisted of peasants who lived close enough to hitch their horses for a one-day round trip between village and town. In addition to this interaction with the surrounding countryside, shtetlekh also were part of a local economic network that included larger and smaller shtetlekh in the same region.

In defining a shtetl, the following clumsy rule probably holds true: a shtetl was big enough to support the basic network of institutions that was essential to Jewish communal life—hence, at least one synagogue, a *mikveh*, a cemetery, schools, and a framework of voluntary associations that performed basic religious and communal functions. This was a key difference between the shtetl and even smaller villages, and the perceived cultural gap between shtetl Jews and village Jews (*yishuvniks*) was a prominent staple of folk humor. On the other hand, what made a shtetl different from a provincial city was that the shtetl was a face-to-face community. It was small enough for almost everyone to be known by name and nickname. Nicknames could be brutal and perpetuated a system that one observer called the "power of the shtetl" to assign everyone a role and a place in the communal universe.[7] As one woman recalled of her shtetl in the 1930s,

> Many in our town had nicknames that were derived either from their occupation, physical appearance or deformities such as Chaim the redhead, Moishe the icon, Faivel cold sore, Eli big belly, Avrum the hernia, Meishl Pick the stutterer, Berl the Copperbeard, Henoch the tin collar (his garment shone like metal for it had not been cleaned since he put it on twenty years earlier). There was Libitchke the maiden. Although she had been married and had children the townsfolk could not forget that Libitchke had married late in life. We had in our shtetl Crutch the tailor who lost a leg and walked with one crutch, Yankl the hunchback, Yosl the latrine, because he had a disagreeable body odor and so on and so on.[8]

These nicknames were but one marker of a social unit that reflected the communal experience of a large part of Polish Jewry between the two wars.

In interwar Poland the shtetl remained an important topic of public discourse and serious study. It represented a collective and identifiable face to face community whose behavior and internal dynamics could be analyzed as part of a wider ongoing debate about the present and future of Polish Jewry. This generic shtetl served as a psychological and conceptual counterpoint to the complex city and as an important barometer of both positive and negative trends within the folk. Jews took heart from the example of Przytyk, a shtetl near Radom, where Jews fought back during a pogrom in March 1936. Minsk Mazowieck, a shtetl near Warsaw, touched off quite different reactions. During the June 1936 pogrom, much of the Jewish population, including the rabbi and many prominent leaders, fled in panic to Warsaw—much to the consternation of Jewish political parties and the press. By the late 1930s, as the threat of Hitler loomed larger, some Jewish intellectuals and writers began to take yet another look at the shtetl. Threatened and beleaguered though it was, it still exemplified the deep roots that the Jews had put down in Eastern Europe. With their backs to the wall, the Jews had to fight harder than before, and the shtetl now symbolized a threatened fortress that the Jews had to protect. A general strike, called by the Bund to protest the Przytyk pogrom, and a notorious trial, where Jews from Przytyk were defendants rather than plaintiffs, enhanced the image of the shetl as the symbol of an embattled people. It was Przytyk that many writers say inspired Mordecai Gebirtig's famous song, "Es Brent" (Our Shtetl Is Burning). It was the shtetl, not the city, that Gebirtig chose to symbolize the plight of the Jewish people.[9]

The shtetl also became an important topic of political debate. In the 1930s Victor Alter, the chief economic spokesman of the Bund, analyzed the socio-economic dynamics of Polish Jewry and, not surprisingly, came to conclusions that supported the Bund's conviction that the Jews' future lay in Poland. Yes, Alter conceded, the economic situation of Polish Jewry was grim but there were real rays of hope—if one turned away from the faltering shtetl and looked at the big urban centers. Polish Jews, acting out of a spontaneous reflex of economic self defense, were fleeing from the shtetl to the big city, from tiny market stands and small workshops to larger urban enterprises. They were leaving for regions sparsely populated by Jews, like the Poznan area. If the shtetl represented a dying past, the city represented a future where Polish Jews would be more secure and more productive.[10] But opponents like Yitshak Lev of the Left *Poalei Tsiyon* were quick to warn the Bund that Polish Jews could not write the shtetl off that easily. It was still a lynchpin of Polish Jewry, its Jewish economy was under heavy attack, and Jews had to rally to its defense.[11] Yitshak Bornstein, one of the chief economists of the Joint Distribution Committee in interwar

Poland, even went against the prevailing wisdom and argued that the shtetl's very vulnerability might also be a source of strength. New policy initiatives and new strategies in the battle against Polish anti-Semitism, Bornstein argued, were much easier to implement in the shtetl than in the city. A small community, whose members knew each other, was also more disciplined and more responsive.[12]

The accessibility of the shtetl as a community that could be studied and mobilized certainly attracted the attention of Jewish scholars in the YIVO (Yiddish Scientific Institute), the center of interdisciplinary scholarship in Yiddish that was founded in Vilna in 1925. The YIVO tried to bring scholars and ordinary Jews together to *zaml*—to collect sources—and to get to know themselves and their lives (in Weinreich's phrase, *tsu derkenen dem haynt*, to know everyday life). Closely allied to the YIVO effort was the *landkentnish* (know the land) movement, spearheaded by the historian Emanuel Ringelblum, the Yiddish writer Michael Bursztyn, and others. The Society for Landkentnish sought to encourage engaged tourism, to organize hikes and excursions, and to take photographs of old synagogues and old cemeteries, and thus to deepen the Polish Jews' ties to the land in which they lived.[13] Both Max Weinreich, the director of the YIVO, and Emanuel Ringelblum were highly pleased when in 1931 a group of teachers and students in the secular Yiddish school in Pruzhany compiled and published a history of their shtetl. The very *process* of *zamling*, of collecting chronicles, documents, records, and photographs of one's own shtetl, could become a pillar, they hoped, of a new Yiddish secular culture.[14] The YIVO did all it could to encourage others to emulate Pruzhany's initiative. To be sure, neither the YIVO nor the *landkentnish* movement neglected the city. Quite the contrary. But they understood that the shtetl remained a dynamic and a vital part of Polish Jewish life.

This new ferment and curiosity produced many important sources for the future historian of the shtetl. One important resource was the *Folkshilf*, the monthly newspaper put out by the CEKABE, the association of free loan societies that was sponsored by the Joint Distribution Committee (JDC). Edited by Emanuel Ringelblum and inspired by Yitshak Giterman, a key director of the JDC, the *Folkshilf* contained comprehensive surveys of the shtetl economy, of efforts to diversify the shtetl economy, and of the shtetl's battle against economic anti-Semitism. (Most of these articles were written by shtetl Jews themselves, and many showed surprising literary skill.) There were also important studies published by the YIVO that appeared in *Yidishe Ekonomik* and in *YIVO Bleter*.

Another key source that reflected the changing society of the shtetl was the weekly newspaper. Such publications contain valuable contemporary accounts that serve as a counterpoint to the nostalgic accounts that were published in many of the post-war memorial books (*yizker bikher*). For example, the memorial book of Glebokie made no mention of grinding poverty. Indeed, it said that most Jews lived well (*di yidn hobn gelebt farmeglekh*).[15] But the weekly shtetl newspaper painted a far bleaker picture and ran detailed accounts of riots by desperately poor Jews who demanded more help from the Jewish community.[16] The memorial book depicted an image of a Jewish community that lived in peace and harmony. But in an editorial from October of 1931, the shtetl newspaper bemoaned the fact that on *Shabes Shuva* (the Sabbath between Rosh Hashona and Yom Kippur) fights had broken out in three different synagogues. "Gentiles like to fight in taverns," the newspaper complained, "We prefer to fight in the synagogue."[17] On Yom Kippur of 1932 a fight over who would lead a service in the synagogue resulted in a mass brawl that spilled into the street.[18] On this, too, the memorial book was completely silent.

Through these sources we can compare the generic shtetl of political and cultural discourse to the actual shtetl of the interwar period. What emerges is a complex picture of social tension and communal flexibility, of economic crisis and resourceful self-defense. Any generalizations about the interwar shtetl have to incorporate an awareness of important regional differences. A shtetl in central Poland with a strong Hasidic presence was quite different from a shtetl near Vilna with no Hasidim at all. A shtetl that had both Hasidim and/or a strong yeshiva would be much more hostile to secular cultural trends than a shtetl that had neither.[19] Shtetlekh near a big city were quite different than shtetlekh in the distant marshes of Polesie.

Regional differences also had political and educational ramifications. Shetlekh in the Kresy (Eastern Poland) were usually strongholds of Zionism and of Tarbut Schools (schools that focused on modern Hebrew culture). In central Poland and in Galicia, a far higher percentage of children attended Polish state schools.[20] Many shtetlekh in central Poland were bastions of the Orthodox, anti-Zionist *Agudat Yisroel*, while in the eastern regions, the *Aguda* was quite weak.[21] Furthermore, it is important to remember that much that happened in the shtetl depended on personal leadership and example. The shtetl needed a cadre of volunteers that could run its vital institutions. The departure of just a few people, either through emigration or through marriage, could have important ramifications.[22] Often what counted was personality rather than politics or ideology. Office did not automatically guarantee leadership and prestige. In many shtetlekh the rabbi did indeed function not only as a religious leader but as a community organizer and as a pillar of strength in a time of crisis. In another town a few miles away, the rabbi might lead a pathetic existence, with little respect or authority.

This face-to-face community also intersected with a clear sense of social status and difference. Seating arrangements in the synagogue, being called to the Torah in the synagogue, the allocation of burial sites in the cemetery—all served to remind the residents of a shtetl of the proper pecking order. Social differences existed even within classes in the shtetl. For example, within the category of artisans, who ranked lower than the independent householders, there were important status gradations that depended on the kind of work that the artisan performed.

Essential to an understanding of how the shtetl worked was not just an awareness of the social gradations but also of the many safety valves that counterbalanced class tensions. A Jew with a grievance against the community could interrupt the reading of the Torah on the Sabbath and demand a public hearing. If a rich man showed too little social responsibility or if he gave too little to charity, then the burial society (*khevra kadisha*) could even the score by hitting the family with an enormous funeral bill. Lowly tailors could assuage the pain of humiliation in the main synagogue by starting their own *minyan* (prayer group). In 1938 one local shtetl newspaper wrote about the tailor's *minyan*:

> Yes it was a minyan for *horepashnikes* [ordinary toilers]. There they did not have to wait for the second class *aliye* [being called to the Torah], for the thin *haftora* [additional readings after the Torah service] that was thrown to them in other synagogues. They elected a president from among their own, and in their own eyes they became the equal of everybody else.[23]

During the interwar period the internal politics of the shtetl underwent a far-reaching transformation thanks to the impact of many new factors that transmitted new influences from the urban centers and that democratized shtetl life. One such organization was the *handverker fareyn*, the artisans' union. The *fareyn* tried to give the despised *baal mlokhe* (artisan) more self respect and inspire him to play a more assertive role in the affairs of the shtetl.[24] It even had a stirring song:

Handverker fun ale fakhn
glaykht di rukns oys
derloybt nisht mer fun aykh tsu lakhn
geyt shtolts, mutik un faroys
zingt un loybt glaykh mit layt
 di arbet nor iz unzer makht
fargest di alte alte tsaytn
der handverker hot tsurik ervakht
(Artisans of all trades, stand tall. Don't let them laugh at you any more. Go
proudly forward and forget the bad old times.)[25]

These new artisans' unions did not have a fixed political affiliation. In
some shtetlekh they cooperated with the Orthodox *Aguda*, in others with
the Bund or the Zionists.

Changing values in the interwar shtetl also led to new attention to the
role of women in communal life. In major cities new women's organizations called for an end to gender discrimination in Jewish life. These calls
had some resonance in the shtetlekh. In February of 1934 an article
appeared in the *Gluboker Vokh* charging that while women bore much of
the everyday burden for running the shtetl's charitable organizations, they
had all too little representation in the shtetl's major institutions. The article began a lively exchange of letters in the newspaper.[26]

The trend to democratization and wider mobilization of the shtetl
community was also reflected in the changing role of the local Jewish
community councils, the *kehilles*. Before World War I these councils—run
by a small clique who handled religious issues and the cemetery—usually
excited little interest among the wider Jewish population. By 1928, however, new government legislation had changed the legal parameters of the
kehilles and had widened their potential to serve as political arenas in the
Jewish community.[27] Elections were often intense and hard fought and
exposed political rifts in the community. Political parties, coalitions of
Hasidim and prayer houses, and personal cliques all contested these elections, which were sometimes marked by violence, especially when the
Orthodox *Agudat Yisroel* used Polish law to overturn Bundist and Zionist
victories. In the shtetl of Sokolow, after the *Aguda* used Article 20 to cancel
a *Poalei Tsiyon* (Labor Zionist) victory, the *Poalei Tsiyon* invaded the
kehilla building and smashed the furniture.[28]

Another focal point of tension in shtetl politics was the *khevre kadisha*,
the burial society. Jews on the outs with the *khevre kadisha*, especially if

they were wealthy, were in for hard bargaining before their loved ones could be buried. Funerals were another potential flashpoint. In Kazimierz Dolny, leftists refused to wear skullcaps at the cemetery and pushed the president of the *khevra kadisha* into a open grave.[29] This theme of violence in shtetl life deserves further study. It rarely got out of hand: shoving and pushing were far more prevalent than beating. Can one see this as a ritualized, implicitly regulated way of registering anger and asserting claims?

Local politics also affected relations with non-Jews, especially with the Poles. On the national level Jews made up no more than 10 percent of the population and had no leverage on the Polish parliament. On the local level, where Jews were often in a majority, their delegates on local town councils were in a better position to help the Jewish population and to secure certain gains at the margins: subsidies for Jewish schools, subventions to local Jewish associations, and the appointment of Jewish councilmen to key positions in local government. But the rules of the game were clear: even when the Jews comprised the majority in the town and paid more than 80 percent of the taxes, they had to let the Poles run the city council and elect a mayor.[30]

Whether on the local town councils or elsewhere, personal relationships in the shtetl allayed some of the tensions of Polish-Jewish conflict. While a common view of the shtetl sees Jewish-gentile contact as minimal, this in fact was not the case. In certain shtetl organizations such as the volunteer fire brigade, Jews and gentiles served together. Jewish and gentile children would study together at the local Polish government school. During the ritual and pageantry of Polish national holidays, Jews would participate along with gentiles. By the same token, local officials might make courtesy visits to Jewish schools and synagogues.

The particular closeness of a face-to-face community left a specific imprint not only on relationships between Jews but also on the interaction of Jews and gentiles. New research in recent years has served as an important reminder that one cannot consider the shtetl as a community whose interaction with non-Jews was limited only to business.[31] As Eva Hoffman has observed,

> Morally and spiritually, the two societies remained resolutely separate, by choice on both sides. Yet they lived in close physical proximity, and, willy nilly, familiarity. In the shtetl pluralism was experienced not as an ideology but as ordinary life. Jews trading horses in a small market town, speaking in haphazard Polish—that was the shtetl. Poles gradually picking up a few

words of Yiddish and bits of Jewish lore—that was also the shtetl. Jewish bands playing at Polish weddings and local aristocrats getting financial advice and loans from their Jewish stewards—all that went into the making of the distinctive, mulchy mix that was shtetl culture. This was where prejudices and bonds were most palpably reenacted—where a Polish peasant might develop a genuine affection for his Jewish neighbor despite negative stereotypes, and conversely, where an act of unfairness or betrayal could be most wounding because it came from a familiar face.[32]

In the late 1930s pogroms and economic boycotts attested to a sharp deterioration in Polish-Jewish relations and to a marked upsurge in anti-Semitism. But one should be careful not to draw too one-sided a picture. Not all local Polish officials allowed anti-Semitic pickets to harass Jewish shopkeepers, and not all peasants heeded the appeals to shun Jewish stores. While newly minted gentile merchants in the shtetlekh had many advantages—including access to easy credit—they still discovered that in many cases driving the Jews out of business was not as easy as they thought.[33]

As the interwar shtetl waged a tough battle against economic anti-Semitism, it was not entirely without resources or allies. Two major institutions that helped the shtetl were the *landsmanshaftn* in the United States and other countries and the Joint Distribution Committee. A study of the organization of Passover relief in 1937 showed that the smaller the shtetl, the larger the role of emigrants in keeping the community afloat. For settlements of fewer than 2,000 Jews, 77 percent of Passover relief funds came from abroad; in communities of more than 10,000 Jews, only 19.4 percent.[34] By the 1930s, help from abroad was a decisive factor in maintaining basic shtetl institutions and in keeping many families economically viable.

In this fight against economic anti-Semitism, one of the most important institutions in the interwar shtetl was the network of free loan societies (*gmiles khesed kases*) developed by the Joint Distribution Committee. By the eve of the war, practically every Jewish settlement in Poland had one. Inspired by Yitshak Giterman, a dynamic director of the JDC in Poland, these free loan societies had an impact far out of proportion to the small loans they were able to give. The *kases* extended small loans to enable Jews to buy licenses or stock a small store for market day. They advanced larger sums to help Jews rebuild their towns after major pogroms. The *kases* also made a major effort to diversify the shtetl economy and to encourage new secondary occupations that might make an important difference at the margins.[35] During World War II, the noted Jewish historian Emanuel Ringelblum looked back on the activity of the *kases* and stressed how much they did to raise Jewish morale. They reminded the shtetl Jew that he was not alone.[36] This dogged belief in the moral and national importance of self-help in the face of seemingly hopeless odds carried over into the early phases of World War II.

The JDC provided seed money for these societies but insisted that eventually at least 50 percent of the capital come from the shtetl itself. This stipulation ensured that the Jewish community felt that it "owned" the *kases*, and it also instilled a sense of dignity and pride. These credit unions helped counterbalance the personal and political infighting that had become such a prominent feature of Polish-Jewish life. Spurred by the JDC and by support from all political factions, the *kases* served as a place where the entire community could come together in a common effort. Often the elections to the boards of these credit societies sparked as much interest as the elections to the *kehilla* itself.[37]

In several key areas, the communal life in the shtetl—despite the growing impact of urbanization—continued to differ markedly from that of the middle-sized and large cities. Despite many conflicts and disputes that marked shtetl life, the bonds created by a face-to-face community had a major impact on philanthropy and the overall sense of mutual responsibility. Unlike the big cities, where many welfare activities had become professionalized and bureaucratized, charity and welfare in the shtetl retained its personal and traditional character. Long established voluntary associations like *lekehm evyonim* (bread for the poor), *bikur kholim* (visiting the sick), and *hakhnoses orkhim* (hospitality for strangers) valiantly struggled to keep the traditional social safety net in place—even if there was growing pressure to think about the dignity of those who were forced to take help.[38] If a Jew suffered a major illness, the shtetl would chip in to send him or her to a larger city for treatment. A leading Yiddish journalist published a study of his native shtetl that contained many pointed criticisms. Nonetheless, he stressed, the shtetl Jews still gave a higher proportion of their disposable income to charity than did Jews in the larger cities.[39] Other sources also attested to the firm bonds of social responsibility. The *Gluboker Lebn*, a weekly newspaper that appeared in a shtetl in Vilna province, ran a not-atypical story about a widow with six children who lost her house and who had nowhere to live. Leading householders in the shtetl led a campaign to help her and publicly challenged friends to donate a given sum.[40] In the same shtetl, when a Jewish woman absconded with the family savings and ran off with a gentile, her children's' classmates raised 25 *zlotys* to help the desperate father.[41] Small shtetlekh sent surprisingly large sums to help the German-Jewish refugees who had been expelled to Poland in late 1938. During World War II, the *Oneg Shabes*, the clandestine archive in the Warsaw ghetto, sponsored questionnaires that asked respondents to explain the discrepancy between the willingness of shtetl Jews and Jews in the big city to help their less fortunate neighbors.

Of all the institutions in the interwar shtetl, few had more of an impact than the new youth movements. Both demography and economics caused the problem of a large number of young men and women with little to do.[42] There was a marked trend towards later marriage.[43] Dowries to start a business, apprenticeships, working in the family store—all these traditional options for shtetl youth became less available in the interwar period. A survey in one shtetl in the Vilna region in 1931 showed that 61 percent of the boys and 83 percent of the girls between the ages of sixteen and twenty had no work.[44]

The youth movements offered a counterculture of lectures and amateur theater, of hikes and discussion groups, of sports and dance. Whatever their ideological differences, the youth movements had much in common.[45] They would rent a room or a *lokal* (meeting place), pool funds for a library, and come together on many weekday evenings and on Saturdays. For many, the *lokal* became a home away from home, a new family that could provide the empathy and companionship that was all too often lacking from parents hard pressed to make ends meet. The youth movements helped break down many of the traditional rules that governed relations between men and women.[46] By organizing Saturday trips to neighboring towns, they helped undermine traditional religious norms in the shtetl. Many members of the youth movements took their politics quite seriously, and ideological rivalries were fierce.[47] On the other hand, whether a given young man joined *Hashomer Ha-tsair* (The Young Watchman) or *Betar*, a revisionist Zionist movement, quite often depended on the presence of a particular young woman that he was courting. But it was the youth movements that offered hope and dignity and that helped break down many traditional prejudices (such as the disdain for physical labor).

The interwar shtetl in Poland was a community of many contrasts. Alongside tension and even intramural violence, one saw idealism, dedication to the wider community, and a readiness to help fellow Jews in need. Jews on their way to morning services in the synagogue passed posters that advertised American style beauty contests and movies like *King Kong* and *Captains Courageous*. Jews heard news of mounting anti-Semitism and then spent a friendly afternoon with a Polish neighbor.

In 1937 a new novel about a shtetl appeared, Michal Bursztyn's *Bay di taykhn fun Mazowie*.[48] On one level, Bursztyn tells a very depressing story that mirrors the worsening situation of Polish Jewry in the late 1930s. The shtetl Smolin (a fictional name) is full of Germans who are waiting for Hitler to come. A loudspeaker in the marketplace carries the ominous news from across the border as well as Hitler's speeches. A feisty Jew who fights back against Polish anti-Semites goes to jail and returns cowed and broken. Worst of all, a pogrom devastates the shtetl. (To evade Polish censorship Bursztyn has the pogrom take place in a Chinese town named Se-Ma-Lin!)

Yet not all is lost. A young Jewish doctor leaves Warsaw to return to the shtetl. Life there, he feels, is more authentic than in the big city. In the shtetl he can make more of a difference. And after the pogrom, as the community buries its victims, an old Jewish truck farmer (*sadovnik*) Hersh Lustig swears that "'the town will be rebuilt. I, Hersh Lustik, give you my word.' His face was blazed with courage in the red sunset."[49]

Bursztyn reminds us that in the late 1930s Polish Jews were not passively waiting for catastrophe to engulf them. They were fighting hard to hold on. In this fight the interwar shtetl played a major role.

NOTES

1. Ignacy Schiper, Aryeh Tartakower, and Aleksander Hafftka, *Zydzi w Polsce Odrodzonej* (Warsaw, 1932, 1933), Vol. 1, p. 4.

2. On this point see Nakhman Meyzl, *Geven amol a lebn* (Buenos Aires, 1951), p. 17.

3. See Celia Stopnicka-Heller, *On the Edge of Destruction: Jews of Poland between the Two World Wars* (New York, 1977); and Jacob Lestchinsky, *Oyfn Rand fun Opgrunt* (Buenos Aires, 1947).

4. Rosa Lehmann, *Symbiosis and Ambivalence: Poles and Jews in a Small Galician Town* (New York, 2001).

5. On this important topic see Dan Miron, *Der imazh fun shtetl* (Tel Aviv, 1981).

6. Sholem Cholawski, *Vifl benkshaft, vifl kheyn* (Tel Aviv, 2000), p. 148. "When I started to work in Rakow, I had a good chance to get to know the Jews of the shtetl. Until that time I had known a *city* like Nieswiezh, with her 4,000 Jews, Lida with 12,000 Jews and Vilna, with 55,000" (emphasis added).

7. Virtually every shtetl memorial book mentions the importance of nick-names in shtetl life. On the role of nicknames as an example of the shtetl's "power," see Hirsh Abramovich, "A Yidish Shtetl in Lite," in *Oyf di khurves fun milkhomes un mehumes: Pinkes fun gegnt-komitet EKOPO*, edited by Moshe Shalit (Vilna, 1931), pp. 362–384.

8. Luba Bat, "Through Laughter and Tears." Personal memoir. Website address is http://freepages.genealogy.rootsweb.com/~cpsa/prvzany/luba_bat.htm.

9. Natan Gross doubts a direct link between the Przytyk pogrom and "Es Brent." The former took place in March of 1936 while Gebirtig wrote his song in 1938. What is significant, Gross believes, is that many Polish Jews automatically linked the song to Przytyk because the Jewish resistance there foreshadowed the theme of *Es Brent*. See Natan Gross, *Zydowski Bard: Gaweda o zyciu I tworczosci Mordechaja Gebirtiga* (Krakow, 2000), pp. 180–185.

10. Viktor Alte, *Antisemityzm gospodarczy w swietle cifr* (Warsaw, 1937), pp. 26–34.

11. Yitshak Lev, "Bundishe Statistik," *Arbeter Tsaytung* (1937), No. 33.

12. Yitshak Bornstein, "Tsu der frage vegn plan fun dem oyfboy fond," *Folkshilf* (March 1936).

13. "*Landkentnish*," Ringelblum wrote, "really means not only learning (*derkenen*) a city's past, its monuments and buildings; it also means getting to know the people (*folk*) with its centuries old folklore and creative traditions." For an important precis of the importance of *landkentnish* for Ringelblum, see E. Ringelblum, "Fun der reaktsiye," *Landkentnish* (1933), No. 1. See also David G. Roskies, "Landkentnish: Yiddish Belles Lettres in the Warsaw Ghetto," in Robert Shapiro, ed., *Individualizing the Holocaust* (New York, 1999), p. 11.

14. "We feel that the writers see proud working Jews. They don't feel that they're guests in Pruzhany. Rather they regard themselves as long established veterans who have put down deep roots in the local area thanks to their work and toil." See Emanuel Ringelblum "An interesanter onheyb," *Literarishe Bleter* (1931), No. 27.

15. Michal and Tsvi Rajak, *Khurbn Glebok* (Buenos Aires, 1956), p. 16.

16. "Hunger demonstratsiye bay der yiddisher kehile in Glubok," *Gluboker lebn*, February 12, 1933. When the police came, Jews asked to be arrested. At least in jail, they argued, they would be able to eat.

17. Shloyme Bagin, "Shande! Shande!" *Gluboker Lebn*, September 25, 1931.

18. "Arum dem Yom-Kiper protses," *Gluboker lebn*, June 2, 1933.

19. Yaffa Eliach, *There Once Was a World: A 900-Year Chronicle of the Shtetl of Eishyshok* (Boston, 1998), p. 111.

20. "Uczniowie Zydzi w szkolach powszechnych," *Biuletyn Ekonomiczno-Statystyczny* (September 1937). While 95 percent of Jewish children attended state schools in Galicia, in Vilna province 56.3 percent of Jewish children attended Jewish schools.

21. Leon Ringelblum, "Di valn tsu di shtotratn in Poyln in 1934," *Dos virtshaftlekhe lebn* (1934), Nos. 8–9, pp. 1–12.

22. Y. V., "Mir zaynen orem in gezelshaftlekhe tuer," *Gluboker shtime*, March 3, 1939; Yankev Dokshitski, "Tsurik in di reyen," *Gluboker vokh*, February 16, 1934.

23. S. Agus, "Shtol," *Gluboker Shtime*, August 12, 1938.

24. See Elimelekh Rak, *Zikhroynes fun a yidishn handverker tuer* (Buenos Aires, 1958).

25. Ibid., p. 151.

26. M. Rubin, "Vi halt es mit der froy in undzer gezelshaftlekhn lebn," *Gluboker vokh*, February 2, 1934.

27. On the details of this legislation see Michal Ringel, "Ustawodawstwo Polski odrodzonej o gminach zydowskich" in *Zydzi w Polsce Odrodzonej*, Vol. 2 (Warsaw, 1932–1933), pp. 242–248. In big cities like Warsaw and Lodz, after *kehilla* elections in the 1930s resulted in Bundist victories, the government replaced the *kehilla* boards with appointed representatives.

28. See Peretz Granatshteyn, *Mayn khorev gevorene shtetl Sokolov* (Buenos Aires, 1946), p. 66. Article 20 disqualified those who openly proclaimed their hostility to religion. It reflected the inclination of the Pilsudski government to support the orthodox *Adudat Yisroel* in Jewish politics.

29. David Shtokfish, ed., *Pinkes Kuzmir* (Tel Aviv, 1970), p. 195.

30. In the local elections in Glebokie in 1934, Jews had to decide whether to join the official government bloc and accept 7 of 15 council seats, or run a separate Jewish list. Many Jews argued that it was humiliating to accept minority status on the council when Jews formed a majority of the town. But the editor of the local Yiddish newspaper reminded his readers that they could only lose a struggle against the local Polish authorities. Polish officials could always manipulate local politics by annexing outlying districts. In the end the Jews accepted the Polish offer. See Shloyme Bagin, "Tsu an eynhaytlekher yidish-kristlekher liste tsu di shtotrat valn," *Gluboker Lebn*, May 18, 1934.

31. See Eva Hoffman, *Shtetl: The Life and Death of a Small Town and the World of Polish Jews* (Boston, 1997); AnnaMaria Orla-Bukowska, "Shtetl Communities: Another Image," *Polin*, Vol. 8 (Oxford, 1995), pp. 89–115; Rosa Lehmann, *Symbiosis and Ambivalence: Poles and Jews in a Small Galician Town* (New York, 2001); and Shimon Redlich, *Together and Apart in Brzezany: Poles, Jews and Ukrainians, 1919–1945* (Bloomington, 2002).

32. Eva Hoffman, *Shtetl*, pp. 12–13.

33. The Jewish economist and journalist Jacob Lestchinsky filed a dispatch on the economic aftermath of the pogrom in Minsk Mazowiecki. He reported that right after the pogrom the Jewish share in the commerce of the town had fallen from 81 percent to 63 percent. But four months later a reporter for the *Varshever radio* asserted that the Jews were holding their own in the town and that while the Polish townspeople felt strong social pressure to avoid Jewish shops, peasants were

ignoring the boycott. Many of the gentile storekeepers could not compete on price with the Jews, and the new Polish local prefect (*starosta*) forbade close picketing of Jewish stores. See Jacob Lestchinsky Archives, Hebrew University, File 286; S. Gotlib, "Der emes vegn di straganes," *Varshever radio*, October 7, 1936. Professor Jerzy Tomaszewski, a noted Polish economic historian, has warned against overestimating the effects of the boycott. See J. Tomaszewski, *Zarys dziejow Zydow w Polsce w latach 1918–1936* (Warsaw, 1990), p. 60. For a more pessimistic view that refers to the crisis of Jewish trade in the Bialystok area, see Menakhem Linder, 'Der khurbm funm yidishn handl in Bialistoker rayon," *Yidishe Ekonomik*, 1937, Nos.1–2.

34. Hersh Shner, "Ankete vegn pesakh shtitse in di yorn 1935–1937," *Yidishe ekonomik* (1937), No. 1.

35. The best source on the *kases* is its monthly newspaper, *Folkshilf.* See also an internal memorandum of the JDC, "Sotsyale arbet in Poyln," June 1936, JDC Archives, Poland, General, No. 326a.

36. Emanuel Ringelblum, *Ksovim fun Geto* (Tel Aviv, 1985), Vol. 2, p. 127.

37. Ibid.

38. The *Gluboker Lebn* ran extensive discussions of how a change in the organization of shtetl philanthropy might show more respect for the dignity of those in need. Organized and institutionalized giving was, in many circumstances, easier to accept than personal handouts. One example cited of a charity that needed to be changed was the *Lekhem Evyonim*, a society that collected food in a pail and distributed it to the poor. Another problem was how to distinguish between Jews who had once been self-sufficient and who now needed help (*gefalene balebatim*) and Jews who had always been poor. See "Arbet un sotsyale hilf," *Gluboker Lebn*, January 29, 1932; "Arum dem Gluboker lekhem evyonim," *Gluboker Lebn*, November 10, 1933. "A beggar might take a piece of bread from a pail, but not *gefalene balebatim* or someone who has lost his job." There were also articles that described the anger of the "traditional poor" when they suspected that the *kehilla* was favoring the *gefalene balebatim*.

39. Abramovich, "A Yidish Shtetl in Lite," pp. 381–384.

40. "Retungs keyt tsu endikn di kleyn shtibele fun der almone mit di yesoymim Kraut," *Gluboker Vokh*, July 6, 1934.

41. "A familyen tragediye vos iz farlofn in Glebok," *Gluboker shtime*, April 15, 1938.

42. In 1930, 24,000 Jewish children in Poland turned 13. In 1938 this number had increased to 45,000. See Jacob Lestchinsky, "Vegn a konstruktivn plan fun hilf far di poylishe yidn," *Yidishe ekonomik*, Vol. 2 (1938), p. 12.

43. See A. Tsinaman and L. Shlamovitsch, "Di yidishe bafelkerung in Horodno," *Dos virtshaftlikhe lebn* (1935), Nos. 8–9, pp. 92–105; Shaul Stampfer, "Marital Patterns in Interwar Poland," Yisrael Gutman, Ezra Mendelsohn, Jehuda Reinharz, and Chone Shmeruk, eds., *The Jews in Poland between the Two World Wars* (Hanover, 1989), p. 196.

44. Shaul Yedidovich, "Di yidishe bafelkerung fun Glebok in tsifern," *YIVO Bleter*, Vol. 2 (1931), pp. 414–420.

45. An excellent source on the youth movements remains Moshe Kligsberg, "Di yidishe yugnt bavegungen in Poyln tsvishn di beyde velt-milkhomes: a sotsyologishe shtudye," in *Studies on Polish Jewry, 1919–1939*, edited by Joshua Fishman (New York, 1974).

46. A hapless father in a shtetl near Vilna, who heard that his daughter was carrying picnic baskets into the forest on Saturday afternoons, replied, "*Male vos zey trogn in vald iz nor a halbe tsore. Di gantse tsore vet zayn ven zey veln onheybn trogn fun vald*" (I'm more worried about what she'll be carrying out of the forest than what she carries into it.) In Yiddish *trogn* means both to carry and to be pregnant. See Abramovich, "A Yidish Shtetl in Lite," p. 370.

47. Perets Granatshteyn, from Sokolow Podlaski, recalled a trip that his *Poalei Tsiyon* youth movement took to a wedding in the neighboring town of Sterdyn. At the wedding the leader of the Sterdyn party youth group began to recruit new members. The brother of the bride, who was a Bundist, objected to the politics and suggested that everyone just relax and have a good time. When Granatshetyn and his friends supported this suggestion, all of the Sterdyn *Poalei Tsiyon* got up and left the wedding in a huff. See Granatshetyn, *Mayn khorev gevorene shtetl Sokolov*, pp. 142–148.

48. This novel was reprinted in Argentina in 1970.

49. Michal Bursztyn, *Bay di taykhn fun Mazovie* (By the Rivers of Mazowia) (Buenos Aires, 1970), p. 210.

7

Looking at the Yiddish Landscape

Representation in Nineteenth-Century Hasidic and Maskilic Literature[1]

Jeremy Dauber

"Once, at the conclusion of the Sabbath, the Besht ordered his stepfather's son-in-law, Rabbi Joseph Ashkenazi, to read him from *Ein Ya'akov* while he lay on the bed and listened. At one place the Besht said Torah concerning a saying in the *Ein Ya'akov*. Then Rabbi Joseph continued to recite the *Ein Ya'akov*, and during the reading Rabbi Joseph envisioned a maggid, whose name was also Rabbi Joseph, who had passed away about three-quarters of a year before that time. He saw him entering the house and dressed in Sabbath clothes and wearing a hat . . . he carried a stick in his hand and he walked as if he were alive. When Rabbi Joseph saw him he became very frightened and the book of *Ein Ya'akov* fell from his hand. The Besht passed his hand over Rabbi Joseph's face, and Rabbi Joseph Ashkenazi saw the dead man no more."

"[Abramovitch] was not dictating; he impersonated, acted like a performer on the stage. In front of my eyes living characters began to hover. They gesticulated, talked, and eventually evaporated."[2]

The two hagiographical accounts above are substantially different in origin and epistemology; the first is by a Hasid telling of a miraculous event; the second a secretary extolling his employer's extraordinary creative talents. While we may detect a shift from miracle to metaphor, however, undeniable similarities in sensibility exist between the two statements—the disciples' sense of their masters' remarkable perceptual powers, powers which give them uncommon ability in presenting to others the way things "really are." Such similarities may suggest the value of a closer examination of the linkages between Hasidic literature and maskilic literature in the nineteenth century, particularly in the pressing question of those authors' larger approaches to questions of representation and realism.

Such an approach flows not only from metaphorical confluence but historical reality: nineteenth-century Eastern European maskilic literature, both directly and explicitly, as in the work of Joseph Perl, and indirectly and implicitly, in works by Israel Aksenfeld and S. Y. Abramovitch, are developed in a polemic framework in which Hasidism plays a major role both as the historical subject of maskilic ire and the creator of literature which both infuriates and inspires. Examinations of that inspiration have often focused on how anti-Hasidic writers appropriate and parody seminal Hasidic works like the *Tales in Praise of the Ba'al Shem Tov* and Rabbi Nachman's *Tales*; a narrower strand of criticism attempts to seek broader literary and stylistic continuities.[3] Such continuities, though, are both inspiring *and* infuriating; conscious maskilic appropriation of Hasidic text, style, and strategy was never an unambiguous act. The complicated adaptation of these processes leads, in turn, to fragmented and ambivalent approaches to this topic within the literature itself.

Beginning with Hasidic literature, we may be able to trace a certain unwillingness or discomfort with firm locations, with particular places, with specific personal descriptions. After tracing this anxiety in the two seminal hasidic texts—the *Shivkhei HaBesht* and Reb Nachman's *Mayses*—we may turn to those texts' closest critic and best student, Joseph Perl, and through him, subsequent maskilic authors: Aksenfeld and Abramovitch.[4] In these maskilic hands, I will argue, the Hasidic uneasiness with direct representation, an uneasiness which stems from specific literary and theological purpose, is both upheld by the maskilim as a literary inheritance and *as such* becomes the locus for the expression of maskilic anxiety over their necessity to engage in what David Roskies has referred to as "creative betrayal," to use literary tools they find personally repugnant to achieve their own polemic ends, particularly given their own genuine interest in adopting the representational strategies of the Western European literature they so admire. As the nineteenth century continues and proponents of the *Haskalah* (Jewish Enlightenment) begin to generate different sorts of ambivalence, this anxiety over representation grows into a symbol of the doubtful efficacy of their literature—a stand-in for their maskilic agenda—to achieve any sort of programmatic goal at all.

To be clear: maskilic anxiety and ambivalence about the adoption of Hasidic literary strategies stems directly from the power of the undeniable influence Western literature had on these writers. Though a critic as perspicacious as Hayim Nachman Bialik could write that readers should not "forget to forget the rules and theory of literature" in studying Abramovitch, and "not to study him by comparison" to other world literatures,[5] Miron's illustration of Abramovitch's debt, direct or indirect, to eighteenth-century and early nineteenth century writers such as Sterne, Scott, Defoe, Richardson, and of course Gogol,[6] and Shmuel Werses' numerous articles on maskilic indebtedness to the German tradition of Wieland, the French tradition exemplified by Montesquieu, the classical tradition of Lucian, and others,[7] have proven such influence beyond doubt. This paper simply hopes to illustrate real thematic and literary connections and continuities within the movements of Hasidism and the *Haskalah* as one aspect of a complex process; to ground maskilic efforts at realistic representation in a wider and earlier literary context; and to argue that the making of these efforts—or, as we will see, the resistance to making them, by constantly typologizing, allegorizing, deconstructing, or questioning them—is itself an essential question in the study of nineteenth century Yiddish literature.

Tales in Praise of the Ba'al Shem Tov

In early nineteenth-century Eastern Europe, traditionalists vouched for the equivalence between reality and representation in the tales purporting to relate the birth, growth, life, and death of the founder of Hasidism, the *Shivkhei HaBesht* (*Tales in Praise of the Ba'al Shem Tov*), first published in Hebrew in Kopust in 1814 and in Yiddish in Korets in 1816. (Though substantive differences exist between the two versions, both were highly influential on subsequent maskilic writers, and both demonstrate analogous treatments of the issues of representation discussed here.) The writer and compiler, striving to perpetuate this equivalence, make great efforts to authenticate the story's sources: tags placed before numerous stories indicate where the writer heard them, for example, and the writer even explicitly notes in his introduction, "Therefore, I was careful to write down all the awesome things that I heard from truthful people. In each case I wrote down from whom I heard it. Thank God, who endowed me with memory, I neither added nor omitted anything. Every word is true, and I did not change a word" (E 4–5; H 5–6).

The very ardency of these claims may arouse suspicion as much as allay it; a close look at the *Tales* raises questions not only about the claim that these stories record historical reality, but about their method of representing it.[8] The *Tales* provide remarkably few descriptions of actual life within the boundaries of the shtetl or other Jewish centers;[9] instead, the *Shivkhei HaBesht*'s tales feature constant displacement and distance. One of the Ba'al Shem Tov's favorite directions is away from the city, towards nature or other idealized, non-spatialized locations like the Land of Israel (E 24, H 24, Y 17).[10] As a child, he runs away from the *melamed* (his teacher) into the woods (E 12, H 13, Y 8); once married, the Ba'al Shem Tov goes to the mountains, where he seals away Rabbi Adam's manuscripts (E 31, H 30, Y 45);[11] later, his beloved spot of prayer is in the fields (E 39, H 37, Y 32).

In those stories where the Ba'al Shem Tov's distance from Jewish locales is minimized, geographically speaking, the text generally accentuates the essential betweenness or marginalization of the Ba'al Shem Tov's proximity to those places. Famously, one of the Ba'al Shem Tov's disguises is that of a coachman (E 26, H 25–26, Y 18), and he seems to possess a coachman's knowledge of the roads and the outlying areas: when Nachman of Kosov tries to avoid the Ba'al Shem Tov, the story tells us that "he changed direction and took a crooked route. For two days he left the road altogether and avoided passing through any village. But the Besht knew the road and he was able to follow him anyway" (E 235, H 205–206). One tale suggests that the Ba'al Shem Tov made his living "keeping a tavern," a temporary stopping point for people between places (E 34, H 32, Y 22). The Ba'al Shem Tov often stops right on the outskirts of cities: after giving an interpretation of a certain *mishna* (rabbinic text), "he traveled for about a verst and stopped to graze the horses in the field," where he is then located by his future disciples (E 39, H 37, Y 32); at another point, the Ba'al Shem Tov is forced to light a tree on fire because "they are still a few versts from that place" where they are going (E 131, H 130, Y 74–75). This phenomenon is not limited to the Ba'al Shem Tov within the work: a common topos in the stories is of a person stopped a short distance from town because of the Sabbath or Yom Kippur, right on the margins and yet unable to enter (see, e.g. E 106, H 93–94; E 221, H 193–194, Y 133).

Even in stories that are set in the shtetl, analogous tendencies towards marginalization or reversal of typical spatial hierarchies are apparent. Not only does the Ba'al Shem Tov, as a *belfer* (one who accompanies children from their homes to school), have a job that is entirely constituted of being *between* places (E 12, H 13, Y 8), but descriptions of him within the synagogue actually place him within "the synagogue vestibule" or encountered "by the mezuzah about to leave"—i.e., in the doorway (E 39, H 37, Y 32; E 150, H 131, Y 76). While the revelation of the Ba'al Shem Tov does take place in a *beys-medresh* (house of study), it takes place at night, and is observed by Rabbi Adam's son who is located behind a special partition (E 16, H 17, Y 12); later, the Ba'al Shem Tov will receive the spirit of Rabbi Akiva at midnight (E 162, H 141, Y 140). This strategy can be summed up by the text's characterization of the pre-revelation Ba'al Shem Tov, who serves as the watchman of the *beys-medresh*: "this was his way: while all the people of the house of study were awake, he slept, and while they slept, he was awake" (E 13, H 14, Y 8). This temporal marginality, this standing outside of time, is perhaps best underlined by the telling detail that one of the few miraculous signs immediately attendant on his death is the stoppage of clocks (E 257, H 225, Y 172).

Temporal marginality is also apparent in the work from the compiler's decision to present stories set not simply in "lived, contemporary" history, but in the mythic past. This past is evoked both explicitly, in tales such as those about the Ba'al Shem Tov's father, Rabbi Eliezer, or implicitly, through inserting the Ba'al Shem Tov or other figures into "local legends" or tales "patterned . . . after the scholar-saints of past ages."[12] Rabbi Eliezer's adventures, for example, are clearly patterned on the Joseph story (E 7–10, H 9–12, Y 5–7), a comparison explicitly acknowledged within the text itself (E 11, H 12, Y 7), and Khone Shmeruk has noted the tale of Rabbi Adam's non–Eastern European provenance (E 13–15, H 14–16, Y 9–11).[13]

This strategy of temporal and locational marginalization can also easily be seen as a representational marginalization, a studied emphasis on the avoidance of description of the central and normative. One reason for this may be seen in the way that these marginalizing strategies are echoed in the text in a metaphorical marginalization within the descriptions of people and things. People are not who they seem to be in the *Shivkhei HaBesht*, the most obvious example, of course, being the Ba'al Shem Tov himself, who is described as having a "mask" that he "puts aside," creating a great light (E 28, H 27, Y 20), and who himself describes his pre-revelation persona as a pretense, a concealment (E 20, H 20, Y 14). It is hardly insignificant that one of the few detailed descriptions of clothes in the *Shivkhei HaBesht* occurs when those clothes are used as a disguise: "[The Ba'al Shem Tov] disguised himself by putting on clothes like those worn by loafers. He put on a short coat and a broad belt, he changed his demeanour and manner of speech, and he went to the holy community of Brody to the house of the rabbi, our master and rabbi, Rabbi Gershon" (E 21, H 21, Y 14).

This discrepancy between image and reality is hardly limited to the Ba'al Shem Tov; in fact, much of the miraculous power ascribed to the Hasidic leader in the text stems from his ability to perceive, and to reveal, who others actually are, instead of what *they* falsely seem to be. The text notes that the Ba'al Shem Tov can see things that others have "lost the power to perceive" (E 159, H 139, Y 167); in the Ba'al Shem Tov's higher powers of perception, we live in a world where borders are thin between both the physical and metaphysical. The Hasidic master illustrates that his perceptual capacities—his ability to represent the world—is the ultimately "correct" one, a fact acknowledged by, variously, those who are temporarily invited to share his perceptual position (though they can do so only briefly), those with privileged knowledge of a particular private datum, and, of course, the mediated reader. Thus Rabbi Gershon, often the reader's stand-in in these tales, has his eyes opened by the Ba'al Shem Tov to see how the dead approach him at times of prayer to ask for his intervention; the former, previously unaware of their thronging presence, falls into a dead faint (E 60–61, H 55, Y 41); similarly, a preacher is unable to see a demon haunting a house (E 182, H 158, Y 97), an *arrendator* (rent-farmer) can be seen with "the Angel of Death dancing behind him," and the Angel of Death is found standing at the head of a bed (E 37, H 35, Y 30 ; E 116, H 101–102, Y 148–149).

Even more importantly, though, is the Ba'al Shem Tov's ability to disregard the common perceptual schism between material essence and moral essence. The Ba'al Shem Tov tells an adulterer that "the sin of adultery is written on his forehead" (E 232, H 203, Y 117), and both animate and inanimate objects in the *Shivkhei HaBesht* behave differently than they "really should" and yet are perceived by the Ba'al Shem Tov as, at least metaphysically speaking, they "really are." For example, the Ba'al Shem Tov can note that a particular bed has been the site of an adulterous affair (E 186, H 162, Y 100–101), or that a particular ring was purchased with money gained from the taking of interest (E 170, H 148, Y 166). Conversely, items which come into contact with transcendent holiness, either in the person of the Ba'al Shem Tov or through proximate location to ceremonies and rituals practiced by his Hasidim, can transcend their physical natures—can, in other words, behave and be characterized in non-representative ways—to express altered metaphysical states. Instances of this phenomenon in the Shivkhei range from the sublime, like the water that trembles in response to the Ba'al Shem Tov's prayer (or, in variant versions, the nearby table or barrels of grain; see E 50–52, H 46–48, Y 69–70), to the more offbeat, like the ax that beats the robber attempting to kill the Ba'al Shem Tov (E 23, H 23, Y 16) or the Ba'al Shem Tov's pipe which puts its robbers to sleep (E 220, H 193, Y 133).

This blurring of the metaphysical and the physical also allows us to refine our understanding of the representation of place. Of the few detailed representations of place, many are of metaphysical locations like Paradise and Gehenna (E 54–57, H 50–53, Y 37–39; E 114–115, H 100–101, Y 153–154): indeed, the Shivkhei's writer explicitly calls attention to his inclusion of an apparently unrelated story about a visit to Gehenna, noting "This story is not about the Ba'al Shem Tov; nevertheless, I include it here because from this story we can learn the fear of heaven" (E 113, H 99). Another lesson, though, is that these classic sites of mystical literature allow for the accentuation of the blurred nature of spatial representation by the author of the Shivkhei HaBesht: a rabbi who has returned from the dead notes that "lower paradise is still touched by corporeality" (E 138, H 120, Y 65). Similarly, places located in dreams are described as more real, more true, than their simple physical counterparts. For example, the wife of Rabbi Abraham, the Maggid's son, dreams of "a huge, beautifully decorated hall (traklin)" (E 98, 99, H 87, 88); a melamed has a dreaming vision of a house and of the Ba'al Shem Tov suggesting a more beautiful world than this one (E 46–48, H 45–46, Y 34–35); and the Ba'al Shem Tov says, in another context, "Do you think it was a dream that you had? Not at all. It was a vision that you saw. I saw it as well and it became a reality before my eyes" (E 54, H 50, Y 71, emphasis mine).

This statement suggests a second aspect of the Ba'al Shem Tov's representative power: he can not only perceive these differences, but can overcome them. He is able to forcibly change other beings from their magically transformed state into their essential natures, often through the mechanism of "elevating their soul" when they have been reincarnated into an abnormal gilgul: examples include a frog, a dog, a fish, and a horse (see, among other sources, E 24–26, H 24–25, Y 17–18; E 133–134, H 116–117, Y 159–160; E 218–219, H 191–192, Y 131–132). In fact, one of the earliest miracles ascribed to him is to defeat Satan himself, whose evil behavior is accomplished through transformation upon transformation: he transforms himself into a sorcerer, who in turn becomes a werewolf

(E 12, H 13, Y 8). Satan, in this treatment, represents the constant efforts to disguise or distance from the essential; in his triumph over Satan, the Ba'al Shem Tov forces him to take on his true form. These transformations can be anagogically seen as a kind of "rewriting" as well: it is the Ba'al Shem Tov who has the power to present things as they are, and he is, indeed, the only author.

The *Shivkhei HaBa'al Shem Tov*, then, constantly attempts to complicate or marginalize not just traditional place and time, but even traditional representation, and to replace it with a new, centralized way of seeing, focusing on a figure who explicitly rejects physical representation for what can be called "essential representation," an in-between mode incorporating metaphysical truths predicated on ideological and theological states. In employing this literary strategy, the work not only expresses Hasidic philosophical beliefs, but also metaphorically recapitulates a move from the margin to the center of both the "historical" Ba'al Shem Tov (as perceived by the text's editor/compiler), as well as the newly empowered Hasidic movement, aware of its marginal origins and moving towards a central position in Jewish life.

Indeed, if the *Shivkhei* is seen as a foundational text of the Zaddikist movement, such marginalization serves as even deeper polemic purpose: it suggests that representation, description at a distance, mediated texts, is no substitute for direct contact with the Zaddik (the mystical master), who is able to perceive "the real truth" and to articulate it. The famous tale that suggests the Ba'al Shem Tov's *toyre* (teachings) cannot be understood once they have been written down by others is a case in point (E 179, H 155–156, Y 93). (In the non-realistic fashion which we have seen, we are not surprised to find that the lesson first appears by seeing a demon walking with a book, and only then following the examination of the book and the discovery that there is none of his Torah in it.) Given the paradoxical implications of the tale, which directly challenge the status of the tales themselves—after all, if these encounters are convincing and compelling because of their charismatic directness, then what does it say to represent them in writing?—we can see that the marginalization of direct representation concretizes the internal contradictions of texts spreading the word of a movement whose essence is direct experiential contact with the Zaddik, and suggests that one must have fidelity not to lying texts, but to the figure who has the power to perceive the essence of things: the Zaddik. Much of this is the case, necessarily, when the author of the text is not the Zaddik himself; the *Shivkhei* are tales of disciples about one who sees, not tales of the seer himself. What occurs when the author is the Zaddik himself is the subject of the next section.

Rabbi Nachman's Mayses (Tales)

In the *Mayses* of Rabbi Nachman of Bratslav, the reader has the opportunity to observe the relatively unmediated spectacle of a Hasidic master's literary endeavor, and, viewed from the limited perspective of representation, the results are at once highly tangential and entirely galvanizing. For if in the *Shivkhei HaBesht* the reader is treated to a theoretical manifesto of the way in which the marginalization of realist tendencies is inextricably connected with "essential representation," in the *Tales* such a movement reaches its apotheosis. For Nachman of Bratslav, a figure obsessed with universal history and redemption, desirous of telling tales of *shevira* (the breaking of the cosmic vessels) and *tikkun* (the re-unification of things), the actual details of Eastern European Jewish life were not merely unnecessary, not simply irrelevant, but in fact actively counterproductive. What mattered were the eternal truths of Jewish history as explained by the Lurianic master narrative, not local squabbles over religious reform or social betterment.[14]

As such, Nachman moves his discussion from the sphere of reality to the sphere of fairy tale, or, if one prefers, myth. If the *Tales in Praise of the Ba'al Shem Tov* tend to accentuate the margins of contemporary Jewish life in order to provoke a longing for its center, constituted as a direct encounter with the Zaddik, Nachman cloaks contemporary Jewish existence in a shell of kings and princes, a spark hidden away within his *kelippa* (shell). Indeed, one of the only tales seemingly located in a realistic traditional Eastern European milieu, "The Tale of the Rabbi's Son,"[15] with its mentions of zaddikim and normal modes of travel over roads, rivers, bridges, and inns, only begins there: by the end of the story, it becomes clear that, in a fashion analogous to the *Shivkhei*, these physical individuals and locales are only the thin veneer beneath which eternal forces both for good and for ill dwell. The merchant who leads the rabbi astray is revealed to be Samael, and the rabbi's son and the zaddik are revealed to be "in the aspect of the 'small light', and . . . in the aspect of the 'great light', and if they had united the Messiah would have come" (E 137). As in the *Shivkhei HaBesht*, we see the blurring between the physical and the metaphysical, where narrative figures are firmly linked to mystical concepts;

here, too, false perception gives way to true perception, realistic representation to essential representation. In this case, however, it is done less through a recorded encounter with the Zaddik than the Zaddik's own created work; Nachman's allegorical structures are quintessentially positioned to serve these purposes, where, for all readerly intents and purposes, there is no essential difference between *mashal* (parable) and *nimshal* (the point of the parable).

This is not to say that Nachman did not recognize that his eternal story had to be applied to local circumstance, and it is hardly coincidental that almost all of the other very few mentions of specific, realistic elements within the *Mayses* appear in the "Tale of the Wise Man and the Simple Man" ("Ma'ase mekhaham vetam," H 62–85, E 143–161), perhaps his most transparent allegory and his clearest rejoinder to the maskilim who he saw regularly towards the end of his life in his town of Uman.[16] When the wise man travels around the world, in contradistinction to tales like "The Tale of the Lost Princess" ("Ma'ase meaveidat bat melekh"), his journey is expressed in terms of specific, terrestrial cities: "They took him along to there [Lagorna], and from there he went off to Italy, and from there to Spain" (H 64, E 145).[17] In fact, those specific elements—place names like Warsaw, Lagorna, Italy, and Spain, merchants who claim their specific origin in Warsaw, and the vaguely realist descriptions of the dress and mode of the Warsaw marketplace ("Meanwhile he observed shop-clerks walking in the marked in their elegant way with their hats and pointed shoes, their elegant gait and clothes"; H 62–63, E 144)—tend to act as symbols of reformist or anti-traditionalist sentiment: they mark the beginning of the wise man's drift towards heresy.

In fact, the transition of representation of real place to false place in the tale, as the wise man begins in Italy and Spain and ends in an illusory mire beaten by demons he refuses to recognize, neatly mirrors Nachman's polemic point: the thrust of Nachman's criticism of the *Haskalah* (Jewish Enlightenment) is that an excess of intellectualism without a proper grounding in the realia of Jewish faith and metaphysics leads to utter illusion, heresy, blindness, and subsequent destruction. Again, it is the metaphysical that, seemingly paradoxically, is perceived as the real, and the objects of the physical world—the material objects that the wise man makes his calling at and his fortune with—which are false. And, once again, it is the zaddik-figure—in this case, the *tam*, whose radical simplicity is, as his name implies, a cover for his imaginative and creative perfection—who is able to transform objects in their essence and see the truth in a world which generates falsehood. For the *tam*, who in eating transforms bread into a variety of foods, water into a variety of beverages, and a pelt into a sheepskin coat, a caftan, and a jacket, is not mistaken in the conventional sense of the term, according to Nachman; rather, he is deeply aware of the irrelevance of diverse material forms in comparison to essential nature. It is not merely because of poverty that the *tam*'s food, drink, and clothing are presented as bread, water, and a pelt; Nachman is stressing the truthful universal at the expense of the lying particular.

Nonetheless, the contradictions which pervade the *Shivkhei HaBesht*—contradictions predicated on the immediacy of the encounter with the Zaddik and his own elevated perceptual status—are present within the composition of the *Tales* and certainly concerning their publication and their interpretation. Though Nachman's amanuensis, Natan Sternhartz, took great pain to ensure that every word of his master's story was properly preserved, early Bratslav writings about the *Tales*, including Natan's own, stress the vital omission of Nachman's own presentation of the tale, as well as the essential inability of all but the zaddik interpreter to delve into the work's full meanings. Natan writes: "For by means of body movement—rocking his head back and forth, winking his eyes and hands gesticulating—it was by these means in particular that the learned [listener] was enlightened to understand just a little; he was amazed at what he beheld, and his eyes perceived from afar the wonders of the Lord and the greatness of his [Nahman's] holy Torah."[18] Conversely, the absence of such opportunities for greater understanding through charismatic encounter would shape Bratslav interpretive approaches for the better part of the next two centuries, creating a rhetoric of the impossibility of total comprehension of the *Tales*.

Ultimately, however, the figuring of these issues into the questions of representation are merely pale reflections of Nachman's essential and essentialist point: that reality as it is perceived by all but the Zaddik is false, and representing it as it is is not merely irrelevant, but perhaps even genuinely harmful.

The Haskalah: An Introduction and Joseph Perl's Megale Temirin

We have seen how Hasidic literature features marginalization of direct representation of Eastern European Jewish realia for at least two different reasons. First, to express a marginality which then leads to a polemic call for a simultaneous embrace of the marginal and a move towards a, if not the, center; and second, to express the struggles of locating a specifically contemporaneous movement within the much larger picture of Jewish history. As we will see, both of these issues are taken up by the work of the *Haskalah*, itself highly polemical, and which also perceived the necessity of grappling with overarching schemes of Jewish past and Jewish future in its polemic battles. However, the different ideological challenges facing the maskilim—particularly challenges stemming from methodological concerns such as using strategies they found abhorrent and, for our concerns, *specifically borrowing techniques from Hasidic literature*—led to an inherent anxiety about those strategies, one which reflects itself in, among other ways, a redoubled questioning of and perpetuation of doubts about direct representation of the realia of Eastern European Jewish life—though for different reasons.

Dan Miron, in his work on Abramovitch, writes that "were Frischmann and Bialik to read him against the background of eighteenth-century or early nineteenth-century fiction, some similarities in technique and manner could not have been overlooked." Miron largely develops this important observation with reference to questions of authenticity—"the urge to present works of fiction as 'true histories'"—questions which, in a radically different epistemological context, we have seen modeled in the debate over the *Shivkhei HaBesht*.[19] One may expand on Miron's insight and suggest that certain aesthetic theories of the period may illuminate trends in maskilic style and representative strategy, both through their influence and the corollary conflicts they generate with other maskilic necessities, particularly the necessity of imitation of Hasidic literature.

In his work, Miron mentions Ian Watt's principle of formal realism, which the latter defines as "the premise, or primary convention, that the novel is a full and authentic report of human experience, and therefore under an obligation to satisfy its reader with such details of the story as the individuality of the actors concerned, the particulars of the times and places of their actions, details which are presented through a more largely referential use of language than is common in other literary forms." Such mimetic reportage, however, was of course purposively shaped: eighteenth-century principles of neoclassical imitation defined art as "an imitation—but an imitation which is only instrumental toward producing effects upon an audience," effects which are both pleasurable and induce virtue. Indeed, those imitations were based on rules of art which, "though empirically derived, were ultimately validated by conforming to that objective structure of norms whose existence guaranteed the rational order and harmony of the universe."[20] In M. H. Abrams' discussion of the mirror as an essential metaphor of popular contemporary aesthetic theories, he notes that "it fostered a preoccupation with the 'truth' of art, or its correspondence, in some fashion, to the matters it is held to reflect." Such didactic imitativeness, predicated on rationalist ideologies, fit well with maskilic agendas.

True, neoclassical aesthetic theory allowed for divergence from strict mimesis to stress the "pleasant and beautiful objects of existing things, . . . objects which are synthesized from parts found separately in nature, . . . the central tendency, or statistical average, of the form of each biological species, . . . the generic human type, rather than the individual, . . . [and] the prominent, uniform, and familiar aspects of the outer and inner world," and it may be that some aspect of the anti-representative trends we observe in maskilic literature, particularly the move towards a type of typological description, participates in this approach. Several factors, however, complicate this picture.

First, as Abrams notes, this "neo-classic stress on the typical, the uniform, the salient, and the familiar" as imitative ideals nonetheless did so through the choice of particulars which most precisely share those universals: "the recommendation of the typical, general, and familiar as basic requirements of art usually turns out to be accompanied by a statement of the need for the leavening qualities of individuality, particularity, and novelty as well . . . in the Age of Johnson, then, we find standards of art running the gamut from a primary emphasis on typicality, generality, and 'large appearances' to the unqualified recommendation of particularity, uniqueness, and a microscopic depiction of detail."[21] More importantly, this divergence, less anti-mimetic than it might first seem, was generally employed to create what critics sometimes called *la belle nature*: nature improved, refined. Clearly, maskilic literature, with its polemic interest in presenting contemporary Jewish life as a portrait of *la nature mauvais*, is already demonstrating a tension between Western European theory and Eastern European practice.

Finally, maskilic writers' polemic and subversive practices meant that their imitative strategies needed to focus not merely on life, but on text and genre. To appeal to audiences unwilling to engage non-traditional texts, they needed to adopt traditional texts' formal features, incorporating not only narratological conventions insisting on the texts' veracity, but more intense and thoroughgoing stylistic perspectives as well—incorporation which creates serious and anxious consequences. Our illustration of the links between these Hasidic texts and maskilic texts will begin with the work of Joseph Perl, the Galician maskil who was obsessed with the *Shivkhei HaBesht* and with Rabbi Nachman's *Mayses*. So much so that his work, both published and unpublished, constitutes specific and explicit reactions to both their popular success and to their historical and ideological claims.[22]

In Perl's *Tales and Letters*, he parodies Nachman's writings, finishing the latter's unfinished "Tale of the Lost Princess" and creating his own "Tale of the Lost Prince." In so doing, he illustrates how Nachman's universal schema of religious redemption through the unification of the Godhead could be neatly subverted into an allegory of the triumph of rationalist endeavor over the forces of Hasidic ignorance.[23] Though these parodic tales were never published, Perl wrote a series of frame letters which suggest how he intended to present them: as tales Nachman told while he was seeing a doctor in Lvov, on the other side of the Galician border, recovering from tuberculosis. The requirements of mimesis, then, constrained Perl's stylistic choices: in the *Tales*, he needed to write sufficiently like Nachman so as not to arouse suspicions of forgery: were he to do otherwise, his whole effort would be ruined.[24]

As a result, the pseudo-*Tales* contain an analogous distancing mechanism to the shtetl as Nachman's *Mayses*, though clearly for very different reasons. It is precisely because of the differences in those reasons that Perl's distancing mechanism collapses at the work's end, and fairly transparent references to the Hasidim and their corrupt economic practices emerge.[25] However, it is difficult to speak definitively about the *Tales and Letters*, as they only exist in unfinished form and were never published, and so our examination of Perl will focus on his main contribution to nineteenth century maskilic literature, *Megale Temirin* (*The Revealer of Secrets*).

Though *Megale Temirin* is generally considered in the annals of Hebrew literature, Perl wrote a Yiddish version of the book as well, a fully finished, elegantly crafted work.[26] Though one can confidently assert that this Yiddish version did not influence future maskilic endeavors (it remained unpublished until the 1930s, and there seems to be no record of its circulation among nineteenth-century maskilim), the book may nonetheless fairly be examined as an example of nineteenth-century maskilic literary endeavor, given its influence on later maskilic authors and its direct link to

Hasidic literature, the one caveat being that the work's influence must necessarily have come from the Hebrew version.

In both versions of *Megale Temirin*, however, Perl seems to have been heavily influenced by Hasidic literature, both in general polemical terms and specifically with regard to representational strategies. True, Perl's disbelief in the authenticity of the tales of the *Shivkhei HaBesht* is eminently clear—beyond their miraculous content, anathema to his largely rationalist sensibilities, the five-decade gap between the Ba'al Shem Tov's death and the *Tales'* publication allowed the expression of grave doubts about the experiential nature of many of the compiler's claims. Nonetheless, Perl's awareness of the *Tales'* popularity once more dictated his usage of and reliance upon certain of the *Shivkhei's* literary strategies. And though *Megale Temirin*, unlike the *Tales and Letters*, does not formally mimic the Hasidic work, many of its structures reinforce the marginalized representation seen in the *Shivkhei*.

First, the novel's epistolary structure removes any claim to objectivity of description as the omniscient narrator disappears, replaced by (generally speaking) the letters of less than perspicacious Hasidim. And these Hasidim can hardly be trusted to provide honest or detailed description as it is, given that Perl has rendered their speech facile, simplistic, and error-prone, stunted and malformed as it is by exposure to the Zaddik. Even the narrator, Ovadia ben Petakhia, is strangely divorced from real life: gifted with the power of invisibility and (seeming) ethereality, he floats above and around of the shtetl, but is certainly not of it.[27]

Just as the Hasidim in *Shivkhei HaBesht* were unable to properly perceive the world around them, the same is true in *Megale Temirin*: while in the former work their blindness came from their distance from the Zaddik, however, here it results from their superstitious proximity to Hasidism in general and to Hasidic texts in particular. For example, the maskil Mordekhai Gold, playing on this confusion, convinces Hasidim in the forest that he is a character from the *Shivkhei*, the demon the Ba'al Shem Tov imprisoned in the woods (L 20, E 57). Hasidim themselves not only fall victim to this confusion, but, because of their corruption, perceptual and financial, perpetuate it: they claim an old clay pipe to be the Ba'al Shem Tov's (L 70, E 127), and pass off tobacco just purchased from a local merchant as a product straight from the Holy Land (L 40, E 50). This is not merely conscious manipulation: the Hasidic perspective on individuals seems to change as a result of the way those individuals are ideologically perceived. Even physical descriptions are affected, like when a Hasid's detailed description of the maskil Mordechai Gold's appearance is loaded with metaphors and references in such a way as to render him a typological antinomian figure (L 8, E 32–33). The results of this perceptual corruption can be literally catastrophic: the rebbe, unable to distinguish between a picture in the maskilic book of the book's author and one of his private secretary, is believed to have "killed" the latter in trying to curse the former (see L 111, E 190; L 123, E 204; and L 125, E 208).

The entire process is elegantly encapsulated in the book's leading metaphor, its very title. The book's title proclaims itself a "revealer of secrets," and the work, according to the title page, "reveals things that have hitherto been secreted away and hidden from all human sight" (title page, E 1). Such language first reminds us of the possibilities of greater perceptions available to Hasidic initiates; but when Perl mentions, in the narrator's introduction, that the secret manuscripts allowing the narrator to gather the letters comprising the book can be found only by those who have lost their way, and that Ovadia does in fact discover the manuscripts after having lost his way at night (Prologue, E 12), we see how neatly Perl has reversed the dynamic, illustrating how seeming sight is really a cover for blindness.

One example may be worth examining at slightly greater length to illustrate Perl's efforts to demonstrate the falsity of Hasidism by demonstrating the falsity of its descriptive or representative actions. At the beginning of *Megale Temirin*, in the "Important Notice," the Hasidic narrator takes great pains to specifically identify the referents to his usage of particular nomenclature:

> Let it be stated emphatically that everywhere this book indicates the designation "Rabbi" (Rov), "Rebe," "Real Rebe," "Tzadek," "Tzadek of the Generation," "Perfect Tzadek," "True Zadek," "Worthy," "Worthy of the Generation," "Real Worthy," "Sage," "Sage of the Generation," "True Sage," "Real Sage," "Scholar," "Prince," "King," "God-fearer," and the like, the reference therein is only to those tzadikim who serve God with *dveykes* (passionate attachment) and *hislayves* (burning enthusiasm) and not to the few "Talmudists" still found in our land, because of our many sins, upon whom light has not yet dawned. (Important Notice, E 7)

This suggests a punctiliousness in Hasidic linguistic and semiotic practice, an effort by the credulous Hasidic narrator to say precisely what he means and identify precisely what is. Later in the text, however, Perl uses precisely this genre of notice in a polemic context to show that Hasidim say exactly what they do *not* mean. In Letter 15, a non-Jewish prince, recognizing that his fellow conversationalist is a Hasid, says: "In that case, I won't lease you the mill because in that book it says you're allowed to cheat us."

The conversation continues, slightly excerpted:

> "Perish the thought!" I cried. "It doesn't say that in this book!" He looked in his *bukh* and says to me, "On Page 14, paragraph 6, doesn't it say this explicitly?!"
>
> I took the holy book and looked at it and cried, "Perish the thought, sir! He wrote here that it's okay to cheat *idolaters*, that is, worshippers of stars and planets, but not *you*!"
>
> When I said this, he went through the roof and he says, "I know you say this, and there's even a Notice about this at the beginning of this book, as all the Jewish authors have, but . . . in your books (he looked in the *bukh* and says), every place where it says "nations," "foreigner," or "non-Jew," it refers to *us*. Even though you say about, "Pray for the well-being of the government," that it refers to fear of God with *dveykes*, why did that Rabbi Nakhmen write in *Kitser Likutay Mohoran* that it's a *mitsve* (good deed) for the tsadek to give a bribe to the idolator? Maybe he also meant 'to give a bribe to idolators who lived eighteen hundred years ago?'" (L 15, E 44)

Perl thus uses Hasidic and traditional literary conventions against themselves, to suggest that literary bad faith, the inherent unreliability of any Hasidic representation, must be extended to other contexts as well. Indeed, if these words in Hasidic texts do not adequately describe their referents, then perhaps words such as "scholar," "true sage," and, of course, "Zaddik" should be taken with more than a grain of salt themselves. Such unreliability is both predicated on active Hasidic malfeasance, as (Perl would like us to presume) in the latter case, and an inherent blindness born of the perceptual corruption which stems from the immersion in Hasidic culture, as in Ovadia's first notice.

Such weakening of the powers of description should not be taken to imply that *Megale Temirin* lacks for descriptions. Quite the contrary; when it comes to characterizations of Hasidic ceremonies,[28] *toyre* (teachings),[29] *pidyonim* (monetary gifts for divine intervention),[30] and the like, Perl's Hasidim are quite voluble and quote such materials at length. Such detailed, almost seemingly transcribed accounts of largely formalized and textualized activities dovetail neatly with *Megale Temirin*'s detailed footnotes, which cite (decontextualized) actual Hasidic textual sources in order to delegitimize them. Indeed, as many critics have noted, it is from Perl's work, here and in his non-fiction *Uber das Wesen der Sekte Hassidism*, that we learn much about contemporary Hasidism, and in fact there are no other extant copies of some of the Hasidic works excerpted in Perl's footnotes.[31] It is this very textuality, however—this attempt to turn a narrative into a pseudo-*sefer* (sacred book)—which again reiterates the marginality of the representational enterprise. The subtitle of Perl's *Uber das Wesen der Sekte Hasidism* claims that work's anti-Hasidic attacks are based on the movement's own works, and critics have noted that such a textualized attack is rare in anti-Hasidic works.

But Perl's textual descriptions may also stem from a desire to marginalize the Hasidic movement by formalistically divorcing it from the "real" shtetl. Up in the air as it is, with letters flying back and forth, and fussily shoved into the library from life through its reams of footnotes, it seems to express its own disconnectedness even while purportedly stressing its own authenticity (aside from the footnotes, the Hebrew version of *Megale Temirin* contains an approbation, acknowledgements, an important notice, a prologue, a lexicon, and a bibliography). In doing so, Perl uses marginalized representation to cast Hasidim as truly marginal to Eastern European Jewish life, as a foreign body attacking Judaism that had to be forcibly removed. In short, *Megale Temirin*, borrowing in this way as in so many others from the target of its parody, the *Shivkhei*, has developed a series of literary and formalistic constraints that cast doubt on the values expressed within the work even as they purportedly strive to perpetuate them.

However, Perl's argument against Hasidic descriptive and representational practices, may be expanded in a way he did not intend: in casting doubt on these particular representative practices, he also unavoidably casts doubt on the entire system of literary representation within the book. Just to take one example—critiques of Hasidic textuality in *Megale Temirin* may become more complicated when one realizes that Perl's antidote to this non-representational Hasidic literature is itself highly textualized: in discussing the *bukh*, the bane of Hasidic existence and Perl's salvific instrument, a Hasid notes that "everything [the author] wrote in this *bukh* he reproduced from their books and he copied everything from their own words," meaning Perl's own approved canon of traditional Jewish literature (L 17, E 53).[32] This seems to be more than using Hasidic letters to display Hasidic bad behavior, kept in secret: rather, it asks whether we can ever know what these stories, or any stories, mean at all.

This "secret" anxiety about the value of direct representation—an ana-gogical stand-in for the anxiety inherent in the subversive use of tradi-tional means and genres by maskilic figures for their polemic purposes—will "reveal" itself in fissures, tensions, and self-contradictions in the two maskilic works we will now take up.

Yisroel Aksenfeld's The Headband

One of the first and most important nineteenth-century Yiddish novels, Yisroel Aksenfeld's *Dos Shterntikhl* (*The Headband*), remains a vital text for anyone interested in varying representations of contemporary Eastern European Jewish life;[33] indeed, Aksenfeld seems to be full of descriptive-ness, often at the expense of novelistic flow, as in his long excurses describ-ing individuals' clothing styles (e.g., Y 158–159, E 146–147), and most famously, in the novel's opening passage, which provides a taxonomy of Jewish domestic arrangements.

> Anyone familiar with our Russian Poland knows what Jews mean by a small *shtetl*, a little town. A small *shtetl* has a few small cabins, and a fair every other Sunday. The Jews deal in liquor, grain, burlap, or tar. Usually, there's one man striving to be a Hassidic rebbe.
>
> A *shtot*, on the other hand, contains several hundred wooden homes (that's what they call a house: a home) and a row of brick shops. There are: a very rich man (a parvenu), several well-to-do storekeepers, a few dealers in fields, hareskins, wax, honey, some big money lenders, who use cash either belonging to the rich man, going halves on the profits, or to the ten-ant farmers and tenant innkeepers in the surrounding area. Such a town has a Polish landowner (the *porits*) with his manor. He owns the town and some ten villages, this entire district being known as a *shlisl*. Some promi-nent Jew, who is held in esteem at the manor, leases the entire town or even the entire district. Such a town also has a Jewish VIP, who is a big shot with the district police chief. Such a town has an intriguer, who is always litigat-ing with the town and the Jewish community administration, even on the level of the provincial government. In such a town, the landowner tries to get a Hassidic rebbe to take up residence, because if Jews come to him from all over, you can sell them vodka, ale, and mead. All these goods belong to the landowner, and so up goes his income. Such a town has a winehouse keeper, a watchmaker, and a doctor, a past cantor and a present cantor, a

broker, a madman, and an abandoned wife (an *agunah*), community bea-
dles, and a caterer. Such a town has a tailor's association, a burial association, a Talmud association, and a free loan association. Such a town has
various types of synagogues: a *shul* (mainly for the Sabbath and holidays), a
bes-medresh (the house of study, for everyday use), and sometimes even a
klaizl (a smaller house of worship) or a *shtibl* (a small hasidic synagogue).
God forbid that anyone should accidentally blurt out the wrong word and
call the town a *shtetl*! He'll instantly be branded as the local smartass or
madman. (Y 21–22, E 49–50)[34]

Though Aksenfeld's detailed descriptions first suggest a commitment to a
school of mimetic descriptiveness, and indeed, Aksenfeld's insistence on
the "literal truthfulness of his plots" is well known,[35] a closer look at the
novel reveals a pervasive doubt over its own representative nature. Even a
cursory look at the passage above, with its constant refrain of "Such a
town . . . ," suggests a movement from prescriptiveness to descriptiveness,
from specific observation towards universalist, typological, and taxonomic
description. The passage's last sentence, apparently mocking the observer's
inability to properly describe his surroundings, may also suggest the privileging of the shared, categorized structure over attempts to encounter
local culture locally, even if mistakenly. The narrator's ironic tone in the
passage, both subscribing to and denying this hierarchy of values, suggests
the ambivalent attitude towards these representative strategies, as well as
revealing continuities of anxiety between Perl and Aksenfeld concerning
the Eastern European Jew's perceptual corruption.

And indeed, the constant effort to efface particularity lends itself to real
questions about the actual value of the descriptions it provides: in Aksenfeld's effort to assert that every town is like this, he forces us to question if
any town is like this. To reinforce this uncertainty, he even names one of
the towns "Nosuchville" (*Lohoyepolie*; Y 22, E 50); "Nosuchville" however,
is not a simply a place that isn't, but the place that infinitely could be:
Aksenfeld takes great pains to tell us that "anything can happen in
Nosuchville," and that "the city has something new every day" (Y 62, E 79).
In stressing the setting's simultaneous location at the heart and outside the
boundaries of Eastern European Jewish life, Aksenfeld evokes Nachman's
Tales as well as Western European and Russian satirical works by writers
such as Butler, More, and Gogol.

Though these onomastic and satirical methodologies may well be
largely drawn from Western literary influences, there is another anti-rep-

resentative trend which is far less likely to be taken from those sources: the subtle way in which Aksenfeld couches his presentation of certain spaces in allusive religious language, thereby creating continuities (if subversive ones) with larger trends in Jewish history and myth. In using this material, however, Aksenfeld's text reveals its own anxieties about the implications of those literary choices. To take one example: it is hardly coincidental that the maskilic character's epiphanic conversion to *Bildung* and *Kultur*, in the city of Breslau, takes place in a garden. Unquestionably, in choosing this paradigmatic newly configured modern space, the apotheosis of Jacob Katz's semi-neutral locale,[36] Aksenfeld is evoking a realistic moment in modern Jewish acculturation; the language in which scene is presented, however, transcends realistic description, jolting the nineteenth century reader into activating reading strategies taken from traditional Jewish text.

First, Mikhel sees "thousands of Germans, men and women, old and young, in fine, festive clothes, strolling out of the town. Where were they heading? Not to a *bes medresh* (house of study) because there was no filthy *bes medresh* in Breslau. Nor to perform *tashlekh*, the rite in which men shake out their pockets into a stream to wash away all their sins for a new year" (Y 93, E 100).[37] Instead, these Germans are returning to an Edenic paradise, entering a classic bourgeois *biergarten*, and Mikhel enters "through the beautiful gates of the garden, along with all of the lords and ladies" (Y 94, E 101). After an extensive description of the garden and Mikhel's participation in its activities, Mikhel wonders: "Just think! For one Polish gulden, he was in Paradise among gentlemen, and such lovely, radiant ladies! . . . He strolled about in Paradise for two whole hours" (Y 96–97, E 103). As this becomes clear, we see that both Mikhel's original suppositions are correct. Aksenfeld presents the hypothesis of *tashlekh* to suggest that in dressing up and making themselves *salonfahig* (socially acceptable), these Jews are not only purifying themselves from the sins of their corrupt community, but are also attending a new kind of *bes medresh*, a school for manners, culture, and behavior.

Notably, Mikhel compares the platform in the middle of the garden to "something like the kind from which the Torah is read in synagogue (if you'll excuse the blasphemous comparison)" (Y 95, E 102). On further reflection, however, it may not be immediately clear which element of the comparison renders the connection "blasphemous": traditional hierarchies naturally privilege the Jewish over the secular, but maskilic subversion often reverses this way of seeing things, considering it artificially constructed, not based on actual perception. Here too we see the fact of perceptual corruption alluded to within the text, harnessed to an anxiety as to whether the text itself by its very nature—by engagement in the strategy of the subversive use of traditional strategies—is also corrupted.

Aksenfeld uses this consciously problematic strategy with regard to time as well as space. In locating the novel's events on or around particular Jewish fast days and holidays, he does not merely take advantage of common cultural conventions to ground his maskilic text in a Jewish continuum, but also reinforces the presentation of a narrative which precariously balances between this time and all time. Mikhel Gravestone is forced out of his marriage to Sheyntse, setting the story's action in notion, on the Tenth of Tevet (Y 33, E 58). Just as this day traditionally commemorates the beginning of the siege of Jerusalem which culminated in the Temple's destruction on the ninth of Av, this action marks the beginning of the siege that will eventually end the dominance of the area's stupid and corrupt Hasidic rebbe. Aksenfeld further develops this schema by dating the first appearance of an apparent poltergeist in the cellar of Markel's saloon to the ninth of Av (Y 71, E 85). By novel's end, when the "poltergeist" is revealed to be merely Mikhel and his beloved Sheyntse secretly meeting in the cellar, and the copy of the Zohar used to "exorcise" them and reinforce the rebbe's power is revealed to be useless, we realize that Aksenfeld has again used dating to suggest symbolic time: the destruction and catastrophic end for believers in such superstition. Indeed, these revelations, along with many others, unfold on the Sabbath of Hanukkah (Y 148, E 139), a time where *pirsumei nisa*, the publicization of the miracle, is mandated to occur—only here the miracle to be publicized is the truth revealed by maskilic writers.

These trends in Aksenfeld's work echo Rabbi Nachman's movement towards symbolic space and time; both writers' works attempt to express the universality of the struggle between good and evil played out in an abstracted setting. True, Aksenfeld's canvas is more localized, given his desire to mythicize a particular contemporary struggle, rather than characterize a universalized metaphysical struggle in corresponding terms. Nonetheless, Aksenfeld's strategies here, in line with so many maskilic strategies, use traditional techniques like this against themselves, begging the question of writerly anxiety towards adoption of such techniques viewed (at least theoretically) as purely instrumental. In this light, the work's leading metaphorical structure—the headband itself—may be interpreted to symbolize not only the commodification of traditional erotic relations, but also maskilic literary strategy, which brings happiness to suffering good people even—and perhaps specifically—under false pretenses and using techniques they find to be problematic, in order to win their beautiful women—that is, unenlightened Eastern European Jewry.[38]

Like so many of the authors we have discussed, Aksenfeld expresses his concerns about adopting these "problematic" techniques by presenting something that is not what it seems to be: the headband Mikhel triumphantly presents Sheyntse is a false one, and Mikhel, though attempting to remain unapologetic, seems defensive in explaining his actions to his father-in-law, Velvele:

> "I enjoyed the story [told about a false headband] more than anyone else did. I, a Jew from Nosuchville, had never known there was such a thing as false pearls. And I thought to myself: 'That's the balm for all the wounds in my heart. I can make my Sheyntse a nice big headband for very little money.' And that's what I did. And I didn't have to hunt for any more business. The small sum I already had was enough for me. I took the stagecoach home and made my—today she's also your—Sheyntse happy. She'll never know the truth, and none of our Jews can tell the difference between real and phony pearls."
>
> "Yes indeed, my wise expert!" said Velvele. "What you've done is ingenious. You got what you wanted with a phony headband. Now why do you carry on about hasidic rebbes fooling people? People want to be fooled. Are they experts, after all? Are they Mikhels? Tell me."
>
> "Don't be offended, father-in-law, but how can you compare my brainstorm to the lies, falsehoods, and deceptions practiced by the Hassidic rebbes?" rejoined Mikhel. "When it comes to worldly things, when people are only after money or silly ornaments or wasteful things, then they deserve to be punished, we ought to fool them. There are lots of fine countries in the world where the women don't have pearl-encrusted horse collars on their heads....And there are so many other silly and crazy things like that. So it's no sin to make fools of people like that." (Y 189–190, E 168–169)

In Mikhel's ardent attempts to distinguish his own "brainstorm" from Hasidic "falsehoods," his fools' pearls from Hasidic rebbes' relics, we see the anxiety of proximate techniques; and in his transformation of his central metaphor into something illusory, Aksenfeld calls into question his entire literary strategy of representation. The resulting uneasiness is only exacerbated by the rash of sudden unmaskings at the end of the novel, where multiple characters reveal that they are not whom they appear to be, in a series of credulity-stretching reunions and revelations which implicate every person in the narrative in wider reunions, their revealed secrets investing the novel's every previous detail with meaning (Y 163–180, E 150–160). This is reminiscent not only of tropes in both the *Shivkhei HaBesht* and *Megale Temirin*, but also of the corollary questions raised by those texts: if things and people aren't what they seem, what are the implications for a movement based on rationalist, neoclassical aesthetic principles of imitation, which says that the literary depiction of something is, in essence, what it is? We must ask if accepting this narrative unproblematically places us in the same situation as Sheyntse, and if Aksenfeld, in desiring his readers to become more like him (or Mikhel, his presumed stand in), wishes us to take apart his novel's claims.

If so, Aksenfeld's *The Headband* becomes a seminal maskilic text not in its certainty, but in its doubt: about itself and about its methods. In adopting these doubtful methods, these authors and their texts necessarily generate some internal stress.[39] These same stresses and fissures will be even more strongly evident in the remaining maskilic text to be considered. Our final author, indeed, will apotheosize this ambivalence, developing it into full-fledged psychosis.

S. Y. Abramovitch: Fishke the Lame

Though this essay's argument is largely dedicated to the relationship between Hasidic and maskilic literature, ending this discussion is impossible without treating the figure who exemplified the transition away from the *Haskalah*: Sholem Yankev Abramovitch, who, in works like "The Mare," carefully and critically anatomizes the failure of the Russian *Haskalah*'s project in a complex allegory. Here, however, we will focus not on Abramovitch's allegorical work but rather on the "mimetic" material which earned him the traditional critical evaluation as the writer who has presented the most powerful and realistic image of Eastern European Jewry; David Frishman's famous remark that were all of Eastern European Jewish life to disappear it could be recreated from Abramovitch's work serves as the most powerful case in point.[40] More recent critics, Dan Miron in particular, have strongly challenged this evaluation;[41] in analyzing the topic in Abramovitch's ostensibly "most realistic" work, *Fishke der Krumer*, we may be able to place such recent critical activity within a historical-literary context, showing how Abramovitch elevates the questions and tensions about representation we have discussed to a new level.[42]

Abramovitch employs a number of complex representational strategies now familiar to us from earlier maskilic works. Mendele's famous taxonomy of the various types of Jewish beggars, for example (Y 80–81, E 237–238), is reminiscent of—but far transcends—Aksenfeld's comparatively demure typology of towns. Indeed, Mendele's taxonomic impulse borders on obsession, and his urge to categorize leads to an apparently studied effort to render realia irrelevant:

> "Reb Alter," I said after I had succeeded in arranging our beggars in the above order from Fishke's description. "Reb Alter, remind me, I beg you, if you remember any other sorts of beggars, who I've forgotten, God forbid, to include on my list."
>
> "What difference would it make?" Alter answered and looked at me like a grown man looks at a boy who is making a fool of himself. "O-vah, he has, God forbid, forgotten! Such an important list! And if you're not included in the list, you can't be a beggar?"
>
> "Don't say that, Reb Alter!" I defended myself. "Our paupers are very conscious of their dignity. They seek honor with all their might. Insult a pauper and he will remind you of it to the end of your days!" (Y 81–82, E 238)

Other similar strategies of description within the novel call this one (and, simultaneously, themselves) into question, their overwhelming and obsessive provision of detail sowing doubt while providing information. The taxonomical impulse towards great specialization of persons, for example, seems weakened by a later characterization where, rather than many people only having one specific type of function, one person has many functions:

> The poorhouse keeper and his family lived there too in a little alcove that was an excuse for a room. Aside from being poorhouse keeper, grave digger, official in the burial society, inspector of the charity hospital, Queen Vashti in the Purim play, a bear during *Simkhes Toyre*, a waiter, a punster at all weddings and circumcisions, he had another business: he made wax candles. (Y 102, E 257)

Even more radically, says Mendele, Jews tend to refer to things as they aren't, illustrating how their language of description, the signifier, is delinked from the conventionally understood signified: "Hence, the janitor of a government school for Jews is known as 'the inspector'; a Jew who delivers letters is 'a post office official"; and a Jew who works in the post office proper is a 'postmaster'" (Y 65, E 223). Simultaneously and contradictorily, certain semantically meaningless sounds can have an infinitude of potential meanings: "ett," for example, "which can signify a lot or a little depending on how adept one is at taking a hint" (Y 20–21, E 178), or "beh," which Mendele describes as follows:

> "In a word, beh has a variety of tastes and all sorts of interpretations, such as, for example: come, if you dare! The goose is cooked! I'm on your side! Do your worst! A plague upon you! A Jewish mind will always divine the proper meaning of "beh" under the given circumstances. The direction in which the beh will be aimed will always be clear." (Y 29, E 186–187)

As such, we begin to see how Abramovitch's seeming commitment to detailed mimetic descriptiveness through a luxurious engagement of varying strategies of description in truth replicates the self-contradictory nature of this description.

Such contradiction is not limited to persons or to speech: Abramovitch and his narratorial surrogates continue to encounter places that contradict simple characterizations of "the way things are," encounters which indicate Abramovitch's development of Aksenfeld's anxieties about both typological and direct representation. In Odessa, for example, Fishke learns that things are different from how, as far as he is concerned, they usually are:

> Everything was new to me, new and strange. I couldn't find a poorhouse like in other Jewish towns. There were no houses to go into either. In our Jewish cities, there are houses—plain houses, nothing fancy, one-story, with the entrance off the street. Push the door, just crack it open, and you're smack in the middle of the house. No big ceremonies, everything you need is right there. . . . But in Odessa, the houses are crazy. (Y 135, E 288–289)

It is natural that Odessa, a center of enlightenment, would differ from Fishke's typical, more traditional, milieux. However, Abramovitch presents this locale as so foreign to the traditional system of description and representation that it shatters any possibilities of Fishke's describing or representing it. As Fishke sums it up: "Everything here is topsy-turvy. It's as if they were trying to make fun of the world" (Y 146, E 298). The Yiddish reads: "*bay aykh is alz vild, khoyzek ingantzn; dayn odes is far mir nisht keyn ort.*" For Fishke, the problems of representing Odessa are so dire that they even result in a denial of the place's existence, if we read the Yiddish literally ("for me, your Odessa is not a place") as well as idiomatically ("your Odessa's not my kind of place"). As one can see from Fishke's meeting with a maskil where he confuses the words "author" and "beggar," with farcically comic results, playing on the phonologically similar *mekhaber/khiber/khaver* (Y 137–138, E 290–291), Odessa's denizens and its visitors do not even share the same basic descriptive vocabulary, and this stands as a reproach to the possibilities for characters—and, by some extension, the writers of those characters—to represent those experiences.

One does not have to visit Odessa, however, to see how Abramovitch marginalizes what seemed to be straightforward strategies of direct representation. When Fishke sings the praise of Glupsk to his beloved hunch-backed girl, his encomia seemingly consists of the fact that in Glupsk, no clear lessons can be learned from perceptions at all:

> The people there are plain folk, with no fancy ceremonies. They all do as they please and nobody cares. For example, well-to-do merchants walk around in rags, dirty and unwashed, and—nothing! Or they go strolling in bright day light in greasy coats, unbuttoned, with coattails flying, and—nothing! Or, on the other hand, you'll sometimes see beggars in velvets and silks and, again—nothing! In short, in Glupsk it's hard to tell the beggars from the rich, either by their dress or their actions. (Y 128, E 281)

Though Fishke's intent is to praise the possibilities of economic liberation—"even I, as you see me sitting here, can become a somebody," he says (Y 128, E 281), we may also take this as Abramovitch's fantasia on the possibilities of liberation from the anxieties of representative description.

Abramovitch goes significantly further in critiquing Jewish descriptive practices than merely observing the delinking of objects and their descriptions, however. In *Fishke der krumer*, Abramovitch reveals his discovery of, and horror at, a particular pathology haunting Eastern European Jewish life and literature: the corruption of perceptual stimuli so that everything is seen as its reverse. We have seen this "reversed perception" in the *Shivkhei*, among other places, but while the *Shivkhei* uses it to indicate the debased perceptions of those distant from the Zaddik, Abramovitch expands its use to implicate not just the people he addresses, but Mendele, and, perhaps, himself as well.

Mendele himself seems aware that the Jewish community as a whole has this problem, as the first sentences of the novel's first chapter indicate: "Just when the bright sun begins to shine proclaiming another summer to the land, when people feel newly born and their hearts fill with joy at the sight of God's glorious world—just then the time for wailing and weeping arrives among Jews" (Y 17, E 174). Aside from traditional Jewry's calendrical subversion of natural, external norms, Mendele notes how Jews debase or deform many natural internal, bodily conditions: he remarks that Jews seem to have been able to "[break] themselves of the vile passion of eating" (Y 25, E 183).[43] This process also extends to the sexual sphere; for example, the novel boasts numerous descriptions of masochistic relationships, where pain is transformed in Jews' eyes into pleasure. When Fishke sees his wife seduced by the red-haired beggar, for example, he remarks: "Sometimes I was very angry, burning mad but at the same time, I don't know why, I was drawn to her. It was like magic. It was like—how can I explain it—like scratching one of those itching sores that I get sometimes. It was pain and pleasure, both together" (Y 87, E 243), and notes that "the more I cooled toward my wife, the more she warmed up to me" (Y 100, E 255).

Characters' perceptions of nature—and their perceptions of those perceptions—are key metaphorical structures in anatomizing this state of perceptual corruption, and Abramovitch's presentation of these perceptions is encapsulated in the novel's first moments, where Mendele's lyrical descriptions of nature are immediately demonized as products of the "Evil Genius"(Y 17, E 174–175). A similar treatment of nature—a first positive perception (that is, one which focuses on nature's beauty) corrupted through a distorted, psychologized lens into a view of the natural world as at best depressing and at worst dangerous is apparent throughout the novel. Running into the forest to look for his lost horses, Mendele remarks, after first providing a realistic, positive description of the forest:

> Fantasy, that terrible prankster and notorious liar, began to play havoc with my thoughts. He shipped me a supply of wild and terrifying images and my mental factory reworked this raw material and made it even more fantastic. In this shipment I found a corpse, the murdered Alter Yaknehoz, and the bones of our horses. My mind refined upon this and developed it into a

fiery red monster and a wolf of tremendous size with huge frightening teeth. (Y 48, E 206)

In Yiddish, Mendele refers to this force haunting him as *der koyekh-hame-dume*, explicitly linking it to creative and imaginative capacity. And indeed, one of Mendele's last observations in the novel concerns his changing perceptions of nature:

> Then I glanced up at the sky. The moon and stars were going their way, but they looked different from before. They were not as friendly. They had become distant and haughty. My heart grew sad and heavy. (Y 161, E 311)

Mendele (and certainly Abramovitch) is aware of the subjectivity of the above description; nature has been confined and delimited to traditional Jewish descriptive practices, its particularly corrupt anthropomorphicizations, with tragic results. This changing perception is adumbrated in its greatest detail in metonymic reference to Mendele's famed Glupsk:

> The green hill of Glupsk is known almost all over the world. There is an ancient folk song, sung by young and old, about it. Mothers and wet-nurses soothe their crying babes and rock them to sleep with it. My own mother, may she thrive in Paradise, also used to sing me this song when I was still in diapers:
>
> > Way up yon green hill,
> > Where the grass grows still,
> > A pair of Germans stand
> > Their long whips in hand.
> > Tall men two are they,
> > But their pants are short,
> > Our Father, our King . . .
>
> This used to be my favorite song. Somehow, my childish mind imagined the green hill to be wondrously beautiful. I used to think that it was not made of common soil like the other hills around my town, but of some indescribably rare and delightful stuff—like Mount Olive or Mount Lebanon—of the soil of the land of Israel. . . .
>
> In later years, when I had outgrown my children's shoes and had seen something of the world, I looked at things with different eyes and under-

stood the true meaning of the little ditty. The green hill was really nothing more than an ordinary hill—not green, but muddy, full of ruts. (Y 157, E 308)

By now, however, we are unable to view Mendele's move from childhood to adulthood, from idealizing Glupsk's beauty to apotheosizing its ugliness, as a simple transition from the "false" to the "true." Not when Abramovitch implicates Mendele's subjectivity throughout the novel. In doing so, he puts not merely traditional society on trial, but himself, and thus the maskilic positions he qualifiedly represents, as well.

We might feel some trepidation about conflating Mendele's anxiety over representation with Abramovitch's positions were it not for the fact that Abramovitch may express similar sentiments himself. In his introduction and dedication to the 1888 version of *Fishke*, Abramovitch (in this section, signed "The Author," it is presumably Abramovitch speaking, though certainty is impossible) writes to Menashe Margolius that his pen is "gaunt and shriveled," and that he seems to be unable to represent Jews in any way other than through the *torbe*, the beggar's sack. He writes:

It has been my lot to descend to the depths, to the cellars of our Jewish life. My stock in trade is: rags and moldy wares. My dealings are with paupers and beggars, the poor wretches of life; with degenerates, cripples, charlatans, and other unfortunates, the dregs of humanity. I always dream of beggars. Before my eyes, I always see a sack soaring—the old, familiar Jewish beggar sack. No matter which way I turn my eyes, the sack is before me. No matter what I say or do, the sack comes soaring up to me! Oy, it's always the sack, the Jewish beggar sack! (Y 14, E 172–173)

Abramovitch's maskilic efforts—constantly associated with questions of stunted, corrupted representation—have led him to real doubts about the literary value of his own polemically charged work. Abramovitch uses Fishke as a leading metaphor to address this question. His self-diagnosed writer's illness is reflected in Fishke, not only physically lame, but literarily so as well: his art is his storytelling ability, and he has a speech defect (Y 83, E 240). Fishke's constant attempts to escape the red-haired bastard and to find romance with the hunchbacked girl correspond to Abramovitch's desire to provide realism without being haunted by the Jewish beggar's sack, by his ideological and polemical constraints, and his hope that he can, indeed, do so.

Both Fishke's crippled stature and his potential for transcendence are expressed in Mendele's description of him: "a creature like so many other wretched souls who appear among us children of Israel, from nowhere, like toadstools after a rainstorm, full-blown, with all their earmarks, without giving the slightest hint that they are budding and about to burst into bloom!" (Y 35, E 193). And it is Abramovitch's rueful awareness that it is he who is the crippled one that yields the explicitly fantastic, fairy-tale resonances of Fishke's description of romantic empowerment:

> Finally, with God's help, she began to move. I lifted her with a power that was not mine and carried her to my corner. I could swear at that moment I walked straight, like other people, without a sign of limping! Slowly, slowly, she opened her eyes and sighed softly. The whole world belonged to me. I felt like the beggar in the fairy tale when his hovel suddenly turns into a huge palace and he finds himself sitting with his queen at a table loaded with food. I took my coat off and quickly wrapped it around my queen, who was shivering with cold. (Y 104, E 258)

The fairy-tale structure, first used by Fishke as metaphor, bleeds into the next level of narration: though the metaphor has ended, the hunchbacked girl remains a "queen." This capacity for narrative transcendence in Fishke's inspiration seems to give Mendele new resolution to attempt to transcend his own limitations, a resolution which fulfills the wishes expressed in the author's preface:

> I promised myself to be more careful in the future, to think twice before speaking once, to do as many of our successful and clever people do—to see and hear only what it pays to notice. From now on, I would utter only words of praise so as to be more popular among the people. (Y 108, E 261)

But Abramovitch and Mendele give us little reason to believe that such a resolution will—or indeed can—be carried out. Significantly, the only individuals in the narrative who seem to be able to escape the constraints of their own selves are the band of beggars; though the indisputed villains of the piece, their transvaluative ability to put on an act whenever they like (Y 90, E 247) and to "ma[ke] fun of the whole world" (Y 89, E 246) engenders veiled jealousy and admiration as it reemphasizes Fishke's (and Mendele's and Abramovitch's) inability to behave likewise. When the red-haired bastard taunts Fishke by throwing him out of the wagon, and saying: "'Folks! Fishke isn't lame at all! He is only acting lame and putting us all to shame, the faker!'" (Y 92, E 248), it is the harshest possible joke: if only one *could* change the way one looks (in both senses of that last word).

Abramovitch's doubt over his own representative strategies is also illustrated in his novel's complex narratological structure. Narratological complexity, as we have seen in Perl's *Megale Temirin*, is part and parcel of both maskilic literature and both the Hasidic and Western traditions that influence it; unlike in the former and (mostly) in the latter, Abramovitch's treatment sows doubt and anxiety rather than reinforcing authenticity. This is clear not merely from the classic distinction between the figures of Abramovitch and Mendele but from Mendele's subsequent split in the novel into two opposing selves who converse (Y 50–52, E 208–210),[44] to say nothing of the possible divisions in the narratorial roles between the Mendele of the introduction, the Mendele of the narrative, and the other narrators within the text: Alter Yaknehoz and especially Fishke. The joint narrative effort of the three, coded as equally subjective, is described in the telling of Fishke's story: "Fishke began again in his fashion, I worked and helped him along in mine, Alter drove us both along in his, and the story continues" (Y 89, E 246).

Mendele muses that "Had a talented writer seen us out that fine morning, he would have found ample material for a poem" (Y72, E 230), and the narratorial fissures and stresses and their role within the novel indicate a commensurate fissure with the engagement of the writer and their art. Late in the novel, Mendele tries to interrupt the story of Fishke with a story of his own, but decides against it, saying: "'Somehow, I don't feel like telling that story today. They can all go to the devil. I hope you don't mind, Reb Alter!'" Alter responds: "'But what kind of manners is it to interrupt someone, to break into his story, to tell your own?'" (Y 123, E 277). This is the essential question of *Fishke der krumer*, and it is a question which can be expanded to investigate how these stresses and interruptions indicate analogous gaps between the maskil or reformist and the subject of reform. Abramovitch truly wrestles with the issue of how and whether he can set himself apart from the group with whom he is taking issue. How could he not, when much of the book mimics his own life experiences, wandering around Podolia and Volhynia with Avreml Khromoy after his orphanhood?

More subtly, Abramovitch hints at these questions onomastically by naming the novel's other main character Alter Yaknehoz. Abramovitch was certainly mindful of the the word *yaknehoz*'s colloquial sense: "goods serv-

ing the religious needs of the people and yielding but little income . . . useless, profitless items."[45] Abramovitch was also certainly well aware, however, of the technical meaning of this technical term: *yaknehoz* is an
acronym for the order of blessings made during the concluding service of
a Sabbath night which immediately leads into a holiday (*yayin, kiddush,
ner, havdala, zman*). On such an occasion, the unusual blessing recited is
"*hamavdil bein kodesh lekodesh*," "one who distinguishes between holy and
holy." But such distinctions are fuzzy and by definition ambiguous; perhaps God can make them, but such power seems beyond not only Alter,
dragged unwillingly into the narrative as Fishke reveals his love interest to
be Alter's daughter, but also Mendele, jolted into the story through a colli-
sion with Alter's wagon.[46] Indeed, the narrative seems to be constructed
from the inside out, as every element becomes linked to every other element. Just as for Alter there is no escape from the past, for Mendele there
is no escape from the story and the mixed lessons that it teaches about the
ambivalent possibilities of art and action.

A final metaphorical structure, employed earlier by Aksenfeld, reinforces Abramovitch's message of self-implication. *Fishke der Krumer*
begins on the seventeenth of Tammuz, the day that the walls of the temple
were breached (Y 17, E 174).[47] Walls are breached here too: Mendele breaks
through the walls between mythic past and realistic present, when he
muses

> about [the Jews'] wisdom, their mode of living, their communal leaders,
> and their sorry condition. My thoughts strayed hither and thither. Before
> me I saw the horned monster, Nebuchadnezzar and his army, bloody bat-
> tles, confusion and commotion. The army tore down walls, smashed out
> doors and windows. Jews, with many packages of wares and old clothes,
> cried for help and mustering their courage—fled. I seized a stick and was
> about to—when boom! I found myself stretched out flat on my back on the
> ground. (Y 19, E 176).

Mendele's oneiric self-projection into historical narrative reminds us, brilliantly, of how easily the walls between narrator and narrative are broken
as well, which, in turn, remind us of the mournful effect such objects of
description have on their ultimate chronicler. Abramovitch had learned
the lessons of the *Haskalah* too well, and they had stunted him and his literature for life. Later Yiddish writers, unaffiliated with the *Haskalah* and
its engagement in turn with Hasidic literature and the representational

anxieties it engendered, far less moored to traditional materials and with primary interlocutors such as modernism, neo-folkism, expressionism, socialist realism, and a host of other movements, would usher in a new era of representation and adopt new literary strategies in depicting Eastern European Jewry. But this is the province of the twentieth century, and thus another topic entirely.

N O T E S

1. The following article first appeared in slightly different form under the title "Looking Again: Representation in Nineteenth-Century Yiddish Literature," in *Prooftexts* Vol. 2, No. 3 (2005), pp. 277–320. I wish to express my gratitude to Indiana University Press for their kind agreement to allow the article to be reprinted here.

2. The former citation is taken from *Die Geschichten vom Ba'al Schem Tov: Schivche ha-Bescht* (Wiesbaden, 1997, Vol. 1: Hebrew, Vol. 2: Yiddish). Translations and citations are from Dan Ben-Amos and Jerome Mintz's translation of the Hebrew version, *In Praise of the Ba'al Shem Tov: The Earliest Collection of Legends About the Founder of Hasidism* (Northvale, NJ, 1993), future references to which will appear in the text as "E" (here, E 124–125), and to the Hebrew and Yiddish versions, where applicable, in the critical editions as "H" and "Y"; here, H 108–109, Y 59–60. The latter is the account of David Eynhorn, Abramovitch's personal secretary; cited in David Aberbach, *Realism, Caricature, and Bias: The Fiction of Mendele Mocher Seforim* (London, 1993), p. 30.

3. For an example of the former approach, see Khone Shmeruk's and Shmuel Werses' introduction to Joseph Perl, *Maasiyot veigrot mitsadikim umeanshei shlomeinu* (Jerusalem, 1969), edited by Khone Shmeruk and Skmuel Werses; an example of the latter approach is apparent in David Roskies' *A Bridge of Longing: The Lost Art of Yiddish Storytelling* (Cambridge, MA, 1995), which begins a wide-ranging discussion of Yiddish writers with an examination of the work of Nachman of Bratslav.

4. Due to time and space constraints, only a few authors could be chosen, and only one work from each could be studied.

5. Cited in Dan Miron, *A Traveler Disguised* (Syracuse, 1996 [2nd ed.]), p. 204. For other early critical discussion, see the fuller article, "Mendele ushloshet hakerakhim," in *Kol Kitvei Kh. N. Bialik* (Tel Aviv, 1947), pp. 236–239; and Y. Klausner, "Pirkei Mendele," *Metsuda*, Vol. 7 (1954), pp. 347–356, esp. p. 348; Klausner cites Bialik explicitly and approvingly.

6. See the discussion in Miron, *Traveler*, pp. 200–218. As Miron himself indicates, other critics have also adopted this comparative approach: see, for example,

Maycr Viner, *Tsu der geshikhte fun der yidisher literature in 19th yorhundert*, Vol. 2 (New York: YKUF, 1946), pp. 5–14 and 32–46; Sh. Niger, *Mendele Moykher Seforim* (Chicago, 1936), pp. 182–183; and N. Mayzel, "Di hashpoes fun der velt-literatur af mendele mo's," in N. Mayzel, ed., *Dos mendele-bukh* (New York, 1959), pp. 364–374, which contains a useful overview of earlier Yiddish criticism on the topic.

7. See, for example, his "Hadei hasatira shel lukianus besifrut hahaskala haivrit," reprinted in his *Megamot vetsurot besifrut hahaskala* (Jerusalem, 1990), pp. 223–249, and "Iyunim bemivne shel 'Megale Temirin' ve 'Bokhen Tsadik,'" *Tarbiz*, Vol. 31 (1962), pp. 377–411.

8. Concomitantly, early attempts to use Hasidic tales to verify or determine real historical events have been replaced by efforts to view them ideologically, as polemical efforts to increase the movement's popularity and influence, or structurally, emphasizing the manipulation of both Jewish and non-Jewish literary and folk topoi to create compelling narrative. For a collection of recent essays reevaluating both the history and literature of Hasidism, see Ada Rapaport-Albert, ed., *Hasidism Reappraised* (London, 1996), and, for our purposes, esp. Karl Erich Grözinger, "The Source Value of the Basic Rescensions of *Shivhei HaBesht*," pp. 354–363. See also Immanuel Etkes, *Baal Hashem: HaBesht—magiya, mistika, hanhaga* (Jerusalem, 2000), esp. pp. 217–265; Ada Rapoport-Albert, "Hagiography with Footnotes: Edifying Tales and the Writing of History in Hasidism," *History and Theory*, Vol. 27 (1987), pp. 119–159; and Moshe Rosman, *Founder of Hasidism: A Quest for the Historical Ba'al Shem Tov* (Berkeley, 1996). For examples of contemporary literary approaches, see Ora Wiskind-Elper, *Tradition and Fantasy in the Tales of Reb Nahman of Bratslav* (Albany, 1998), and Yoav Elstein, *Haekstaza vehasipur hakhasidi* (Ramat-Gan, 1998).

9. This is not to say that there are *no* such descriptive elements: as Ben-Amos and Mintz suggest in their introduction, arrangements such as "the particulars of business arrangements and the precarious circumstances of keeping the *arrendeh*, the privilege received from the master of the estate to mill grain or distill liquor or to collect taxes" are there as well (p. xxvii).

10. Even in the description of place, vagueness abounds. The Ba'al Shem Tov becomes a successful *melamed* and judges cases in "a community near the community of Brody" (E 19, H 19, Y 13). A city, many of whose citizens are adulterers, is given no name and no identifying details (E 99–101, H 88–89, Y 71–72).

11. Elijah's first revelation to the Ba'al Shem Tov takes place halfway up a mountain, and even the the Ba'al Shem Tov's links to Elijah are related to the transcendence of normal spatial boundaries: according to the text, the Ba'al Shem Tov once noted that he "expected to ascend to heaven in a storm like Elijah the prophet" (E 169, H 167).

12. See Ben Amos and Mintz, *Shivkhei HaBesht*, Introduction, p. xxv.

13. Khone Shmeruk's proof, in his "Hasipurim shel Reb Adam Baal Shem vegilguleihem benuskhaot sefer *Shivkhei HaBesht*," in *Sifrut yidish bepolin:*

mekhkarim veiyunim historiim (Jerusalem, 1981), pp. 119–146, obtains notwith-standing the compiler's efforts to give the work authenticity by saying where he heard the tale.

14. On Nachman of Bratslav and his tales more generally, see, in addition to the sources cited above, Arthur Green, *Tormented Master: A Life of Rabbi Nach-man of Bratslav* (University, Alabama, 1979); Mendel Piekarz, *Khasidut bratslav: prakim bekhayei mekhollela uviketaveha* (Jerusalem, 1995); Roskies, *Bridge of Long-ing*, pp. 20–55; Arnold Band, Introduction, in Arnold Band, ed. and trans., *Nah-man of Bratslav: The Tales* (New York, 1978), pp. 9–48; idem., "The Function of the Enigmatic in Two Hasidic Tales," in Joseph Dan and Frank Talmadge, eds., *Studies in Jewish Mysticism* (Cambridge, MA, 1978), pp. 185–210; Sh. Niger, "R[eb] Nakhman Bratslaver un zayne sipurey-mayses," in idem., *Bleter-geshikhte fun der yidisher literatur* (New York, 1959), pp. 111–177; and now the collection of studies, *God's Voice From the Void: Old and New Studies in Bratslav Hasidism* (Albany, 2002), edited by Shaul Magid.

15. The *Sipurei Mayses* were first published in a bilingual edition in Ostrog in 1815. Though a critical bilingual edition of the *Sipurei Mayses* is a desideratum, Bratslav Hasidim have put out numerous bilingual editions of the work which are, for polemic reasons, quite similar to the original, such as *Sefer Sippurei Ma'asiyot* (Jerusalem, 1975). In this edition, "Ma'ase merav uben yakhid" appears on pp. 58–61; all future page references will appear in the text by the letter H; translations, taken from Band, *Nahman of Bratslav: The Tales*, will be prefaced by an E.

16. See Khayim Liberman, "R[eb] Nakhman Bratslaver un di umaner mas-kilim," in *Ohel Rokhl* (New York, 1980), Vol. 2, pp. 161–197.

17. Similarly, in "The Tale of the Cripple," the eponymous cripple mentions traveling to Leipzig, from where roads go to Breslau. "Ma'ase mekhiger," H 23–24, E 83–84.

18. Cited in Roskies, *A Bridge of Longing*, p. 29; see his discussion there as well as that of Piekarz, *Khasidut bratslav*, pp. 160–184.

19. Miron, *Traveler*, pp. 205–207. See also pp. 215–218, where he discusses "the relation between the pretense of literary veracity in the writings of nineteenth-century Yiddish novelists and their general intellectual commitment to the ideas of the *Haskalah* . . . allegedly lacking in stylistic dignity and barred from aesthetic self-sufficiency, a Yiddish narrative had to possess the merit of being unequivo-cally true."

20. Ian Watt, *The Rise of the Novel* (Berkeley, 1957); for our purposes, see esp. pp. 9–34; quotation from p. 32.

21. On this notion of neoclassical imitation, compare M. H. Abrams, *The Mir-ror and the Lamp: Romantic Theory and the Critical Tradition* (New York, 1953), esp. pp. 13–46. Quotations from pp. 14, 17, 34, 37–39, and 40. Though Abrams is primarily focused on poetry, many of the theoretical considerations advanced

here apply to prose as well; compare also Watt, pp. 15–17, for a slightly more detailed description of the prevalence of "realistic particularity."

22. On Perl more generally, see now Jeremy Dauber, *Antonio's Devils: Writers of the Jewish Enlightenment and the Birth of Modern Hebrew and Yiddish Literature* (Stanford, 2004), pp. 209–310, and the sources cited there.

23. This material has been published in a critical edition edited by Khone Shmeruk and Shmuel Werses; see Perl, *Maasiyot veigrot mitsadikim umeanshei shlomeinu*. For discussion and analysis, see Shmeruk and Werses' introduction, as well as Dauber, *Antonio Devils*, pp. 228–251.

24. Such an argument relies on the assumption that Perl indeed wrote this material for publication for a wide audience, as opposed to simply attempting to preach to the choir and to amuse his fellow maskilim. Such assumptions about audience are never quite as certain in the case of the *Haskalah* (Jewish Enlightenment) as they are often assumed to be; in the case of Perl, whose decision to withhold a Yiddish version of *Megale Temirin*, presumably a more polemically effective work than the actually published Hebrew *Megale Temirin*, these assumptions may be very uncertain indeed.

25. Admittedly, it might be argued that such explicit mentions merely echo Nachman's comparatively more explicit mentions of the maskilim in certain of his tales.

26. *Sefer Megale Temirin* was published in Vienna by Anton Schmid in 1817. The Yiddish version may be found in Zelig Kalmanovitch, ed., *Yoysef Perls yidishe ksovim* (Vilna, 1937). Translations are taken from Dov Taylor's translation of the Hebrew version: *Joseph Perl's Revealer of Secrets: The First Hebrew Novel* (Boulder, 1997). References will be given to both the letter number, preceded by L, and to Taylor's translation, referred to as E.

27. Critics have often commented on Ovadia's invisibility, but less attention has been paid to his ability to travel through the air (Prologue, E 13), which parodically renders him a *luftmensh*, not a Hasidic wonderworker with the ability of *kefitsat hederekh*, shortening of the way. It may also be worth noting in passing how much traveling back and forth appears in the narrative: see, for example, L 54, E 99.

28. See, for example, the description of the Hasidic new moon ceremony (L 9, E 34); what may be a celebration of the *Simkhat beit hashoeiva* (L 34, E 74–75); a description of a Lag B'omer ceremony (L 45, E 87); and a dream interpretation ceremony (L 60, E 109).

29. There are, for example, numerological wordplays or *gimatries* (L 23, E 63–64), and *toyre* (L 62, E 114; L 84, E 150; and L 114, E 193–194). In one case (L 104, E 178–179), the Hasidic *toyre* is explicitly juxtaposed with scientific or rational ideas.

30. See, for example, L 19, E 55–56.

31. For one early seminal observation in this regard, see Simon Dubnow, "Der ershter kamf fun haskole kegn khsides," *YIVO-Bleter*, Vol. 1 (1930), pp. 4–8.

32. On *Megale Temirin* as a "battle of the books," see Dauber, *Antonio's Devils*, pp. 275–285, and especially L 60, E 110, L 77, and E 139–140, where the Ba'al Shem Tov is "shown" to be holier than Elijah based on extensive textual comparison of I–II Kings and the *Shivkhei HaBesht*.

33. *Dos Shterntikhl's* precise date of composition is unknown; it was probably written in the late 1830s or 1840s, and published in 1861. The edition used here is Isroel Aksenfeld, *Dos Shterntikhl* (Buenos Aires, 1971), referred to in the text subsequently as Y; translations are taken from Joachim Neugroschel, *The Headband*, in Joachim Neugroschel, ed., *The Shtetl* (New York, 1979), referred to as E. On Aksenfeld, see Viner, Vol. 1, pp. 65–207; Saul Ginzburg, "New Material Regarding Israel Aksenfeld," *YIVO Annual*, Vol. 5 (1950), pp. 172–183; and Zalman Reyzen, *Fun Mendelson biz Mendele* (Warsaw, 1923), pp. 355–374.

34. A similarly styled narratorial statement of abstracted truth, focusing on the role of the broker in Jewish society and comparing it to in Germany, Russia, and Poland, can be found in Y. Aksenfeld, *Dos Shterntikhl*, pp. 67–68, and J. Neugroschel, *The Shtetl*, pp. 82–83.

35. See Miron, *Traveler*, pp. 212–213 for discussion, where he makes the same point about Isaac Mayer Dik. Compare also Viner, *Tsu der geshikhte fun der yiddisher literatur 19th yorhundert*, Vol. 2, p. 197, who praises Aksenfeld's "reportorial preciseness."

36. Compare Jacob Katz, *Out of the Ghetto: The Social Background of Jewish Emancipation* (New York, 1978 [2nd ed.]), esp. pp. 42–46; I am grateful to David Roskies for this suggestion.

37. The explanation of *tashlekh* is Neugroschel's addition.

38. For alternative readings of the headband metaphor, see Dan Miron, *Bein khazon leemet* (Jerusalem, 1979), esp. p. 199, and his "Folklore and Antifolklore in the Yiddish Fiction of the *Haskalah*," in *The Image of the Shtetl and Other Studies of Modern Jewish Literary Imagination* (Syracuse, 2000), pp. 49–80, esp. pp. 65–67 and 78–79.

39. One can see these stresses at their height in a series of maskilic stories about an encounter between a man and a *gilgul*, a wandering, transmigrated spirit; versions of these stories, written by A. B. Gotlober, Isaac Erter, and Isaac Mayer Dik (the last essentially a translation of Erter's work), themselves call into question the mechanism by which they make their reformist points—namely, the supernatural testimony of a being against whose existence maskilim (and, more importantly, some of the stories) militate. I hope to examine this more closely in a separate article.

40. David Frishman, "Mendele Moykher Sefarim," *Kol Kitvei David Frishman* (Warsaw, 1931), Vol. 6, p. 74.

41. See, for example, the essays in his *Der imazh fun shtetl: dray literarishe shtudyes* (Tel Aviv, 1981), esp. pp. 19–138, and the altered, abridged version which appears as the title essay of his *Image of the Shtetl*, pp. 1–48.

42. The compositional history of *Fishke der krumer* is complex; Abramovitch published a first Yiddish version in 1869, but subsequently produced a significantly revised and expanded version in 1888. (A Hebrew version, with a first draft translated by Bialik and refined by Abramovitch, appeared in 1901.) This essay refers to the 1888 Yiddish version. Citations are taken both from Mendele Moykher Seforim, *Geklibene verk* (New York, 1947), Vol. 3, pp. 13–161 (referred to hereafter in the texts as Y); and Gerald Stillman's translation in Marvin Zuckerman, Gerald Stillman, and Marion Herbst, eds., *Selected Works of Mendele Moykher-Sforim* (Malibu, CA, 1991), pp. 171–312 (referred to hereafter in the texts as E). On Abramovitch in general and *Fishke* in particular, see the sources cited above, as well as Niger, *Mendele Moykher Seforim*, pp. 139–153.

43. The only aspects of nature, for Abramovitch, that Jews *are* in tune with are grotesque ones: the description of Alter's enormous nose and the sound it makes becomes an opportunity for Abramovitch to comment on how Jews seem to humorously reflect nature's thaw (Y 20, E 177) and the way that Jews are natural sweaters, remarking that "the very gist of Jewishness is to be found in this fiery nature" and once more linking this phenomenon to Jewish suffering, asking "Who, among all the seventy nations of the world, has sweated more than the Jew?" (Y 24, E 181). Compare Bialik, p. 236.

44. On narratological divisions in Abramovitch's work generally and *Fishke der krumer* in particular, compare *Traveler*, passim, as well as Jeffrey Fleck, "Mendele in Pieces," *Prooftexts*, Vol. 3, no. 2 (1983), pp. 169–188, and N. Mayzel, "Di grenetzn tsvishn Sh.-Y. Abamovitch un mendele mo's," in *Dos mendele-bukh*, pp. 294–325.

45. Stillman, Glossary, p. 430.

46. All stories seem to be linked to one another, too: after Alter tells his tale, Mendele says: "The way your story ended with the disbanding of the fair reminded me of a very interesting tale which I can't forget to this very day. It's a story about a bathhouse and it ends just like yours. There's not even a hair's breadth of difference between them, except the other story is short" (Y 34, E 192). This despite the fact that the stories are highly different. Compare also Gershon Shaked, *Bein sechok ledema* (Ramat Gan, 1974 [2nd ed.], esp. pp. 120–124, and Menakhem Perry, "Haanalogiya umekoma bemivne haroman shel mendele mo's," *Hasifrut*, Vol. 1, No. 1 (1968), pp. 65–100, esp. pp. 72–76.

47. For an extensive look at Abramovitch's use of holidays and of seasons throughout his oeuvre, see Shmuel Werses, "Khagim uzemanim beyetsirat mendele," in Shmuel Werses, *Mimendele ad hazaz* (Jerusalem, 1987), pp. 87–102, esp. pp. 96–99; on time in the novel more generally, see Watt, *The Rise of the Novel*, pp. 21–22.

8

Imagined Geography
The Shtetl, Myth, and Reality

Israel Bartal

The Map of the City

When in 1911 the Hebrew writer David Frischmann came to evaluate the
work of Sholem Yankev Abramovitsch (better known as Mendele Moykher
Sforim), he saw Abramovitsch as first and foremost a Jewish draftsman.
For him, Mendele was the great painter who described in minute detail
and with great precision the lives of Jews in the first half of the nineteenth
century:

> How well did Mendele draw our life in the Diaspora! He took the full life of
> the Jew in the street of the Russian shtetl during the first half of the last cen-
> tury, and also a bit of the second half of that century, and has given us a
> large canvas with all manner of detail, great and small, with every precision,
> great and small, so that even if we are now somewhat remote from them he
> compels us to go back and relive in our imagination those terrible times. Let
> us assume, for example, that a flood has totally wiped out the shtetl world,
> with all its inhabitants, and has eradicated every memory, every relic, every
> survivor. . . . Only Mendele's four great stories remain. . . . On the basis of
> these relics, a scholar who wished to reconstruct a picture of the lives of
> Jews in the street of a Russian shtetl during the first half of the nineteenth
> century would be able to do so, without the smallest tit or jottle missing."[1]

In Frischmann's opinion, Abramovitch's writing is a unique and authentic
Jewish phenomenon, and the fictional world depicted in his works is a
faithful reflection of the real world of the shtetl: It represents the historical

reality of Jewish life in the Russian Pale of Settlement. This radical approach to literary fiction has been disputed by many, since it plays down the impact of the author's critical-maskilic mind on his image of the shtetl.

Mendele Moykher Sforim carried on a literary tradition that went back to the beginning of the *Haskalah* movement in Eastern Europe. That movement, which reached the Pale of Settlement at the start of the nineteenth century, focused its literary criticism on the traditional Jewish society as reflected in a stereotype of the Jewish community. Authors created a fictional "city" that was presented as the archetype and embodiment of every aspect of Jewish existence. The profile of this shtetl was drawn to suit all those aspects of Jewish life that the maskilim considered to be flawed and in need of reform: from the architecture of the houses and layout of the streets through the stench of the river that ran by the town. The authors and their readers were intimately familiar with the reality from which they drew the materials for their fictional town. From this reality they selected certain elements, which they highlighted, and blotted out others that were an equally inseparable part of the real Jewish world. In later years, after the Jewish intellectuals born in the towns of Eastern Europe had moved away from their native districts, physically and psychologically, the bitter maskilic rejection of the Jewish small town was replaced by a nostalgic idealization of it. Sometimes the old rejection and new nostalgia mingled to create an ambivalent blend. In any case, however, we must not consider the literary depiction of Eastern European *shtetlekh* to be a historical document, as Frischmann did with Mendele's stories. The image of the shtetl in modern Jewish literature is quite different from the historical reality on which the authors drew. That historical reality is also very different from the image of the shtetl in modern Jewish collective memory. Or, as Eva Hoffman has put it:

> The Shtetl, in the absence of living actualities, has become a trope, a metaphor frozen in time. In our minds, it tends to be unchanging, filled always with the same Sabbaths, the dybbuks, the fear of Cossacks, the family warmth. But although it is true that the shtetl changed reluctantly and slowly, it was not exempt from the forces of accident, conflict, and development—in other words, from history.[2]

In this chapter we focus on a central aspect of the gulf between the literary fiction created by Jewish authors and the reality of the Jewish small town: its geography, or, in plain words, the literary map of the shtetl vis-à-vis the historical map.

Let us begin with the map sketched by Mendele in his Hebrew story, "*Beseter ra'am*" (1887). This story, written after the pogroms of 1881–1882, is certainly one of the most complete examples of a literary map of the shtetl in the spirit of the *Haskalah* (Jewish Enlightenment). Mendele writes as follows:

> I will lay it before your eyes in its color and form and you will see it as it is. Kislon is an all-Jewish town in every detail. The builders' art is despised there and its rules are never followed. Its houses do not stand upright, arrogantly challenging heaven, but are low. Some of them tilt precariously and their roofs are buried in the ground. There is no paint or trimming on the outside. . . . The precept of building a parapet at the edge of the roof, with pipes to carry off the rainwater, is not observed here. On the other hand, the custom is to collect slops outside the door, and pigs come and wallow up to their ears in the mud and mire, for their benefit and pleasure, and make the place stink.[3]

A remarkably similar description of a shtetl can be found at the beginning of Sholom Aleichem's series of tales, *Di Shtot fun di kleyne mentshelekh* (*The Town of the Small People*). He, like Mendele, highlights the lack of planning. The houses were not built according to a blueprint and are totally devoid of charm. Sholom Aleichem goes farther, however, to describe the layout of the entire town as a total muddle:

> The town of the small Jews to which I will bring you, dear reader, lies in the center of the famous Pale of Settlement. In the center of that blessed region, where our brethren the Jews are so numerous, they live crowded together like herring in a barrel and are fruitful and multiply. The name of this industrious town is Kasrilevke. . . . The town of the small Jews is far away from the world of the Holy One Blessed Be He. In a God-forsaken corner, a place not trodden by human beings, it has been standing there for many years, dreaming its dreams and sunk in its thoughts, forlorn and preoccupied with itself. It seems to have nothing to do with everything in the outside world, . . . such as culture, education, progress, and the like. . . . You want to know what Kasrilevke looks like? . . . The houses themselves are small mud huts, low and rickety, and look like ancient gravestones in an

ancient cemetery. . . . Don't look for streets and marketplaces in Kasrilevke. When the city was built, they did not lay it out with a builder's rule or sketch it with a compass, or leave any space between the houses. Why should any empty and desolate space stand idle, when you can build a house there? . . . There are also streets in Kasrilevke—big streets and little streets, long streets and short streets, not to mention lanes and alleys and cul-de-sacs. You may say that those streets are not very straight; that they are twisting and curving and wind about, running up hill and down dale, full of trenches and pits, cellars and caves, back lots and courtyards.[4]

The literary shtetl in these two excerpts seems to be the product of spontaneous generation. Its form seems to be derived from a combination of the Jews' unique mentality and the needs of everyday life. The proclivity for disorder and chaos and the absence of any feeling for aesthetics (a legacy of the maskilic criticism of Jewish life) combined with the decisive influence of economics to shape the geography of the shtetl. This is a source of the zigzags and twists in its lines, which were determined by topographic conditions and not planned rationally by a professional engineer. This also explains the crowding together of the buildings, which grew up as it were of themselves, directly linked to the reproductive processes of the population. The shtetl of Mendele and Sholom Aleichem resembles a living organism. Sholom Aleichem even compares the appearance of Kasrilevke to "a sunflower overflowing with seeds"[5] (and also to noodles on a wooden pastry board). The past of his shtetl is distinctly ahistorical, and so is its historical geography. It is true that in his work Sholom Aleichem gave an important place to the encounter between the inhabitants of the small town in the Pale of Settlement with the modern world. He even published a series of short sketches about the "progress" that had reached his childhood town, and wrote in the introduction:

Let everyone on earth know that Kasrilevke is a reformed town, where nothing is lacking: hotels and guesthouses, restaurants and taverns, and it even has a theater. This is not the town we knew in days of yore. The major advances made by the big world have also made its way to this city and changed its face totally."[6]

Sholom Aleichem even represented these sketches as a tourist guide to "cities and countries." But that same town "we knew in days of yore" became fixed in the literary work as a monolith of collective memory that lasted from antiquity to the day when the people of Kasrilevke were awakened by the whistle of the steam locomotive and passed from the realm of myth to that of history. Such organic growth, which was compatible with the traditional collective memory—which was distinctly ahistorical—was not suited to the history of the Jewish shtetl in Eastern Europe. The literary image of the shtetl obliterated the historical facts and distorted the geographical maps. We can learn about the great difference between the mythical geography of the town and the earthly map of the Jewish shtetl by examining three types of historical sources: (a) historical documents that deal with the founding of cities in Eastern Europe; (b) maps of cities and towns; (c) the descriptions of the shtetl in the memoir literature.

Historical Documents

Written historical sources about the founding of urban settlements in Eastern Europe contain vast amounts of information about the meticulous planning of the town or new neighborhood. For example, in his studies of the community of Pinsk in White Russia, Mordechai Nadav reconstructed the list of the householders (99 before 1648) and showed, on the basis of a document dated 1650, the layout of the residential areas in the city. The historical core of the Jewish community was located on lands belonging to the castle; from there it spread to the area under the jurisdiction of the bishop and the lands of churches and monasteries.[7] According to an 1864 city map, the great synagogue of Pinsk was at the very center of the ancient core of the community, with the Catholic cathedral and the Russian Orthodox monastery on one side and the large Greek Orthodox church on the other.[8] Relying on historical sources about the town of Opatow, Gerson Hundert discovered that "The gap separating Jews and Christians was larger than the physical distance between the two neighborhoods."[9]

Not only was the Jewish town built according to a plan, and sometimes several plans (corresponding to the jurisdiction of this or that landowner within the boundaries of the town); the Jewish residential areas were mixed with those of their Christian neighbors. The town plan generally did not provide for any intentional segregation of Jewish homes. Christian religious establishments and Jewish public buildings stood side by side. It is extremely difficult to reconcile the material from the sources with Mendele's statement that "Kislon is an all-Jewish town in every detail."[10]

City Maps

A study of the maps of Eastern European towns reveals a grid of straight lines. What is more, in many of them the original urban nucleus surrounds a square or rectangular market plaza and includes churches, courthouses, a municipal building, and other non-Jewish institutions. See, for example, the plan of the town of Lezask in western Galicia: the streets run in straight lines, and the marketplace is rectangular; the Catholic cathedral stands on one side of the marketplace, and the rabbi's house on the other. Similar maps can be found all over the vast territory of what had been the Polish-Lithuanian Commonwealth before the partitions of the kingdom. It seems far-fetched to describe this as an impenetrable labyrinth or write the following (also from the aforementioned description by Sholom Aleichem):

> Don't worry about the people of Kasrilevke themselves. A man from Kasrilevke, who lives in the town of Kasrilevke, among his brothers the people of Kasrilevke, will never lose his way or get lost. Everyone will find his way home, to his wife and children, like a bird that flies straight back to its nest and fledglings.[11]

Note once again the irrational character of the map of Kasrilevke, which the author implies to his readers. People are guided by their instincts, not by map coordinates. This town is like a cluster of nests, and the bird that feeds its young flies from the source of food (the market) back to the nest using primordial instincts and animal senses.

But the fact is that even towns that were not built as part of a settlement project by some Polish landowner, but were founded in the nineteenth century on territories that Russia annexed from the Ottoman Empire, did not sprout up like mushrooms in southern Ukraine. They were built according to a master plan and preserved at least the simple layout of a main street (a road between two towns) with houses on either side.

Memoirs

Even though memoirs contain a large admixture of fiction, they generally include lengthy and detailed descriptions of the map of the shtetl, lists of buildings and institutions, clear distinctions among different areas, and information about population groups and where they lived. What is more, the memoirists clearly distinguish among the historical stages in the development of the urban map—stages that were engraved in the memories of the townsfolk and alluded to in the names of streets or designations of different neighborhoods. When Isaac Leib Peretz wanted to characterize the distinctive traits of the Jews in his birthplace, Zamosc, he did not eradicate the non-Jewish milieu from the city map or present it in terms borrowed from the world of flora or fauna. Zamosc, like many of the cities and towns founded by the Polish gentry, was the result of fastidious planning, and its original streets were straight as a ruler:

> Zamosc is a distinct, middle-class Jewish kingdom. It is a city with a sizeable market square and side streets as well. Two whole streets are paved. Standing in the middle of the market, at the point where the two paved streets meet, you face the watchtower of the town hall, and there you have the distinct, middle-class Jewish kingdom. You also have a narrow alley leading to the market, and another narrow alley leading to the gateway to the Lublin highway.[12]

Peretz goes on to provide detailed descriptions of the castle, the church, the marketplace, the hospital, and other institutions. As if to make this description more tangible, he writes, "here I've described everything around, like a chalk diagram on the blackboard."[13] A critical reader is apt to ask whether there is any room for a comparison between an old and carefully planned fortress town like Zamosc and the literary descriptions of Kasrilevke or Kabtzansk? If, however, we compare the histories of towns all over Eastern Europe, we find that it is hard to speak about a lack of planning or a "wild" growth of the town plan.

On the contrary, the cities and towns founded by the Polish gentry over a period of centuries in various parts of the Polish-Lithuanian Kingdom were built according to master plans. The towns of New Russia, too, founded in the nineteenth century, were, as mentioned above, built according to plans. The town was a product of colonization processes, and its original nucleus was set up all at once. What is more, in many cases the Jews lived in the ancient heart of the town, so that precisely the municipal institutions typical of the premodern Christian city were adjacent to the Jewish core of the town! The Jews ran shops on the main street or had stalls at the fairs held in the market square. In both cases these were planned commercial precincts in which the nobleman who owned the town leased space out.

It is interesting to note that contemporary scholars who study the memoirs of Eastern European Jews have also failed to recognize the difference between the shtetl of literary fiction and that implied by the memoirs. For example, David Assaf, in his introduction to Yehezkel Kotik's memoirs about his birthplace, Kamenets-Litovsk, writes as follows:

> The topography of Kamenets is no different than that portrayed in many descriptions of Jewish communities in the Pale of Settlement. Kotik describes the main sites and institutions in the town (such as the nobleman's estate and the churches, the synagogues and *batei midrash*, the bathhouse and the *mikveh*, the poorhouse and the *talmud torah*, the river and the cemetery) . . .[14]

The "descriptions" to which Assaf refers are those in the literary works of nineteenth- and twentieth-century authors (from the Yiddish *Haskalah* literature through Soviet-Yiddish writing). As we have seen in Mendele's and Sholom Aleichem's descriptions, there were no Christian "sites and institutions" in the shtetl of myth. Not only were there no straight lines on the maps of Kabtzansk and Kasrilevke; there was no church, landowner's mansion, or town hall. How, then, was this imaginary geography, which became a fixture of later Jewish collective memory and has even found a home in serious historical writing, born?

I believe that three factors played a part in the development of the "classic" image of the shtetl and its imaginary cartography:

1. The eradication from the literary memory of the town's Polish past;
2. The blurring of the geographical and demographical dimensions between big city and small town;
3. The sharpening of the opposition between the Jewish urban settlement and its non-Jewish rural surroundings.

The Obliteration of the Polish Past

All signs of the "recent" historical past were obliterated from the imaginary map of the shtetl. Sholom Aleichem and Mendele painted a "present" in which every residue of the sites of economic activity rooted in the feudal period has been eliminated without a trace. What is more, the geography of their imaginary towns omits the Polish nobility and its decisive role in the planning of the town and its survival for centuries. The autochthonous Ukrainians, White Russians, and other ethnic groups fill in the Poles' place in the works. The *poretz* (Polish noblemen) survives, if at all, in the folktales recounted by the old people of Sholom Aleichem's literary town. This imaginary town has no history, and its map has no historical geography. It was created from a post-feudal "present" that had ostensibly existed since the earliest times. It is true that the abolition of serfdom in Russia in 1861 and the failure of the Polish uprising of 1863 led to a dramatic decline in the power of the Polish gentry. Rapid transformation affected the economic life of shtetl Jews, and the age-old leasehold system withered away. But the physical map of the shtetl did not change with equal speed. The old plan survived the social and economic changes for some time, but the Jewish writers chose to remove it from their imagined geography. Hence, the literary representation of the shtetl geography reflected the political and economic changes but not necessarily the physical ones.

But there was another dimension to the obliteration of any trace of the Poles from the shtetl environment. The banishing of the Polish gentry and erasure of its memory from the mythical map of the shtetl were indeed appropriate for two authors who adopted Russian imperial discourse and saw the Polish element in Jewish history as a decadent relic that got in the way of progress. Mendele and Sholom Aleichem, who had absorbed the values of the *Haskalah*, internalized the ideas of the westernizing camp in Russia and were inclined to identify the Polish nobility as a conservative factor that exerted an anti-rational influence. This picture is at variance with the actual political and cultural endeavors of some of the Polish landowners in the Pale of Settlement and their relations with the pioneers of the *Haskalah*. The contrast between the imaginary shtetl, from which the Polish historical and geographical element has been erased, and the complex historical reality of Jewish-Polish relations in the Russian Empire comes to the fore in the difference between the descriptions of the shtetl in the autobiographical writings of Mendele and Sholom Aleichem and in their fictional writings. For example, in his autobiographical "Shloyme Reb Hayim's," Mendele writes at length about his father's close relations with a Polish landowner who lived near the town of Kapuli in White Russia. We learn that the father spoke and wrote fluent Polish![15] Of course if the Polish landowners were incompatible with progress, rationalism, and the Enlightenment, why would they plan cities with straight boulevards? The marketplace was the only feature of the historical map of the feudal town that survived in these two authors' imaginary geography. This marketplace, which had frequently remained in the same location since the days when the town was under the direct control of the Polish landlord, becomes the main place where Jews and peasant farmers rub against one another in the literary town. There are no Polish landowners to be seen in the marketplaces of Mendele and Sholom Aleichem. Only peasants come there. By contrast, the marketplace of Kamenets-Litovsk in Kotik's memoirs is bustling with *pritsim* (noblemen).[16] So is the Zamosc marketplace in I. L. Peretz's memoirs.

City or Town?

How do the authors remember their birthplaces? Was it a large town, or a small settlement? There are three Yiddish words for a Jewish urban settlement: *shtot, shtetl,* and *shtetale.* Scrutiny of the vast amount of literature that deals with Jewish communities in Eastern Europe reveals unmistakably that the three terms are used interchangeably by authors, memoirists, and historians. Sholom Aleichem calls his Kasrilevke "*di shtot fun di kleyne mentshelekh*"—"the *city* of the little people." Voronka in the Ukraine (the town where he was born), from which he drew many details of Kasrilevke, was a rather small place at the end of the nineteenth century—but he calls it "a city." A native and former resident of Kalarash, a county seat in Bessarabia, wrote: "Despite its three main streets, with a number of side alleys, the government institutions and charitable institutions, a significant number of synagogues, some of them large and imposing, with a train station serving the entire region—nevertheless it was my small town."[17] According to the 1897 census, there were 4,593 Jews living in Kalarash.[18] A contemporary historian has written, in a book on the Grodno community and its fate during the Holocaust: "I have chosen a *town* of average size."[19] Grodno, now in Belarus, was home to 21,159 Jews in 1931. It was one of the leading Jewish communities of historical Lithuania and became an important industrial center and hotbed of the Jewish labor movement—and yet it is referred to as a "town."

The tendency to reduce the size of the Jewish town, a tendency that gains momentum as it turns from a real historical venue into a mythical site, is found both in literature and in the nostalgic collective memory. The miniaturization of the Jewish urban entity makes it possible to present a world that is simpler, more homogeneous, and more Jewish. This enhances the contrast between the big city, which is heterogeneous and indifferent, and the long-rooted organic community. The historical demography of the Jewish town is very different from its literary demography. This difference also influenced the portrayal of the imaginary geography we are dealing with here. Just as there are no distinctions of Hasidim and Misnagdim (the opponents of Hasidism) in the mythical shtetl, so too it has no neighborhoods with mixed populations. The inhabitants of this storybook town constitute a collective with collective traits; the geography of the town is correspondingly an aggregate of all the institutions and sites that maintain this collective existence, from birth to death.

Thus Sholom Aleichem, noting one geographical site in the center of the shtetl, offers us the particular essence of Kasrilevke:

> A large and broad field, more or less a semi-circle, or perhaps a square, located in the heart of the city center, where you find all the shops and stores. . . . That is the place of the market every morning, when throngs of non-Jewish farmers and their wives come into the city and bring all sorts of edible commodities to its residents. . . . And in that very same field, the she-goats and he-goats of the community gather in their families. . . . That is also where you will find the synagogues and *batei midrash* and the other holy institutions of the town, plus the *hadorim* and *talmudei torah*. . . . A special corner was allotted for the bathhouse, the place where Jewish women immerse and purify themselves in the *mikve*, and also for the poorhouse, where poor Jews go to die.[20]

A single parcel of land in the center of the small town can encompass every aspect of Jewish life, both material and spiritual.

Town and Country

The sharpening of the distinction between the Jewish urban community and its rural surroundings also left a significant impress on the literary map. The historical town had an original core with buildings, streets, and residential compounds, in which Jews and Christians were frequently next-door neighbors. In the literary shtetl of Mendele and Sholom Aleichem, the center is all-Jewish, and the Christians live on the outskirts or in the nearby villages.

A typical example of this distinction between fiction and historical geography is the priest's garden in Sholom Aleichem's shtetl. In the story of Motel, the orphaned cantor, the wonderful garden next to the Jewish boy's house, from which he filches fruit, belongs to Menashe *der royfe* (the healer) and his penny-pinching wife; in the real Voronka, the fruit is stolen from the priest's garden on *Tisha b'Av*[21] (a fast day) of all days! The priest lives in the center of town, his daughter sees the Jewish boy picking pears in her father's yard, and the priest sics his dog on the lad and rips his cap off his head. The priest's garden, a familiar and frequent place to be found in every town in Eastern Europe, was generally located next to the town church. Kotik, too, writes in his memoirs about such a garden, which was "beautiful, full of blossoming fruit trees and lovely and fragrant flowers. The scents that wafted from the priest's yard were so intense that no Jewish nose could stand them and your head got dizzy."[22] Kotik's family rented the tavern from the priest who owned the garden and lived right next to it.

In the literary works, the complex ethnic mosaic of the city, in which Jews, Poles, and Russians or other nationalities lived together, has been replaced by an ethno-geographic segregation: the Jews in the center of town, the *goyim* in the suburbs and surrounding villages. There is a kernel of truth in this: more non-Jews lived on the outskirts of town. This does not mean, though, that the center of town was exclusively Jewish. The literary map deliberately obliterates the presence of the Christian urban population from the Jewish heart of the shtetl. It identifies the non-Jewish world with the countryside, thereby intensifying the distinctly urban identity of Eastern European Jewry. The urban experience, the legacy of hundreds of years of colonization in the heart of a foreign and hostile population, did not reflect the demographic and geographic truth. It did, however, express the profound internal truth of alienation from the countryside outside the town. This alienation was very familiar to Mendele and Sholom Aleichem. They gave it expression in the imaginary geography of Kabtzansk and Kasrilevke.

The literary geography of the shtetl was born in the social and economic crisis that beset the world in which the traditional Jewish society of Eastern Europe had been living for hundreds of years. This world was based on a broad and complicated network of reciprocal relations between the Polish gentry and the Jewish communities. The historical

Jewish shtetl was born, grew, and flourished as an essential organ of this network. The map of the town, with its streets and buildings, did not spring up spontaneously; it was drawn by the partnership between the nobleman and the *kahal*—the organized community. With the demise of the feudal economy and the decline in the political power of the Polish gentry (during the second half of the nineteenth century), the shtetl remained the last relic of a strange and alien era. Within a few years, sometimes no more than a decade or two, the feudal town with its medieval layout went through a process of rapid and aggressive urbanization. Otherwise it lost its economic primacy and was abandoned by most of its Jews. The new metropolis, a product of the nineteenth century, became the utter antithesis of the waning town—not only in its demographic, social, and economic reality, but also in literary fiction. The sleepy town, sunk in its dreams about the riches of its glorious past, was depicted as the opposite pole of the vibrant metropolis, where lifestyles are remade, and values, opinions, and beliefs are transformed. The real geographic map gave way to an ahistorical map that was entirely Jewish—a densely populated shtetl, chaotic and disordered, surrounded by an alien and hostile gentile population.

NOTES

1. D. Frischmann, *On Literature* (Warsaw and New York, 1938), p. 74 (Hebrew). This review had been rewritten and changed several times by David Frischmann. On the place of Frischmann's interpretation of Mendele's "historical reality," see Israel Bartal, *Non-Jews and Gentile Society in East European Hebrew and Yiddish Literature, 1856–1914* (Ph.D. dissertation, The Hebrew University, Jerusalem 1980), p. 319, n. 1 (Hebrew).

2. Eva Hoffman, *Shtetl: The History of a Small Town and an Extinguished World* (London, 1999), p. 80.

3. *Mendele's Collected Works* (Tel Aviv, 1954), p. 377 (Hebrew).

4. Sholom Aleichem, "The Town of the Small People," *Collected Works*, Vol. 7 (New York, 1944), pp. 9–15 (Yiddish).

5. Ibid, p. 14.

6. Sholom Aleichem, "The New Kasrilevke," *Collected Works*, Vol. 5 (New York, 1944), p. 61 (Yiddish).

7. Mordechai Nadav, *History of the Jews of Pinsk, 1506–1941*, Vol. 1, 1506–1880 (Tel Aviv and Haifa, 1973), pp. 47–48 (Hebrew).

8. Ibid., pp. 296–297.

9. G. D. Hundert, *The Jews in a Polish Private Town: The Case of Opatow in the 18th Century* (Baltimore, 1992), p.45.

10. *Mendele's Collected Works*, p. 377

11. Sholom Aleichem, "The Town of the Small People," p. 15.

12. Isaac Leib Peretz, *My Memoirs*, translated from the Yiddish by Fred Goldberg (New York, 1964), p. 99.

13. This sentence (two words in Yiddish) is missing from Goldberg's English translation! See the original Yiddish: Isaac Leib Peretz, Mayne Zikhroynes (*My Memories*) (Warsaw, 1965), p. 65.

14. Y. Kotik, *What I Have Seen: The Memoires of Yehezkel Kotik*, edited by David Assaf (Tel Aviv, 1999), p. 61 (Hebrew).

15. *Mendele's Collected Works*, p. 292.

16. Y. Kotik, *What I Have Seen*, pp. 95–97.

17. A. Haruvi, "The Shtetl Where I was Born," in *The Kalarash Book* (Tel Aviv, 1966), p. 15 (Hebrew).

18. Ibid., p. 35.

19. T. Patal-Kena'any, *It's Not The Same Grodno: The Grodno Community in War and Holocaust, 1939–1943* (Jerusalem, 1991), p. 11 (Hebrew).

20. Sholom Aleichem, "The Town of the Small People," pp. 15–16.

21. *Tisha b'Av*—the ninth day of the month of Av—is the traditional day of mourning in the Jewish calendar. It commemorates the destruction by the Babylonians of the First Temple in Jerusalem in 586 B.C.E., and also the destruction of the Second Temple by the Romans in 70 C.E.

22. Y. Kotik, *What I Have Seen*, p. 101.

9

Gender and the Disintegration of the Shtetl in Modern Hebrew and Yiddish Literature

Naomi Seidman

The classical period of modern Hebrew and Yiddish literature, which took the shtetl as a central subject, also coincided with its decline in the face of such forces as secularization, industrialization, and emigration. The writers who describe the shtetl, almost without exception, themselves traced the route from shtetl to metropolis, with all that this implied. It is no wonder, then, that, as Dan Miron argues in "The Literary Image of the Shtetl," the literature of the shtetl is everywhere shaped by the motif of exodus and exile.[1] But Miron warns us against reading this literature as strictly mimetic, a faithful reflection of either broad socio-historical forces or individual biographical realities. The works of Hebrew and Yiddish literature written by *"di klassiker"*—S. Y. Abramovitsh, Sholem Aleichem, and Y. L. Peretz—present a transparently fictional, highly stylized shtetl, drawing upon a relatively limited pallet of recurring motifs and a shared metaphorical gestalt. These literary shtetlekh differ from their historical counterparts; the *klassiker*, for instance, typically present the shtetl as pure Jewish space—a *yidishe melukhe* (a Jewish state), in L. Shapiro's ironic formulation—thus marginalizing or expunging the Christian presence so visible in any actual Eastern European town. Sholem Aleichem's literary Kasrilevke "was depicted as an exclusively Jewish enclave, an unalloyed entity," Miron writes, although Voronke, Sholem Aleichem's hometown and ostensible model for Kasrilevke, could hardly be characterized that way. Ignoring the economic dependence of towns like Voronke on the non-Jewish population and the visible presence within them of churches, Christian

cemeteries and, on fair days, throngs of peasants, Sholem Aleichem created a fictional shtetl that "consisted of Jewish stuff and formed a Jewish
universe."[2]

The "Judaization" of the literary shtetl of the classical period is bolstered and shaped, in Miron's analysis, by three discursively linked components that appear, virtually without exception, in these narratives: the fire,
the departure, and the appearance of a stranger. There is, of course, some
basis for these literary phenomena in the social and material realities of
small-town Jewish life (shtetl homes, for instance, were typically built of
wood and other combustible material, making fire a terrifying and peri-
odic occurrence). Nevertheless, the motifs of conflagration, exodus, and
the appearance of a stranger are actually three "submetaphors in a larger
metaphorical gestalt," to quote Miron. Taken together, they function as
referents to the largest patterns of Jewish history and as intertextual links
to the classical Jewish sources: the flames signify the repeated destruction
of the Temple and Jerusalem, the departure scene refers either to the Exodus from Egypt or the various expulsions from the Land of Israel, and the
stranger speaks to Jewish messianic hopes. These three motifs, Miron
argues, together construct the literary shtetl as an Eastern European
Jerusalem, a tiny, exiled *yerushalayim shel mata* (this-worldly Jerusalem),
in which the national-religious drama of destruction, exile and redemption continues to unfold. "The shtetl was Jerusalem in her fallen state,"
Miron writes, "and yet it was still Jerusalem—the Jewish polity par excellence."[3]

In his analysis of the second of these "submetaphors," Miron lists a
number of motifs that regularly accompany descriptions of the departure
scene: "dybbuks, devils and ghosts," which presumably signify the mournful and uncanny dimension of the exodus. Miron also mentions "widows
and *agunot*, deserted women who 'sit solitary and weep sore into the
night, the tears on their cheeks.'"[4] Miron does not spell it out, but the
implication of these last two related motifs is clear enough: the widows
and *agunot* (deserted wives or "grass widows" who may not remarry) who
recur in these scenes of departure function not so much as unfortunate
individuals in a broadly mimetic canvas of social upheaval as richly symbolic emblems of national lamentation and bereavement. The *agunah* is a
literary figure, in Miron's reading, an intertextual allusion to the humiliated woman who is the city of Jerusalem in Lamentations, or, more specifically, the bride whose husband the king deserts in *Lamentations Rabbah*
3: 21 (as well as a number of parallel sources). Here is the *aggada*:

R. Abba bar Kahana said:

It is like a king who married a woman and wrote her a large marriage settlement (*ketubah*). He wrote her: So many bridal–chambers I am building for you; so much jewelry I make for you; so much gold and silver I give you. Then he left her for many years and journeyed to the provinces. Her neighbors used to taunt her and say to her: Hasn't your husband abandoned you? Go! Marry another man. She would weep and sigh, and afterward she would enter her bridal-chamber and read her marriage-settlement and sigh [with relief]. Many years and days later the king returned. He said to her: I am amazed that you have waited for me all these years! She replied: My master, O king! If not for the large wedding-settlement you wrote me, my neighbors long ago would have led me astray.[5]

While the *agunah* is a symbol of national destruction in both the *aggadic* literature and in the literature of the shtetl, she functions somewhat differently in each of these cases. In the parable that depicts Israel as an abandoned bride, the *agunah* is a metaphorical vehicle for the Jewish people as God's rejected bride, and the story of her marriage gone sour is an allegory for the rift between God and his people. The writers of the classical shtetl literature, on the other hand, produce not parables but broadly mimetic (if tragicomic and satirical) fiction; within this genre, the *agunah* connects the contemporary scene with a larger, national drama of exile—that is, she functions *both* as a metonym for nineteenth-century social upheaval *and* as a metaphor in a national-religious epic.

In the first of these functions, the *agunah* represents the historical situation of women and marriage in the disintegration of the shtetl. Her presence is shorthand for the differential effects for men and women of the processes of modernization, immigration, and urbanization. In the second of these functions (the one Miron places at the forefront of his analysis), the *agunah* refers not to the particular situation of Jewish women in nineteenth-century Eastern Europe but rather to the Jewish people as a whole in its (dysfunctional) "marital" relation to God.[6] The metaphorical use of the *agunah*, I would point out, evacuates the figure of its specifically *female* situation, since she refers to a collective dominated by men even if it figured as feminine. In Roland Barthes' terms, the *agunah* becomes a "turnstile of form and meaning," in which "its form is empty but present, its meaning absent but full."[7] This is rendered explicit in the *nimshal* (solution) that adumbrates the parable. After identifying the neighbor women as the nations of the world, the passage continues: "the people of Israel enter their synagogues and houses of study, and there they read in the Torah, 'I will look with favor upon you, and make you fertile. . . . I will establish my abode in your midst, and I will not spurn you' (Lev. 26: 9, 11), and they console themselves."[8] The bridal-chamber, then, represents the synagogues and houses of study that hold the Torah, Israel's *ketubah* (wedding contract); in the explication, the female space of the bridal-chamber is transformed *in toto* into prototypically male territory. By contrast, in the mobilization of the *agunah* in modern Jewish literature, the femininity of her plight continues to register.

Although Miron tucks the *agunah* within a catalog of secondary motifs, desertion seems to me a crucial component of the literature of the shtetl, and in particular of the exodus scene. This is certainly the case, at least, for the first two examples Miron provides of people leaving the shtetl: the first is the departure of Benjamin and Senderl from Tunyadevka in S. Y. Abramovitsh's 1878 Yiddish novella, *The Brief Travels of Benjamin the Third*; the second is the departure to the big city of Mendele Moykher Seforim and the *melamed* (teacher) Reb Leyb in Abramovitsh's 1894 Hebrew short story, "In the Days of Earthquake."[9] In both of these fictional works, the departure of the protagonists involves not only the desertion of their wives, but also the comic reconstitution of the spousal relationship between the two male traveling partners; clearly, then, not only the Jewish national narrative but also marriage and gender are at stake. The second chapter of *Benjamin the Third*, which describes Benjamin's initial abortive flight from Tunyadevka, brings the motif of *aginut* to the surface—it is entitled "How Benjamin Became a Martyr and Zelda an Agunah." The *agunah* may be an ostensibly accidental "by-product" of a departure narrative that hinges on its male protagonists, but she nevertheless has a strikingly constant role.

As Miron readily acknowledges is the case with the "submetaphors" of fire, departure, and the appearance of a stranger, the "secondary" literary motif of wife-desertion has some basis in historical reality. The social processes summarized in the phrase "the disintegration of the shtetl" occurred in distinct ways for different classes, geographical regions, and generations; as a number of historians have argued, it also shook the basic unit of community life, the family, to its core, changing the traditional relationship of parents and children, women and men. Describing the disruptive impact to the family of the *Haskalah*, the nineteenth-century Jewish "Enlightenment," Lucy Dawidowicz writes:

Quarrels between traditionalists and modernists frequently divided families as well as communities: marriages were dissolved, wives abandoned. Husbands who turned maskilim were often forced by traditionalist in-laws to divorce their wives even when the couple lived in harmony, while other maskilim fled inflexible in-laws and tearful wives, seeking "progress" and "light."[10]

Solomon Maimon can serve as precursor in this regard as in so many others: in leaving Eastern Europe for Mendelssohn's Berlin, the *ilui* (child prodigy) turned maskil (enlightened person) left a wife and family with barely a backward glance.[11] As Bluma Goldstein has pointed out, Maimon, who abandoned wife and family in search of *bildung*, could serve as prime example for how masculine "enlightenment" did not preclude a blindness to women's predicament.[12]

The pattern of abandonment is evident throughout nineteenth-century *Haskalah* autobiography. Surveying the autobiographical writings of such maskilim as Abraham Ber Gottlober and Moses Leib Lilienblum, Paula Hyman writes that

> women (both wives and mothers-in-law) figured in [these autobiographies] as obstacles to self-realization and modernization. For young men raised in the traditional Jewish community and yearning to break free, women represented the burden of tradition and the familial obligations it imposed upon young men before they had the opportunity to realize their dreams of intellectual growth.[13]

In the struggle between tradition and modernity, women were often aligned with tradition; there is a grim logic, then, to the fact that in the movements of Jewish modernity, they sometimes found themselves left behind.[14]

The other face of the *Haskalah* link of women and tradition, though, is a feminist or proto-feminist one, in which women are primarily the *victims* of the traditional way of life, rather than the perpetrators of its worst evils.[15] Yehuda Leib Gordon's seminal poem of 1868, "The Tip of the Yod," focuses its attention squarely on the plight of the woman abandoned in the social upheavals of the nineteenth century. But while his heroine, Bat Shua, is the victim, at least in part, of urbanization and immigration, Gordon, the exemplary maskil, heaps blame not on these forces but solely on those of tradition. The poetic narrative tells the story of a young woman who is married off to a man she does not love and is then denied a divorce from him. In the poem, a Jewish version of the kingdom lost for want of a nail, Bat Shua becomes an *agunah* when a rabbi rules that her divorce is invalid because the document contains a misspelled word—her first husband has signed his name "Hillel" with the "defective" rather than the "plene" spelling, and so the *yod*, the smallest (and most insignificant, Gordon implies) letter, is missing. Since her husband has since been lost at sea, the "mistake" is irreversible, and Bat Shua cannot be set free to marry the man she loves. The poem foregrounds what is perhaps the clearest and most tragic example of the gender asymmetry and hierarchy in Jewish law (or, as Gordon might rather view it, in its hair-splitting rabbinic interpretations): the asymmetrical right of men to divorce women, and the subjection of the woman who cannot obtain a legal divorce or whose husband has disappeared.[16] By contrast to the stasis and rigidity of the traditional world, the young man who introduces Bat Shua to the joys of modern romance sweeps into town on a wave of progress; he is the manager of the railroad construction project. Nevertheless, the poem suggests that modernity too has its victims: first among them is Bat Shua's father, whose living as a post-stationmaster is destroyed by the new railroad. Ultimately, by poem's end, Bat Shua herself has joined the anonymous masses of poor streaming through the train station, the detritus of a traditional society in ruins.

Miron's warning against a strictly mimetic reading of the classical shtetl literature applies at least as much to such transparently fictional *Haskalah* texts as "The Tip of the Yod" as Michael Stanislawski has insisted.[17] Gordon's poem is not realism but rather biting satire, and Bat Shua is not a three-dimensional character but rather a cudgel raised against the forces of Jewish orthodoxy. The *klassiker* avoided the explicit axe-grinding of the *Haskalah*; their narratives of the shtetl, moreover, are marked by an ambivalence toward tradition absent from Gordon's scathing critique. The trail of *agunot* left in the wake of the literature of the shtetl, I will argue, is the very sign of this ambivalence—victim and victimizer both, the *agunah* indeed embodies the past in its nagging demands and impossible claims.

Although wife-abandonment was a social problem of significant dimensions during the period in which the classical shtetl literature was produced, the figure of the *agunah* must be distinguished from her "actual" counterparts. Historically, men deserted children along with wives—Maimon's son accompanies his wife in pursuit of a *get* (divorce) from her "enlightened" husband, and the *Forward*'s "Gallery of Disappeared Men" includes the pleas of children to their missing fathers along-side those of their mothers. In the *literature* of masculine departure from the shtetl, however, children are either silent or entirely absent. By reducing the desertion drama to its two principals, husband and wife, shtetl literature envisions it as a struggle between mythical opposites. The husband and wife function, in part, as sexual archetypes or stereotypes, with the *luftmentsh* (the impractical) husband shaking off the abuse of his shrewish wife. The husband-wife polarity in these narratives, however, serves a range of themes that far exceeds the strict category of gender roles. Sholem Aleichem's *Menachem Mendel* (1892–1909), in its epistolary symmetry, provides perhaps the most transparent example: Menachem Mendel signifies Odessa and the "London" stock market, urbanization and emigration; Sheyne Sheyndel signifies Kasrilevka and its marketplace, tradition and the past. In this system, Menachem Mendel's failure to return to his family in Kasrilevke is propelled by the unstoppable machinery of modernity itself. If it is historically accurate, as we have seen, to say that in the departure from the shtetl, women and children were sometimes left behind, my point is rather that in the *literature* that describes the departure from the shtetl, what is left behind is gendered as feminine and emblematized by the figure of a woman.

Without minimizing the relevance in this context of the *aggadic* literature on desertion, I would argue that the departure scene in shtetl literature must also be understood as drawing upon another set of literary conventions—from the European romance—to which it stands in negative or parodic relation. The geographical distance between the shtetl and the modern metropolis in which Hebrew and Yiddish literature arose was also a cultural gap between traditional Jewish literature and the secular European models Hebrew and Yiddish writers strove to emulate. The context for the emergence of modern Hebrew and Yiddish literature, I would thus argue, includes not only the "echo chamber" of the classical Jewish library and the historical resonances of the Jewish national epic, but also a range of conventions and assumptions about what it meant to write modern European literature. A secular Jewish literature on the European model, needed romance—the very Hebrew and Yiddish terms for the novel, *roman*, encode the romantic demands of the genre. Thus, it is no surprise that the depiction of the skirmishes of modernity are cast, increasingly throughout the nineteenth century, as heterosexual drama, as a struggle between a man and a woman, or even more classically, as a man caught between two women—one who represents the old way and one the new. Exemplary of this latter approach is Reuven Braudes' 1888 novel *The Two Extremes*, which pits the traditional wife whom the protagonist has left behind in the shtetl against the alluring and sophisticated young woman in the city to which he has come, and then, in moderate maskilic fashion and as the title implies, attempts to find a compromise between the two.

The pressure of European romantic conventions on the literature of the shtetl is nowhere more evident, though, than in *The Brief Travels of Benjamin the Third*, the best known of Abramovitsh's works and a central text of nineteenth-century Yiddish literature (and in a later self-translation, of Hebrew literature as well). The novella recounts the mock-heroic adventures of two ragged Jews, Benjamin and Senderl, who venture from their backwoods shtetl in the Pale of Settlement in search of the legendary and heroic "Red Jews," using the often fantastic medieval literature of Jewish exploration as their eminently unreliable guide. Benjamin and Senderl are parodic versions of Don Quixote and Sancho Panza (Cervantes' novel is itself, of course, a parody of the chivalric romance); the novella was translated into Polish as *The Jewish Don Quixote*. In contrast with Quixote's emblematically European pursuit of love and honor, Benjamin and Senderl are married men in flight from their shrewish wives. The Jewish world, Abramovitsh's parody implies, has no room for the romance and chivalry on which European literature rests. In *The Jewish Don Quixote*, the knights and squires are all married, their true bonds are with each other, and the dragons they fear most are their domineering wives.

Abramovitsh's Jewish parody of the Christian European romance is thus also a satire on Jewish gender relations. *Benjamin the Third* implicitly contrasts the "proper" heterosexuality of European literary convention with a traditional Jewish world in which romance is absent, gender is turned on its head, and emasculated Jewish men are beaten by their shrewish wives. These motifs are most explicit precisely in the scenes involving the departure from the shtetl: the first of these, the chapter entitled "Benjamin Finds a Help-Meet and Is Coupled with Senderl di *yidene*," is a cross-gendered parody of a seduction scene, with Benjamin playing the illicit lover and Sender the seduced housewife, fearful of her abusive mate and drawn to the sweet-talking new man attempting to entice her to leave him:

> When Benjamin came to Senderl he found him sitting on the dairy bench, peeling potatoes. One cheek looked inflamed, while one of his eyes was

black and blue and scratched as if someone had clawed at him. He sat there dejected and crestfallen, like that young woman whose husband abandoned her and went abroad, or like a woman whose husband has just slapped her. (*Vi a yugend, vos der man ihrer hot zi avekgevorfen un iz avekgegangen lemedinas hayam, oder vi an isha, vos der man hot ihr derlangt a patsch.*)

Senderl's wife wasn't at home.

"Good morning, Senderl! Why so blue, dear?" Benjamin said as he came in, pointing at Senderl's cheek. "Did she get you again? Where is she, that woman?"

"She's at the market."

"Great!" Benjamin shrieked with joy. "Stop peeling those potatoes, darling, and let me be alone with you in there. . . . no one's in there, I hope? I don't want anyone chaperoning us now—I want to have a heart-to-heart talk with you, I can't wait any longer, my blood is boiling and I long for you. Come with me quickly. I don't want her coming in before we've finished."[18]

Senderl is compared in this passage not only to an abandoned woman, but explicitly to the young woman in *Lamentations Rabbah* whose husband also goes off *lemedinas hayam* (translated earlier in this essay as "to the provinces"). The second simile, in its radical drop in register, "like a woman whose husband has just slapped her," returns us to the comic and human dimension of the parable; this is someone mourning not her *abandonment* by a beloved spouse, but rather the unhappy proximity of an abusive one. While the first simile makes the sanctioned move of comparing a Jewish man, or the masculine Jewish collective, to God's bride, the second simile exposes the *wrongness* of Senderl's plight in terms of proper gender relations, in which it is presumably the woman's role to be slapped by her man. The rabbinic literature provides the pathos of the scene and links it to the exile of the Jewish people, but it is silent, as David Stern has astutely recognized, on the question of what motivates the king to leave his bride.[19] It is the modern critique of traditional Jewish gender roles—"like a woman whose husband has just slapped her"—which provides both the motivation and even poetic justification for Senderl's desertion of his wife, the act that immediately follows this scene. The metaphorical application of *aginut* to a male figure here justifies the production of a non-metaphorical *agunah*, for whom the story finds no classical Jewish resonance and not a shred of sympathy. Thus, although Abramovitsh's narrative mimetically points to the social problem of wife-abandonment, it remains caught up in the rabbinic logic that associates the pathos of desertion with the plight of Jewish men.

Earlier in this essay, I glossed over a difficulty with the integration of the figure of the *agunah* into the departure scene. Miron describes the departure as having two possible faces: exodus and exile. In the context of Miron's powerful and concise argument, this second category is strangely out of focus, comprising as it does both the triumphant flight from tyranny and the forced displacement from home. The use of the *agunah* in *Benjamin the Third*, even more curiously, bridges the two sides of the category. On the one hand, the departure of Benjamin and Senderl, as Miron argues, is a triumphant escape from captivity, "a brilliant parody of the biblical story of the Israelites' hasty escape from their house of bondage."[20] Miron does not say so explicitly, but foremost of the oppressions in this house of bondage is shtetl marriage, and the part of Pharaoh is played by the protagonists' wives. The biblical account of exodus, however, provides no images of wife-desertion; on the contrary, the *topos* of the *agunah* at play in the lengthy passage quoted above is taken entirely from the literature of *exile*. This slippage is not, it seems to me, accidental. From one perspective, the escape of Benjamin and Senderl is a triumph; they are victims, after all, and there is some warrant for figuring their debasement, in the fallen world of the Eastern European Diaspora, to that of the ultimate Jewish exile—the *agunah*. But they also act as the bridegroom—God—in the rabbinic literature, creating exile and oppression in their flight. Just as the *agunah* is a paradoxical figure, most anchored to her husband in his absence, the *agunah* in Abramovitsh's novella is an uncanny figure as well, a figure for both the men and their wives, linked with and divided from her spouse in a circle of victimization and abandonment.

In a powerful meditation on the characteristic ambivalence of shtetl literature, Miron describes the construction of the shtetl as a

> tremendously potent myth that nourished and sustained an alienated, nostalgic, modern Jewish community . . . The old home had always been both warm and stuffy, both intimate and cramped. Above all, it was tragically weak and vulnerable . . . Thus, although its desertion was obligatory, it was also the source of perpetual guilt. The shtetl image wrought in the works of the great Yiddish masters subtly expressed the pain of the parting and assuaged the guilt qualms . . . In the shtetl image a personal gap between one's past loyalties and present commitments, between childhood and adulthood, between innocence and experience, was narrowed and healed.[21]

The literature of the shtetl indeed emerges from its abandonment and loss, but, I would argue, it does not always heal these wounds. The figure of the *agunah* haunting the departures of Benjamin and Senderl, Mendele and Reb Leyb, testifies to the difficulty of mediating between the narratives of exodus and exile, between the triumphant, painful move into modernity and the nagging, glorious claims of the past.[22]

Although Dvora Baron was that rare figure in her time, a Hebrew woman writer, she shared the move from shtetl to city that is part of the collective biography of her generation—leaving her Lithuanian hometown of Ouzda in 1902 at the age of fifteen. As with the *klassiker*, Baron's stories have sometimes been read as straightforward shtetl ethnography; it is clear to me, though, that they can more fruitfully be read within the intertextual and metaphorical gestalt that Miron sees as underlying the classic literature of the shtetl. But where the *klassiker* mobilize the *agunah* as pointing to the larger national resonances of their narrative, Baron's stories function as critiques of both rabbinic hermeneutics and the modern literary uses to which it is put. "Agunah" (1927), her central story on the theme of the *agunah*, can be read, more particularly, as a response to Agnon's 1908 "Agunot," his first major publication and, literally, his signature piece (Agnon took his pen name from the story). "Agunot," to begin with Agnon's story, uses the concept of *aginut* to describe the existential and erotic alienation of its characters. This appropriation of a female figure drawn from Jewish tradition as an existential symbol is part of Agnon's modernist poetics, in which midrashic and mystical literature is mined for material that can speak to modern Jewish, and human, concerns. While the *aggada* uses the figures of husband and wife as allegories for a purely religious and national narrative, Agnon, by contrast, simultaneously activates the human/sexual and metaphysical levels of the trope. Erotic alienation is not the vehicle for the disruption of a cosmic relationship; it is for Agnon another face of the same phenomenon. Where earlier Hebrew writers had taken the *talush*, the "uprooted" young man, as the symbol for the collective alienation of a generation, Agnon reaches further into the Jewish past for his token of identification, drawing upon a female figure to symbolize the existential dislocation of his own life and of his generation. The *talush* is cut off; the *agunah*, however, is also enchained by and to the past that has rejected her.[23] For Agnon, then, the *agunah* serves as a powerful symbol not only for alienation, but also for what might be called an alienated entanglement, or an entangled estrangement.

Baron's "Agunah" describes the visit of a traveling preacher to a shtetl, focusing more particularly on a woman (named Dinah, as is the protagonist of Agnon's story) who is listening to the preacher expound on the very *aggada* alluded to in *Benjamin the Third* and elaborated in Agnon's "Agunot." The preacher recounts the story of the young princess who marries a king who lavishes gifts on her. "Then one day the king grew angry at her, stood up and demolished the canopies, ripped off her jewelry and clothing and then left her and sailed off to a land across the sea." The preacher keeps close to *Lamentations Rabbah* here, but does not quote it: the king's absence is still unexplained, but it is preceded by an abusive outburst—in the *aggada*, he leaves on his journey for no apparent reason. The neighbor women, in the sermon, pity the *agunah* but do not sexually tempt her, saying, "Woe is this poor woman, for what her husband has done to her."[24] The preacher, wrapping up his sermon, summarily expounds the parable's allegorical interpretation, describing how Israel, lost in the darkness of exile, will return to her long-absent husband, God, but Dinah remains transfixed on the literal level of the story (and on the moment before the satisfying denouement), wondering until late in the night what happened to the unfortunate bride. Finally, she turns to her husband across the dark, dank bedroom:

> "Raphael," she stretches a gaunt hand through the air. "You understood what he was getting at, there, in the synagogue: What happened to her? What happened to the agunah? Did he come back to her, the husband? Did he come back?"
>
> There is no reply. He, the old man, is not asleep, but he does not answer.
>
> "That's what they're like, always," she shakes her head, as it were, to the fairy-tale princess, gesturing with her head that she means "them," men, and then she turns back toward the wall, toward the window.
>
> The house is suffused with a damp chill and the smell of rot, a damp, moldy smell, and the night that peers through the window from outside is dark, very dark.[25]

The story implies that Dinah's situation is truly that of an *agunah*, even if she technically has a husband. She is dependent on him even to understand the meaning of her own situation, a meaning he withholds in the form of intellectual abandonment. Wife-desertion here becomes the extreme instantiation of patriarchal norms that govern the everyday structure of traditional life: the exclusion of women from Torah study, the denigration of women's relation to the tradition, and the primacy of male intellectual community over family relations. Thus, Baron's story returns the parable to the specific situation of women, resisting the long tradition of reading the sexual conflict of such midrashic narratives as signifying the relationship between a (masculine) national collective and its (masculine) divinity. In this new midrash, Dinah's "misreading" from ignorance is reread by the narrator as an act of resistance. Together, the two readers privilege the literal over the allegorical, the female over the male perspective, and the darkness of the socio-political exile of women over the national tragedy of the Jewish Diaspora. The Hebrew secular modernism that rescues sacred texts from desexualized and conventional allegorical readings is rediscovered in this story in an unexpected place—in the traditional Jewish woman's ignorance of—or freedom from—the accretions of traditional hermeneutics.

But it is in one of her earliest short stories that Baron most radically challenged the narratives of women's abandonment. "Fedka," published in both Hebrew and Yiddish in 1909, includes in the space of a dozen pages all three of Miron's shtetl motifs: a fire, departure, and the appearance of a mysterious stranger. The last of these is Fedka, the gentile postman of the title, about whom the Jewish women repeat the sort of miracle-stories that accompany the "appearance of a stranger" (prototypically Elijah the prophet):

No one knows where he's from, who he is, what he is. There are some who even doubt that he's a Christian:

"The man, he must have been a Jew. If he converted, it was only so that he'd be allowed to tear open envelopes on Sabbath."

Others protest:

"Fedka was never a Jew in his life, but what it is, he worked for a long time in rich Jewish houses. Once he was in terrible danger and the Jews he worked for saved him, and he swore from then on to be good to Jews."

And they assure everyone:

"From the day he took the position as postman in the shtetl, no bad news from abroad ever came through the mail."[26]

This shtetl guarded by a saintly and mysterious gentile postman is also unusual in another respect. Where Abramovitsh and Sholem Aleichem imagine shtetlekh populated entirely by paupers and beggars, Baron peoples this shtetl with Zelda's and Sheyne Sheindel's, that is, "women whose husbands have wandered abroad." The only masculine exceptions are "either little children or dried up old people."[27] Yet "Fedka" resists both the pathetic and the grotesque modes of the desertion scene, showing us neither the *agunah* who "weeps sore in the night", nor the outraged virago pursuing her browbeaten husband with a frying pan. Instead, she imagines a female population collectively in love with the postman, Fedka, who fully returns their affection and ardor. Fedka, of course, has the important function of bringing the mail, all of it from America; but instead of Fedka being merely the vehicle for the important relationship between the women and their husbands in America, his postal deliveries become the occasion for the ongoing flirtation between the handsome postman and the Jewish women who depend on him for a range of masculine and gentile services: unscrewing recalcitrant bottles, opening letters on *shabbes*, and, the story hints, sexual services, as well. On the Sabbath, Fedka delivers the mail in the afternoon, just in time for the post-cholent nap.

> The shutters are closed, the house is stifling and dark. Women and girls dressed in nightgowns and slips try to scurry away, but Fedka hushes them, waving his arms: "Sh . . ." As if absentmindedly his hand grazes a soft heaving breast; on his face he suddenly feels a panting breath that makes his blood sizzle: "Fedka-a-a . . ."[28]

If only he could make kiddush for them, the women marvel, his perfection would be complete.

In "Fedka," Baron reverses the perspective, near universal, that privileges the masculine journey over the experiences of the women left behind, uncovering a store of hidden pleasures in a shtetl emptied of Jewish men. "Fedka" both mobilizes and undoes the metaphorical structure that, in the classic shtetl literature, views the shtetl as a fallen Jerusalem. Resisting the Judaizing of the shtetl, Baron places her gentile hero within each of the three "submetaphors" that structure her story as they do that of the *klassiker*: Fedka is the mysterious visitor who appears in the Jewish section of town to rescue the inhabitants from the fire that threatens to engulf them. Fedka is also the only man to remain in town when the Jewish husbands have departed. By describing the mutual attraction between this non-Jew and the women left behind, Baron in effect gives subversive voice to the "neighbor women" of *Lamentations Rabbah*, who urge the *agunah* to see her husband's absence as license to look elsewhere. As David Stern points out, the suggestion of the neighbors may be not a taunt but "a perfectly accurate view of the state of the marriage" and "a perfectly neighborly gesture"; it is Stern's reading of the *mashal* (parable) as a parable of critique of the divine "husband" that finds expression in Baron's narrative.[29] *Lamentations Rabbah* ultimately prescribes the text—*ketubah* and Torah both—as a substitute for husbandly affections; Baron, by contrast, presents us with the postman as erotic substitute for the texts he delivers. Baron, then, takes up a suggestion offered not only by the neighbors, but also indeed by the rabbis themselves, that an abandoned woman might find her comfort where she can.

Baron's radical rereading of *Lamentations Rabbah* is also a rereading of the *agunah* in the classic literature of the shtetl. The feminine shtetl, in the classic departure scene, had been cast as backward and sexually stultifying; the shtetl in "Fedka," by contrast, is the stage for an erotic scenario that dissolves both ethnic borders and the ineluctable narrative of progress. Privileging the present over the absent, the visible over the textual, Baron also invites us to read the grand religious narrative of Jewish exile as having prematurely foreclosed the possible pleasures of Diaspora, and the erotic company of gentiles. In focusing on the women left behind rather than the men who have traveled on, Baron invites us to read both modernity and the Jewish national epic entirely differently.

Notes

1. Dan Miron, "The Literary Image of the Shtetl," in his study *The Image of the Shtetl and Other Studies of Modern Jewish Literary Imagination* (Syracuse, 2000), pp. 1–48.

2. Ibid., p. 3.

3. Ibid., p. 33.

4. Ibid.

5. *Eikah Rabbah* 3: 21, translated by David Stern, quoted in David Stern, *Parables in Midrash: Narrative and Exegesis in Rabbinic Literature* (Cambridge, MA, 1991), p. 57.

6. For a discussion on the appropriation of the specific historical situations of individuals who are made to serve national symbolic ends, see Roland Barthes, "Myth Today," in *Mythologies*, translated by Annette Lavers (New York, 1972; original 1957), pp. 109–159.

7. Ibid., p. 124.

8. *Eikah Rabbah* 3: 21, Stern, p. 57.

9. Miron, "The Literary Image of the Shtetl," p. 20.

10. Lucy Dawidowicz, "Introduction," *The Golden Tradition: Jewish Life and Thought in Eastern Europe*, ed. Lucy Dawidowicz (New York, 1967), p. 27–28.

11. Salomon Maimon, *Lebensgeschichte* (An Autobiography), ed. Moses Hadas (New York, 1975).

12. See Bluma Goldstein, "Doubly Exiled in Germany: Deserted Wives/Agunes in Glikl Hameln's Memoirs and Salomon Maimon's Autobiography" (paper presented at the Association of Jewish Studies, Boston, 1992). This paper is part of a book-length project of reading the narratives of abandoned women in Jewish literature and culture, including the work on Abramovitsh and Rabinovitsh (see also note 18) and on the problem of desertion in immigrant America.

13. Paula Hyman, *Gender and Assimilation in Modern Jewish History: The Roles and Representation of Women* (Seattle, 1995), p. 61.

14. As historians have shown, the massive wave of immigration that began in the nineteenth century produced its own disruptions of the Jewish family. As evidence we can take the gender imbalance of the immigrant population (57% male, 43% female, in the years 1880–1914), the work of the National Desertion Bureau, and the *New York Forward*'s "Galeria fun farshvindener mener" (The Gallery of Husbands Who Disappeared), a two-page spread that featured photos and descriptions of men who had deserted their wives. For the statistics on immigration, see Paula Hyman, *Gender and Assimilation* in *Modern Jewish History: The Roles and Representation of Women* (Seattle, 1995), p. 61. On the National Desertion Bureau and "The Gallery of Disappeared Men" see Bluma Goldstein's upcoming work on the *agunah* in modern Jewish literature and culture entitled *Enforced Marginality: Jewish Narratives on Abandoned Women* (Berkeley, 2006).

15. As Lilienblum's autobiography suggests, one man could sometimes display both "faces" of the *Haskalah* attitude toward women. Thus, in an 1871 letter from Odessa to his wife in Vilkomir, Lilienblum justifies his having left her by explaining that the rabbis viewed women as filth, born only to serve men; given the ways their marriage was degrading to her, they were better off apart! For a discussion of this letter and Lilienblum's sense of his family as "an encumbrance," see Alan Mintz, *"Banished from Their Fathers' Table": Loss of Faith and Hebrew Autobiography* (Bloomington, 1989), pp. 43–44. As Mintz rhetorically asks, "What could be more pathetic than Lilienblum's writing a long poem on the occasion of the tenth anniversary of his marriage called 'A Prisoner's Lament'?" (p. 213, note 13).

16. Yehuda Leib Gordon, "The Tip of the Yod," in *The Complete Works of Yehuda Leib Gordon*, Vol. 1 (Tel Aviv, 1960), pp. 129–139 [Hebrew]. For a biography of Gordon and an analysis of "The Tip of the Yod," see Michael Stanislawski, *For Whom Do I Toil: Judah Leib Gordon and the Crisis of Russian Jewry* (New York, 1988). Stanislawski argues that "The Tip of the Yod" gives such an

exaggeratedly dark picture of Jewish women's plight that it must be understood as parody.

17. Stanislawski, *For Whom Do I Toil*, p. 127.

18. Abramovitsh, *The Complete Works of Mendele Mokher Sforim*, Vol. 6 (New York, 1920), p. 21 [Yiddish].

19. Stern asks

Why must the king leave his wife in the first place? Why must he journey to the foreign provinces? If these questions are never answered in the course of the *mashal*, neither are a host of others: Does it ever enter the king's mind that, after he departs, the wicked neighbors will test and torment his wife? . . . if his promises are sincere, why is the king, upon his return, so astonished at her faithfulness? . . . Is the king's unexplained absence really an act of unjustified and gratuitous cruelty to his hapless wife?

As Stern makes clear, he asks these questions not to answer them but "to show that the doubts they express are indeed raised by the mashal's critique." In Stern's reading, the *mashal* is as much a parable of complaint as of praise and consolation. Stern, *Parables in Midrash*, p. 60.

20. Miron, "The Literary Image of the Shtetl," p. 23.

21. Ibid., p. xii.

22. Given that an impossible mediation is at stake in this literature, it is no surprise that those narratives that deal most explicitly with modernity and wife-abandonment, *Benjamin the Third* and *Menachem Mendel*, are both unfinished works.

23. It has sometimes been noted that "Agunot" contains no actual *agunah*, the term is metaphorically displaced from abandonment to an alienation shared by men and women. But critics have failed to notice that there is in fact an *agunah* in the story, the wife of the rabbi who goes off in voluntary exile "to redeem lost souls."

He washed his hands, drew on this mantle, took up his staff and his wallet, and, calling to his wife, said, "My daughter, seek not after me in my going forth, for the doom of exile has been levied upon me, to redeem the forsaken in love." He kissed the mezuzah, and slipped away. They sought him, and did not find him. [S. Y. Agnon, "*Agunot*," in *The Complete Stories of Shmuel Yosef Agnon: These and These* (Tel Aviv, 1966), p. 415 [Hebrew]. This story appears in English in B. Hochman's translation in S. Y. Agnon, *Twenty-One Stories*, ed. Nahum Glatzer (New York, 1970).]

The wife is not mentioned again—the narrative is interested in thematizing not her loss, but rather his exile; it is not her condition that becomes portentous and emblematic, but his. While Agnon's title reminds us of the problem of *aginut*, the narrative ends by exalting, once again, the masculine traveler over the woman he leaves behind.

24. Baron, "Deserted Wife," in *The First Day and Other Stories*, ed. Chana Kronfeld and Naomi Seidman, translated by Naomi Seidman with Chana Kronfeld (Berkeley, 2001), p. 94.

25. Ibid., p. 98.

26. Baron, "Fedka," in *The First Day*, p. 187.

27. Ibid., p. 179.

28. Ibid., p. 186.

29. Stern, *Parables in Midrash*, p. 62.

10

Rediscovering the Shtetl as a New Reality
David Bergelson and Itsik Kipnis

Mikhail Krutikov

The realistic novel was the predominant genre in Yiddish literature in interwar Europe. The novels by such well-known authors as Sholem Asch, David Bergelson, Der Nister, Moyshe Kulbak, I. J. Singer, and Zalman Shneur firmly secured the place of Yiddish literature as part of *Weltliteratur*. Many of these novels have little, if anything at all, to do with the shtetl. The major Yiddish novelists who entered literature on the eve or in the wake of World War I and the October Revolution and matured during the interwar period were eager to affirm their newly acquired urban cultural status by creating memorable pictures of past and present Jewish life the cities as diverse as Warsaw, St. Petersburg, Lodz, Berdichev, Minsk, Berlin, New York, London, Antwerp, and Jerusalem. Besides the city, Yiddish writers of that time daringly explored unfamiliar terrains of North and South America, South Africa, and the Russian Far East. Yet, when it came to depicting the shtetl, the clarity and confidence of realistic representation would often be blurred by sentimentalist nostalgia or disfigured by expressionist fragmentation. For a Jewish author writing in the aftermath of the great European upheavals of 1914–1921, depicting the shtetl sometimes presented a greater artistic challenge than portraying the city. The traditional nineteenth-century "image of the shtetl," so perceptively analyzed by Dan Miron in his seminal essay,[1] no longer fit reality and had to be adjusted to the situation of rapid social, economic, and cultural decline.

Before proceeding with our discussion of the representation of the shtetl in David Bergelson's and Itsik Kipnis's works, we first need to clarify the use of certain key terms. "Realism" may be described as a way of depicting reality which is "true to life," but it would be more difficult to give a more exact definition of this style because each culture and each epoch may have its own views of realism. In the following analysis of two important Yiddish novels of the 1920s I draw upon the ideas of Elisabeth Deeds Ermarth, which are developed in her study of the English novel. According to Ermarth, realism as an artistic method is based on a presumption that the author and the reader share certain basic views of space and time: namely, the time-space continuum is perceived as homogeneous, uniform, stable, and commonly accessible. Neither the writer nor the reader is supposed to question these conventions. This consensus, Ermarth tells us, "implies a unity in human experience which assures us that we all inhabit the same world and that the same meanings are available to everyone. Disagreement is only an accident of position."[2] In English literature, a realistic novel typically is narrated by a third-person voice in the past tense, although sometimes the narrator may speak in first-person. The narrator in realistic fiction "transgresses the boundaries of individuality not only between persons but also between persons and texts."[3] It is, of course, not always easy to draw clear lines separating between the realist novels and the non-realist ones. More useful would be to identify realistic elements and aspects in a literary text, which can appear side by side with non-realist ones.

Realism has always held a special place in the Yiddish literary system. Some critics and writers emphasized the mimetic value of Yiddish as the language of the masses, as opposed to the aristocratic Hebrew of the learned elite. The Soviet scholar Meir Wiener celebrated the creation of modern Yiddish literature by the radical Enlighteners (maskilim) out of the need to reach out to the broad popular audience. Wiener regarded the appearance of Yiddish realism in the first half of nineteenth century as the moment of truth in Jewish cultural history, when for the first time in thousands of years Jews became capable of expressing themselves in their natural vernacular idiom. From this perspective, the three founding fathers of modern Yiddish literature—Mendele Moykher Sforim, Sholem Aleichem, and I. L. Peretz—were the greatest Yiddish writers, unsurpassed in their realist representation of the shtetl Jewish life. But, as Dan Miron warns us, we should not mistake their artistic images for a historical or anthropological reproduction of the shtetl. What the three Yiddish classical writers created—and to them Miron adds a fourth one, the Hebrew author S. Y. Agnon—was not a photograph but "a double-tiered visionary image, a metaphor as rich as any in the annals of literary toponymy." Thus, Sh. Ya. Abramovitsh created in his Mendele novels a metaphorical universe, with the fictive town of Glupsk as its capital and numerous shtetlekh with telling names such as Kabtsansk, Tsvuyachits, Tuneyadevke, and Bezlyudov as its provinces, which were not part of the real world dominated by big cities. The difference between myth and reality would become especially clear when a character like Fishke the Lame or Benyomin the Third occasionally ventured from the Glupsk country into the territory of the real Russian Empire, only to realize the huge difference between the two worlds. The classical image of the shtetl was based not on the consensus between the author and the reader in the sense of a universal convention that Ermarth finds in the nineteenth-century English realistic novel, but on a close cultural bond between a Yiddish writer and his reader, which was rooted in the shared religious metaphors of Jerusalem, exile, and redemption.

The first Russian Revolution of 1905–1907, accompanied by the mass involvement of the shtetl youth in radical politics on the one hand and by the wave of anti-Jewish pogroms on the other, brought about a radical revision of Yiddish literary conventions. The experience of the revolution created a new language and new imagery for representing reality. Mass upheavals, violence, and disturbances were no longer to be seen as part of the eternal cyclical paradigm of Jewish history, but as a new phenomenon, an unprecedented historical transformation that was to change the Jewish condition once and for all. The new realistic style borrowed its images and concepts not from the tradition but from the contemporary political discourse, newspaper reports, and socialist propaganda, replacing the dominant Jewish *Weltanschauung*, with its idiosyncratic mixture of sentimentality, irony, resentment, and faith, by a new universalistic one, which was straightforward, earnest, optimistic, and detached from the daily concerns of the shtetl life. The passing away of Peretz, Sholem Aleichem, and Abramovitsh within three years during World War I marked the end of the classical era. The shtetl was incorporated into the world as the result of the violent development of European history and could no longer be realistically perceived as a separate universe. In the wake of the World War I, the October Revolution, the Russian Civil War, and the Soviet-Polish War, Yiddish writers in Eastern Europe were especially interested in testing the limits of the shtetl against those unprecedented waves of violence. "When the shtetl was focused on, to the exclusion of the cities or the larger geopolitical scene, total destruction suddenly became a real possibility," as David Roskies sums up the challenge posed by reality to

Yiddish literature of that period.[4] In two examples taken from the works of the leading Ukrainian-Yiddish authors, Itsik Kipnis and David Bergelson, I will attempt to demonstrate how the totality of the catastrophic experience led to the emergence of a new realistic vision of the shtetl that was no longer excluded from the space-time continuum of the new reality.

Publication of Itsik Kipnis's short novel *Hadoshim un teg* (*Days and Months*) in 1926 was a remarkable event in Soviet Yiddish literature. It was the first prose work that addressed the recent events from the Civil War in Ukraine from a Soviet perspective. The book was introduced by the leading Yiddish critic, Isaac Nusinov, who praised it for its truthful depiction of the war and tried to shield the young author from possible accusations in petit-bourgeois nationalism. The novel was warmly received outside the Soviet Union as well: in his *Lexicon of Yiddish Literature* Zalman Reyzen called the book "one of the most important phenomena in the new Soviet Yiddish prose that signals the return to the tradition of simplicity and naturalness of artistic realism in Yiddish literature"; David Bergelson characterized the main character of the book as a new incarnation of Sholem Aleichem's Motl, the Cantor's son who did not go to America but stayed in Kasrilevke throughout the entire Civil War.[5] Nevertheless, Kipnis was chastised by proletarian critics and forced to revise the book for the Russian translation that appeared in 1930. The book figured at Kipnis's trial in 1950 as evidence of "anti-Soviet and nationalist agitation," for which he was sentenced to ten years of forced labor. The accusation was dismissed, and the writer was released in 1957, when a Deputy General Prosecutor of the Soviet Union decided that it was wrong to punish the writer for a book published twenty-four years earlier, "especially as he had already been subject to literary criticism and reprimanded at that time."[6]

Khadoshim un teg, which is subtitled "A Chronicle," is a first-person account of the events in the author's native Volhynian shtetl in during the Civil War, when the Red Army fought against various anarchist and nationalist guerrilla gangs. The title points to the contrast between two modes of time, which, Roskies explains, include "idyllic time—the quiet joy of a newlywed couple in the sleepy but prosperous shtetl of Sloveshne—[which] is measured in months"; and "tragic time—the terror of the pogrom itself and of its aftermaths—[which] is measured in days." As Roskies observes in his brief but penetrating analysis of the novel, the narrator's "sense of split time" is used as an artistic device for expressing the full weight of terror experienced by the Jewish population of the shtetl.[7] The novel opens on a sweet and naïve note, with Isaac telling about the overwhelming state of happiness he experiences after the marriage with his beloved Buzi. Her name of course immediately refers the reader to Sholem Aleichem's *Shir hashirim*, a lyrical poem in prose about teenage love. *Khadoshim un teg* is replete with Sholem Aleichem references, which serve a dual purpose: to establish a connection with the classical literary tradition and at the same time to highlight the difference between the shtetl before and after the war.

The narrative voice, like the narrative time, possesses two different modes: "the sophisticated narrator, capable of . . . richly metaphoric language, and the naïve narrator, who is taken in by surface realities."[8] During the initial peaceful few months represented in the novel, we slowly become familiar with the shtetl with the help of the narrator, a worker in the shtetl tannery industry. He is a proletarian by choice: rather than being a foreman in his father's own tannery and taking part in exploiting workers, he prefers to work as a wage laborer for someone else. The young couple enjoys the pastoral routine of work and love. As befits a conscious proletarian, Isaac is indifferent to religion, likes Yiddish literature, and even expresses some signs of sympathy to the Zionist ideals, albeit not without some irony. But practical Zionism is associated for him with the petit-bourgeois class of *balebatim* (house-owners).

At the beginning of the new era the shtetl tries to continue living in its own mythological space:

"who doesn't know that in Russia it's already a year since the great revolution? Of course we know that. But in our place no revolutions have yet taken place. Here one only hears stories. The shoemakers are making shoes, the tailors are doing tailoring, the shop owners are keeping their stores open . . . One even feels some sense of 'salvation coming to Jews' . . . But in the meantime our shtetl still isn't aware of anything."

"ver veyst nisht, az in rusland iz shoyn a yor nokh der groyser revolyutsye? Avade veysn mir! Ober in undzere mekoymes gufe zenen nokh keyne shum revolyutses nisht forgekumen. Bay undz hert men bloyz mayses. Di shuster shustern zikh, di shnayder—shnaydern, di kremer halt di kleytn ofn . . . zet ir, di nodl baym shnayder geyt afile gringer fun hant:— m'filt epes "yeshues oyf yidn" . . . ober dervayl veyst nokh undzer shtetl fun gornisht."[9]

The new reality of class struggle has not yet captured the shtetl: when the workers sing *marselyeze*, it still sounds like a *mayse*, and the shtetl bourgeoisie still believe that the new authorities can be placated.

Using his peculiar pseudo-naïve idiom, Isaac chalenges the traditional concept of the shtetl as an isolated space. "Some people say that Sloveshne is the end of the world. But it's a big lie. If we travel for about 50 to 60 vyorst from any end of the town, we will reach a railroad. And with the railroad, the entire world already lies open." (*Andere zogn, az mit Sloveshne endikt zikh shoyn di velt. S'iz ober a groyser lign. Fun velkhn ek shtot s'zol nisht zayn, ven mir forn op a 50–60 vyorst, trefn mir a ban. Un mitn ban iz dokh shoyn fray di velt* [p. 43].) For Isaac, Sloveshne is open "out to all four sides." These outward ways are marked by the tanneries, which he defines as "our source of livelihood" (*undzer hayes*), located on the periphery of the shtetl like town fortifications. Each tannery merits a detailed technical description. In addition, on three sides the shtetl is surrounded by a belt of young birch groves. These groves serve as the shtetl promenade and pasture. Beyond this natural shtetl border lie woods and fields, punctuated by small villages and hamlets. By shifting the emphasis from the commercial center to the productive periphery of the shtetl, Kipnis creates a new image of the shtetl as an open space integrated into the surrounding landcape, as opposed to the classical model of the shtetl as a closed space with the market place as its center, which was developed by Mendele, Sholem Aleichem, and Peretz. The significance of this shift becomes evident in the second part, where the time mode suddenly changes from idyllic to tragic.

Indeed, small industry and trade play now a more important role in shtetl life than the traditional commerce that has all but collapsed in the time of the war shortages. Because peasants now rarely come to the shtetl, shtetl Jews, among them Isaac's mother-in-law, have to go out to the country to exchange scarce goods for food. In the times like this, shtetl workers make a better living than merchants because big city industry lies in ruins and is not able to satisfy the demand for basic necessities such as clothing, shoes, harness, and kitchenware. The industrious Sloveshne tanners manage to negotiate a relatively good deal with the powers that be. They go to the neighboring shtetl Ovruch to work for the local commander of the Ukrainian nationalist militia under the command of Simon Petlyura, who not only provides Jewish workers with safe conduct, but also promises to punish the perpetrators of the pogrom in Ovruch. In the end, however, he not only does not honor his promise but also brutally murders the most prominent Ovruch Jews before leaving the town.

The signs of the looming pogrom multiply as the narrative progresses. Every innocent detail conceals a dangerous potential that become manifest during the pogrom. As Roskies observes, "the Gentiles, seemingly nonexistent at the outset, are strategically introduced at the midpoint of the narrative, and from there Kipnis builds a rise-and-fall pattern of terrifying intensity."[10] Kipnis portrays gentiles not as flat stereotypical figures in the tradition of the classical shtetl literature, but as real and problematic characters. At first they appear cooperative, familiar, and even friendly, but their treacherous nature reveals itself gradually as the pogrom comes closer. Like Petlyura's commander, the new head of the Soviet militia reassures Jews that they are safe, but when the pogrom breaks out, he turns out to be one of its leading perpetrators. The pogrom seems inevitable simply because it is in the air: "actually, nothing is clear, but all the talks are about pogrom" (*eygntlekh, veyst men dokh fun gornisht, nor redn redt men fun a pogrom*) [p. 83]). The pogrom eventually begins on a Tuesday, when most men are away at work in the villages, and goes on till Saturday, when a Red Army regiment comes and punishes the pogromists. The worst atrocities happen at night, whereas during the day the shtetl looks quiet as usual, and only "our streets are crossed over by thin threads of fear" (*di gasn zaynen bay undz ale ibergekreytst mit fedimlekh fun shrek* [p. 117]).

Isaac and his family survive thanks to their cunning, instinctive sense of space. Every night they find the right place to hide, first in orchards and the surrounding groves, then with peasants in neighboring villages. They survive on the periphery of the shtetl space, whereas in the central part Jews face certain death and devastation. The pogrom shakes up Isaac's view of the world, so that he now questions the traditional Jewish quietist position: "So, when will they kill *shikses*? For no particular reason, grown-up *shikses*? Simple girls, such as the daughter of Naftole-Yoshke who lives at the river, the dressmaker, and, in general, anyone who simply turns up under their hand—and with no real intention to kill?" (*"iz ven zhe vet men umbrengen shikses? Azoy zikh, un groyse shikses? Ot azelkhe proste, vi Naftole-Yoshkes meydl fun untern taykh, di shnayderke un, biklal, velkhe s'veln nor kumen unter der hant—vos keyner klaybt zikh nisht koylen"* [p. 145]). It was this passage that would put Kipnis in trouble with the Soviet vigilantes of political correctness for over twenty-five years.

After the pogrom Isaac feels estranged from the Sloveshne Jews who show passivity and helplessness before the danger. On Friday, when the shtetl is taken over by the pogromists, the Jews are forced to bury their dead. "They worked till darkness, and at night they all sang *lekhu neranena* ("come, let us sing to the Lord") at the cemetery" (*Biz nakht hot men gearbet, un in ovnt hobn ale gezungen 'lkhu neranena' oyfn heylikn ort* [p. 164]).

It is only thanks to one courageous Jewish man who secretly runs to Ovruch on the Friday night and comes back with a Red Army regiment on Saturday that the shtetl is rescued. The retaliation is swift and brutal, the Reds killed many perpetrators on the spot, and the gentiles accept this as normal, although not without a grudge: "all right, we had to pay head for a head, but not more, it's a waste to lose such healthy *goyim* (gentiles), mostly young men, washed, all well-matched. And those Jews who were killed were not all so first-rate. They were old people, women, children" (*"nu, meyle farfaln, m'hot opgetsolt a kop far a kop, nor mer nisht, an aveyre azelkhe gezunte goyim. Di merste teyl yunge, ibergevashene, ayns in eyns. Un di yidn, vos men hot geharget, zenen dokh nisht geven ale keyn briyes. S'zenen dokh geven alte, geven vayber, geven kinder"* [p. 170]). Because the Red Army appears as the only feasible alternative to Jewish passivity, Isaac, along with other Jewish workers, decides to join it in order to defend Jews in other shtetlekh from counter-revolutionary gangs. Isaac leaves Sloveshne for good, and after the war settles in a big city. But he is still uncertain as he completes his chronicle about five years after the events: "I don't know whether I am clever or foolish that I am now writing down these lines for memory" (*"Ikh veys nisht, tsi ikh bin a kluger, tsi a nar mit dem, vos ikh farshrayb itst ot do shures far an ondenk"* [p. 183]).

The image of the shtetl in *Khadoshim un teg* differs in some important ways from the classical shtetl archetype. The imitation of Sholem Aleichem's style turns out to be a parody that destroys the mythological shtetl artistically when the real shtetl has been destroyed physically. Sholem Aleichem's Motl was an eternal teenager whose development was arrested by his emigration to America; Kipnis's Isaac matures during the five days of the pogrom and becomes a Red Army soldier. In Sholem Aleichem's Kasrilevke all productive activity turned into travesty, like Pinye's plan to make ink or *kvas*; Sloveshne is dominated by its tanning industry which produces real goods. The Jewish calendar and life cycle ruled supreme in Kasrilevke, whereas Sloveshne lives according to a new timetable of revolutionary wars.

The first Soviet edition of *Khadoshim un teg* was preceded by an introduction by Isaac Nusinov, a leading Soviet authority on Yiddish and world literature. Nusinov characterized the style of the novella as "primitive" and pointed out that the young author was not capable of reaching a degree of artistic generalization that was necessary for a representation of the Civil War from the "conscious" Marxist point of view, especially when it came to nationalist "bias." But Nusinov recognized that Kipnis succeeded in producing an adequate picture of the "primitive" reality of the backward shtetl by portraying both Jews and Ukrainians as passive objects of the revolution rather than its active subjects.[11]

The novella was warmly received outside the Soviet Union, particularly by the left-wing critics, and was republished by the prestigious Kletskin press in Vilno in 1929. In his *Lexicon of Yiddish Literature* Zalman Reyzen called the book "one of the most important phenomena in the new Soviet Yiddish prose that signals the return to the tradition of simplicity and naturalness of artistic realism in Yiddish literature."[12] Nusinov's discriminating criticism did not shield Kipnis from more vicious attacks and accusations of "petit-bourgeois nationalism" by some Soviet proletarian critics.[13]

"*Khadoshim un teg* is an interesting, fresh, and I would even say an original work," wrote Shmuel Niger, the leading American critic of the time, in 1927.[14] Niger's only reservation regarding the book concerned its "mixed" style. Kipnis was good, according to Niger, in the "lyrical" parts where he spoke with the passionate, naïve and ironic voice of a young artisan in love; he was less good where he assumed the tone of the detached chronicler.[15] The stylistic dualism of the novella was explored with more subtlety by David Roskies. Already the title of *Khadoshim un teg* implies a contrast between two modes of time, which Roskies distinguishes as idyllic and tragic: "idyllic time—the quiet joy of a newlywed couple in the sleepy but prosperous shtetl of Sloveshne—is measured in months; tragic time—the terror of the pogrom itself and of its aftermaths—is measured in days." The narrator's "sense of time split in half" is used, Roskies explains, as an artistic device for expressing the full weight of terror experienced by the Jewish population of the shtetl.[16] The narrative voice, like the narrative time, possesses two different modes: " the sophisticated narrator, capable of [. . .] richly metaphoric language, and the naïve narrator, who is taken in by surface realities.[17] Strangely enough, this point could still be missed by such a perceptive reader as David Bergelson.

When *Khadoshim un teg* came out in the second, "improved" edition in Vilno Kletskin farlag in 1929, it was reviewed by David Bergelson in the Warsaw weekly *Literarishe bleter*.[18] Echoing Nusinov, Bergelson stressed the close genetic link between Kipnis and Sholem Aleichem. Kipnis took up Sholem Aleichem's narrative where Sholem Aleichem made a wrong turn, taking his young hero out of his native shtetl of Kasrilevke to America and losing him there for Yiddish literature. The prototype of Kipnis's Isaac is Sholem Aleichem's Motl, who in this case "iz geblibn in der heym un hot durkhgemakht mit Kasrilevke ir nayem gilgul" (had stayed at home and made a new round of transformation with Kasrilevke).[19] The orientation toward Sholem Aleichem's aesthetics determined both strengths and weaknesses of Kipnis's novella.

Bergelson noted that Kipnis went one step further from his mentor by emancipating his hero from the dominating authorial narrative voice. His protagonist "hot zikh oysgelernt tsu dertseyln vegn zikh un vegn arumike mit zayn eygenem moyl, on der hilf funem groysn kinstler Sholem Aleykhem" (learned to talk about himself and about people around him with his own mouth, without the help of the great artist Sholem Aleichem).[20] As a point of departure for his story, Kipnis brought together in marriage two of Sholem Aleichem's favourite characters, Isaac/Motl and Buzi from the story "Song of Songs." Bergelson especially praised Kipnis's style, which he found better than Sholem Aleichem's in its colourful and "organic" characterization of the Jewish artisan. Unlike Sholem Aleichem, Kipnis was himself part of this social group: the artisans have "oysgeteylt" (delegated) their writer from their midst to tell the story of his love— Bergelson pointed out somewhat haughtily, perhaps being aware of his own bourgeois background.[21]

Yet this kind of a naïve character was anachronistic and no longer adequate to the new reality, Bergelson argued. His main deficiency lay in his limited petit-bourgeois mentality that limited his class consciousness. To the life-and-death question of the revolutionary time, "mit vemen bistu?" (with whom are you?) he answered: "ikh, mit vemen ikh bin? I hob khasene gehat . . ." (me, with whom I am? I've just got married...).[22] The ideological backwardness of the author led to the artistic weakness of his work. The petit-bourgeois worldview that was still relevant in 1890 and enabled Sholem Aleichem to create Kasrilevke as a "synthetic" shtetl, was no longer adequate in the situation of 1919, which reduced the significance of Sloveshne to a mere local case study. But, Bergelson added, Sloveshne was nevertheless the best portrait of the shtetl in the revolution and war in contemporary Yiddish literature. Kipnis's folk-style simplicity in the depiction of the pogrom was far superior, Bergelson concluded, to pathetic sentimentalism of the American author Lamed Shapiro and other modernists.[23]

In his review of Kipnis's novel, Bergelson elaborated on some of the arguments from his earlier essay on Sholem Aleichem, which appeared in the New York communist daily *Morgn-frayhayt* in 1926. In that essay Bergelson argued that both the strengths and the weaknesses of Sholem

Aleichem's style resulted from the fact that Sholem Aleichem embodied the collective creativity of the Jewish people. Speaking in the voice of the collective, Sholem Aleichem remained insensitive to such phenomena as individual psychology, female beauty, or the beauty of nature because the Yiddish language of the people did not possess adequate linguistic and artistic resources.

Instead, Sholem Aleichem excelled in the depiction of grief, suffering, and death, because he could draw on the wealth of the folk idiom: "do filt zikh, vi laykht Sholem Aleykem hot genumen verter fun rekhts un fun links, mamesh geshart mit di lopetes" (one feels here how easily Sholem Aleichem could utilize words, he literally shoveled them).[24] Bergelson's conclusion was categorical: "a shrayber is a sholiyekh-tsibur, a yoyresh un a forshteyer fun gresere, oder klenere masn" (a writer is a messenger, an heir to, and a representative of, greater or smaller masses).[25] This statement, which signaled Bergelson's shift towards communism, fully conformed with the official Soviet doctrine of the late 1920s–early 1930s, according to which the artistic capacity of a writer to express reality is fully determined by his class background.

The same class-deterministic approach informed Bergelson's reading of Kipnis's novella. Although Bergelson's essay appeared in Poland, it followed the general line of Soviet criticism that regarded Kipnis as a voice of the Jewish petit-bourgeoisie. A contemporary reader might wonder how a writer as subtle and intelligent as Bergelson could miss the subversive irony of Kipnis's pseudo-naïve stylization of Sholem Aleichem's style. Bergelson seems to have fallen into the traps that Kipnis deliberately set up for his ideological critics.

In fact, rather than imitating Sholem Aleichem style, Kipnis subjected it to a critical interrogation against the new reality of war and revolution. Jewish calendar and life cycle ruled supreme in Kasrilevke, but Sloveshne lived according to a new timetable of revolutionary wars. In contrast to Sholem Aleichem, in Kipnis's novel, as Roskies noted, "[m]yth and the language of faith play no mitigating role whatsoever, whether because Soviet Yiddish politics would not allow for them or because Kipnis himself rejected the mythic component of Sholem Aleichem's legacy."[26] One might only speculate that Bergelson may have deliberately ignored the depth of Kipnis's prose by caricaturing him as Sholem Aleichem's epigone because Bergelson had himself just published his own revolutionary novel which manifested a complete break with the old tradition of shtetl representation.

David Bergelson's third novel, *Midas-hadin* (*Measure of Judgment*), marks the watershed between the modernist and socialist realist periods in the writer's creativity. Written while Bergelson still lived outside the Soviet Union, it came out simultaneously in Kiev and Vilna, being one of the few works of interwar Yiddish literature published both in the Soviet Union and abroad.[27] In it Bergelson makes an attempt to accept the ideological perspective of the Revolution and to celebrate it artistically, but still without adopting the normative discourse that was already becoming obligatory for writers working in the Soviet Union. The experimental character of the novel is evident in its name. To choose a Jewish religious concept as a title was untypical for Bergelson, who normally used for this purpose words denoting time or space, either literally, as in *At the Dnieper* or *In a Backward Town*, or metaphorically, as in *Descent, When All Is Said and Done*, or *In Darkened Times*, or simply named his works after their main characters or events.

As follows from his critique of Kipnis, Bergelson was not satisfied by the contemporary state of the Soviet Yiddish prose and aspired to the role of the leading revolutionary writer, not an easy task for someone who was living abroad and was not a member of the Communist party. Susan Slotnik believes that Bergelson succeeded in his endeavor: "It is in *Midas-hadin* that his concept of Marxism and the Marxist view of history achieved sufficient clarity and cohesiveness to sustain a novel-length work.[28] But in the following statement Slotnik, probably inadvertently, casts some doubt on the "clarity and cohesiveness" of Bergelson's Marxism: the recognition of the revolution "is presented, not as an emotional or even intellectual process, but rather as a quasi-religious one."[29] As I will try to demonstrate, it is precisely Bergelson's artistic experiment at reconciling the Marxist, class-deterministic, vision of the revolution with a quasi-religious one, rooted in the Jewish mystical tradition, that makes *Midas-hadin* both problematic and interesting.

The unusual title offers a clue to the novel's symbolic meaning that is concealed under the surface of its obvious pro-Soviet ideological message. The action takes place in a new space that has been created as a result of the Revolution and the Civil War. The revolutionary space is defined by the invisible but dangerous border that separates not just two states but two worlds: the Soviet revolutionary world of the future, and the Polish bourgeois world of the past. The border is guarded by a group of revolutionary soldiers based in the former Russian Orthodox convent of Kamino-Balke. Between the center of revolutionary power and the border are Jewish shtetlekh and Ukrainian villages, swarming with all sorts of people desperate to "steal themselves over the border" and leave the land of the Revolution behind. The shtetl Golikhovlke, once a center of local trade and commerce, now subsists exclusively on the illegal traffic of people crossing the border to Poland. Golikhovke has turned into a ghost town which sleeps during the day and comes alive at night, when local wagon drivers take refugees to the border.

If the traditional image of the shtetl was that of a "Jerusalem in exile," to use Miron's formula, then Bergelson models Golikhovke after Sodom.[30] A decent person cannot even buy food there: "'they cook and bake here not for people like us—they make a party for those who come here to cross the border'" ("*'m'kokht un m'bakt nit far azelkhe vi ir—do makht ment 'hasene' yene, vos kumen aher ganvenen di grenets'*" [pp. 145–146]), a local girl explains to a Red Army soldier who passes thorugh the shtetl on his way from the border to Kamino-Balke. As Susan Slotnik points out in her study of Bergelson's novels, there is no politically neutral space in *Midas hadin*: "Golikhovke is the home of one counterrevolutionary element: those who smuggle goods and people over the border for their livelihood," whereas the other aspect of the opposition, the Socialist-Revolutionaries who prepare an anti-Soviet peasant rebellion, is associated with the various villages in the vicinity.[31] The shtetl is the point of conflict between two adversary powers, the Bolshevik revolutionary dictatorship of Kamino-Balke and the ripening rebellion that is nested in villages and hamlets near the border. The countryside is represented as the source of insecurity and danger; which needs to be eliminated by revolutionary force. But neither side is favorably disposed towards the shtetl Jews.

The novel's main character is Filipov, the gentile commander of the Kamino-Balke regiment, who has been sent to the area to put an end to the illegal cross-border traffic. Filipov embodies the strictness of revolutionary judgment: as a "prophet and messenger of the revolution,"[32] as Slotnik characterizes him, he "carries in him a cold iron drop of justice, which decides whether to shoot prisoners or not" (*trogt in zikh a kaltn, ayzernem tropn yoysher, vos bashlist, shisn arestantn, tsi neyn*) [p. 107]). A unique figure in the world of Bergelson's writing, Filipov is a one-dimensional character fully determined by his ideological commitment to the cause of revolution.[33] His mind is programmed to such an extent that he does not remember his own birthday—"as if I were born in October," he tells his comrade (p. 243). From the moment he joins the revolutionary struggle, he changes his real name, Anastasyev, for the revolutionary pseudonym Filipov. But his physique is not able to meet the high demands of his mission. Filipov suffers from a severe chronic inflammation in his neck, so that his enemies and even some of his colleagues secretly hope that he would die before he gets a chance to dispense revolutionary justice to them.

Bergelson repeatedly stresses the mystical, superhuman aspect of Filipov's personality, which he represents by means of religious symbolism. Filipov's revolutionary consciousness is concentrated in an "iron drop" inside him, which instructs him what to do in critical situations (p. 240), not unlike the legendary device of *urim vetumim* (the breastplate) through which God revealed His will to the High Priest in the Jerusalem Temple. The comrades perceive Filipov as "an iron man and a tzaddik [righteous man]," whereas his enemies find this combination impossible: "I've never seen yet a tzaddik from iron" (p. 177). At the end, however, even the iron man is worn out by the burden of his responsibility for the Revolution and decides to meet his death, setting off alone in a suicide mission to fight counter-revolutionary bandits in the woods. His heroic death helps to mobilize the demoralized forces of the Revolution, so that the reader can be assured in their final victory.

The subversive use of religious discourse in the novel is an essential part of Bergelson's realistic technique. He deliberately brings together elements that traditionally belong to completely different symbolic realms in order to demonstrate the overwhelming power of the new revolutionary reality. Filipov turns the former monastery of Kamino-Balke into a prison and fills it with people who in normal life would never find themselves in the same room. Here we see a number of Jews—a merchant, Reb Arn, with his business assistant; a former Red Army soldier; an anti-Bolshevik Socialist-Revolutionary; and a watchmaker—as well as two Polish prostitutes, a Russian Orthodox priest, and a Ukrainian bandit. All these people have been caught attempting to cross the border illegally and are now awaiting judgment. The revolutionary committee meets on a Friday night, but the sentence is not announced until a day later. On the Friday afternoon the religious Reb Arn has bribed a guard to get him a *challah* (braided bread) for the Shabbat. When the *challah* eventually arrives on the late Sabbath afternoon, he invites his fellow Jewish inmates to celebrate with him the departure of the holy day. When darkness falls, the executors come to take him together with the two Polish girls to be shot. Reb Arn, who has been preparing himself to die as a pious Jew for the sanctification of God's name, takes it as a grave offence that he will be executed in the company of two prostitutes. Susan Slotnik perceptively interprets this detail as an allusion to the two thieves who were crucified with Christ (p. 252).

One can easily imagine how such a scene could have been presented by Sholem Asch, who would of course relish the melodramatic situation wherein an observant Jewish merchant and Catholic-Polish prostitutes are murdered together by the cruel Russian Bolsheviks. Bergelson, however, destroys all national and religious sentimentalism with one cruel touch. Before leaving the cell, Reb Arn quietly tells his assistant where he hid the money that he made by smuggling his leather merchandise. Bergelson skillfully plays on the reader's expectations of a yet another heroic act of *kiddush ha-shem* (martyrdom), which was made popular by Asch, only to turn them upside down by exposing the "true" mercantile essence of traditional piety. This final episode leaves a strong impression on other people in the cell. Reb Arn gets metonymically reduced in the memory of his assistant to his five golden teeth, which have "forever weakened and profaned all the beautiful religious teaching that one pronounces over the Shabbat khale before death" (*hobn oyf eybik farshvakht un vokhedik gemakht ale sheyne toyres, vos men zogt farn toyt oyf shabesdike khales* [p. 132]). Bergelson methodically revises traditional religious values and exposes them as corrupt, selfish, and cynical.

As a new totality, the Revolution has no room for personal autonomy. It enforces a new consensus upon the fragmented society of frightened individuals who can no longer maintain traditional bonds of family, friendship, community, or business. "'These days, if you've known someone from yesterday, it doesn't mean that you know him today'" (*"Hayntike tsaytn, az du konst a mentshn fun nekhtn, heyst es nokh nisht, az du konst im haynt"* [p. 34]), remarks Doctor Babitski, a disappointed *intelligent* and a former radical. Bergelson creates the new reality using the conventional device of the impersonal narrator who maintains a distance from the events through past-tense narration. The narrator sees through the characters' minds and coldly exposes their weakness and selfishness. He methodically identifies, exposes, and deconstructs myths, symbols, and metaphors that were inherent in the pre-Revolutionary way of life.

Bergelson's innovative narrative technique can be illustrated by the use of word *tseylem*—Hebrew and Yiddish for "cross"—which carries obvious negative connotations in the traditional Jewish discourse. This word is more than once associated with Filipov: he was raised in the poor working suburb by his pious grandmother, a *groyse tseylemnitse* (a devout Christian) (p. 244); pursuing the smugglers, he has *ibertseylemt* (literally, "crossed over") the way of smugglers with two shots from his gun. The wife of a White officer who attempts to cross the border has strange eyes, "with a woman figure sitting deep in each eye, and each woman has a cross on her chest" (p. 15). The priest in the prison cell crosses his mouth as yawns in his sleep hearing the Sabbath blessing over the meal. The most poignant subversion of both Christianity and Judaism is probably the oxymoron *koshere tseylemlekh* (Kosher cross). In Bergelson's use, the word *tseylem* loses its traditional Christian meaning but retains an aura of danger, estrangement, and mysticism. Bergelson can use a religious reference in a deliberately improper way in order both to ridicule traditional religious observance and to characterize the counter-revolutionary nature of a person. He makes a bandit, who fills himself with vodka before going into action, say "every time a new *asher-yoytser* [blessing over vodka]" (p. 204)—which denotes that the bandit needs periodically to relieve himself, an action which is metonymically described as saying the traditional Jewish blessing after such an act. The overall ideological message created by the multiple allusions of this kind is simple and straightforward: religion, whether Christian or Jewish, is associated with the counter-Revolution. Bergelson's artistic inventiveness in his uses and abuses of religious imagery makes this message look fresh and convincing.

The traditional shtetl crumbles and falls apart under the pressure of the Revolution together with the whole old world. Here again, Bergelson's descriptions of landscape and nature are charged with religious imagery, which deliberately mixes Judaism and Christianity. An ordinary sunset is transformed under Bergelson's pen into a mystical vision:

> First the darkness obscures the valley, the old mill and the little bridge, then the marketplace, the rooftops that dig their way into the mountainside and rise up, higher and higher, like the rungs of a ladder. Finally the darkness engorges the mountain itself, [and] the old Catholic church. There it remains suspended, as though before a translucent wall, still waiting, as though for *havdole* [the ceremony of separation at the end of Shabbath]. Without a single light, enveloped in [the darkness], Golikhovke lies waiting with bated breath . . . At the same time, there, on the church, where a flange of sky is still bright, someone is scrambling up to its topmost point and staring down on all the inhabitants of Golikhovke: Now what is going on in Kamino-Balke, in the old monastery of bygone days?[34]

Zi farfintstert frier dem tol, di alte mil mitn brikl, dernokh dem mark, di dekher, vos grobn zikh ayn in barg un shtaygn, shtaygn, vi di shtaplen fun a layter. Tsuletst farshlingt di fintster dem barg aleyn, dem altn katoylishn kloyster. Dort blaybt zi hengen, vi far a durkhzikhtiker vant, vos vart nokh vi oyf havdole . . . Eyngehilt in ir ligt golikhovke on a likht un vart mit fartayetn otem . . . glakh dort, oyfn kloyster, vu a breg fun himl iz nokh hel, drapet zikh emetser oyfn same shpits un kukt zikh ayn far ale golikhovker: Vos tut zikh itst in gevezenem altn monastir—in kamino-balke? (pp. 22–23)

Night is the time when the enemies of the Revolution come out. Darkness provides them with a cover and blurs all religious, national, and social differences. The marketplace, the mill, Jewish houses, and the Catholic church are all united in their dark hatred of the Revolution that resides in the Kamino-Balke monastery. Describing the shtetl, Bergelson often switches over to present-time narration, which enables him to create an impressionistic effect of uncertainty and fragmentation as opposed to the logical clarity of the revolutionary world-view. The objective past-tense narration from a single standpoint located safely in the future, when the Revolution has already triumphed, gives way to a multitude of present-tense voices that form the "chorus," the "voice of Golikhovke." The crowd of shtetl inhabitants comments, argues, and exchanges news in "a series of short sentences, uttered by anonymous individuals."[35] The chorus offers the ordinary, petit-bourgeois response of the population to extraordinary events that befall the shtetl, such as military action, acts of terror, and executions. This change of the narrative tense and the abandoning of the uniform perspective, which was a characteristic feature of Bergelson's style in his earlier works, acquires now not only an aesthetic but also an ideological significance, serving as an illustration of what Slotnik calls "the thesis of historical determinism and revolutionary 'truth.'"[36]

The special kind of omniscient narrator is an innovative feature of the novel. Despite his assumed "stance of objectivity," Bergelson's narrator is not impartial.[37] He understands the old world well, but does not sympathize with its sorrow. We can see reality as reflected in the consciousness of several characters, the chief "center of consciousness" being the protagonist, Doctor Babitski, a disappointed and depressive man who wants to be left alone but is always drawn into the middle of activity. It is through his eyes that we see the mystical revelation of the new regime as a Kabbalistic image of cold fire over the seat of the Bolshevik power: "they are cold flames of *midas-hadin*, little fires, whose master is 'he,' Filipov, a mine worker—they are the flames of that strange strict new world" (*"zey zaynen kalte fayern fun midas-hadin, fayerlekh, iber velkhe es iz balebos 'er,' Filipov, an arbeter fun shakhtes—zey zaynen fayern fun epes a modner nayer shtrenger velt"* [p. 79]).

The cold energy of *midas-hadin* that emanates from Filipov sets him apart from the word and turns him into an agent of destruction: "now he was full of the *midas-hadin* of the 'great justice,' cold and alien to everybody around him and to himslef" (*"itst iz er geven ful mit midas-hadin funem 'groysn gerekht,' alts eyns kalt un alts eyns vayt tsu ale arumike punkt vi tsu zikh aleyn"* [p. 240–241]). It seems that the Revolution has brought about a separation between the two mystical powers that normally coexist in a balance, *midas-harakhamim* (the power of mercy) and *midas-hadin*. Mercy—*rakhmones*—has no place in the new world of strict revolutionary justice. As one of the characters explains, Filipov is one of those people who cannot have the pleasure of *rakhmones*. By contrast, Babitski hears the word *rakhmones* mentioned in the crowd of women, wives, and daughters of the prisoners in Kamino-Balke, who wait for days in front of the closed gates of the former monastery.

Midas-hadin is not a realistic novel in the traditional sense. Unlike the nineteenth-century Russian, English, or French realists who depicted a relatively stable world, Bergelson depicts a radically new reality not yet familiar to his reader or to himself. "The narrator tries to depict the new by the means of a language that is made out of the associations with the old"—so Novershtern describes Bergelson's narrative technique.[38] By using such a conventional realistic device as impersonal past-tense narration, Bergelson implies a temporal and spatial continuity between the past and the present, something which hardly corresponds to the real experience of his readership of that time. The objectivity of the narrative style imposes new ideological conventions that in fact can be highly contentious for anyone who does not automatically share the revolutionary world-view. The new objectivity is based on the revealed absolute truth of the Revolution which is contrasted to the passive objectivity of the old "bourgeois" world, which is represented by Dr. Babitski's position of neutrality and non-participation. Thus, the objective narrative perspective helps to legitimize violence as the law of the Revolution.

And yet it would be an oversimplification to identify the position taken by David Bergelson as the author with the point of view of the narrator. Through the impersonal past-tense narration Bergelson shows us an unreal experimental world ruled by *midas-hadin* alone. It is a metaphysical construction not unlike the universe of Kafka's fiction—indeed, the Kamino-Balke monastery resembles the Castle both as a dark architectural fantasy and as a metaphysical source of power. This new universe has no room for the traditional shtetl mode of living on trading, negotiating, bargaining, and arguing which necessarily involves compromise and the recognition of the other. Shtetl life is conveyed through the present-tense narration devoid of a definite ideological point of view. Here we hear a polyphonic chorus of voices which belong to real people of flesh and blood. The reader who recognizes the conflict between the two types of narration will discover a mystical parable beyond the realistic surface, a nightmare vision of the world ruled solely by the power of strict judgment, unmitigated by the vital influence of mercy and compassion. Here the new metaphor of the shtetl as Sodom replaces the classical "shtetl as Jerusalem" metaphor.

Kipnis and Bergelson, each in his own way, conducted an intensive dialogue with Yiddish literary tradition. They used realism as an instrument of deconstruction of old stereotypes and conventions. The story of the destruction of the shtetl by the combined forces of gentile violence outside and Jewish degradation inside serves for them as a case study in the comprehensive world collapse during the series of catastrophes of 1914–1921. Bergelson and Kipnis strip the shtetl of its mythological aura and forcefully push it into the hostile reality. Their contemporaries outside the Soviet sphere of ideological influence, among them such different writers as the Yiddish authors Sholem Asch, Lamed Shapiro, the Yiddish and Hebrew author Zalman Shneur, and the Hebrew authors Shmule Yosef Agnon and Haim Hazaz, employed the opposite strategy of sticking to the traditional image of the shtetl as a self-contained unit, the symbolic chronotope of Jewish existence. They explored, each in his own way, the growing tension between the *yidishe melukhe* (Jewish kingdom, which is also the title of Lamed Shapiro's popular novella) and its increasingly hostile environment, but they did not adopt a uniform narrative perspective for both. This may help to explain the artistic "double standard" that many Yiddish authors applied to the representation of the shtetl and the city. Whereas city fiction—the novels *Three Cities* and *East River* by Asch, the collection of novellas *Nyu-yorkish* and the unfinished novel *Der amerikaner shed* by Lamed Shapiro, the novels *The Brothers Ashkenazi* and *The Family Carnovski* by I. J. Singer, as well as Bashevis's novel *The Family Moskat*—belongs unquestionably to the European realistic tradition, the shtetl stories and novels by the same authors—such as Asch's *Kiddush hashem* and *Thilim-yid* (*Salvation*), Shapiro's *Di yidishe melukhe* (*In the Dead Town*), Zalman Shneur's collection *Shklover yidn* (*The Jews of Shklov*), I. J. Singer's novel *Yoshe Kalb*, and Bashevis's *Satan in Goray*—present the shtetl as a symbolic rather than a realistic space.

The shtetl myth was probably the greatest invention of modern Jewish imagination. As Dan Miron tells us, "the shtetl has based its existence not only on the Jewish religion and *halakhah* but also on Jewish myths and metaphors. It had developed its own Jewish self-image, which had conditioned its perception of time and space."[39] Yet after World War I, literature had outgrown its myth of the shtetl origin, and young writers were looking for ways to overcome limitations imposed by it on their creativity. Miron describes this process in terms of a transformation of poetic devices: from the metaphorical vision of the shtetl as it was created by the generation of the classical writers to the metonymic "deflation" of the shtetl myth by the post-classical authors that was started by Itche-Meir Weissenberg and David Bergelson in their post–1905 fiction. According to Miron, the young generation shifted the balance between "the observed metonymy" and "the intuited metaphor," which was carefully maintained in the works of the classical Yiddish literature. After 1905 this classicist poise was no longer sustainable, and the split between the neo-romantic metaphoric and the opposite naturalistic metonymic representation of the shtetl became visible in the two different novellas under the same title *A Shtetl*, by Asch and Weissenberg respectively.

Although Miron admits that the metonymic "countervision" of the shtetl in works by Bergelson, Markish, Weissenberg, and others deserves attention in its own right, he believes that "within a comprehensive historical perspective it forms a mere foil, a contrasting backdrop against which the contours of the richer and more complex vision of the *klassiker* stands out."[40] What this essay has tried to demonstrate is that in the best works of the post-classical period we can find a new metaphorization of the shtetl based not on its special position as Jerusalem in exile, but on its relationships with the real world around it. For Bergelson the underlying metaphor is *midas-hadin*, a world devoid of *midas-harakhamim*. Kipnis, drawing upon Sholem Aleichem's archetype of Jewish character, creates a new figure of a *folks-mentsh* (an ordinary Jew), an eternal and indestructible hero capable of overcoming obstacles and surviving disasters without losing his Jewish soul.

NOTES

1. "The Literary Image of the Shtetl," in Dan Miron, *The Image of the Shtetl and Other Studies of Modern Jewish Literary Imagination* (Syracuse, 2000), pp. 1–48.

2. Elizabeth Deeds Ermarth, *Realism and Consensus in the English Novel: Time, Space and Narrative* (Edinburgh, 1998), p. 65.

3. Ibid., p. 67.

4. David G. Roskies, *Against the Apocalypse: Responses to Catastrophe in Modern Jewish Culture* (Cambridge, MA, 1984), p. 123.

5. Zalman Reyzen, *Leksikon fun der yidisher literatur, prese un filologye*, Vol. 3 (Vilna, 1929), col. 642.

6. The documents related to Kipnis's trial are published in the Ukrainian journal *Z arkhiviv VUChK, GPU, NKVD, KGB*, No. 3/4, 1998, p. 298.

7. Roskies, *Against the Apocalypse*, 183–184.

8. Ibid., 183.

9. Itsik Kipnis, *Khadoshim un teg un andere dertseylungen* (Tel Aviv, 1973), p. 26.

10. Roskies, *Against the Apocalypse*, 184.

11. Yitskhok Nusinov, "A vinkle fun yor 1919," in *Itsik Kipnis, Khadoshim un teg: a khronik* (Kiev, 1926), pp. 6–8.

12. Zalman Reyzen, *Leksikon fun der yidisher literatur, prese un filologye*, Vol. 3 (Vilna, 1929), col. 642.

13. The critical responses to the first publication of *Khadoshim un teg* are summarized by Shmuel Niger in his 1927 review "I. Kipnis—'Khadoshim un teg,'" in Shmuel Niger, *Yidishe shrayber in Sovetn-farband* (New York, 1958), pp. 132–133.

14. Ibid., p. 136.

15. Ibid.

16. Roskies, *Against the Apocalypse*, pp. 183–184.

17. Ibid., p. 183.

18. David Bergelson, "Kipnises *Khadoshim un teg*," *Literarishe bleter*, Vol. 29 (272), 1929, pp. 558–560.

19. Ibid., p. 558

20. Ibid.

21. Ibid., p. 559.

22. Ibid.

23. Ibid.

24. David Bergleson, "Sholem Aleykhem un di folks-shprakh," *Morgn-frayhayt*, 29, August 1926. I would like to express my thanks to Gennady Estraikh for drawing my attention to this article.

25. Ibid.

26. Roskies, *Against the Apocalypse*, p. 185.

27. References are given according to David Bergelson, *Midas-hadin* (Vilna, 1929).

28. Susan Ann Slotnik, "The Novel Form in the Works of David Bergelson" (Ph.D. diss., Columbia University, 1978), p. 241.

29. Ibid.

30. Bergelson was not the first Yiddish author to compare a shtetl to Sodom. We find this comparison already in Mendele's novel *The Magic Ring* (Mendele Moykher-Sforim, Geklibene verk, Vol. 4 [New York, 1946], p. 262). Six years after the publication of *Midas-hadin* Isaac Bashevis developed this nucleus image into a full-size antinomian nightmare in his first novel *Satan in Goray* (Warsaw, 1935).

31. Slotnik, "The Novel Form in the Works of David Bergelson," p. 242.

32. Slotnik, p. 233.

33. Avraham Novershtern, "Aspektim mivniim baproza shel David Bergelson mereshitah ad 'midas-hadin'" (Ph.D. diss., Hebrew University, 1981), pp. 51–52.

34. I am grateful to Joseph Sherman for providing me with this translation.

35. Ibid., p. 302.

36. Ibid., p. 329.

37. Ibid., p. 288.

38. Novershtern, *Aspektim mivniim*, p. 32.

39. Dan Miron, *The Image of the Shtetl and Other Studies of Modern Jewish Literary Imagination* (Syracuse, 2000), p. 45.

40. Ibid.

11

Agnon's Synthetic Shtetl

Arnold J. Band

"I tell you, 'Rabi Binyomin,' that Mendele's style is not
the last word in Hebrew fiction."

In a retrospective article written in 1933, the addressee of this statement,
"Rabbi Binyomin" (the Hebrew author Yehoshua Radler-Feldman), recalls
his meetings with Agnon in Jaffa in 1908–11, when both were young, aspir-
ing writers. In one memorable scene, the two were walking along the
Mediterranean shore when Agnon protested that Mendele's style, for all its
monumental stature, did not lend itself to the description of nuanced psychological states and, as such, was not "the last word in Hebrew fiction."[1]
The implication, of course, was that he (Agnon) would do better. The
author, recording this event after Agnon had published the four volumes
of the first edition of his collected works in 1931, implies that Agnon had
indeed succeeded in forging a new prose idiom in Hebrew, something that
transcended Mendele, even though in 1911, when Agnon expressed these
aspirations, "Rabi Binyomin" thought his claims presumptuous.

While the sequence of events in this reminiscence might not be entirely
accurate, the statements and descriptions of personalities and sentiments
have a ring of authenticity and coherence. Mendele, after all, was the giant
of modern Hebrew prose fiction in those days, and every young writer had
to confront this looming figure who had recently published his three-vol-
ume collected Hebrew fiction in 1910. Some aped him, but others like
Brenner, Agnon, Gnessin, and Shofman found their own individual styles
and voices. When Agnon protested against Mendele, he was not merely
seeking a more adequate linguistic medium to express psychological real-

ism. Mendele's Hebrew style was the quintessence of the Europeanization of Hebrew prose. Despite Mendele's richly textured Jewish ambiance and his dazzling mastery of Hebrew sources, his syntax and modes of narration are those one would recognize in the great nineteenth-century European authors. As a dedicated proponent of *Haskalah* (the Jewish Enlightenment), his use of this Europeanized style was, in itself, an ideological statement; his portrayal of Jewish life in "the shtetl" was predominantly—often mordantly—satiric. In rebelling against Mendele, Agnon was not only exploring new modes of expression; he was making a statement about Jewish history.

I enclose the term "shtetl" in quotation marks throughout this chapter, since it should be abundantly evident by now that it is a problematic term, open to a host of interpretations. More often than not, the "shtetl" is an imagined construct based on literary description either in Hebrew or in Yiddish, and even when treated by historians, it is the product of historiographic reconstruction, by no means free of imagining.[2] As such, the "shtetl" is less a specific place than a shorthand way of referring to the life of Jews in Eastern Europe in the late-nineteenth and early twentieth centuries. In this sense the "shtetl" is always a synthesis of facts, memory, and imagination. Agnon, we shall argue, is one of the leading creators of this synthetic world; his portrayal is based on both a complicated empathy and a prodigious erudition. While some descriptions are attentive to discriminations between the *dorf* (the village), the *shtetl* (the town), and the *shtot* (the city), many references to, or representations of the "shtetl" really refer vaguely to Jewish life as lived in a wide range of settings in Eastern Europe from about 1830 to 1939. Agnon is usually very punctilious is his use of the terms: *ayara* (the *shtetl*), *kefar* (*dorf*), and *ir* (*shtot*), as was Berdiczewski, for instance, before him.

During his long writing career covering about sixty-five years (1903–1968), Agnon wrote thousands of pages about the "shtetl" in his fiction, his memoiristic pieces, and his historical memorializations—three genres which often crossed and merged. To discuss these "shtetl" forays adequately would take an extensive study, beyond the scope of this chapter. A productive project for the current volume is to focus our attention on a remarkable decision Agnon made, apparently in 1911, subsequent to the above-recorded conversation with Rabi Binyomin. In 1911 Agnon worked on "Vehaya he'akov lemishor" ("*And the Crooked Shall Become Straight*"), which Brenner published at his own expense in 1912.[3] In this lengthy story, really a novella, one finds for the first time the characteristic

Agnonic style and voice which he maintained throughout his entire career, even when writing about themes having nothing to do with the "shtetl." His choice of both style and theme in this period was crucial for the development of his career and reveals much about his attitude towards Jewish history. What interests me, therefore, are the ideological implications of the choice of both theme and style. And since the choice of theme, its setting in a so-called "shtetl," is easier to handle than the question of style, because the object of representation is simpler to present than the mode of representation, we shall pursue that track first.

The new technique Agnon adopted in 1911 was highly original. This choice involved two moves. First, he chose the milieu of the "shtetl" as the arena of dramatic action with attention to psychological nuance rather than the object of satire. Second, he wrote his story in the language that aspires to reproduce the thought patterns of a learned narrator—that is, a late rabbinic Hebrew couched in a Yiddish language milieu. He was, in essence, using the language medium of that imagined world to convey the themes and plots dealing with that world. He was trying to write about that world in its own language, from within, with deep respect for its cultural richness and textual density. That is the inherent claim of this Agnonic style. The narrator's voice is that of a learned "shtetl" Jew, wise to the ways of the greater world, but not alienated from it.

To truly understand exactly how deliberate this choice was, one has to study the styles of the seventy pieces he published in the seven years before "Vehaya he'akov lemishor." Those stories and essays are written in an entirely different style, one closer to the normative Hebrew prose style of the turn of the twentieth century. Most of these were, to be sure, embarrassingly clumsy and were published only because the editor of a provincial newspaper often has to fill space. Those published in Jaffa attest to experiments in more serious writing, usually macabre, neo-romantic tales of frustrated love, bizarre deaths, strange women—all conveyed in an agitated, often lush, Hebrew prose style. Agnon himself obviously realized that this was not the medium he was seeking, and after the success of "Vehaya he'akov lemishor" he scrapped most of what he had previously written and either rewrote or totally discarded every line he had published. Few of these seventy items were ever republished in the many collections of his works.[4]

The technique worked wonders even in the first story in which it was used: "Vehaya he'akov lemishor." The author faced a crucial choice in writing this story: in the society described, mid-nineteenth century Galicia, the norms of traditional piety and the bourgeois ethic are at odds. The hero, Menashe Hayyim, a pious shopkeeper of some means, is forced into bankruptcy by a new competitor. To recoup his capital, he reluctantly takes to the road as an itinerant beggar armed with a letter of recommendation certifying his identity, his former position in society, and his rectitude. While this seemingly bizarre technique for recovering lost capital was not unheard of in earlier centuries, it had become the butt of satire by the nineteenth century. Begging for funds even for acceptable charities like family support and dowries for indigent brides were stock subjects of satire in the works of such seminal authors as Mendele. Agnon's story is thus a deliberate deviation from Mendele's narrative technique: it is more attentive to psychological realism or to bourgeois attitudes, and it strives to achieve effects that are less formally and formalistically rabbinic, less balanced in their syntax. By refusing to avoid both late-rabbinic or Hasidic locutions and Yiddish speech patterns, he shaped an ambiguous, flexible style which allows for multiple perspectives. With this style Agnon could fuse the pious with the bourgeois and neutralize the satirical Mendelean bite.

Since Menashe Hayyim is conceived as a person and not a type, he can lose both status and identity, themes Agnon learned from his reading in European literature. The hero succumbs to temptation once he has recouped some of his money and sells his letter to another beggar. As one might anticipate, he then loses his money and all his possessions and must return to the road to beg, sans letter of recommendation. The beggar who bought the letter naturally dies and is buried as Menashe Hayyim: the latter's wife, now a widow, remarries and bears children which she could not do previously when married to Menashe Hayyim. When the hero finally returns home, he finds his wife both married and a mother. Here, too, Agnon dwells upon the conflict inherent in the situation: according to Jewish law, Menashe Hayyim should reveal that he is alive, thus embarrassing his wife and condemning her child to bastardry; but since he loves his wife (love, we should note, is a bourgeois-romantic sentiment), he leaves town beset by the guilt of his concealment. He spends the last days of his life living in a cemetery where, by chance, he finds the cemetery guard inscribing his name on a handsome gravestone which his wife, thinking that the beggar carrying the letter was indeed her husband, had ordered to memorialize him. Several days later, happy in the thought that his wife still loves him and that he had resisted the temptation to reveal the truth, thereby ruining her life, Menashe Hayyim dies, and the guard, who knows the story, places over his grave the stone ordered by his wife for the beggar's grave which she thought was his.

Even in bald plot-outline, this novella does not sound like the pious tale it was taken to be by most critics for over thirty years: the quasi-rabbinic style, as well as the pious milieu succeeded in deflecting the reader from such obvious—today—topoi as the loss of identity and the descent into hell, let alone the ambiguous ending in the graveyard or the hero's impotence. Kurzweil noticed in the early 1950s that there are, indeed, many discordant elements in the story, but following his theological bias, he read the story and much of modern Hebrew literature as a literary manifestation of secularism.[5] The story, for him, is a tragedy. Kurzweil, however, did not address the totality of the story, or the title which—taken from Isaiah 40—implies that "the crooked is made straight"; the ending clearly vindicates the hero and restores the reader's confidence in the possibility of justice in this world. Menashe Hayyim does die happy in the knowledge that he has been rewarded with the two gifts most important to him: assurance of his wife's continuing love for him and confidence that he would have his posterity even if it were merely his name on a tombstone.

The story, Dickensian in its narrative twists and psychological insights, is set in the market towns and villages of Eastern Galicia, in the world that we refer to as "the shtetl." In that world, most of the characters are Jews, and since the time of the action is the mid-nineteenth century, they are pious Jews. While there are few prodigiously learned Jews in this story, it is not the world of Sholom Aleichem's Menahem Mendel or Tevya. And while significant scenes take place at the time of a major commercial fair, a *yarid*, the world of the novella is pre-industrial. To capture both the flavor and thought patterns of that world, Agnon invented this peculiar manneristic style we now recognize as characteristically Agnonic, a fitting vehicle for the portrayal of the rich personal life of Jews of the period. Fundamentally, his attitude towards that world is less ideological (Mendele) or nostalgic (Peretz) than it is aesthetic: it is primarily the setting for a story he wants to tell.

And yet, insofar as the choice of style implied a definite ideological position, Agnon's own negotiation with Jewish history, it is a deliberate act of what we now call "dissimulation," the opposite of assimilation. It implies acceptance, not rejection of the mores and values of the world of Jewish piety and erudition. "Vehaya he'akov lemishor" takes place, as noted, sometime in the middle of the nineteenth century, but this is not the only period of so-called "shtetl" life that Agnon used as a setting.

Without trying to be exhaustive, it is worth presenting some cardinal examples of other periods. In doing so, we should also note the wide range of topics he was inspired to treat in his fictions.

Several of his stories set in the "shtetl" take place during his youth in Buczacz, the real "shtetl" in Eastern Galicia where Agnon was raised, roughly in the first decade of the twentieth century. Often the town is referred to as "Shibush"—a comic metathesis of letters implying the "mistaken" life of the characters. While "Bine'urenu uvizkenenu" (With Our Youths and Our Elders, 1920) is a political satire, such stories as "Bidemi Yameha" (In the Midst of Her Days, 1923) or the novel *Sippur Pashut* (*A Simple Story*, 1935) use the themes of unrequited or uncommon love to energize a plot that highlights the fears and aspirations of the small-town Jewish bourgeoisie. These Jews, while living in a world where many Jews are still pious, have little to do with the concerns or practices of pious Jews. And yet, the most sustained creative effort of Agnon's early career, *Hakhnasat Kallah* (*The Bridal Canopy*, 1929–30), moves back in history to about 1825 and concentrates on a world of exclusively pious Jews. Its hero, Reb Yudel, comes from Brody, a substantial trading city by that time, but he is unaware of the commercial life of the town and spends most of the novel wandering about the small market towns and villages of Galicia seeking dowry contributions for his daughters. Less than ten years later, in 1938–39, Agnon produced his novel, *Oreah Nata Lalun* (*A Guest for the Night*), a powerful description of the ravages of World War I on his imagined "shtetl," Shibush. The description of both physical and spiritual desolation is so relentless, that many readers mistakenly read the novel as a prophecy of the Shoah rather than the imaginative recreation of the deplorable state of the "shtetl" in the interwar period.

After the Shoah, between 1945 and 1965, Agnon devoted much of his energy to writing stories or accounts of the life in his own "shtetl," Buczacz, which had been destroyed with most of its Jews in 1941. These pieces were assembled by his daughter after his death in three sizeable volumes—*Ir umelo'a* (*The City and the Fullness Thereof*, 1973), *Lifnim min hahomah* (*Within the Wall*, 1975), and *Korot Batenu* (*The Beams of Our Homes*, 1979)—and comprise his eloquent memorial to the actual "shtetl," Buczacz, the source of much of his inspiration. I cite the memorialization aspect of these volumes since critics writing on Agnon often are amazed at the paucity of his literary reaction to the Shoah because they do not look into these hefty collections. In fact, one can argue that these volumes comprise the greatest of all *yizker bikher* (memorial volumes). These volumes have never been properly studied, but given Agnon's encylopedic historical knowledge of his own "shtetl," of Galician Jewry, and of the intellectual and religious life of East European Jews, it is not rash to suggest that our comprehension of what we call "shtetl" literature is woefully incomplete without a serious study of these volumes.

Turning from the world represented to the mode of representation, we should note, at first, that the specific style Agnon fashioned in writing "Vehaya he'akov lemishor," immediately directs the reader to a world of texts and textuality, and a specific textuality at that, one that embodies in all its features a traditional, recognizable milieu. No competent reader of Hebrew could conceivably miss the multifarious implications of this style. Realizing he could never fashion a neutral text, "free" of referentiality to previous texts—for such is the nature of the Hebrew language in the beginning of the century and, to a lesser degree, even today—Agnon fashioned an artful pastiche of an older style so convincingly that it took most readers some thirty years to realize that under the "pious" text of the novella lay a subtext which qualified, ironized, or even subverted the text. The seemingly "pious" text can thus be used for a variety of purposes: as a mask hiding or modifying the author's bold or revelatory sentiments on religion or sensuality; or as a mediating barrier that allows the author to distance himself from too direct and immediate responses to the dynamic, demanding events of contemporary Jewish history. Without it, Agnon's "negotiation" with Jewish history would have been impossible since he, as a writer of fiction, would have been overwhelmed by the flood of events.

"Negotiations with Jewish history" is a phrase that requires some elaboration here. It refers to an author's use of material taken from earlier authors. By talking of "negotiation," we restore the author and treat him as an active agent rather than a passive receptor of influences. "Negotiation" assumes that there is an active, on-going process in which the "other side," the classical texts alluded to or echoed, are active in that they force the author to yield to them. The process of negotiation, then, is dynamic and complex. The author—Agnon, for instance—negotiates with a text which he has already activated by his reading. What makes the Agnonic text so intriguing is that a careful reading brings you to the conclusion that the author is supremely conscious of his negotiations with the text, and, inasmuch as these are historical Jewish texts, the concrete manifestations of what we ordinarily call Jewish history, he is negotiating with Jewish history.

For the reader, then, reading an Agnonic text is also a "negotiation with Jewish history" and should be perceived as such. Inasmuch as Agnon is so patently conscious of the historical contexts of his linguistic sources and fictive situations, the reader must also possess some expertise in these historical contexts. Agnon's text insists, unlike any other Jewish text that I know of, that the reader respect the depth and density of Jewish traditional texts and mores. An awareness of this interpretive requirement should free us of some of the subjectivity that is an inevitable component of the interpretive act. In dealing with the text of an author so linguistically manipulative as Agnon, such awareness of historical controls is not only advisable—it. is imperative. We should realize, in addition, that almost every story has more than one published version and that the narrator's perspective—and personality—might change from work to work, from version to version of the same work, and even from phrase to phrase in the same sentence.

In suggesting that Agnon "negotiates with Jewish history," we do not imply that Agnon tries to render faithful representations of specific moments in Jewish history. The contrary is true: he was too shrewd a writer to succumb to that temptation. His writing career, we should remember, embraced one of the most turbulent centuries in Jewish history. To have lived through that period in some of the most important centers of Jewish historical experience—Galicia, Jerusalem, Germany—and to survive it as a writer in control of his materials is, in itself, a tour de force of the human imagination. I would argue that Agnon succeeded in doing so precisely because he fashioned a synthetic mode of narrative discourse that was not based on the norms of Hebrew discourse which we usually associate with the regeneration of modern Hebrew literature. These norms, to be sure, could not be fashioned after Hebrew speech norms at the beginning of this century, because few people spoke Hebrew then, even in Eretz Yisrael of the Second Aliyah. Since, however, Hebrew was in an advanced stage of "revival" and had already established a viable modern literary tradition by 1905, there were what one might call evolving "quasi-speech" norms, and the major Hebrew prose writers strived to shape and/or approach those norms. In general, Hebrew writers from the last decade of the nineteenth century on linked Hebrew with the national revival movement and, specifically, the creation of a Hebrew community in Palestine. Agnon, on the contrary, persisted in refining his highly literary style which enabled him to keep his distance from the world. This manneristic or synthetic style is both a resistance to the hegemony of a ruling culture and a device for containing the centrifugal, contradictory sentiments of the modernist sensibility. Agnon's choice of a style, which was historically regressive in certain aspects, implies a deliberate literary and ideological stance towards dissimilaton, not assimilation.

When we fuse this formulation of Agnon's narrative voice with the notion of the "shtetl" as a literary—or historiographic—synthesis rather than a historical reality, we realize that he succeeded brilliantly in creating the "shtetl" in its most profound and varied manifestations. Shrewdly, he has the narrator give us the "shtetl" in its own voice, at least as Agnon wanted to synthesize it: in a learned Hebrew echoing a Yiddish milieu, in an acceptance of everything that world had to offer, in an act of dissimilation, not assimilation. This acceptance is by no means uncritical, but even when it is piercingly caustic, it accords the "shtetl" the respect of rendition in its own terms. This virtual "shtetl" has become for many readers the only "shtetl" they know just as *Fiddler on a Roof* has become for many Americans the only "shtetl" they know.

The comparison of Agnon with *Fiddler* is not gratuitous; it highlights the concluding point of this essay. The stark comparison is informative. Sing a few bars of any of the charming Broadway songs of *Fiddler*, and you evoke in the American audience warm sentimental feelings about something called the "shtetl." This response requires no previous knowledge of Jewish life or culture. It questions nothing, challenges nobody, and merely builds on vague stereotypes that distort any plausible historical reality. But read out loud in Hebrew the first line of Agnon's little story, "Ma'ase ha'ez": *"Ma'ase bezaken shehaya gone'ah milibo. Ba'u vesha'alu larof'im. Amru sheyishteh halav izim"* ("This is the story about an old man who should groan from his heart. They went to consult the doctors. They said he should drink goat's milk"). A simple, adequate reading requires not only knowledge of Hebrew, but some sensitivity to the intertextual resonances the author exploits to tell his story. In brief: the author challenges the reader, requires both erudition and work, and thus operates in the intellectual milieu of the "shtetl," as he conceives it, a world of dense Jewish life, where even his simplest characters have significant Jewish literacy. If, as we have argued, what we call the "shtetl" today is primarily the product of literary representations of all sorts and levels, these very sources determine the image of the "shtetl" we present and, indeed, cherish. And to the extent that they are memorials, they, like all memorials, generate and shape memory. The differences we have cited are not merely academic, but ultimately existential and fateful. And the stakes are high.

Notes

1. Yehoshua Radler-Feldman, *Mishpehot sofrim: partsufim* (Tel Aviv, 1961), p. 280.

2. Dan Miron, *The Image of the Shtetl and Other Studies of the Modern Jewish Literary Imagination* (Syracuse, 2000)

3. The story was first published in *HaPoel hatsai'r* (Jaffa), Vols. 7–10 and 12–16 (Jan. 9, Jan. 24, Feb. 11, Mar. 19, May 2, May 19). It was published as a separate volume in 1912, 1919, and subsequently in Agnon's collected stories, in both the 1931 and 1953 editions.

4. For a treatment of Agnon's writing before 1912, see my *Nostalgia and Nightmare* (Berkeley and Los Angeles, 1968), pp. 29–82.

5. Baruch Kurzweil, *Masot 'at sipure Agnon* (Tel Aviv, 1963), chs. 3 and 18.

12

The Image of the Shtetl in Contemporary Polish Fiction

Katarzyna Więcławska

In post–World War I Polish literature, the motif of the shtetl, represented as a part of the Jewish world, the realm of Jewish culture and custom, is recursive, yet marginal. This fact might seem paradoxical, especially if we are to consider the historical context of the Polish literary tradition, which places Polish writers in the position of witnesses of Jewish life and tragic death in Eastern Europe. True, this role of a careful witness was not really undertaken on a larger scale. And yet, though many complicated and painful matters are still to be reconsidered, contemporary Polish literature that does deal with Jewish issues, including the shtetl image, might be of particular interest for Polish and Jewish readers. In what way is the shtetl retrieved and saved in Polish literary memory—as the essence of Jewishness, the mixture of cultures, or maybe the land of fantasy infiltrating the real? What is the face of the contemporary myth? What are its sources?

As Eugenia Prokop-Janiec notices,[1] each period in the history of Polish literature brings its own specific picture of the shtetl and its inhabitants, a picture that reflects not only the historical and cultural trends of that time but also the experiences of a given writer in relation to the shtetl. Positivist and Enlightenment views of the shtetl saw it as a Jewish ghetto, a backward, superstitious, and isolated environment, the relic of the epoch destined to undergo economic and cultural transformations or to decline and disappear altogether. Such a picture is, with time, interspersed with descriptions of both the most fundamental and the exotic aspects of Jewish culture and religion and portraits of the most typical members of the shtetl community. The interwar period witnesses quite an opposite variation of the shtetl motif, presented now as the land of peaceful, idyllic childhood, where Jewish tradition guarantees the safety and integration of the Jewish community. The shtetl theme in that form is undertaken mostly by Polish-Jewish writers (those who speak as Jews in the Polish language), who describe the little towns as everlasting homelands of their imagination and identity, though heading for their inevitable fall in the contemporary world. The prewar literary shtetl image is an interesting complement to Polish literature in general, touching upon the problem of coexistence of Poles and Jews. The shtetl becomes a place of cultural and economic encounter of ethnic groups living next to each other rather than together in a very restricted area.

After World War II, the shtetl, for obvious reasons, is moved into the sphere of historical themes and viewed by writers from such a perspective. The first reaction to the tragic end of the shtetl community in Polish fiction can be found in the works of those writers who emphasized their Jewishness even before the war, like Julian Stryjkowski or Kalman Segal, and those who, like Adolf Rudnicki, turned towards Jewish topics primarily after the Holocaust. Some of them survived the Holocaust outside Poland and then considered commemorating the Jewish world, which so tragically passed away, as their basic moral duty. Their fiction became the background for contemporary Polish literature that deals with the shtetl motif. The growing interest of the Poles in multi-culturalism, specifically in Jewish culture and the history of Jews in Poland, stimulated the return of the shtetl in the works of the last witnesses of these times, both Poles and Polish Jews—Andrzej Kuśniewicz, Bogdan Wojdowski, Stanisław Benski—as well as the generation of writers who knew the little towns just from literature, documents, reports—Władysław Paźniewski, Hanna Krall, Piotr Szewc. This second group's case might be especially worth examining as they undertake a theme demanding not only knowledge but also subtlety in reaching beyond stereotypes, superstitions, idealization, and the barrier of time in order to grasp the vague truth.

Considerable differences can be noticed between the prose of writers of Jewish origins (e.g., Stryjkowski) who published their works before and after World War II and Polish fiction preoccupied with the shtetl image that has been written by both Poles and Polish Jews within the last two decades. The former writers seem to be deeply rooted in the shtetl culture, and from that position they are able to document the shtetl's decline in the economic, social, and moral sense. They point to the decadence and the decay of Jewish tradition and religiousness, which thus far had upheld their ethnic identity. Their shtetl is heading for disaster; it is infiltrated with death. For Polish writers of the last decades of the twentieth century, the shtetl is a land of memory, and as such it becomes an autonomous, private territory of their imagination, and it is governed by its own laws which allow for the mixture of realism and fantasy. The little town turns into a magic world belonging to the past, but, at the same time, lasting in the writer's imagination and teeming with life in all its variety. Such visions of the shtetl world are not untouched by the spirit of the Holocaust. Nevertheless, this tragedy is often treated in an allusive way. It casts a spell over the fictional shtetl, surrounding it with the atmosphere of anxiety and fear.

In analyzing the way the shtetl is presented in recent Polish literature, we focus here on the treatment of time, the conventions of spatial description, and the figures that populate the little town, as well as its Jewishness. Both Polish writers, like Kuśniewicz or Szewc, as well as Polish-Jewish ones, like Wojdowski or Benski, offer diversified approaches to the shtetl in respect to these categories. Their fiction, therefore, offers interesting examples of literary attempts to bring back to life the places and people that have disappeared.

The time in which the writers place their shtetl is one of the most powerful factors creating the atmosphere of the story and revealing their own relation to the presented reality. Szewc, the youngest of the writers mentioned, in his novel *Zagłada* (*Annihilation*),[2] chooses one summer day of 1934 as the time in which to portray his home town of Zamość. The choice of the day is incidental—it is just one of many similar days slowly going by in the life of Zamość inhabitants. Nothing special happens that day, people carry on their everyday duties and act in the same predictable way. The narrator, who creates the atmosphere of monotony, even boredom, seems to be fascinated with such a reality. He hunts down various quickly fleeting moments, scenes, "scrubs of time and space." In Szewc's novel each picture, flash of light, sound, or smell turns out to be equally important for the general image of the world—the moment in which a butterfly flies over the narrator's head or a goat wags its tail, the janitor raises his hand or the dancing Hasidim disappear in the distance. The writer wants to catch and save forever each of those transient scenes, as if he were taking a photo. The world of Zamość, 1934, preserved in the literary photography, is dominated by the present, which seems lasting, while the future and the past seem almost unreal. The reader has an impression that nothing here can ever change. The flow of time comes to a halt, just like a fly caught in a lump of amber. The narrator seems to confirm such a thought: "What is going to happen next? We need to rely on the order of things and events. It's unalterable, ever right."[3] So does this idyllic, peaceful world correspond to the title "annihilation"? This is the real point of Szewc's novel. His true aim is to immerse the reader in the experience of the slow, monotonous passage of time in the fiction, which seems to annihilate reality. It is this literary world, however, which, though it allows for saving the scraps of time, is nothing more than illusion, as the title itself indicates. In Polish the word *zagłada* (translated into English as "annihilation") means almost the same as "Holocaust." The portrait of the shtetl community is therefore overshadowed by its future tragic fate. The historical perspective which infiltrates the reader's perception of the novel makes it clear that the Zamość of Szewc's story can only be partially encountered and only by means of literature.

Another interesting variation of the return to the shtetl can be found in Andrzej Kuśniewicz's novel *Nawrócenie* (*Turning Back*).[4] The author describes here a little Galician town, probably Sambor, of the interwar period. He bases his fiction on his own memories of life in such a shtetl at that time. However, this return to the past has a specific character. "Turning back," as the writer explains, "is different from going back because it does not necessarily mean the return to the path you've followed, you can stray from it, right or left, wherever."[5] So Kuśniewicz's return to the interwar shtetl is no longer an attempt to reconstruct that world but rather to revive his own memory by means of imagination. He admits that human memory records just episodes, scenes, touching events; it cannot offer a complete picture of a shtetl. Therefore, the realistic portrait of the little town in his book intermingles with fantasy, dream, a whole chain of literary associations. It can suddenly turn out that the narrator, a young schoolboy rambling about the town, is in fact traveling on the elephant's back through India while the characters of Kipling's novels or Polish and Ukrainian legends appear somewhere within the shtetl limits. The writer's "turning back" has also another deeper meaning. In one of the interviews published in the Polish magazine *Literatura*,[6] Kuśniewicz states that the novel is not an attempt to go back to a given period of time. It is rather a turning back towards his Jewish neighbors and friends murdered during the war, and thus his personal act of devotion to them.

The shtetl in Kuśniewicz's and Szewc's fiction is still a world accessible to the reader either through memory or imagination. In Wojdowski's story "Pascha" ("Passover")[7] it becomes almost a fairy-tale land, which is devoid of even most general time references and does not belong to the presented reality. It is just the scenery of a play in a Jewish theatre in postwar Warsaw, constructed of the most cliched, stereotypical landmarks of shtetl topography. Its existence is limited to the time the play lasts. Then the shtetl disappears forever, making one of the viewers, old Jew Leib, dream about an idyllic shtetl life.

The time distance that separates contemporary Polish and Polish-Jewish writers from the prewar period when shtetlekh still existed, has an impact on the way the shtetl space and the people who used to live there are described. The artists all seem to be aware of the threat that hangs over the attempts to revive the world gone forever, best expressed by Kuśniewicz: "*A należy pamiętać, że utracone zawsze olbrzymieje i obrasta w legendy i mity*" ("You need to bear in mind that what has been lost grows in stature and is slowly transformed into a myth or legend"). Having to rely on memories as well as on literary and historical sources, they try to present the barrier of time as something unavoidable, and the incompleteness of the shtetl portrait as something natural. They focus on those elements of reality that move their imagination or stimulate their memory to the greatest extent. The shtetl world constructed in that way is the land of carefully chosen details, but it can be supplemented with fantastic, surreal visions any time.

The shtetl as described by Szewc in *Annihilation* and in his latest novella, *Zmierzchy i poranki* (*Dusks and Dawns*),[8] is in terms of its spatial description one of the most original portraits of this place in Polish literature. Szewc's concern for detail makes Stryjkowski compare his prose to Proust's as well as to Schulz's way of presenting the world, as a sudden escape into surrealism, which is especially characteristic of the latter. Szewc decides not to introduce plots into his books, and the characters that appear in them are all equally important, presented at incidentally chosen moments of their lives, without any psychological insight. The narrator assumes a role of a careful observer, gathering facts and recording pictures and scenes. Therefore *Annihilation* gives the impression of a literary photo album of prewar Zamość. However, the tricky point about these old photographs is the fact that they are all teeming with life. The reader is taken by the narrator to the very center of each scene, surrounded with sounds, smells, changing colors, shifting light, allowed even to look into the thoughts of the characters. Everything in the shtetl is worth portraying—Mr. Baum's doves over the market square, dirty table tops in Mr. Rozenzweig's bar, sun beams reflected on a windowsill. All these literary photos create a detailed topography of the town in which it becomes easy to recognize Zamość. The narrator gives a precise layout and names the streets, mentions local landmarks like Rynek Solny, Brama Lwowska, the Łabuńka River, and identifies neighboring villages. As Bogumiła Kaniewska notices,[9] this little town turns out to be the center and the model of the universe for its inhabitants. Szewc's shtetl has its central point—the market square, the so-called "Town's Eye"—and its limits—the town's outskirts, beyond which the world ends, becomes unreal. Just as fleeting moments are the essence of time, the very place where one spends one's life is the core of space and constitutes the whole world. The human being is thus never given the opportunity to experience the world extensively, just a fragment of it: "For the policemen, for Mr. Hersze Baum, for Kazimiera M., and Mr. Daniłowski, the lawyer, for the people present in the market now and for all other inhabitants, their town is the model of the universe in its microcosmic scale."[10] These fragments of reality or the universe are the topics of Szewc's literary photos.

With time and space constituting the main "characters" of Szewc's novellas, the human protagonists appearing in both books are, quite naturally, schematically presented. They are both Jews and Poles involved in their everyday monotonous activities—Mr. Baum spends another day in his shop, policemen stroll around the town, Mr. Rozenzweig serves at his bar as always, a local prostitute Kazimiera is getting bored at home. People act as usual, experience similar emotions—love, anger, boredom. However, they are all immersed in the flow of time, doomed to perish, albeit unaware of their doom as yet. It is the narrator who wishes to save a short moment of their existence, to cheat time.

Kuśniewicz's shtetl is in some aspects similar to the portrait of Zamość by Szewc. Here, as well, the reader encounters a narrator who functions as a guide to the shtetl. Nevertheless, this trip round the town has a completely different character as the main criterion for choosing the scenes, places, events, and people that are described is the narrator's memory. The narrator is now an old man who wants to recreate the time of his childhood and youth during a meeting with old friends in Paris. He enters the prewar shtetl as a young boy, the descendant of a local Galician aristocratic family, a little alienated from the town youth, sometimes funny in his attempts to emphasize his superiority and originality. Such a manner offers him a good opportunity to assume the role of an observer. At the same time, it foregrounds the fact that the shtetl image created here in a flow of scenes and events is important for the narrator only: his descriptions of meetings with friends, first loves, school, local entertainments are all interspersed with his thoughts, fantasies, and monologues. The shtetl space serves only as a very detailed backdrop for these descriptions. Moreover, Kuśniewicz focuses on the multicultural character of the shtetl community, the symbiosis of Poles, Jews, and Ukrainians involved in normal everyday contacts so typical for people living in the same place—friendship, business, gossip, minor quarrels (of a personal rather than an ethnic or a national character). The shtetl Jews, with their traditions, customs, and religion, are at the center of the narrator's attention; he feels attracted by their intentional isolation in the most central religious and cultural domains of their lives and by the atmosphere of ancient dignity surrounding their culture. However, he admits that his interest is more that of a tourist admiring a world that is exotic to him; he does not try to enter the very essence of Jewish beliefs and lifestyle. He also maintains a distance towards the shadow of the Holocaust hanging over the shtetl. As a man who used to live among the people so cruelly murdered, he is not able to cope with the tragedy—words are not enough for him to express the loss. The characters appearing on the streets of the shtetl in his novel, his past Jewish acquaintances who are probably all dead now, urge him to face the truth. The narrator is not able to, according to his own words, "enter the medias res of the apocalypse." As a result, Kuśniewicz recreates his shtetl as a safe and almost idyllic place, the homeland of people of different nationalities peacefully coexisting. History, with its pogroms, anti-Semitism, and the Holocaust, is intentionally left aside, and the shtetl becomes a myth.

The myth of the Arcadian little town is also present in Wojdowski's story "Passover." Leib, the Jew left in Warsaw after the war, dreams about returning to the shtetl, imagining its harmony and order, its old, established morality, simplicity of life, and closer contacts with God: "In a little town people fear less, they are less evil, even the devils are less powerful than anywhere else."[11] However, even in the play about the shtetl he watches, the little town is the world of the dead.

The majority of the shtetl images in contemporary Polish fiction concern prewar times, as is the case of Wojdowski, Kuśniewicz, and Szewc. Stanisław Benski's novel *Ocaleni* (*The Survivors*)[12] is an exception in that it offers a picture of the shtetl immediately after the war. A young Holocaust survivor, Michał, returns to his home town of Soligród, which before the war was inhabited by almost six thousand Jews. Now the whole Jewish quarter has been destroyed, and there is no one left here except for a Jewish boy saved by a Polish woman. The narrator is shocked by what he sees, the shtetl loses its realistic character for him:

> When I returned from the camp our shtetl was completely empty. I looked at houses that didn't look like houses, at streets that didn't look like streets, and I saw people who didn't look like people. And there was a skinny nanny-goat that didn't look like a nag goat, and flowers that didn't look like flowers and a sky that wasn't a sky. I wandered around the nonstreets, I hung around the nonmarket on which stood the nonchurch and the non-town-hall and a single nonbench. At Grobelna street there was a synagogue that wasn't there, but it alone existed for me, as did our one-story house which wasn't there either.[13]

As he walks through the town just after the catastrophe, watching the last traces of Jewish presence disappear, he witnesses the end of the shtetl world.

An important aspect of the shtetl image in contemporary Polish fiction is its Jewishness: presenting Jews as shtetl inhabitants, this fiction treats their daily life, customs, religion, and surroundings, as well as Polish-Jewish relations in a limited town space. In the novels by Kuśniewicz and Szewc the Jewish world of the shtetl is preserved with faithfulness to detail. Nevertheless, their world is described by an outsider, not a real member of the community. The narrators maintain distance towards Jewishness, aware of their inability to understand fully the rules governing the lives of Jewish people or the true meaning of their rituals, customs, and beliefs. They can share neither the Jews' ancient past and traditions nor their tragic destiny, which casts a shadow over the apparently safe and monotonous shtetl existence. The Jewish world, though admired, is at the same time a mystery which can be shown only from the outside, as in Szewc's "photography" or in a story related many years after the actual events took place. An alternative to such a presentation of the shtetl involves reducing its space to the most basic elements and choosing characters who are most typical of the Jewish community, yet only portrayed in broad and not fully detailed terms, as in the case of Wojdowski's fiction. His theatrical shtetl is clearly just a reminiscence of the past, not at all the portrait of the place and people living there. Benski's shtetl is also devoid of any traces of Jewishness—it is a destroyed and depopulated town, but still a home of the narrator. However, his world, closed forever in the boy's past, remains inaccessible to the reader.

When we consider the image of the shtetl in Polish literature, we find that it steadily moves towards the sphere of the myth and legend. True, it still remains as a presence in the fiction of the last witnesses of its actual existence, the writers like Kuśniewicz, who used to live in shtetlekh and knew the Jews there personally. It also stimulates the imagination of younger writers born after the war, like Szewc, for whom the Jewish world is already a part of history, with some exotic tones. Nevertheless, in the case of both perspectives, the shtetl with time eludes realistic presentation. The topography of the towns is often perfectly retained, with exact street names given along with detailed descriptions of buildings and interiors. The same can be said about the characters populating the literary shtetl: not only are they named, but they are usually also carefully described, with attention to their interests, jobs, daily routines, and appearance; sometimes the reader is given the direct access to their thoughts. However, the shtetl world lacks authenticity, vivid emotions, the overwhelming sense of its uniqueness so characteristic for the shtetl portrait in the fiction of older generation of writers, like Stryjkowski. These older literary works serve as a basis, a point of artistic reference and the source of inspiration for the younger writers. Szewc's indebtness to Stryjkowski is probably the clearest example here. For Szewc, his collaboration and long interview with Stryjkowski, published as *Ocalony na wschodzie* (*Saved in the East*),[14] might have been a sort of artistic impulse. But the barrier of time can only partly be crossed by the writers publishing their works within the last two decades of the twentieth century, and what is beyond their knowledge or memory must be reconstituted in fantastic transformations or shrouded in silence. Their personal interest in history and emotional response towards the lost world of Polish Jewry produces a desperate attempt to enter these times once again. This, in turn, makes their shtetl a symbolic space of Polish-Jewish encounters, which in the historical sense comes too late.

David Roskies in his article "The Shtetl in Jewish Collective Memory,"[15] notes that the East-European little town has always been a myth in Jewish-American literature. Nonetheless, the manner of its representation definitely underwent a change after World War II. Before, it served as a source of national identity, an idealized or criticized homeland. After the war, the shtetl became the community of the dead demanding commemoration, as in *yizkher* books, Theo Richmond's *Konin*,[16] or Eva Hoffman's *Shtetl*.[17] In Polish literature, in turn, the shtetl, an integral part of Polish prewar reality, became a myth, and one that some people would prefer to forget, yet others have chosen to maintain. The new wave of interest in Jewish culture, however, has recently brought about the appearance of semi-documentary books dealing with the history of different towns or cities like Kielce, Kalisz, and Lublin.[18] Contemporary Polish fiction proves that the shtetl motif can still be represented from new perspectives adopted by artists searching for the vaguely explored areas of their country's history.

NOTES

1. Eugenia Prokopówna, "The Image of the Shtetl in Polish Literature," *Polin*, Vol. 4 (Oxford, 1998), pp. 129–141.

2. Piotr Szewc, *Zagłada (Annihilation)* (Warsaw, 1993).

3. Ibid., p. 85.

4. Andrzej Kuśniewicz, *Nawrócenie (Turning Back)* (Krakow, 1987).

5. *Nawrócenie*, p. 10; translation by Katarzyna Więcławska.

6. *Literatura*, No. 12 (1990), pp. 26–27.

7. Bogdan Wojdowski, *Krzywe Drogi (Winding Roads)* (Warsaw, 1987).

8. Piotr Szewc, *Zmierzchy i poranki (Dusks and Dawns)* (Krakow, 2000).

9. Bogumiła Kaniewska, "Listopadowa jest tu gdzie była . . .- o *Zagładzie* Piotra Szewca," *Polonistyka*, No. 1 (1999), pp. 24–28.

10. Szewc, *Zagłada*, p. 17.

11. B. Wojdowski, *Krzywe Drogi*, p. 29.

12. Stanisław Benski, *Ocaleni (Survivors)* (Warsaw, 1986).

13. Quoted in Antony Polonsky and Monika Adamczyk-Garbowska, eds., *Contemporary Jewish Writing in Poland, An Anthology* (Lincoln, 2001), p. 194.

14. *Ocalony na Wschodzie* (Montricher, 1991).

15. David Roskies, *The Jewish Search for a Usable Past* (Bloomington, 1999), pp. 41–67.

16. Theo Richmond, *Konin* (St. Ives, 1995).

17. Eva Hoffman, *The Shtetl* (Boston, 1997).

18. See for example Jerzy Bojarski, ed., *Ścieżki pamięci (Paths of Memory)*, Wydawnictwo "Norbertinum" (Lublin, 2002).

13

Sarny and Rokitno in the Holocaust
A Case Study of Two Townships in Wolyn (Volhynia)

Yehuda Bauer

This chapter presents a detailed study of two shtetlekh in the 1930s and during the Holocaust. While a significant minority of East European Jews lived and died in these townships, very few such studies of them have been made to date. While I therefore do not here draw general conclusions regarding all shtetlekh, I hope that this and similar works may in the future serve as a basis for such generalizations.

There exists a great deal of literature about the nineteenth-century shtetl, much of it of great literary and historical value, some of it nostalgic in nature, presenting the shtetl as the quintessence of traditional Jewish life. The question is whether this is an accurate description of life in the shtetlekh in the period examined here. In the present study, in the absence of an agreed sociological definition, the shtetl is defined as an East European township with between 1,000 and 15,000 Jews, who formed at least a third of the population, and in which the lives of Jews were largely determined by the Jewish calendar and by a structure of traditional voluntary Jewish organizations and self-government. Eastern Europe is a huge area, with many hundreds, if not more, shtetlekh. Therefore, the research of which this chapter is a part concentrates on Western Belarus and the Western Ukraine, lands that were under Polish rule in the pre–1939 era, and the emphasis is on the internal life of these communities and their relationships with the surrounding non-Jews. We will deal with Polish, Soviet, and late-German policies, but only as the context in which these shtetlekh lived and died. While Polish and Soviet governmental attitudes are well researched, as is the genocidal policy of the German occupants after June 1941, Jewish life in the 1930s and Jewish reactions during Soviet and then mainly German times, are less well known. For the whole area of these former eastern Polish marches (*kresy*), only one monograph has been published to date.[1]

The two shtetlekh analyzed here are Rokitno and Sarny (all name-spellings are prewar—i.e, Polish), in Wolyn (Volhynia), one of the two (then) Polish provinces with a Ukrainian majority.[2] Rokitno had a population of some 2,000–2,500 Jews in 1940, in an overall population of about 5,000;[3] Sarny had 4,950 Jews in 1937, out of a population of about 11,000.[4] Sarny is a railway hub, and the railway eastward, towards Kiev, passes Rokitno, which lies about 12 kilometers west from what was then the Soviet border. The Sarny province (including Rokitno) is in the north of Wolyn, adjoining the Polesie area of forests and marshes to the north, which is unlike the more open, but hilly, country towards the south.

There is a major problem of sources. Polish, Soviet, and German materials on the internal life of the small east–Polish Jewish communities are either nonexistent, or very sparse, as the outside powers had little interest in their inner workings. The Poles were interested only in Jewish political parties and their loyalty or otherwise to Poland; the Soviets, during their period of rule between September 1939 and June 1941, destroyed the internal organized Jewish life. The Germans had no interest in the inner life of these communities at all. There are very few diaries, and none for the two shtetlekh presented here. The main sources are postwar testimonies of survivors, and these, like all post-factum oral testimonies, present problems that have been abundantly discussed in the relevant literature. My position is that when there is a relatively large number of converging testimonies, they present a solid historical foundation for analysis. For very specific reasons, there are many testimonies for these two places, probably up to a hundred testimonies from Rokitno, and several dozens from Sarny, and this makes it possible to draw tentative conclusions about the historical development in these shtetlekh in the period under review. The Memorial Books for the two communities are an important source, and they are quoted when there is no contradiction between them and other testimonies.

Poland was stricken by the Great Depression of the 1930s, and the Polish government's policy was to squeeze out the Jewish element, mainly lower and middling middle class—peddlers, shopkeepers, craftsmen—by favoring ethnic Poles and encouraging an anti-Jewish boycott. The result of this policy was a fairly radical impoverishment of Polish Jews, many of whom were seeking a way to leave Poland, but had nowhere to go: the

United States was closed, after the passing of the 1924 immigration laws, immigration to Palestine was severely restricted by the British Mandatory government after the outbreak of the Arab rebellion in late 1935, and Western Europe had no place for Jews either. There were three major Jewish political movements in Poland in the 1930s: the Zionists, split into a large number of mutually hostile factions; the Orthodox, represented largely by the *Agudas Yisroel* party; and the socialist, anti-Zionist, and anti-religious Bund (*Allgemeyner Yiddisher Arbeterbund*).

In the late 1930s, the Bund was gaining the upper hand, and important research has argued that in 1938–39 about 38% of Jews voted for the Bund in elections within Jewish communities; 36% voted for the different Zionist parties; and 23% for the Orthodox.[5] The figures may not be accurate (the author of the study could not find figures for a number of communities, and not all Jews voted), but they do indicate a clear trend. The Zionists could no longer offer emigration to Palestine as a solution, because British policies there severely restricted Jewish immigration in the late 1930s, and the Orthodox had no real answer to the burning questions of survival in Poland. The possibility of an alliance with the Polish socialists (the PPS), which would work for an egalitarian Polish socialist state in which Jews would enjoy a cultural autonomy, seemed a way out. The decline of the Zionists and the Orthodox was especially marked in the large cities and in Central Poland However, in the *kresy* the Bund was weak, and the Zionists continued to dominate, probably because of the relative absence there of industry and a working class, Jewish or Polish. The decline of Orthodox influence is also very marked, though there were exceptions here and there (and some of the influential rabbis in the *kresy*, including Sarny and Rokitno, were supporters of Zionism). This does not mean to say that most Jews did not keep the Sabbath, keep kosher homes, or visit synagogues, at least during the holidays. But a person could belong to a secular Zionist group or vote for the Bund or even demonstrate against the rabbis, and yet observe these basic traditions. However, the religious ties were definitely loosening, especially with the younger generation, many of whom were members of decidedly secular Zionist youth movements. These younger people may have argued with their elders, but respect for parents was such that convinced Marxist youths would go to the synagogue because their parents did. In a very typical incident in the shtetl of Kurzeniec, in Belarus, a member of the Marxist-Zionist *Hashomer Hatzair* youth movement, whose mother had been an active Communist, but whose father was strictly observant, was asked in a postwar interview when he received the call (by another member of *Hashomer Hatzair*) to join the forest partisan group of which he was a member. His answer was: on a Friday evening, after the blessing of the candles.[6]

This characterization holds true also for the two shtetlekh examined here. Sarny was a new town; a tiny village by that name,[7] which had been owned by an aristocratic landowner, General Dzerzinsky, and which included a few Jewish families, gave its name to a new town established by a Tsarist government decision on May 10, 1903, following the building of railway lines, and a railway hub in 1901. Jews were permitted to settle there. In fact, Jewish entrepreneurs, mainly in the logging business, then traders, peddlers, craftsmen, and some professionals, built the town and originally constituted about half of its 14,000 inhabitants prior to World War I. Ukrainians and Poles, including some intelligentsia, joined them.[8] Orthodoxy was strong in Sarny until after World War I and exercised some influence afterwards, as well, but the main rabbinical figures tended to support Zionism. There were seven synagogues in Sarny, and the central local rabbinical figures were Rabbis Aharon Kunda, a Hasid, and Rabbi Moshe Hechtman, a *misnaged* (traditional non-Hasidic Orthodox)—both were killed in the Holocaust. But Rabbis Israel, Moshe, and Eliezer Perlov (the last died in 1922) of the Karlin-Stolin Hasidic "dynasty" were the ones who commanded the majority of support among the followers of Hasidism in both shtetlekh, and their synagogue was the largest in Sarny. Rabbi Shmuel Pachnik and his son Yosef (Yossele) of Berezna also opened a synagogue in the town. Their membership consisted of the poorer elements. Supporters of the Hasidim of Stepan, another town in the area, were also active, and most were pro-Zionist. The head of a Stolin Hasidic yeshiva (*Or Yisroel*) in Sarny, Mendel Kostrometzky, emigrated to Palestine.[9] Zionist influence spread in Sarny before 1914, and the war strengthened Zionism. The first immigrants to Palestine went there prior to the war, but in 1921 a whole group emigrated. Thereafter, immigration to Palestine was officially supported by the community.[10]

Rokitno, too, was a new town—there was an old village by that name, with a few isolated Jewish families, and a Belgian glass producing company found that there was kaolin and sand in the neighborhood.[11] They built a glass factory, employing Poles almost exclusively. The factory owners persuaded (bribed) the builders of the railway to Kiev to have the line pass the plant. Next to the railway station a new town was built late in the nineteenth century, which ultimately adopted the name of the village, and in which a growing population of Jews were employed as craftsmen, shopkeepers, accountants, peddlers, and traders. There were very few intellectuals, and among those few, a family of pharmacists, who also served the glass factory, stood out.

In the wake of the Russian Revolution some Communist influence began to be felt in both shtetlekh. Despite this, in Rokitno it was the Bund that initially gained many adherents, opening a library and a school. However, in the 1920s, Zionists gained the upper hand; a Hebrew *Tarbut* school was founded and built between 1928 and 1931. It served some of the outlying villages as well, and we are told that 90% of the township's children attended it. Because it taught in Hebrew (until 1932 in the Ashkenazic pronunciation), children began talking Hebrew on the streets. The left-radical *Hashomer Hatzair*, founded in 1926 by a Hebrew teacher, as well as the right-wing *Betar* (from 1928) and the leftist *Hechalutz Hatzair*, claimed the allegiances of most Rokitno Jewish youths. Some members of *Hashomer Hatzair* went over to *Hechalutz* and *Betar* in the 1930s, but then *Betar* weakened later in the decade. Rokitno Jews of the older generation were suspicious of the leftist movements, yet *Hechalutz* continued to flourish. A training farm for pioneers to go to Palestine to join kibbutzim was founded at Klosowo, in the Sarny district, and became a point of attraction for the youths in the two shtetlekh. The old Orthodox primary school, the Talmud-Torah *cheder*, continued to exist, but its graduates mostly joined the secular youth movements. Some of the older generation still adhered to the Hasidic way of life, but community leadership in the 1930s was decidedly Zionist; the Bund disappeared. Quite a number of the youngsters emigrated to Palestine from 1925 on, though the exact figure is impossible to establish.[12]

Rokitno Jews were largely poor, especially many of the craftsmen; at best, they lived a lower–middle-class life. There was a small number of wealthier merchants, as in most other shtetlekh. Towards the end of the 1930s, the community head was Aharon Slutzky, a moderate Zionist and a well-respected personality. There were three, then only two, synagogues, and while organized religion did not dominate local politics, the rabbi, Joseph Aharon Shamess, originally a merchant, though with a rabbinical education, was very popular. He, too, identified as a supporter of Zionism.[13]

A similar situation prevailed in Sarny, which of course was larger and was a county administrative seat—under the Poles, the Soviets, and the Germans. There was some minor industry in the town, and again, mainly Polish workers were employed. The Bund did maintain a presence there even in the 1930s, but became very weak, with the Zionists dominating the political and cultural landscape. A *Tarbut* school became the most popular educational institution. Originally founded in 1921, the school building was built between 1928 and 1931, and it claimed to have 600 pupils in the thirties, or 90% of the town's children. While an attempt to establish a *Tarbut* high school failed, there was a Polish high school in town which accepted a very limited number of Jewish pupils.[14] Cultural life centered on four libraries, a drama circle, and visiting theater companies.

Until 1924, there was actually no community structure in Sarny, and officially, the rabbi was someone from the northern town of Dabrowica. Then elections took place, and Sarny became responsible for the smaller communities around it.[15] The community head was Shmaryahu Gershonok, a merchant and an intellectual from Bobruisk in Eastern Belorussia and, of course, a Zionist.[16] The same youth movements as in Rokitno were active here.[17] There was very little acculturation with Polish civilization—98.9% of Wolyn Jews reported Yiddish or Hebrew as their language. Within the Zionist camp, the Left enjoyed a majority, as the 1929 elections showed.[18] There was a small Communist core in Sarny, who tried to organize apprentices, but was brutally suppressed by the Polish authorities. Its members spent years in jails, and the Stalinist dissolution of the Polish Communist Party in 1938 sealed their demise—until the Soviets came.

The majority of the population in the Sarny area was Ukrainian, mostly peasants. There was a Ukrainian minority in the two townships, with a few intellectual leaders, mainly doctors and lawyers. The majority of non-Jews were Polish, both working-class people and local politicians, government officials, and policemen, with a number of craftsmen and merchants who competed with the Jews. Most Ukrainians were Russian Orthodox, a few were Greek Catholics (Uniates). During the 1930s, the Ukrainian national movement, led mainly by people from Eastern Galicia, gained ground, as it opposed the anti-Ukrainian policy of the Polish government. They were radically anti-Soviet as well, and they demanded an independent Ukraine, first of all in the two Polish-dominated Ukrainian provinces, to extend later to all of the Soviet Ukraine. In this endeavor, they veered towards Nazi Germany as the only power that could make their political dreams come true. At the first congress of the Ukrainian National Movement in Berlin in 1929, the final aim was spelled out: removal of all "foreigners" (Jews and Poles) from Ukrainian lands. In 1940, the movement split into two factions, one led by Andrej Melnik, and one by Stepan Bandera. Their avowed anti-Semitism was based on a long history that identified the Jews as the go-betweens of Ukrainian peasants and the hated Polish lords, and on the massive murder of Jews in the immediate post–World War I period. Yet in the 1930s, most ordinary Ukrainians' relations with the Jews seemed to be quite friendly, and Jews were more apprehensive about the increasing anti-Semitism of urban Poles than about the Ukrainians. In Wolyn, there were two religious minorities among the Ukrainians that were to play an important role during the Holocaust: the Baptists (locally called *Shtundists*, or, erroneously, *Subbotniki* [Sabbath observers]), and the Old Believers (*Staroveryi*, also sometimes identified by the Jews, erroneously, as *Subbotniki*). The Baptists, whose presence was the result of the activity of German missionaries in the nineteenth century, numbered a few thousand in all of Wolyn. Straddling the Polish-Soviet border, especially north of Rokitno in the marshy areas of Polesie, there were a number of isolated villages of Old Believers, who formed what was basically a fundamentalist sect opposed to the official church and, before 1917, to the Tsarist regime. Very few Jewish survivors were found who were not saved, at some point, by the *Shtundists* or the Old Believers, both of whom saw in the Jews God's people, whose rescue would guarantee them a place in heaven.[19]

Poles, too, lived not only in the towns, but also in villages. Some of these were old Polish settlements; others were planted in the area by the interwar Polish government which tried to Polonize the region. Relations with the Ukrainian majority were tense. Polish villages tended to appear in small clusters;[20] anti-Semitism among these peasants was not widespread, as they saw in the Jews another minority that had to defend itself against the Ukrainians. Especially in the area some 18 kilometers southwest of Rokitno, there was such a cluster of three villages—Okopy, Budki Borowskie, and Dolhan—with another village, Netreba, in which a number of Ukrainians had converted to Catholicism, and in effect joined the Poles.[21] Near Sarny there was Karpilowka, and there were some other Polish villages. There were also some Jewish villages, such as Tulip, north of Rokitno. In addition, there were Czechs in villages, who had settled in the region in the nineteenth century. They, too, maintained good relations with the Jews, for the same reasons as the Poles, but also because they had not brought anti-Semitism with them from their country of origin.

In the last two years before the outbreak of war, the economic crisis deepened, affecting Wolyn and including the two townships. Unemployment was hidden, because the closeness of the Jewish family structure protected individuals who had no visible source of income. Some professions could be engaged in only outside of the winter months (brick-laying, house-painting). The decline of the Polish market affected all merchants, and the increasing poverty of the Ukrainian peasants made life for Jewish peddlers and shopkeepers very difficult.

The invasion of Poland by the Germans brought with it bombardments by the *Luftwaffe*, which hit both shtetlekh, but especially Sarny because of its importance as a railway hub. Lives were lost, and then a flood of refugees from German-occupied Poland hit Wolyn. In Rokitno, the refugees became almost one-fourth of the Jewish population, in Sarny even more (as I will detail below). On and after September 17, 1939, Soviet forces occupied the *kresy*—they arrived in the two shtetlekh in the first days of their invasion (Sarny, on the nineteenth, Rokitno, on the seventeenth)—in the wake of the secret protocols signed between Germany and the Soviet Union after their pact of August 23, 1939.

In Rokitno, the Soviets were welcomed "enthusiastically," and not only by Jews.[22] In Sarny, those who owed taxes to the Polish government, youths who hoped for educational opportunities, and others were happy.[23] Given the alternative of German conquest, the Soviets were preferable. The few Jewish Communists, more in Sarny than in Rokitno, came out of hiding and expected to receive important positions in the local administration. A local militia was set up, with many Jews joining it. However, after a few weeks, those Jews who were nominated for administrative posts (and the militia) were removed, and Ukrainians were selected in their stead. The Soviet authorities organized an Assembly for the Ukrainian areas, in which Jews—and Poles—were underrepresented[24] so as to recruit Ukrainian support for the new regime. Among the few Jews who were selected by the Soviets to be members of the Assembly, which voted to join the Soviet Union, was a woman from Rokitno, Mushka Schuster. She was the wife of a very poor building worker, who was employed most winters; they lived in a small wooden house on someone else's property. She had no choice but to do what she was told, and was sent to Lwow to vote for the annexation, after which she returned and was ignored by the Soviets until the Germans came. The Germans were looking for Communists, and local Ukrainians told them about Mushka Schuster. She was arrested, interrogated, tortured, brought to Rovno, and shot there. Ukrainian nationalist vengeance against Jewish Communists had thus been wrought.[25]

When the Soviets came, the Jewish communities dissolved everywhere in the *kresy*, and often without any overt Soviet pressure. In Sarny, the community secretary was ordered to transfer the property of the community to the municipality.[26] All over the *kresy*, synagogues closed, though there was no actual order to close them—however, heavy taxes were imposed, and the faithful could not or did not find the courage to raise the money to keep them open. Rokitno and Sarny were somewhat different from other places: the two Rokitno synagogues were not closed, nor were the synagogues in Sarny. When the ritual bath was closed in Sarny, Hasidim built a private one in the yard of the synagogue that was left alone.[27] But after a while this opposition weakened; Jews worked on the Sabbath and on holidays.

Zionist and Bundist organizations dissolved, often without any orders—a hint was enough. Teaching Hebrew was forbidden, and Hebrew—and Orthodox—schools became Yiddish, Russian, or Ukrainian schools, often with principals who were brought in from the "old" Soviet Union. All schools had to adopt Soviet curricula. In both shtetlekh, some of the Zionist and Orthodox teachers now preached Stalinism to young pupils who in many cases tried, unsuccessfully, to rebel against what they saw as betrayal.[28] Nevertheless, reading survivors' accounts, one gains the impression that Soviet schooling did leave an impact on impressionable youngsters, and of course, the Soviet regime opened up educational opportunities to Jewish youth that had not been dreamt of under the Polish government. Rokitno survivors tell us about higher education that they began, and about openings in government employment. These latter were deeply resented by Ukrainians and Poles, who did not like to see Jews in any official positions.

What is to some degree surprising is the ease with which traditions and institutions that had roots going back for centuries collapsed like houses of cards. There were attempts, here and there, and reportedly in Rokitno as well,[29] to form small underground groups that tried to maintain a Zionist presence. But these were very few, and did not have much support from the local Jews, who just tried to make ends meet and survive in the new regime. During the first weeks of the new regime, and through the Soviet manipulation of the exchange rate of rubles for Polish *zloty*, shops were stripped bare of their goods by Soviet soldiers and civilians starving for things they could not get back at home (Germans did the same after they occupied the area).[30] A serious shortage of even basic goods aided in developing a flourishing black market. Shops and businesses were nationalized, but former traders—in their vast majority Jews—had an advantage over others, and often managed to hoard goods and sell them in small quantities. If they were caught, they faced deportation to Siberia.[31]

Most people found some type of work, and middle-class people, mainly merchants, were employed in state-run shops—sometimes in their own previous establishments—or in some cases fled to small villages to escape the attention of the security police. Craftsmen were told to establish cooperatives, or *artels*, and received a certain minimum income from there. That did not suffice, of course, and testimonies tell us that whoever did not steal, had nothing to eat.[32] The consensus among survivors is that due to the corruption and manipulation of the Soviet bureaucracy, Jews generally did not suffer economic deprivation under the Soviets.

Masses of refuges arrived in Wolyn after the Soviet occupation, from German-occupied Poland, probably around 50,000–60,000. Waves of deportations of people who were considered to be unreliable or opposed to the regime took place. Relatively more Jews than Ukrainians or Poles were deported, and most of these were refugees who had come from German-occupied Poland.[33] In addition, some 4,000 young Jewish men agreed to work in the mines of the Donbas, in Eastern Ukraine, but the conditions there were so terrible that many tried to escape.[34] In Rokitno, probably some 400 people, mostly refugees, were deported to Siberia, which of course saved the lives of most of them, but they could not have known that at the time. Only three local "bourgeois" families are reported to have been deported.[35] In Sarny, an estimated 2,000 refugees arrived, and most of them were deported.[36] The local Jewish population remained largely intact, and paradoxically, when the Germans came, the community was revived, more or less in the shape it had had before the arrival of the Soviets.

As everywhere else in the *kresy*, the Soviet occupation sharpened the opposition of the local population against the Jews, who were accused, especially by the Ukrainians, of having supported the regime and served as its handmaidens. In actual fact, there is little evidence to substantiate this charge, especially as many Ukrainians were enthusiastic partisans of the Soviets. Most governmental jobs, and especially those in the security services, went to "Easterners"—that is, Ukrainians and Russians who were sent from the "old" Soviet Union to guide matters in the new territories. Jews tended to be underrepresented in all these positions. But the propaganda of the underground nationalists was effective in Rokitno and Sarny just as much as elsewhere in Wolyn, though there is no evidence in the two shtetlekh of nationalist emissaries preparing the local population for the arrival of the Germans (as there is in some places in Eastern Galicia); however, many Ukrainians did not need outside propaganda to make them into ardent nationalists.

The German invasion of the Soviet Union on June 22, 1941, came as many young Jews were serving, or had just been recruited into, the Red Army.[37] In some cases, this enabled these young men to withdraw with the Soviets, but most of them probably did not survive (no statistics are available).[38] In Wolyn, the Soviets put up a strong resistance to the Germans, and a heavy tank battle was fought in the Rovno region on June 26–28, before the Soviets finally retreated. The northeastern corner, where Sarny and Rokitno lie, was conquered in early July,[39] but as the German armored troops marched through, and even after the infantry divisions followed them, the more remote areas saw few if any Germans in the first weeks after the Soviet retreat.[40] In fact, there were villages north of Rokitno, in the Polesie area, which were not visited by Germans until the late fall of 1941. It is well known that German forces were overextended, and Ukrainian collaboration was very welcome.

In the brief period between the German invasion and the occupation of the Sarny area, many Jews tried to flee into the "old" Soviet Union. However, during the first few days, Soviet guards on the old Polish-Soviet border prevented refugees from crossing, saying that they were spreading panic and were being disloyal to the Soviet Union. Apparently, the border was opened on June 26. Others tried to join the Red Army, but even those who were accepted, or had been serving before the invasion, were removed from the fighting units in October–December 1941; impressed into labor battalions, many of them were forced to clear mines and do menial jobs on the frontline, and many were killed there. From all of Wolyn, some 15,000 Jews managed to flee into the unoccupied territories, but it is unclear how many of them survived the war. From Rokitno, possibly some 200 Jews managed to escape.[41] One testimony even has it that "they [the Soviets] announced immediately that everyone who could, should move . . . some Ukrainians left as well." The addition of "we knew that to stay would mean certain death" is probably hindsight.[42]

After the withdrawal of the Soviets, and before the arrival of the Germans, pogroms by Ukrainians erupted in many areas of Wolyn. In Sarny, there were three days of looting, before the Germans put an end to it. In Rokitno, both Poles and Ukrainian villagers went on a looting rampage, but the Jews organized self-defense, and little damage was done, though the head of the Jewish self-defense was killed.[43]

The first wave of mass killings in Wolyn was perpetrated by *Einsatzgruppe* (EG) C, especially by *Einsatzkommando* (EK) 5 and *Sonderkommando* (SK) 4a (under Paul Blobel). Some 15,000 men were murdered in accordance with the prevailing Nazi ideology that spread throughout the newly occupied Soviet territories and identified Jews, and especially Jewish men and intelligentsia, with the Bolshevik regime. However, the Sarny region was not affected, and no mass murders took place there at that time. Further mass killings, this time not of men capable of working, but mainly of women, children, and the elderly, took place in Wolyn during the winter months, when some 30,000 Jews were murdered.[44] Again, the two shtetlekh were not affected. The reason may have been that the local German commanders, in this case the regional command at Lutzk, had a great deal of leeway as to when and how the local Jews should be murdered. Also, German murder squads were overextended, and the relative remoteness of the region did not make a special effort on their part worthwhile.

Orders were issued to mark the Jews with armbands on July 8 in Sarny and a month later in Rokitno. On September 9, the order, for all of Wolyn, came that Jews should wear a yellow badge instead, but this was enforced in Sarny on October 1 (Yom Kippur) only, when all the Jews were forced to attend a roll call in a public square.

In Rokitno, no Germans were in evidence until August. In the meantime, a Ukrainian shoemaker by the name of Retzlav,[45] who was of part-German parentage and a drunkard, was charged by the German command in Sarny to establish a police unit. He gave jobs to his Ukrainian and Polish friends and ordered Jewish representatives to appear before him. Quite naturally, Aharon Slutzky and two other former prewar Jewish councilors accepted the task of representing the Jewish community. Retzlav humiliated them, beat them, and then accepted a massive bribe, promising not to harm the Jews any more.[46]

The Germans divided the territories differently from either the Poles or the Soviets. After a brief interim period of military rule, they instituted a civilian government (on September 1, 1941). They attached the area of Southern Polesie, which included Brest-Litowsk, Stolin, Pinsk, and Kobrin, to Wolyn, calling the whole *Generalbezirk Wolhynien-Podolien* and putting it under the administration of *Generalkommissar* Heinrich Schoene.[47] This was now part of the *Generalkommissariat Ukraine*, under Erich Koch. The region was divided into 12 areas (*Gebiete*), each with a *Gebietskommissar*—including Heinz Krökel, the acting *Gebietskommissar* for the Sarny region[48]—and in larger towns, German *Stadtkommissars* were appointed. A Ukrainian attempt to establish Ukrainian rule was quickly aborted. Local SIPO (*Sicherheitspolizei*) command posts were established (usually out of former EG personnel), including one in Sarny, under Albert Schumacher (the local SS und *Polizeigebietsführer*), but they were very thinly manned; the main German force that was used to murder the Jews, under SIPO leadership, was battalion 320 of the ORPO (*Ordnungspolizei*) based in Rovno. In 1942, they were joined by battalions no. 305 and 315 (all three belonged to Regiment no. 11). German forces were insufficient and were supplemented by three Ukrainian battalions (*Schutzmänner*), each with about 600 men—no. 102, in Krzemieniec, and nos. 104 and 114. In November 1942, as the activities of partisans in northern Wolyn and Polesie were increasing, two more were added: nos. 105 and 106 (the latter in Sarny), but this came after the main murder actions against the Jews. In addition, there were 1,407 German gendarmes in all of Wolyn, and 11,870 Ukrainian policemen,[49] so it is hardly surprising that in Rokitno there appear to have been no more than 12 German gendarmes.[50]

After marking the Jews, the Germans proceeded to rob them of their property. In Sarny, on August 15, 1941, in October, and then again in January, 1942, huge amounts of gold (48 kilograms in August, 5 gold rubles per head in October, 35 kilograms in January) were demanded, as "contributions."[51] In Rokitno—88,000 gold rubles. Later, 3 kilograms of gold were demanded. In both places—as practically everywhere else in Europe—the leadership thought that providing the money would stave off worse persecutions. In Rokitno, as in some other places in Eastern Europe, a religious interdiction (*cherem*) was issued against those who refused to pay their share.[52] All livestock, such as cows, horses, fowl, and so on (most Jews owned some livestock), was confiscated, as were carts, bicycles, and the like.[53] In early 1942, a group of 30 S.S.-men (SIPO or ORPO, the identity is uncertain) is reported to have arrived in Rokitno with a civilian, a *Kreislandwirt* (area agricultural expert) named Ditsch, who stayed behind and became a feared oppressor of Jews.[54]

Forced labor was introduced immediately after the Germans' arrival. The mass killings of the first months, not just in Wolyn, produced a labor shortage, and Jewish slave-labor was widely used; Sarny and Rokitno were no exceptions. In Rokitno, log-cutting, work in the glass factory, field work, and so on, were supervised largely by soldier members of the *Todt* (German military labor) organization. In late December 1941, 68 Jews from the Sarny area, among them 14 from Rokitno, were sent to Vinnitsa, for forced labor, apparently to build Hitler's headquarters there. Two men fled, and returned to Rokitno.[55] In Sarny, the Germans demanded 300 men and 100 women for various types of hard labor. Later, they tortured the

Jews by forcing them to destroy a wall in the town with their bare hands within eight days. Another, purely sadistic torture was to force the women to carry bricks from one end of town to the other, to no purpose whatsoever.[56]

The *Judenräte* in the two townships differed from each other.[57] In Sarny, the *Judenrat* head was Shmaryahu Gershonok, the 70-year-old (in 1941) respected former head of the community; his secretary, Hermann Neumann, however, was a refugee lawyer, from Kalisz in Western Poland, the intermediary with the Germans, who was completely taken in by them. There was criticism of the *Judenrat*, mainly of Neumann.[58] The Ukrainian municipal authorities were outright murderous.[59] A Jewish order-police was established, under Yonah Margalit (or Margulies), and there is criticism of him in one testimony, though he later became a leading member of the underground.[60]

In Rokitno, Aharon Slutzky, 48 years old, became the *Judenrat* head, and the general view of the *Judenrat* and the small Jewish police group was positive.[61] The *Judenrat* had to guarantee with their lives that no Jew would escape from Rokitno, as the Germans were wary about the possibility of resistance by partisans right from the beginning. The synagogues were closed down, but then reopened, though public prayer was officially forbidden. Workers received permits that enabled them to receive larger food rations.

Food was strictly rationed. While Jewish forced laborers in Rokitno originally received half a kilo of bread a day, others of course received much less. But then the workers' ration was later reduced to 100 grams a day.[62] In Sarny, the ration was 100 grams a day for workers, 80 grams for the rest, and there was actual starvation in the ghetto, which was established on April 15, 1942, with 15 persons to a room. Such crowding became even worse when the Germans brought in Jews from the small neighboring villages, and the number of ghetto residents increased to about 6,000.[63] In addition, the Germans established a separate small ghetto for a number of craftsmen and their families—a procedure that they followed in many other places as well. However, when the final liquidation came, these craftsmen were murdered together with the main ghetto.

Life in Rokitno became progressively more difficult, and food was scarce. Nevertheless, unlike in Sarny, we seldom hear about actual starvation. Contacts with the local population were maintained, despite orders to the contrary. Some parents tried to organize education for their children, and there is a report that speaks of groups of 3–5 children who were being taught "Hebrew and Torah" by former teachers and older, non-working, people.[64]

Two testimonies tell us that a number of Jewish women were raped by Polish, Ukrainian, and German policemen (*gendarmes*).[65] This may or may not be true.

On May 1, 1942, a ghetto was established in Rokitno, though one without walls, with eight persons to one room. A small group of Jewish order-police was also set up at that time. The food ration (for the non-working population, apparently) dropped to 40 grams of bread a day.

There were no organized, communal attempts at education or cultural life in either shtetl. In Sarny, "the youth met in small groups, but there was no particular content at these meetings." News about mass-murder actions in the general area spread in the spring of 1942 and was confirmed by some 50 families of the ghetto of Davidhorodok, who were sent to Sarny by the Germans.[66] As a result, people in Sarny built hideouts (we don't hear about this in Rokitno), but these proved to be ineffective when the time came. There was an illegal radio in the ghetto through which news was spread.[67]

The murder of the two communities took place in August 1942, on the twenty-sixth for Rokitno and on the twenty-seventh for Sarny. Characteristically, the order of the *Generalkommissar* of the Bezirk, in Lutzk, to liquidate all Jewish ghettoes within six weeks was issued *after* the murder in the two townships; it came on August 31, in the wake of a meeting of German officials in Lutzk on August 29–31. To act first, and confirm the decision to do so later, was a common Nazi practice. In Sarny, German and Ukrainian policemen were supplemented by some 200 members of the *Todt* organization, which was charged with building and repairing, but was also used for murder actions against Jews. Prior to the mass murder, rumor spread that a German police station in the area, in Ostarky, was annihilated by partisans, who were reported to have killed 20 Germans.[68] If this indeed took place, it may have constituted an additional incentive for the Germans to annihilate the area's ghettos.

In Sarny, a tragic discussion took place on the eve of the mass murder. A resistance group was created apparently at the very last minute. Consisting of former members of Zionist groups, together with refugee strongmen (*shlegers*), many probably with a criminal background, it included the head of the Jewish Police, Yonah Margalit, a former teacher in the Hebrew school. Together they organized themselves into three groups that were poised to burn the ghetto and enable people to escape to the nearby forests.[69] They had the blessing of Gershonok. However, when the Germans concentrated forces in Sarny and the Jews became suspicious, the *Judenrat's* secretary, Neumann, argued that he had received assurances from the acting *Gebietskommissar* of Sarny, Krökel, that no harm would befall the Jews. The potential rebels decided that they could not take upon themselves the responsibility of acting, and thereby sentencing the ghetto to death, if there was a reasonable chance that nothing would happen; the rebellion was aborted.[70]

On and after August 24, the Germans concentrated all the Jews from the Sarny district in Sarny; some 14,000 Jews and 100 Roma (Gypsies) were also brought in. Some three days of thirst and starvation followed, as the Jews were guarded by Germans and Ukrainians armed to the teeth.[71] There was a wooden structure in the enclosure, and the Gypsies and some Jews were kept inside. On August 27, the Jews of Sarny were driven out of their homes and forced to join the others in the enclosure. The first to be taken out to be killed, on that day, were the recently arrived Rokitno Jews. Soon, automatic fire was heard from the nearby forest. Now there was no further doubt about the Germans' intentions, and two members of the Sarny underground, Yosef Gendelman and the smith Tendler, who had managed to smuggle in his wire-cutter, rushed to the fence and cut it. At the same time the Gypsies set fire to their barracks—the actions may have been coordinated—and in the ensuing commotion, while some 500–1,000 Jews escaped, about 2,500 were killed on the spot by automatic fire. The rest were then taken out to the forest and killed there. After the massacre, German and Ukrainian police and members of the *Todt* organization searched Sarny and murdered Jews trying to hide. "Almost all the Christian population, Ukrainian as well as Polish, participated in killing the Jews."[72]

In Rokitno, there had been two roll calls of all the Jews (on March 12 and March 17, 1942) before the final liquidation, possibly in order to lull any suspicions on the part of the victims.[73] When the third roll call was ordered, for August 26, members of the *Judenrat* calmed the people by saying that after the assembly on a cattle market, near the railway, they would be sent home again.[74] The Germans prepared railway carriages to transport the Rokitno Jews to Sarny and kill them there. All came—contrary to the situation in Sarny, we don't hear of people hiding. The roll call yielded 1,638 (some survivors say 1,631) present.[75] The Ukrainian and Polish police, under the command of *Oberwachmeister* of the *Gendarmerie Sokolowski*, possibly a Polish *Volksdeutscher* from Silesia (or Berlin), guarded the assembled Jews, but they left one side of the square open, whether intentionally or not is not clear.[76] Ukrainian militiamen from one of the battalions mentioned above then marched into positions near the square. According to a number of testimonies, there was also a Latvian unit.[77] A Jewish woman, Mindl Eisenberg (known as "Mindl Cossack" because of her physique and courage), saw this and screamed "Jews, they have come to kill us."[78] The militia and the German gendarmes began shooting, and then a disorganized, panicked, mass attempt to escape ensued, in which hundreds managed to run to the adjoining forest—the estimates vary between 400 and 900. Many women with small children were among them, but of these, only a few managed to escape the pursuers.[79] Families were torn apart, and groups of Jews began wandering through the dense forests. In the shtetl, the rest, variously estimated at between 800 and 1,200, were herded into the cattle wagons. Between 100 and 300 were killed on the spot. There are no German or Polish accounts, and the survivors could not reconcile their different impressions of the numbers involved.

The escapees from the two shtetlekh tried to survive in the dense forests that cover northern Wolyn. In the summer of 1942, there were no partisan detachments in Wolyn, with the exception of the unit of Dmitri M. Medvedev, an NKVD (Soviet secret police) officer, whose unit of some 150 men (including, oddly enough, some Spanish Republicans who had found refuge in the Soviet Union) had been parachuted into northern Wolyn and engaged in sabotage and intelligence work. Medvedev was no anti-Semite (his mother was Jewish), and at first he accepted Jewish refugees, but then he could not cope with unarmed civilians. He took a number of young men into his unit, and directed the others to other units further north, in the Pripjet marshes on the Wolyn-Polesie-Belorussian border.[80]

During the times of the ghetto in both places, and even more so afterwards, the relationships between the Jews and their Ukrainian and Polish neighbors were of absolutely crucial importance. In 1940, at its meeting in German-occupied Cracow, the OUN, the Ukrainian nationalistic movement, split, with the majority siding with Stepan Bandera. They prepared the ground for a Ukrainian rebellion against the Soviets who were then in control of Wolyn and sent a locally well-known leader, Maxim Borovets, a.k.a. "Taras Bulba" (the name of the hero of the novel by Nikolai Gogol), to the northeast, into the Sarny district, in early August 1940. Borovets, from Dubno, had been a stone-quarry owner and engineer, with not unfriendly ties with Rokitno Jews, especially the pharmacists of the Soltzman family. A radical, anti-Soviet nationalist, arrested by the Poles before the war, he was nominated by the Soviets to be in charge of a stone quarry near Sarny. At first he tried to see whether the Soviets would support Ukrainian nationalism. When he realized that they would not, he decided to support the Germans. He organized his supporters when the Germans invaded and went over to them with weapons taken from the Soviets. He then cooperated with the German-initiated Ukrainian version of the German *Einsatzgruppen*, the *Pokhilni grupy*, and tried to set up a Ukrainian administration. He was nominated as commander of the Ukrainian militia in Sarny county in the summer of 1941.[81] The Germans used such Ukrainian initiatives to recruit their Ukrainian militia, police, and local governments. They were aided by the Orthodox clergy, especially Bishop Polikarp of Lutzk. Borovets-Bulba developed his armed groups, known as the *Bulbovtsy* and numbering some 2,000 men, in the Sarny area. Their main mission was to kill Soviet partisans and Jews, and they started by murdering all the Jews of the township of Olevsk, beyond the former Soviet border, east of Rokitno. In November 1941, the Germans ordered him to disband his units. Bulba obeyed, but withdrew to his own base in Borovoye with dozens of his men. In February 1942, he offered to the Germans to fight the growing Soviet partisan movement, and when he was refused, set up his Ukrainian partisan army. However, parallel to his effort, the Bandera nationalists (Bandera himself had been arrested by the Germans in 1941) penetrated the forests, and a rivalry developed between the groups, both calling themselves the Ukraina Povstan'ska Armio (UPA [Ukrainian Insurgent Army]). There were 4,000 *Bulbovtsy* in the forests by then. In March, 1943, some 6,000 Ukrainians, many of them from the German-controlled militia and police, joined the two branches of the UPA; in late 1942, the *Bulbovtsy* began murdering Poles wherever they could. Under their influence, most Ukrainians in the area turned violently anti-Jewish (and, later, anti-Polish). For the escapees from the two shtetlekh, this meant that their lives were in constant danger from the locals. In mid-1943, the *Bulbovtsy* suffered serious reverses at the hand of the Soviet partisans, and were forced to join forces with their Bandera rivals (the *Banderovtsy*).[82]

The Soviet partisan movement was originally divided into several types of units. Some were controlled by the Party, some by the Army, some by the NKVD, and some directly by the Supreme Command of the partisan movement, set up in May 1942, under Panteleimon Ponomarenko, the secretary of the Belorussian Party. Soviet soldiers—some of them escapees from POW camps, others remnants of units defeated by the Germans—local Party activists, anti-German peasants, Jews, some Poles, and other soldiers parachuted into the area by the Soviet Army, made up the detachments. In the Polesie area (northern Wolyn and Southern Belorussia), units were set up by Dimitry Popov, an escaped Soviet officer, Jozef Sobiesak, a Pole, Mikola Konieshchuk ('Kruk'), a Ukrainian (his detachment was composed mostly of Jews), and Sergei Korchev, a Russian, whose second-in-command was Alek Abuyev, a Jew. All these were combined in late 1942 by the Soviet Colonel Anton Brinski. They penetrated the Sarny district and sent some of their units to the Rovno area further south. When the unit grew larger, separate regiments were formed, and then all were combined in the Brinski partisan brigade (in early 1943). Near the Brinski brigade, a second large partisan division developed under Alexander N. Saburov, another high NKVD officer, and Jews from the Sarny district reached those units (including the Pleskonosov detachment, which contained a number of Jews) as well.[83] In March 1943, in addition to the Medvedev unit, another NKVD unit was parachuted into the area, under Nikolai Prokopiuk. These NKVD units were controlled, separately from Soviet-held territory by the NKVD chief Timofey Strokach. In the end, all partisan units in the Ukraine came under the control of the Party, via the Central Partisan Command, and the most important commanders became members of the Central Committee of the Ukrainian Party (Alexander Saburov and Alexei Fyodorov). Further north of the Sarny area, a Jewish detachment under Moshe Gildenman ("Dyadya [Uncle] Misha") from the shtetl of Korets formed in September 1942, and some Jews from the Sarny district joined it.[84] Another Jewish unit formed in Berezno, in the Sarny district, but failed to maintain itself. Further south, in the Rovno district, another partisan brigade under Colonel, later General, Vasili A. Begma (former Party secretary of Rovno county), also took in some Jews from the Sarny area. In 1943, the famed partisan division of Sidor A. Kovpak fought its way from Belorussia, through northern Ukraine, to the Drohobycz oilfields in the East Galician Carpathian foothills. Kovpak, who was no anti-Semite either, accepted a number of Jews into his units, but most of them perished in the hard-fought battles in Eastern Galicia.[85] There, his units were defeated and dispersed by the Germans, and the remnants had to make their way, in many small groups, back to the north. Only few Jews survived this ordeal.[86] By 1943, there were areas north of Rokitno (e.g., Belezowo and other villages) that were under full partisan control. One report has it that a Jewish Soviet officer warned peasants in one village that if they denounced Jews to the Germans, the village would be burned down.[87]

There were Jewish families in many of the small villages, especially those in the forests and marshes. The case of Berezowo, 45 kilometers northwest of Rokitno, may serve as an example. There were 18 Jewish families in the village, and some 500–600 Ukrainians and Belorussians in the area (most of the surrounding smaller villages were in fact Belorussian). There was no house of prayer, and the Jews used to pray in the house of the Jewish elder, Israel Berezowski. Jews there barely knew how to read and write, and their education consisted in learning to read the prayer book. The relatively wealthier families sent their children to the *Tarbut* school in Rokitno. When the Soviets came, the witness went to attend a teachers' seminar in Dabrowica. For four to five months after the Soviet retreat, "we did not see any Germans at all," until some 60 Ukrainian policemen arrived from Rokitno to supervise the whole area. They murdered a whole Jewish community of 30 people in the village of Wojkiewicze, some 30 kilometers away. But there were also local policemen, and these protected the Berezowo Jews for a while. A Jew by the name of Brick became the Jewish representative. In the end, 303 Jews were concentrated in the village by the Ukrainians, and no one was permitted to leave. The Jews had heard about the mass murder in Rokitno, but by that time the Ukrainian commander realized that the Ukrainians were simply being used by the Germans, and he desisted from murdering the local Jews. A troop of German security police came, 10 of them stayed in the village, and they organized the murder of those Jews who did not escape to the forests. The murder action took place two days before the Jewish New Year (1942). The number of survivors cannot be determined.[88]

Most Jewish young men, and a number of women, managed to find partisans who accepted them, if they survived the first extremely harsh and difficult weeks or months in primitive dugouts. There was a lot of anti-Semitism in these Soviet units, usually (though not always) reined in by the commanders, and there were Jews who fell victim to the bullets of their own comrades-in-arms.[89] However, there were also units where there was no anti-Semitism at all (as shown above).[90] Women generally, and Jewish women in particular, were often sexually exploited by their officers and had no choice but to submit. Others were held in great esteem as fighters, nurses, or providers of essential services, so that the overall picture is contradictory. There is, however, a very clear divide between the Ukrainian and the Belorussian areas. There was very definitely less anti-

Jewishness in the latter, and on the whole, Jews who managed to get to the partisan detachments, especially in Belorussia, had a fair chance of survival. The problem for many was how to survive until they found such partisans.[91]

For some Jews, keeping the religious commandments was a must, and in some cases they overcame great obstacles to do so. Practically all Jews, whether they considered themselves observant or not, kept Pesach and fasted and prayed on Yom Kippur.[92]

Escapees from Rokitno went either north, into the Polesian marshes, and looked for partisans, or southwest, to the area of the three Polish villages mentioned above. The Polish peasants, who had been living there for many generations, saw in the Jews poor creatures persecuted by the enemies of the Poles: the Ukrainian nationalists and the Germans. All of them were basically friendly to the Jews, especially the Catholic priest, Ludwik Wolodarczyk, and the local schoolteacher, Felicja Masojada, who organized a Polish resistance group that established contact with Soviet partisans (who were beginning to be active further north) as early as the summer of 1942. The three villages (and the fourth, Netreba, which was part-Polish) were on the edge of the thick forests in that area, and many Jews hid there. They spent the nights in makeshift dugouts in the forest and begged for food—and sometimes worked for it—during the day. Early in 1943, a Polish unit formed within the Soviet partisan movement (part of the Rovno brigade, a regiment commanded by Fyodorov "of Rovno"), led by Roman Satanowski; of the original 80 members, 30 were Jews (after the war it turned out that he was a Jew), and additional Jews joined that unit, while others joined other Soviet units. Father Wolodarczyk even mediated between some of the Jews—especially the Rokitno pharmacist, Yakov Soltzman[93]—and the partisans. These Polish villagers were pro-Soviet for the simple reason that there was no one else who could save them from the *Bulbovtsy*—and, indeed, the *Bulbovtsy* in the end burned their villages and murdered many Poles; the rest fled into the forests and joined the Jews who were hiding there. During 1943, Ukrainian nationalists murdered tens of thousands of Poles in Wolyn, especially in the northern areas.[94] The four Polish villages mentioned, and both Wolodarczyk and Masojada, were among the victims.[95] Many cases of Polish rescuers are mentioned by the survivors. In one case in Sarny, according to a survivor, a Polish woman named Anna Studzynska rescued a bloodied Torah scroll from a dying beadle.[96] In addition, three Polish or part-Polish villages in the area—Karpilowka, Malinsk, and Maloszki—where Polish peasants offered help to escaping Jews, are mentioned.[97]

Generally, survivors from Eastern Galicia and Wolyn tell us that the Ukrainians were overwhelmingly and murderously anti-Jewish, with few exceptions.[98] There can be no doubt that most Ukrainians were either totally indifferent to the fate of their Jewish neighbors, or indeed violently anti-Semitic. However, there appear to be important differences between different geographical areas. Thus, a typical survivor testimony says that "one has to note that the attitude of the peasants towards us was relatively good. There was no case of hurting Jews or denouncing them, anywhere in the Belezowo area" north of Rokitno.[99] Another survivor testified that "there were those who were hostile, and there were others who saved many, whether by supplying food or in other ways."[100] Most survivors were helped, at one or another time, by more than one Ukrainian,[101] and one must remember that helping Jews was not only punishable by death at German hands, but that *Banderovtsy* and *Bulbovtsy* killed Ukrainian helpers of Jews as well.[102] On the other hand, one must always remember that those who were murdered by Ukrainians, or denounced by them to the militia or to Germans, as well as those who were robbed and then sent to die in the forest, left no testimonies behind—and they are the overwhelming majority.

As to the motives for Jews to fight in partisan detachments, obviously the instinct of self-preservation was primary. However, the burning urge to take revenge for the killing of loved ones was also an active incentive, as many testimonies indicate. During the war, and after liberation, Jewish partisans killed Ukrainian collaborators and murderers of Jews wherever they could, sometimes in the barbaric fashions they had learnt from the murderers.[103] In Rokitno, this was also facilitated by the fact that the township was actually conquered by Soviet partisans, under the command of General Saburov, on January 2 (or 4, according to others), 1944. About 200 survivors gathered there, or about 13% of the 1,638 who had been there in August 1942—the highest survival rate in Wolyn. A number of them joined the Red Army.[104] Sarny was liberated on January 11; there were about 100 survivors, or about 2%. The town was bombed by German airplanes after its liberation, and much of what was left was destroyed.

In 1946, the remaining Jews of Sarny and Rokitno left for Poland (as did the local Poles).

· · ·

The two shtetlach analyzed here were new, founded at the end of the nineteenth century. The question whether that had any impact on the behavior of the Jews during the Holocaust has to be answered negatively. In other places in the *kresy* such as Buczacz, Krzemieniec, or Kosow Huculski—all of them old established Jewish communities—Jews did not behave any differently from the way they did in Baranowicze, Sarny or Rokitno. In the new towns, however, there was a great deal of difference.

Sarny and Rokitno were typical of many other shtetlekh in the *kresy* in terms of the modernization process of Jewish life in the 1920s and 1930s. While traditional Orthodoxy declined, Zionism, and especially the Hebrew educational system and the youth movements, became predominant; the Bund became a negligible quantity, as did the Communists. The socioeconomic picture resembles that of other shtetlekh: a few wealthier merchants, very little industry or none, and a struggling middle class of merchants. Below them were the peddlers, small shopkeepers, and, mainly, the craftsmen, who together formed the majority of the population. There had been migration, mainly to the United States, before and immediately after World War I, and some immigration to Palestine in the interwar period, chiefly influenced by the *kibbutz-hachsharah* of the left-wing Zionist youth movements at Klosowo in the Sarny area. However, at the same time, in both shtetlekh, the traditional premodern social structure persisted, in the form of the various voluntary organizations that ensured social welfare and in the form of the community's autonomy maintained through an oligarchic system established in the preceding centuries. The rabbinate fulfilled an important integrative role, meshing with the increasing secularization despite a lively controversy. For the Orthodox element, the Hasidic "courts" of the region were still of great importance. The Polish government's exclusionary economic policies hit mainly the middle class. The relationship with the surrounding populations, Ukrainians and Poles, was generally reasonable, but old enmities were just under the surface. No direct evidence was found of the effects of World War I and postwar massacres and brutalities that were commonplace in Wolyn between 1914 and 1921, but it is highly unlikely that these had been forgotten.[105] The rise of radical Ukrainian nationalism targeted Jews, Poles, and Soviets, all of whom were to be eliminated. The nationalists identified with National Socialist Germany.

The occupation of the area by the Soviets in September 1939 opened educational opportunities for the Jews and enabled them, for the first time, to occupy positions, albeit generally inferior ones, in mostly local government. Since the alternative to Soviet rule was German occupation, Jews welcomed the Soviets as liberators. This increased the hatred of Poles and most Ukrainians towards Jews, though Soviet rule meant the destruction of the age-old Jewish communal structures, the abolition of autochthonous Jewish education, the pauperization and persecution of what once was the Jewish middle class, and the regimentation of the craftsmen. There was little opposition to these Soviet policies, and the speedy collapse of the Jewish institutions is somewhat surprising, though a very weak opposition seems to have been more marked in Sarny and Rokitno than elsewhere, perhaps because of the relative remoteness of the townships from centers of authority. Proportionately more Jews were deported to Siberian camps from the *kresy* than Poles or Ukrainians, though most of the Jewish deportees were refugees from Nazi-occupied Poland, and only a minority were former Jewish communal and political leaders and wealthier merchants. Because of the corrupt nature of the Soviet regime, Jews were generally able to make a living with the help of a grey or black market and bribes to the officials. All this applied to the two shtetlekh as well.

After the occupation of the area by the Germans, the same administration was introduced in the Sarny area as elsewhere, and the German policies did not differ from parallel policies elsewhere in the occupied areas of the Soviet Union. The individuals who became the rulers of the area, including those who became the oppressors and the murderers of the Jews, were part of a consensus of Germans who accepted the liquidation of the Jews as a necessary and positive policy and were willing, with few exceptions,[106] to murder every Jewish man, woman, and child without any apparent hesitation. Some of them were corrupt, and that may have mitigated their policies temporarily. No extreme sadists were reported. The murder was organized, it seems, from the regional center, in Lutzk.

The communities that had been dissolved by the Soviets rebounded, paradoxically, as a result of the German conquest. In both shtetlekh, it was the Jewish community that selected its leadership which became the *Judenrat*. In both cases it was the same group of individuals who had led the prewar community, and the heads of the *Judenrat* in both cases were the former heads of the *kehillah* (the Jewish community). In Sarny, the *Judenrat* head was a decent old man whose influence was declining; a refugee from the West became the go-between with the Germans, and a negative influence on the community, whereas the head of the Jewish police became an active member of the resistance. This is quite different from other shtetlekh, such as Buczacz and Krzemieniec in the south of the *kresy* and Baranowicze in the north. In Rokitno, the head of the *Judenrat* received high marks for integrity and self-sacrifice, although in the end the *Judenrat* fell for the deceptions of the Germans. There are, therefore, obvious differences between the two shtetlekh in this regard; these cannot be explained by objective circumstances, but only, perhaps, by the characters of the individuals concerned and by the chance of their being where they were at the time.

There were no attempts, in either shtetl, to organize social welfare, smuggling of food, health aid, or education (though there were some private educational initiatives in Rokitno). While there were remnants of religious life, especially in Rokitno, religious observance seems to have taken place in the homes only, and that is understandable, given the violent oppression by Germans and Ukrainians. In these small places, social welfare or organized smuggling of food was hardly possible, and in Rokitno perhaps even unnecessary, given the closeness of the township to the agricultural surroundings and the closely knit nature of the communities. There were no morale-building cultural activities. What has elsewhere been called *amidah* (standing up against German policies, armed and unarmed) took a completely different form from what we have learnt about in large centers such as Warsaw, Lodz, Bialystok, Vilna, etc. If one considers hiding and/or escaping into the forest as an active Jewish reaction—and this is what is proposed here—then the individual initiatives to do so were an expression of the refusal to surrender. Such initiatives were fairly massive, in both communities. They were of course made easier by the proximity of the dense forests and the fact that there were Soviet partisans whose movement began to develop a few months after the liquidation of the two shtetlekh. Polish peasants, Baptists, Old Believers (*Staroveryi*), and a number of Ukrainian peasants who were willing to endanger themselves made it possible for a small minority to survive until they could join the partisans or be helped by them.

The mass escapes from Rokitno and Sarny seem, at first glance, to be very unusual, and in a way they are, but similar escapes took place elsewhere, mainly in the Belorussian areas to the north of Wolyn (Lachwa, Kleck, Mir, Dvorets, and others). As mentioned above, there were the forests that made the escapes possible. But that factor, in itself, while necessary, was not sufficient. It was the Jewish initiative to make use of the opportunity of escape that made it so. Escapes like that did not happen in other places, where the opportunity existed, but was not taken up—in

Krzemieniec, for instance, or Kossow in Eastern Galicia, and probably elsewhere as well.

It has been noted that while the testimonies used generally describe the Ukrainians as hostile and murderous, which was probably true in most cases, there seem to have been quite a number of exceptions, so that a generalization regarding the heinous behavior of the Ukrainians during the war cannot be accepted without qualification.

One can also conclude that no generalization is possible regarding either Jewish leadership or Jewish reactions in comparable circumstances, despite the fact that the Germans, the Poles, the Ukrainians, the Belorussians, and the others were the same and had similar attitudes.

Systematic research on the Jewish partisans in the *kresy* is still very sketchy.[107] The numbers involved are still more guesswork than anything else. What is clear from the story of the two shtetlekh is that the further north (and into Belorussia) people fled, the greater the chances of meeting partisans, from the early autumn of 1942 on. While there was quite a lot of anti-Semitism, sometimes murderous, among the partisans, this diminished as time went on, largely due to of the influence of the Soviet Communist leadership. The participation of large numbers of Jews in partisan detachments meant an opportunity of taking revenge on the Germans and their collaborators, and that was undoubtedly the main motivation of these fighters. It is hard to imagine the brutality of this type of war. No prisoners were taken—or rather, they were taken, interrogated, and killed. Collaborators, or even suspected collaborators, met the same fate. Jews saw in the Soviet regime their rescuers and saviors, and rightly so. Many identified with the Communist ideology that was inculcated by the regime's representatives, but many others, while not actively opposed to the regime, became disillusioned and wanted to get away, mostly to Palestine, as soon as the war was over. We are talking here of areas that were Polish before the war, where the impact of the past, with its Jewish cultural, political, and religious experience, made itself felt. Many emigrants were the Jewish Communists who, after the war and sometimes years after its end, made their way out of the Soviet paradise. And yet, their loyalty towards and friendship with their former Russian, Ukrainian, or Belorussian comrades and commanders remained very strong.

It has to be stressed that for the Jews, the Soviet regime and the Red Army were the only hope for survival, and that in this their reaction was the opposite of that of most Ukrainians and of course most Poles. It is this historical memory that explains much of the deep cleavage that exists today between Jews and members of East European nations who experienced the Soviets as foreign and hostile occupants.

The extant literature on the Jewish "family camps" in the forests is in its infancy. There was no hard and fast borderline between these "camps"—which actually, mostly, just primitive dugouts (*zemlianky*) in the forest—and the partisans. Many are the testimonies, including those from the two shtetlekh, that document the frequent transition from one to the other. These family camps could not survive without some help from the peasants, and this is another proof of the complicated relationship of the Jews with the Ukrainian population. On the other hand, many did not survive, partly because someone betrayed them, and that someone was usually a Ukrainian peasant, sometimes even a whole village.

The end of shtetl life in the *kresy* meant the demise of one of the most important sources of contemporary Jewish life, and through that, of contemporary culture generally. The study of Jewish reactions to the genocidal policies, within their historical context, are of importance both for the surviving Jewish people and for the understanding of victims' reactions to genocide generally.

Further research may perhaps add to or correct the conclusions reached here.

Notes

1. Shimon Redlich, *Together and Apart in Brzezany* (Bloomington, 2002).

2. The other being Eastern Galicia.

3. There are no reliable figures on Rokitno. Shmuel Spector, *The Holocaust of Volhynian Jews, 1941–1944* (Jerusalem, 1990), p. 53, has 2,000 for the Soviet period, excluding refugees from the West. In some of the testimonies, there are estimates of up to 3,500.

4. Ibid., p. 14.

5. Joseph Marcus, *Social and Political History of the Jews in Poland, 1919–1939* (Berlin, 1983), p. 469.

6. Yehuda Bauer, "Kurzeniec," *Moreshet* (English version) (Tel Aviv, 2003), pp. 132–157. The name of the witness was Zalman Gurevich.

7. The name means deer in Russian and was adopted because these were abundant in the forests there.

8. *Sefer Yizkor leKehillat Sarny (Memorial Book for the Sarny Community)*, Yosef Kariv, ed. (Tel Aviv, 1961), pp. 13, 27–28. Henceforth cited as Sarny.

9. Ibid., p. 228.

10. Ibid., pp. 35–40, 70, 173. Memoirists claim that hundreds immigrated to Palestine between the wars.

11. The town was originally called Okhotnikov, to immortalize a Russian landowner of that name, but it soon reverted to the name of the village. The factory was founded by a Jew from Belgium named Rosenberg, then was owned by the Polish General Zawadski, then passed into the hands of two Jewish owners, Pflanzreich and Ronglewski, from Warsaw. Aharon Zunder, from the Sarny area, apparently bought him out (Memoirs of Alex Levin, Canada, unpublished, copy in the possession of Chaim Bar-Or, Haifa, p. 5; henceforth cited as Alex Levin).

12. *Rokitna (Volin) Vehasviva*, by Eliezer Leoni, ed. (Tel Aviv, 1967), pp. 49–52, 58–82, 85–105; henceforth cited as Rokitno. An English translation, by Lora Metelits Hull, can be found at www.jewishgen.org/Yiskor/rokitnoye/rokitnoye.hmtl.

13. There was a small group of Communists in Rokitno. A testimony by a former Communist, Joseph Gendelman, in the *Rokitno Memorial Book* (Rokitno, pp. 191–192), claims that the group was founded in 1925 and organized strikes of poor workers. The merchants, he says, called the police, and he and others were sentenced to long terms of imprisonment. Liberated by the outbreak of war in 1939, he became a member of the town council under the Soviets, and then escaped into the Soviet Union when the Germans invaded.

14. Sarny, p. 195.

15. The rabbi from Dabrowica was Yakov Lieberson.

16. From 1932, he was deputy head, and from 1936 he was head of the community. The official rabbi was Nachum Pachnik (from Berezna). Rabbis Kunda and Hechtman remained responsible for their respective communities.

17. *Hashomer Hatzair* was founded in 1921, and the others—*Hechalutz, Hechalutz Hatzair, Gordonia, Betar, Freiheit* (another leftist movement), *Hashomer Hadati* (religious Zionists)—followed.

18. Sarny, p. 210.

19. There are many testimonies about the *Shtundists*, e.g., in Rokitno, pp. 289, 307, and elsewhere. For instance, one testimony (p. 307) tells us about three Baptists who rescued a whole group of Jewish partisans during a German attack by leading them through the Polesian swamps, at the risk of their own lives. On the Old Believers, see Asher Binder, YV 03/3364, and Moshe Trossman and others, YV 2005 (cited as Trossman 2005). However, it seems that in other areas of the Ukraine, Old Believers were less friendly to Jews. We don't know most of the names of the rescuers; an exception is a peasant by the name of Zachar Nikichuk from Ostichowo in the Polesie marshes (Sarny, p. 355).

20. There were 745 Polish villages in Wolyn. Tadeusz Piotrowski, *Genocide and Rescue in Wolyn* (Jefferson, NC, 2000), p.7.

21. Bronislaw Janik, *Bylo Ich Trzy* (Warszawa, 1970). A number of Jewish testimonies confirm the story of the friendly attitude of these Polish peasants and

especially mention one peasant, Juzek (Jozef) Zaleski (Rokitno, p. 309), as well as the priest and a teacher (see n. 93 below).

22. Rokitno, pp. 237–242. For a detailed account of the Soviet occupation, see Jan T. Gross, *Revolution from Abroad* (Princeton, 1988), p. 202.

23. Sarny, 267. But the Soviets then demanded the taxes Jews owed to the Poles for themselves! See also Andrzej Zbikowski, "Why Did Jews Welcome the Soviet Armies?" *Polin*, Vol. 13 (London, 2000), pp. 62–73.

24. Sixty out of 1,500 delegates were Jews—i.e., 4%—whereas the proportion of Jews among the population was 10% (Spector, op. cit., p. 25; Rokitno, pp. 243–245).

25. Rokitno, pp. 253–254; Yissaschar Trossman, YV-03/3477.

26. Sarny, p. 266.

27. Rokitno, p. 239. "The Zionist parties and the youth movements disbanded voluntarily. Here and there underground meetings were held" (p. 244).

28. Sarny, p. 267. Rokitno, pp. 106–108, 237–242. The once-popular Hebrew teacher Mordechai Gendelman in Rokitno was arrested and, when released, is said to have declared that "Hebrew is a rotten language." One of the memoirists in the Rokitno Book, Baruch Shchori, a Hebrew teacher, tells us that he became the principal of a Ukrainian school and taught his pupils the Stalin Constitution of 1936.

29. Rokitno, pp. 248–249. Apparently, only 8 members of youth movements made it to then-neutral Vilna, and of these some managed to reach Palestine in early 1941.

30. See Goetz Aly, *Hitlers Volksstaat* (Berlin, 2005), for the way the Nazis bought up goods everywhere using local currency which they obtained by effectively robbing the local economies.

31. Rokitno, p. 246. Batsheva Fishman, daughter of a trader from the shtetl of Lachwa, who had fled to Rokitno with the help of Jewish soldiers in the Red Army, reports that "something like heavy mourning enveloped" her.

32. Sarny, p. 268. "I cannot complain" about life under the Soviets (Survivors of the Shoah Foundation [henceforth cited as SF], Shmuel Levin-04224).

33. Over half of the refugees were deported, leaving probably around 24,000 in the area. Together with natural increase from 1931 on (estimated at 9%), the total number of Jews in Wolyn when the Germans came was around 250,000 (Spector, op. cit., pp. 1–10). "Every day, trainloads packed with refugees passed" the Rokitno rail station on their way to Siberia—surely a vastly exaggerated account, but indicative of the mood among many Rokitno Jews (Rokitno, p. 246). According to Polish figures, 52% of the deportees were Poles, 30% Jewish, and 18% Ukrainian and Belorussian (Gross, op. cit., p. 199). The Jews constituted about 10% of the total population, the Poles about 25%. Thus three times more Jews were deported than was their percentage of the population while twice the number of Poles were deported relative to their percentage of the population. And Ukrainians and

Belorussians were under-represented among the deportees. These statistics refute the argument that Jews were the rulers of this area under the Soviet regime and were preferred by it to other groups in the community. For details, see Gross, op. cit., passim.

34. Spector, p. 27.

35. Asher Binder, YV 03/3364. They were the Shulman, Gitelman, and Gol-ubovich families (Alex Levin), p. 8.

36. Sarny, pp. 79, 270. Only about 4 or 5 local families were deported.

37. Rokitno, p. 247.

38. Rokitno, pp. 251–253. Young men tried to escape also because it was gener-ally assumed they would be in danger from the Germans, whereas women, chil-dren, and old people would not be bothered. There were Jews in both places who remembered the friendly German soldiers who had been in the area during and after World War I and thought that there would be no danger from the Germans (e.g., SF-Alexander (Alex) Levin-4150, Shmuel Levin-04224).

39. Sarny was occupied between July 5 and 9, Rokitno on July 15 or 17 (Spector, pp. 47, 55).

40. This resulted in contradictory statements as to the actual date the Germans occupied the townships: it depended on whether the witnesses described the withdrawal of the Soviets and the passage of German armor, or the actual occu-pation by German infantry.

41. Shmuel Levin (YV M/E 141, a testimony from 1946) says there were 1,800 Jews left when the Germans came.

42. Michael Kravtsov, Fortunoff Library, Yale, T-1924. Another testimony claims that the Soviets handed out passes for evacuation to some people, which would agree with other sources (Sarny, p. 272).

43. Rokitno, p. 242.

44. Spector, op. cit., p. 115. In some instances, Ukrainian intellectuals—mainly doctors—demanded the liquidation of Jews.

45. I have not been able to find out his first name.

46. Rokitno, pp. 260–263. Asher Binder, YV 03/3364. It is reported that Rabbi Shamess demanded, in the synagogue, that unity be maintained and that that would save the Jews.

47. His headquarters was first in Brest; in June 1942, he moved to Lutsk.

48. YV TR-11/01235.

49. Spector, p. 175. On Ukrainian collaboration in the murder of Jews, see Dieter Pohl, "Ukrainische Hilfskräfte beim Mord an den Juden," in Gerhard Paul, ed., Die Täter der Shoah (Göttingen, 2002), pp. 205–234.

50. These gendarmes were led by Oberwachmeister König and included a par-ticularly sadistic gendarme named Henkel. However, generally speaking, the Ger-man gendarmes were less of a danger than the Ukrainian policemen (Rokitno, pp. 262–264, and YV TR11/01235). In the early 1960s the German investigating

authorities were unable to establish the first names of these individuals, nor the name of the *Oberwachmeister* Sokolowski in Rokitno (see n. 76 below).

51. Sarny, p. 274.

52. Rokitno, pp. 265–267; Alexander (Alex) Levin, SF-4150; and in many other testimonies. The "contributions," as they were called, from Rokitno were sent to Sarny.

53. Sarny, p. 273.

54. Rokitno, p. 269; YV TR11/01235. Postwar German efforts to find him (and his first name) were unsuccessful.

55. Rokitno, p. 338–339. One of the two was Asher Binder, a former *Hashomer Hatzair* member and a refugee from Western Poland, where he had been on a Zionist *hachsharah* (farm in preparation for immigration to Palestine) and who later became a well-known partisan.

56. Sarny, pp. 272, 312.

57. A survey of views of survivors regarding the *Judenräte* in all of Wolyn yielded positive evaluations for two-thirds of the 45 places where there were sufficient numbers of survivors to provide testimony; one-fifth were negative; and the rest were contradictory. Views on the Jewish Police in 33 places yielded slightly more than 50% positive evaluations (Spector, p. 167). If this is true, it would corroborate Aharon Weiss' findings about *Judenräte* in the *Generalgouvernement*, and thus put another nail in the coffin of purely condemnatory views of the *Judenrat* as an institution. Spector reports that about one-third of *Judenrat* heads were former leaders of their communities. Sarny and Rokitno fit into this mold.

58. "The Jewish Council was a tool in German hands" (Sarny, p. 274). Yet on the next page we find: "one should recollect, with appreciation, the people who fulfilled their role in the Jewish Council, the late Mr. Gershonok, a noble man, especially"; Moshe Pickman, another *Judenrat* member, is said to have been a good man (Sarny, p. 284).

59. The mayor was one Mariniuk, the man responsible for Jewish forced labor was Kazik Kostrun, and the head of the police, one Batuchin, was, so the witnesses say, a murderer (Sarny, p. 273).

60. *Yiddishe Caitung*, Tel Aviv, September 8, 1955. Margalit was a graduate of *Betar*.

61. The *Judenrat* "consisted of very decent people" (Jacob Soltzman, YV—03/1594). "It is possible to say that the *Judenrat* in Rokitno was 100% ok" (Mordechai Shulner, YV 03/1366—this despite the fact that in the winter of 1941–42, 15 Jews, supposedly master craftsmen, were selected by the *Judenrat* to be sent away; only 3 returned (Rokitno, p. 270). "Thanks to the *Judenrat*, many managed to save themselves and to flee to the forests" (Ita Gompel, YV M.I.Q. 377; see also Trossman, YV 2005).

62. Rokitno, p. 262. Seventy grams, according to Shmuel Levin, YV M/E 141.

63. Sarny, pp. 273, 312. Some sources say that the date of establishing the ghetto was April 2–4, 1942.

64. But there appears also to have been one former *Tarbut* teacher, who taught children (Rokitno, p. 326; see also Spector, p. 140).

65. Rokitno, p. 263; and YV-M/E 141. A report of the Israeli police of July 6, 1964, summarizing a number of testimonies for German judicial authorities, claims that 2 girls were raped. This becomes 25 girls in Shmuel Levin's testimony of July 9, 1946 (both found at YV TR 11/01235). There is no further corroboration of the story, though there are similar stories from Baranowicze (see my article, "Kurzeniec," op. cit.), and Krzemieniec (see Yehuda Bauer, "Buczacz and Krzemieniec," *Yad Vashem Studies*, Vol. 33 (2005), pp. 245–306). Rape was certainly not German standard policy, given Nazi racial ideology; but local helpers of the Germans and occasionally German troops and policemen, including SS personnel, were guilty of such outrages.

66. Killings in the small villages of the area preceded the massacres in the two shtetlekh. Thus, the Jewish village of Tupik, north of Rokitno, was liquidated (Rokitno, pp. 264, 292) a short time before Rokitno itself. But in a place like Glinna, in the same area, the Germans only arrived in early 1943, and the Jews could flee. According to Moshe Trossman, most of the Glinna peasants were *Sunnotniks* (i.e., *Staroveryi*) (SF-51503–13).

67. Sarny, p. 355. The radio was hidden by Simcha Morok (Sarny, pp. 354–364).

68. Rokitno, p. 273. YV M/E 1313, testimony of Chaim Pinchuk. I have not been able to verify this story.

69. According to Yitzhak Geller, who claims to have been the head of the resistance, they had 3 rifles, some handguns, and grenades. They planned to take additional weapons from the Ukrainian police by force, destroy the electricity plant, and set fire to the town. One of the groups was commanded by Tendler, who later was the person who is said to have enabled the flight to the forest of large numbers of Jews (Sarny, pp. 275–276, 316). The *shlegers* (strongmen, the core of the underground) were led by a former boxer.

70. Sarny, p. 308. The story is confirmed by a number of other witnesses (e.g., Sarny, p. 321), though Pinchas Neumann says that the *Judenrat* secretary, Neuman (no relation of the witness) "had the interests of the Jews at heart." The preparations for resistance bring up an interesting sidelight: there seem to have been moral scruples as to the killing of Ukrainian murderers. Joshua Friedman (Fortunoff Library, Yale, tape T-2484) killed a Ukrainian with a knife in order to escape, and comments: "If I wouldn't have done it, you know what would have happened." However, he said this in 1993, and the scruples may have arisen much later than in 1942.

71. The German in command was local SIPO chief Albert Schumacher, and the deputy commander of the Ukrainian policemen was one Sirozhka (I have not

been able to find out details about him) (Sarny, p. 278). Rabbi Nachum from Dabrowica is said to have declared there that these were the days of the coming of the Messiah (Israel Pinchuk, YV M.49. E – 717).

72. Spector, p. 195; Sarny, pp. 276, 314–315. There are several versions of who cut the fence. One has it that Gendelman was helped by a Gypsy (Rom). Another, that two girls were sent to divert the attention of the guards from the fence and that another man, a refugee from Poland by the name of Migdal, brought the scissors. Actually, these versions are not necessarily incompatible. Tandler's or Tendler's first name was probably Yehuda or Berl. One witness (Joseph Bennem, SF-48329) claims to have taken the scissors from Gendelman and then cut the fence; he also claims that they were helped by a friendly German who agreed not to shoot at them initially. There are quite a number of testimonies by escapees. Some of these appear to have been driven to despair and wanted to commit suicide. In one case, a Ukrainian peasant (Zacharko Andrua) prevented a Jew from suicide because he had pangs of conscience for having killed a Jew previously (Sarny, p. 281).

73. The dates are mentioned in the testimony of Berl Roitman (YV—M/E 334). However, another witness says there was yet another roll-call "two weeks after Yom Kippur," 1941 (YV M/E 141). Another testimony tells us that the *Judenrat* was warned by someone who had access to a German, that an "action" was going to take place. The *Judenrat* refused to believe (Rokitno, p. 318). Asher Binder (YV 03/3364) says that "there were non-Jews who said, on the eve of the roll-call—flee to the forests." Others report that they did not trust the German announcement, and that they prepared for the worst (e.g., Levin, SF-4150; Issaschar Trossman).

74. Nachum Katznelson, a *Judenrat* member, is mentioned (Rokitno, p. 314).

75. After the deportations by the Soviets, some 2,000–2,100 remained. Of these, some were sent to do forced labor in Vinnitsa, some were murdered, and there were more "natural" deaths than births. The figure of 1,631–1,638 can be taken as being accurate.

76. Some witnesses (Soltzman, YV-03/1594), and Moshe Trossman (YV, 2005), say that Sokolowski was a decent man. Issaschar Trossman says he came to the square with his arm in a bandage, and did not shoot (Trossman, YV 2005).

77. "The Latvians were the worst" (Soltzman, ibid.).

78. Trossman, YV-03/3477 and SF-51503; exactly what Mindl yelled is not clear: some say she screamed "Shma Yisroel," others, "Antloift!" (run away!). Mindl's son survived.

79. Local peasants received rewards for bringing in Jews to be killed; the rewards are variously said to have been one or more kilo of salt, or larger amounts (10 kilo) of sugar (e.g., Sarny, p. 280).

80. Rokitno, p.p. 304–306. In the various Trossman testimonies (see nn. 61, 66, and 78 above), there is the story of their relationship with the Medvedev group,

and it does not redound to the credit of the Jewish escapees. Medvedev could not deal with over 100 Jewish refugees, and he provided them with an armed escort, cattle, horses, wagons, and 18 rifles, and directed them into the Belorussian areas. However, on the way, discipline broke down, people made off with cattle and horses and rifles, and the rest failed to cross into Belorussia. The escorts went back to Medvedev, and then returned to tell the Jews that they had to fend for themselves. The Trossmans made their way to Glinna (they had arranged to met there in case of trouble before the "action" in Rokitno).

81. Rokitno, pp. 254–256.

82. Spector, pp. 244–269; Yakov Soltzman (YV 03/1259) has a very slightly divergent, but basically parallel story.

83. Rokitno, p. 307; and Trossman, YV-03/3477; see also Sarny, pp. 347–349. Pleskonosov, apparently also an NKVD man, was friendly to Jews (see Issaschar Trossman, in Trossman, YV 2005); Trossman and his father became partisans in his detachment (otriad).

84. Trossman, YV-03/3477; Rokitno, p. 306.

85. There are several testimonies of Jewish survivors from Kovpak's retreat (e.g., Joseph Bennem, SF-48329)

86. John A. Armstrong, ed., *Soviet Partisans in World War II* (Madison, 1964), passim. Joseph Bennem, SF-48329.

87. Rokitno, p. 286.

88. Ruchama Oliker, YV—0.3/3402, born 1923; the testimony is from 1969. Oliker ultimately joined the Kovpak partisans and was the only woman in her company (no. 7, first regiment) fighting as an ordinary soldier. See also Yitshak Surowitch, born 1936, YV M/E 1907, testimony from 1946. The Baptist peasant who saved him and the remnant of his family, according to Yitshak, "got sick with fear, but he said that we would be killed anyway [if he did not save them], so come in, and if the bad time comes, we will all suffer together." Berezowo and Belezowo are two separate places.

89. "Many of the Jewish partisans fell by bullets shot by their Russian comrades-in-arms" (Sarny, p. 284).

90. Asher Binder (YV 03/3364) was a member of a 50-man detachment (with 6 Jews) commanded by a Ukrainian, Vassili Yeremchuk, and he says there was not anti-Semitism at all there.

91. One testimony (YV M/E 141) tells us of an adventurous escape from Sarny, when two Jews hid in the house occupied by Germans who were shooting at the escapees, and then made their way to the forests. On the way, they killed two Ukrainians who wanted to hand them over to the Germans with pocket-knives. Peculiarly enough, there is an exactly parallel story from Rokitno: two young brothers escaped into the house from which the Germans and Ukrainians were shooting at the Jews and escaped by the back door (Levin, SF-4150, Shmuel Levin-04224).

92. Trossman, YV-03/3477. Near Belezowo, in the marshes north of Rokitno, some 80–90 Jews assembled on Yom Kippur in 1943, Trossman tells us. This is confirmed by Asher Binder, YV 03/3364.

93. Yakov Soltzman, YV-03/1594. The testimony is from 1959, when Soltzman was 62 years old. He was first helped by a Polish acquaintance from Rokitno, and joined Satanowski in May 1943. The priest and the teacher are mentioned in a number of testimonies.

94. Piotrowski, passim.

95. The positive attitude of the Polish peasants towards the hiding Jews appears in a number of testimonies (e.g., Rokitno, p. 320). Srul (Yisroel) Weiner, born 1928, tells us how he escaped, wounded in the head, and found his three sisters, aged 10, 3 1/2, and 2, and walked with them to the Polish villages. "We received food from the Polish peasants, and wintered in the forest." His eldest sister asked him to leave them to die, but he refused and held out until liberation (YV M/E 160; the testimony is from 1946). The testimony of Tzvi Olshansky, a well-known Jewish partisan, corroborates Weiner's story in every detail (Sarny, pp. 355–365). In 1943, Olshansky threatened the head of the nearest Ukrainian village (apparently after the Polish villages had been liquidated) that if he did not take care of the four children, he and his community would be killed by the partisans. This made it possible for the children to survive. See also Levin, SF-4150; Alex Levin, op. cit., p. 13ff.; and Trossman, YV 2005. Polish peasants also occasionally helped a unique group of five children, among them Alex Levin, his brother, and Chaim Svetchnik (Bar-Or), who survived, miraculously, in hideouts in the forest. Chaim Bar-Or lost his mother and sister there, and they had to bury them with their bare hands. They survived (ibid.).

96. Sarny, pp. 368–369, and 375–376.

97. Ibid., pp. 329–330.

98. E.g. Mordechai Shulner, YV 03/1366.

99. Rokitno, p. 294. In Glinna (a village in the swamps north of Rokitno, with a Jewish population going back possibly some 500 years or more), Retzlav came with a troop of 20 policemen at the beginning of German rule and incited the peasants against the Jews. Probably as a result of this, there was a case of a farmer denouncing a Jew. The Jewish partisan Asher Binder killed him (pp. 294–295). The case of Glinna is fascinating. The Trossman family and other Rokitno Jews hid in the forests nearby and were helped mainly by the *staorveryi*. Moshe Trossman said that the other Ukrainians were all murderers, but then adds that some helped (Trossman, YV 2005).

100. Sioma Gendelman, YV 03/7662.

101. E.g., Rokitno, p. 322. A number of Ukrainian rescuers are mentioned by name, such as Miron and Ivan Borisowicz, Chvedor Menisowicz (Rokitno, pp. 334–335). In Sarny, the Anuszkewicz family (apparently, some of them identified as Ukrainians, others as Poles) rescued a number of Jews (Sarny, pp. 336–347).

Alex Levin (op. cit., p. 13) relates that he and his brothers decided, out of desperation, to return from the forest near the Polish villages to Rokitno. On the way, they met a number of Ukrainian peasants on their wagons, who warned them not to do so because they would be killed. In other words, they rescued them.

102. In one instance, a Jew who escaped from the massacre in Sarny, which occurred on a Ukrainian holiday, was running through a Ukrainian street and was greeted—in broad daylight—by a Ukrainian wishing him "good health." He comments, "If all were like him we could have survived" (Joshua Friedman, Fortunoff Library, Yale, tape T-2484). Some survivors remembered the names of their rescuers, Poles or Ukraninians, but most did not, or remembered only their first names (e.g., Rokitno, p. 286). A testimony relating to the village of Kisorycz, near Rokitno, tells us that a young Jewish boy, Yakov Kanishkov, was saved by a known anti-Semite who took pity on the child, brought him to the forest, and told him where to run to find partisans. This deed of the Ukrainian (whose name is not known) was found out in the village, and the man and his whole family were burned to death by the *Bulbovtsy* (Rokitno, p. 156–157).

103. E.g., Rokitno, pp. 338–339, 345–350. Israel Pinchuk, YV M. 49. E 717, became an NKVD officer and was involved in punishing collaborators. Another example is that of Berl Bick (Sarny, pp. 333–334). Individuals survived in the most odd ways. Thus, a Rokitno Jew by the name of Chaim Ben-David (YV 03/3288) claims that he served in the Red Army, was taken prisoner, escaped three times, assumed a Polish identity, married a Polish woman, and became a German soldier in Lithuania, serving as a tailor in a unit. His testimony is accompanied by a document showing him as a German corporal. The Sarny survivor Avraham Feinberg relates a particularly gruesome story in his testimony (Sarny, pp. 352–353). Some of the avengers were themselves killed by the *Banderovtsy*, who waged a brutal war against the Soviets until about 1947 (e.g., Yehiel Trossman, father of Moshe and Issaschar).

104. Shmuel Levin (YV M/E 141) became an officer and was among the Soviet soldiers who conquered Berlin.

105. See Piotr Wrobel, "Violence and Society after the First World War," *Journal of Modern European History*, Vol. 1, No. 1 (2003), pp. 125–145.

106. Some exceptions were mentioned in the testimonies: one witness, Mordechai Shulner (YV 03/1366), reports that a German (probably a gendarme, possibly a Communist), provided food to him and his family in Rokitno. Another witness, Feige Schwartz, was rescued by a German from Cologne, Paul Redinger, during the mass murder in Sarny. With the help of another German, he protected her from German patrols. After she hid in the house of a Polish woman, he found her, gave her food, and promised the Polish woman to help her if she protected the witness and another Jewish girl. He then continued to supply food to her until he was sent to the front and disappeared (Sarny, pp. 322–329). A third case, also in Sarny, is mentioned by survivor Aryeh Turkewicz, of an "elderly" German,

probably a *Todt* worker, who supervised some Jewish laborers; when one of them, a certain Moshe Goldman, was accidentally injured, the German carried him to his home, called for medical help, and helped out with food, as well as visiting Goldman a number of times until he got well (Sarny, p. 317). Two other cases are mentioned by Joseph Bennem (SF-48329) of friendly treatment by Germans in a military store in Sarny, and of a German whom he persuaded not to fire at the escapees from the Sarny concentration enclosure on the day of the mass murder.

107. Shalom Cholavsky has authored a first overall description of Jewish partisans in Belorussia in his Hebrew-language book, *Meri Velohama Partisanit* (Jerusalem, 2001). There are some detailed accounts of specific units and places, such as the Bielsky partisans, the Mir rebellion, and others, and a number of general hagiographic accounts that have to be treated with some skepticism.

14

The World of the Shtetl

Elie Wiesel

Whenever I think of the Shtetl, small colorful Jewish kingdom so rich in memories, I am filled with pity and sadness.

I think of those men and women who created it, nourished it, and kept it alive. I think of the known and unknown, the sacred and the profane, the impoverished tutors and their mischievous pupils, the joyous innkeepers and their weary customers, the beggars and their songs, as well as the princes in disguise, carriers of ancient melodies and eternally renewed dreams of hope and redemption. How did they manage for such a lengthy period in history to overcome so many threats and perils from a world that could not understand them?

In my mind, I see them again, defenseless citizens, living on love and faith, in the streets of the shtetl somewhere in Poland, Romania, Hungary, the Ukraine: in short, in all the regions of Eastern and Central Europe where history's turbulent winds brought them, often by force, as if to plant there a variety of aspirations and regrets without which no culture could ever exist.

Since when has the shtetl existed, at least under this name? Whose idea was it? Who was its first builder? Heaven knows, history does not. In those times of ancient calendars, kings and rulers (who could no longer dwell in boredom) found both pleasure and interest in chasing their Jews from one province to another, from one country to another, only to invite them back so as to help their national economy and, at the same time, divert the anger of the population towards them.

I hope the reader will not mind my dealing with this theme from neither a sociological nor an anthropological viewpoint. Rather, my goal is to indulge in an evocation or a meditation on memory.

The reason is simple. Though buried in the ashes of recent history, the shtetl remains very much alive to some of us whose numbers continually decrease. Oh yes, we are the last remnant of these Jewish communities that the cruelties of the twentieth century have destroyed forever but whose traces can still be found in some memories and words, strangely dispersed, as if determined to go on haunting a world that wants to forget.

Like most survivors, I live in fear. What will happen when the last witness is no longer here to testify, or simply to tell the tale? Who will he or she be? What will become of his or her burning images, tears, and whispers? What will it mean when there is no longer anyone who can say, "The shtetl? You want to know what it was like living and dying there? Listen, I come from a shtetl . . ."?

What makes a place inhabited by Jews . . . a shtetl? Literally, the word means "a small city." So it may be accurate to call a city of ten or fifteen thousand Jews a shtetl. But what about a locality of only two thousand? Or a village numbering no more than 120? How is a shtetl to be measured, by what characteristics is it recognized? Only by its picturesque or exotic aspects? Why is Chagall's Vitebsk a shtetl, whereas Saloniki, with its exiled Jews from Spain and Portugal, is not? The fact is that the shtetl belongs to the Ashkenazi world of Eastern Europe—but what was its beginnings? Again, no precise date seems to be available. All we know is that a Jewish presence in Western Europe can be traced to the destruction of Jerusalem by the Romans who brought many of the city's Jews back to Italy, France, and Germany. As for Eastern Europe, chronicles tell of Jews, during the persecutions linked to the first Crusade in 1096, fleeing Prague and Cracow. Since then, Jews came and left, and returned again to Poland where they knew periods of relative happiness and distress. In 1261, King Boleslav the Pious published his "Statute of Kalisz" guaranteeing Jews many important rights. For example, it prohibited Christians from falsely accusing Jews of blood libel. The King went as far as to threaten transgressors with the same punishment Jews would have received, had the accusations been founded.

Another Polish king known for his kindness towards Jews was Casimar the Great, who reigned in the mid-fourteenth century. Some people think he protected the Jews because he had a Jewish mistress, Estherke. Just like her namesake in the Megillah, she was a strong, positive influence on him.

In general, the living conditions of Jews depended on the mood and character of the kings and the economic situation in the land. In other words, Jews never knew what tomorrow would bring. They endured many pogroms, some worse than others. One example is the massacres conducted by the bloodthirsty mobs under Hetman Bogdan Chmielnitzki in

1648, when most Jewish communities were decimated. At least seventy to eighty thousand Jews were murdered. In the chronicles of the time, one reads scenes of such brutality that, in Sholem Asch's words, one's faith in humanity may be lost. The chronicles also contain halakhic elements that reveal historical events. For example, in a shtetl ravaged by a tempest of fire and blood, the few survivors confronted a heartbreaking dilemma: what should the orphaned community rebuild first, the house of prayer or the cemetery?

Such was the fate of hundreds of communities. The enemy would suddenly emerge with sword in hand, and in a frenzy of hatred, he would behead men, women, and children in the streets, in poorly barricaded homes, caves, and attics. The murderers would leave only when they thought the last Jew was dead. Then as if out of nowhere, a man, woman, or adolescent would appear. Haggard, in mourning, he or she would try to find a way amid the ruins. Then they would begin digging graves. They would bury the dead, say *kaddish*, and life would once again begin flowing, binding the abandoned survivors into a community. They would rebuild their homes, open schools, arrange weddings and circumcisions, celebrate holidays, fast on Tisha b'Av and Yom Kippur, dance on Simhat Torah, and make their children study Talmud: all that, while waiting for the next catastrophe. That was life in the shtetl. While the calm lasted, and even during the storm, great books were written, important lessons offered. At one point, the *Vaad Arbaa Ha-aratzot*, the Council of the Four Lands, was established. As the highest authority, it dealt with urgent issues in organized Jewish life that were not covered by traditional or ancient law. Its so-called *hetér iska*, authorizing Jewish bankers to ask for interest on loans (which was forbidden in the Bible), is still displayed in every bank in Israel.

Then, in the middle of the last century, the brackets of respite and renewal irrevocably closed because our fiercest and bloodiest enemy wanted them to remain so. Of all Hitler's pledges to his bewitched nation, the only one he almost fulfilled was that concerning his plan to annihilate the Jewish people and erase it from the surface of the earth. I say "almost" for, thanks to the Allied armies and their bravery, he lost the war. But when we evoke the shtetl, we must omit the "almost." Tragically, there Hitler's victory seems total. The shtetl is gone. Forever. Granted, Jewish life can be found elsewhere: in Europe, in the United States, in the former Soviet Union, and especially in Israel where it welcomes us with a face shining with hope. Oh yes, Jewish life is once again flourishing, vibrant with creativity. But the life of the shtetl belongs to the past.

Need I say that I miss it? Must I say aloud what, in many of my writings, I repeat in whispers? The shtetl is my childhood. I remain attached to it. And faithful.

Let us try to revisit it together. No matter where it is located on the map, the shtetl has few geographical frontiers. Swallowed by Carpathian mountains or rivers, dominated by Polish princes, or governed by Romanian landowners, it is built on the same social structures, contains the same impulses and resources, the same attachment to a collective destiny both dark and glorious. In other words, in its broad outlines, the shtetl is one and the same everywhere.

In Yitzhak Leiboush Peretz's Hasidic tales as well as I. J. Singer's novels, the same characters are plagued by the same worries, stifle the same cries, and recite the same prayers composed in ecstasy. No need to question them: young and old, rich and poor, satisfied and dissatisfied, what they have in common is their Jewishness. When asked to identify him- or herself, a Jew in Hungary, Poland, or Romania will say not say, "I am a Hungarian, Romanian, or Pole of Jewish origin or faith," but "I am Jewish." How did they create a life apart, a separate Jewish identity? Was it the essential part of their heritage? Of their collective consciousness perhaps? Clearly, their Jewishness was at the heart of their commitment to religion and history. Whenever a son or daughter would leave home for study or work in a great city or abroad, the parents' blessing would always be accompanied by a plea: "Do not forget that you are Jewish!" For them, being Jewish also had an ethical imperative. It meant that there are things a Jew cannot, must not do. "*S'past nisht*" was a common Jewish expression from the shtetl: it is not nice. Not nice for a Jew to say or do certain things, in certain ways. And then, too, whatever a Jew did implicated other Jews. That explains the need of Jews not to bring shame on their fellow Jews, not to endanger them. That was a frequent argument governing Jewish behavior in the shtetl. A Jew from the shtetl thinks of other Jews even after leaving the shtetl—even when the shtetl ceased to exist. In the shtetl, the Jew felt that the entire world was looking upon him, and passing judgment on his actions.

And indeed, for the anti-Semite, every Jew was responsible for all Jews. That is why solidarity was a defining theme of shtetl life. When accusing a single Jew of cheating, the anti-Semite indicts all Jews. When accusing of a Jew being disloyal, the anti-Semite shouts: all Jews are traitors. Needless to say, all these accusations were baseless, fabrications of poisoned minds and tongues.

Does this mean the shtetl was an anti-Sodom, a city of no evil? Does this mean that all its inhabitants were saints? Of course not. Since 1516 we have known that Utopia is a place that does not exist. The absolute is a divine attribute, not a human one. As everywhere else, among the inhabitants of the shtetl, good and wretched men could be found. Some were pure, others were not. Some were innocent, others were guilty. But, in the shtetl people had no illusions about each other's shortcomings. Speaking of Yankel, they would say: "Ah, you mean Yankel-the-thief?" Or: "Ourke-the-liar?" I remember: in the little town, there was an informer. That must have been his profession. He had red hair and wore brown leather boots. Whenever he would appear in *shul*, people would lower their voices. He did not mind. He knew that we knew. Somehow he was not ostracized. Not a single person was hurt because of him. Was this because the overwhelming majority of Jews in the town were Hasid and Hasidism teaches us compassion for the sinner?

Hasidism. Let me seize the opportunity to elaborate on this movement which grew to become the spiritual symbol of the shtetl for nearly two centuries.

It can be said that Hasidism was born in the shtetl and could not have been born anywhere else. It is in isolated and impoverished villages and hamlets that Rabbi Israel Baal Shem Tov, the Master of the Good Name, known as the Besht, gathered his first friends, allies, disciples, and followers. It is said that he personally visited more than 280 of them, attracting by his mere presence simple men and women in need of strength as well as scholars in search of transcendence. In big cities, people were too busy and perhaps too tired to go and hear a wandering preacher, a teller of tales, who came not to reprimand but to reassure. The Besht, in the beginning, took children to school, addressed women in market places, neglecting no occasion to create and broaden his network of solidarity and companionship, and thus save thousands of families and hundreds of small communities from despair. One must remember: for the Jewish villagers and inhabitants of small forsaken communities, exile had become unbearable. Resignation would have made the separation irrevocable, had it not been for the Besht.

It is in the shtetl that Hasidism flourished. Elsewhere, in the big cities, the Establishment exerted its powerful influence in matters of economic welfare and intellectual development to such a degree that it gave villagers the feeling of being pushed away, despised. For them, for their survival, the Hasidic message was essential, even vital. What was its content? That God listens even to those men and women who do not know the mysteries of Kabbalah. That God is present everywhere, in all our endeavors, in all our aspirations, not only in study but also in prayer: both lead to God. One many attain truth by way of the heart as well as the mind. The illiterate shepherd with a warm heart is for God as important as the learned man whose knowledge is rooted in books.

A Rabbi Moshe-Leib Sassover, a Rabbi Zousia of Onipol, a Rabbi Levi-Yitzhak Berditchever could not have emerged in Troyes, Odessa, or Vilna where biblical study and Talmudic research involved a dazzling elite, itself dazzled by inspired teachers endowed with charismatic powers. There, Hasidic Masters were not needed.

They *were* needed in the shtetl where tired and sad Jews had to be told that what a Talmudic scholar accomplishes in a thousand pages of commentary, a devout Hasid can obtain by reciting with fervor one prayer alone, the simplest of all: the *Shma Israel* (Hear O' Israel). What mattered was the *kavvana*, the purity of intent.

A story: One day, the Besht summoned his close disciples and told them that it was time to do the necessary thing so as to hasten Redemption. One must not wait any longer. They had better be ready to knock at the highest and most secret gates, all inaccessible to the common mortal, break the lock, and allow the Messiah to come and save those who believed in him. The Besht knew what had to be done: he knew the place, the time, and the words. Thus his disciples received from him precise instructions for the days and nights ahead.

They would meet on the first day of the first week of the month of Elul, somewhere in the forest. Burning with enthusiasm and mastering their impatience, the Besht's disciples followed his instructions to the letter. They fasted from Sunday to Friday, prayed with particular *kavvana*, recited at midnight the litanies known only to the initiated, spent hours concentrating on certain combinations of divine names, ever-careful not to allow any impure thoughts to enter their minds, invoked memories ancestors— until the day arrived.

From near and far, they converged upon the secret place in the forest. But the Besht was not there. Precious moments turned into anguished hours. Silently, not daring to look at one another, the disciples wondered whether they had done something wrong. Were they unworthy of their sacred task? Perhaps they misunderstood or misinterpreted some of the

Master's directions: were they responsible for the failure of the entire undertaking? They were close to despair when the Besht appeared, breathless: "Do not feel guilty," he told them. "You have not done anything wrong. This morning, as I left the village on my way to be here with you, I heard a child crying in a house nearby. I opened the door. The room was empty. I looking to my right, to my left: nobody. Only the child, in his cradle. He was weeping: his mother must have gone to do an errand. His tears broke my heart. So I stayed a while to calm him. I sang for him. When I stopped, he cried again. So I went on singing. Oh, I knew, with all my heart and soul, I knew that you were waiting for me, and that the Messiah himself was waiting, but what could I do? I thought, when a Jewish child cries, one must not leave him; when a lonely Jewish child is so unhappy that he is shedding tears, the Messiah will have to wait."

I will share another tale: it happened on Rosh Hashana, the first day of the New Year, before or during the Mussaf service. The hour was near for Reb Mendel, the appointed man, to blow the *shofar* which would permit the holy community of Israel to plead before the celestial tribunal. Reb Mendel was waiting for the Besht's order. But the Besht was preoccupied because Satan, in heaven, had erected obstacles to interfere with the prayers. So he used all his inner resources and appealed to his ancestors, imploring them to help him vanquish Satan. In vain. Satan remained vigorous and his barricade unmovable. The Besht increased his effort, reciting prayers used for emergencies only. Still nothing. As for the faithful, they felt the gravity of the situation. They were about to burst into tears when, all of a sudden, the delicate sound of a flute pierced the silence: it was a young shepherd who played. Naturally, after the shock subsided, he was reprimanded by the faithful: didn't he know that it is forbidden to play musical instruments on such a holy day? But the Besht quieted them down. "Why did you want to play?" he asked the flutist. "I don't know how to pray," answered the young shepherd. "I don't even know how to read. But like everybody here, I wanted to do something for God, and tell Him that I love Him. That's why I played a tune for Him." Then, the Besht, his sadness gone, spoke to his disciples of his joy: "What I couldn't do with my prayers, this young shepherd did with his tune. He vanquished Satan. Now let us proceed with the sacred service. Blow the *shofar*, Reb Mendel!"

Adversaries of Hasidism denigrate such tales, describing them as anti-intellectual, unworthy of the Jewish tradition which emphasizes learning. That was the major complaint leveled at ignorance. Unfair, say the supporters of Hasidism. All of the Besht's closest disciples and friends—the

Maggid of Mezeritch, Rebbe Pinhas of Koretz, among others—had high standing in the scholarly community.

In truth, the Besht had one goal: to sustain the Jew by showing that his or her links to the great community of Israel are indestructible. As Rabbi Aharon of Karlin used to say: "If you don't know the Zohar, study Talmud. You don't know the Talmud? Open the Bible. You don't know the Bible? Say Psalms. You don't know Psalms? Shama Israel, you know? No? Then just think of our people and love one another. That will be sufficient."

You may ask: is that really sufficient? Answer: as a beginning, that will be sufficient. After all, to love one's fellow man is a biblical commandment. That would lead the Hasid to look for it in the text. And study its commentaries. And climb the ladder of knowledge higher and higher. What was important was not to give up.

In the shtetl, one often had reason to doubt and despair. But then the Besht came and declared: Stop! Take hold of yourselves! The people of Israel need each and every one of you—and so does the God of Israel.

A Hasidic Master would never say to his disciple: you study too much, you spend too much time buried in books. Quite the contrary, he would say to him: you have not studied enough yet, continue; learn more, always more; but remember: study alone is not enough, it must bring you closer to others.

That is why, until the very last day of the shtetl, Hasidic *shtible'h* (prayer houses) existed in every small city, in every village, even in places where there was no local rebbe. In my little town, there were Hasidim belonging to many rebbes who would, on occasion, come to spend a few days and evenings with them. And then the entire town would join them for services or "Tisch" on Shabbat. To be together, that was what Hasidism wanted. To be able to evoke common experiences and events one or the other has witnessed at the court of his Master. *Dibouk Haverim*, the obligation to be attached to friends, was—and still is—to hasidim as important a principle as *emunat tzadikim*, faith in the just teacher.

Let us be frank: when we speak of the shtetl and Hasidim's boundless faith in the *tsaddik*, we must not fail to recall that it also had those who believed in the occult. People believed not only in the intercession of rebbes but also in the evil activities of Satan's envoys. They were feared for their malevolent tricks and deeds. They were supposed to curse certain homes, turn friends into enemies, steal newborns. People also believed in virgins being possessed by dead souls or *dybbuks*, which very few rebbes could exorcise. All those legends on the powers of King Ashmedai's wife,

Lilith; and on the little devils lurking in the woods on nocturnal voyages; and on the dead who rise from their graves at midnight, go to the synagogue, and read from Scripture. Woe to the passerby who, if summoned by them, does not enter going backwards. I myself remember how I used to tremble when I had to use the sidewalk near the cemetery.

Though terrified, we did not let anything interfere with our studies. A shtetl without its schools—or *cheder*—was inconceivable. The poorest of the poor saved enough, or nearly enough, to pay his children's tutor. Education began at age three, when the father would envelop his son in his *talit* and bring him to *cheder*. For the little boy, *cheder* did not represent a kindergarten where he could play with his peers, but the first alien and probably hostile environment, far from his parents. There he would face a teacher with a long beard and, at times, a nasty look in his eye if a pupil resisted repeating after him: *aleph, béit, gimmel . . .*

Usually, in spite of the honey candy given to him for every letter, as a promise of the Torah's sweetness, the little boy would begin to cry. He would worry that once he was through with the *Aleph-Béit*, he would have to open the Five Books of Moses, the commentaries of Rashi, the Talmud, and multitudes of commentaries on commentaries. In other words: he would fear that there would be no end to study! Well, little boy from the shtetl, that's how it is, that's how it has always been. Ask your father and grandfathers, ask thirty centuries of fathers, and they will tell you: the study of Torah has a beginning but no end!

The passion for learning, which is an essential part of the Jewish tradition, did not begin in the shtetl, but it existed there. I never saw my father or any of my uncles go anywhere without a book under their arms. What was the worst insult burled at a person? That he is an *am-haretz*, an ignoramus. Who is respected? A *talmid khakham*, a scholar. To describe him, we make use of several words: *Ben Torah*, son or man of Torah; *illui*, someone with an oceanic memory; *harif*, someone with a penetrating intelligence; and, of course, *gaon*—a genius.

Here, too, we ought to acknowledge reality: not all children aspired to dedicate their lives to study. Some became merchants, others shoemakers, tailors, woodcutters, barbers or . . . beggars. There were those who, fed up with the difficulties at home or anti-Semitic provocations in the street, responded to the call of an easier life in the Western world. Some went to study medicine in France or to work with an uncle in America. A few doctors came back and stayed in my town until the end. Then there were those youngsters who, influenced by Communist agitators,

ran away to Russia or stayed home to work clandestinely for the communist revolution aimed at transforming society by destroying its structures—at that time few people were aware of Stalin's cruelty and innate
anti-Semitism. How many future Communist leaders actually came from
the world of the shtetl, and even from the world of the yeshiva? At the
origin of their political commitment was the misery of their communities. Was their communism a form of rebellion against their parents?
Possibly. But it may also have been intended to spare them further
anguish, suffering, and humiliation. This point must always be remembered: though we love to celebrate life in the shtetl, from the economical
viewpoint, it was far from easy.

I remember my first return to my little town twenty years after I had
left it. I remember the shock I felt upon discovering how poor the Jews of
my town were. I walked around familiar streets and squares, entering
homes of friends I remembered from my childhood. What transformed
them into wretched dwellings? Oh, I knew that there were poor people in
our midst, but not that there were so many. Nor did I know that even
those who were considered wealthy were in fact poor. For instance, my
own family. In my childish view, I never thought we were poor. Well, we
were not. We owned our own house, we had a store. True, we had no running water, no bathroom, no toilet—so what! One could live very well
without such things. Anyway, we were properly dressed. (On Wednesdays
all the beggars would be fed in the courtyard.) So why complain? It was
only two or three generations later that I understood how mistaken I had
been. Certain images resurfaced: my parents, on a long winter night, discussing whether they could afford to buy new clothes for the children or a
new stove when our old one broke down, or whether they could plan a
trip to the mountains. As in everything in life, wealth in the shtetl was relative; only the poverty of the poor was not.

And yet. On Shabbat, if poverty did not vanish altogether, it was diminished. One can never speak enough about what Shabbat was like in the
shtetl—and what it did for its inhabitants. Shabbat helped people endure
the other six days of the week, days that were often grey and dark, and
heavy with sorrow and anxiety. Hence the anticipation of Shabbat, which,
actually, began much earlier. Thursday-evening or early Friday-morning,
the housewife would already be busy preparing the challah, gefilte fish,
and *cholent*, the traditional elements of a Shabbat meal in the shtetl. The
white tablecloth, the white shirt: everything had to be ready. And all that
belonged to the housewife's domain. One easily forgets that we owe her

the gift Shabbat represents which we call *Shabbat hamalka*, the Shabbat Queen. We couldn't wait for the arrival.

With the approach of Shabbat, business was conducted in haste. Shopkeepers and their customers were equally in a hurry to go home. Men would go to the ritual bath, the *mikveh*. Get dressed. Get ready. And worthy of welcoming the Shabbat, already on the horizon. The first to spot her would be the *shammes* (the beadle): he would go from store to store and from home to home, shouting: "*Yidden, greit zich zu Shabbes!*" "Jews, ready yourselves for the Sabbath!" "*Yidden, s'is bald Shabbes oif the welt!*" "Jews, it's almost Sabbath in the world!" At home, one did not need those reminders: the mother, mine too, lit the candles honoring Shabbat, one for each member of the family, and blessed them silently, with gestures of grace and tenderness. Suddenly, her face would be illuminated by a light coming from another world, from another time, a light at once frail and eternal. And her beauty multiplied sevenfold, so much so, that even now as I write these words, I remember the tears that welled up in my throat.

In the *shul* (synagogue) also, everything seemed different. More luminous, the candelabras. More serene, the faces. More melodious, the prayers. The Talmud is right: on Shabbat, one gains an additional soul, the *neshama yetera*.

Then, at the end of the service, worshippers would rush towards the visitors in our *shul*. If there were none, the *shammes* would shout, "Are there strangers here?" It was forbidden to allow anyone to be alone for the Shabbat meal. Often, people would fight over a visitor. It was an honor to invite him or her to their table. I myself can hardly remember a Shabbat without an honored guest in our home.

Whenever my maternal grandfather, Reb Dodye, was with us, we felt doubly honored. And I triply . . . I have sworn never to forget him. Nor his return from the Shabbat-eve office. He would stop at the threshold, kiss the *mezuzah*, and, his face burning with delight, start the Wizsnitzer *Sholem aleikhem malakhei hasharet*, be blessed, angels in the service of peace. And it was as if peace had now reigned over heaven and earth, a peace that brought together men and women of all nations, of all ages, a dream in which Shabbat remains the inspiring symbol.

The end of Shabbat was marked by my mother and grandmother. Shortly before the *havdalah* ceremony which separates light from darkness and the sacredness of Shabbat from the rest of the week, both women, as all mothers, would recite the special prayer attributed to the great Rebbe

Lévi-Yitzhak of Berditchev: *Gott foun Avrohom, Yitzhok oon Yaakov*, God of Abaham, Isaac and Jacob, extend your protection over Thy children and ours . . . When the prayer ends, the *havdalah* begins.

Whereupon another song takes hold of my memory: *Bobeshi zog nokh nit God foun Avrohom* . . . (Grandma, do not say [the prayer] God of Abraham) A child pleads with his grandmother not to recite her prayer, not yet, pleads with her to wait a bit longer. The sun hasn't set yet in the west, let Shabbat last a while longer . . .

The child loves Shabbat and refuses to leave it behind—or to be left behind.

Which reminds me of an old Hasid or an old rebbe who, during the mystical Third Meal (on Shabbat afternoon), does in his way what the grandmother is implored to do in hers. He sings a song: "When *ich wolt gehat koiech*, if I had the strength, *wolt ich in di gassen gelofen*, I would run through the streets, and *Ich wolt gesrien hoiech*, and I would yell with all my might, *Shabess heiligere shabess*. Holy, holy Sabbath . . ." And legend has it that as long as he sang, the Shabbat remained with him and his followers. So he sang . . . and he sang . . .

Yiddish was of course the language of the shtetl—a language that dates back to the high Middle Ages. Feverish, rich in meaning and fantasy, it carries better than any other tongue the life and dreams of the shtetl. There are Yiddish words that have no equivalent in any other language: *cholent* is something other than a hot plate; *yarmelke* is something other than a *kipah*; *yossem* is something other than an orphan; and *rakhmoness* is something other than *rakhmanut* or compassion. (By the way: did you know that *cholent* is French? During Napoleon's invasion of Russia, the troops used to keep their food warm on a slow fire: *chaud-lent* . . . Similarly, the names *Yente* or *Beile* in Yiddish come from Spanish and French: *Yente* comes from *Gentila*, and *Beile* from *Bella* . . .)

I have said it often, I love speaking Yiddish. There are songs and lullabies that can be sung only in Yiddish: prayers that only Jewish grandmothers can whisper at dusk, stories whose charm and secrets, sadness and nostalgia can be conveyed in Yiddish alone—though I imagine Sephardi Jews could offer Ladino that same praise. I love Yiddish because it has been with me from the cradle. It was in Yiddish that I spoke my first words and expressed my first fears. It was in Yiddish that I greeted the Shabbat. I did not say "*Shabbat shalom*" but "*gut Shabes*."

This immense love for Shabbat in the shtetl has often inspired Yiddish literature—and some anecdotes as well.

It is Friday afternoon. An old villager returns home from the *mikveh*. It is snowing but he doesn't mind. Soon it will be Shabbes. He will rest, eat well, meet friends in *shul*. Suddenly, he notices Ivan, freezing while pushing his sleigh with heavy sacks of coal on it. So he thinks to himself: ah, how clever of Uncle Jacob; and how silly of Uncle Esau. The Talmud says they decided to divide among themselves both worlds created for man: Jacob will get the world to come, whereas Esau chose the world below. And look at Esau! What did he get? He works hard day after day, endures the bitterness of a laborious existence, whereas I am given to savor the joy and serenity of Shabbat: well, who of the two brothers made a better deal? Sometime afterwards, the old villager had to travel to Vienna, either on business or for medical reasons. He was put up at one of the good hotels. And for the first time in his life he discovered luxury: big halls with flowers on every table, well heated rooms, golden chandeliers, the most exotic fruits, lavish bathrooms with showers and marble tubs . . . So he examined the material aspect of non-Jewish life, and thought to himself: well, well, having now seen Esau's world, I think I can say that Uncle Esau was not such an idiot after all . . .

Shtetl humor. You may ask: isn't Jewish humor everywhere the same? No, in the shtetl, humor was sharper, funnier, yet never offensive. It illustrated the taste for self-ridicule. One laughed at oneself more than at others.

Listen, for instance, to a brief exchange by Sholem Aleichem between a father and his young son:

- Moishele, be nice; close the window; it is cold outside.
And Moishele answers:

- Papa, if I close the window, will it be warmer outside?

A Hasidic anecdote: a future rebbe is received by an illustrious Master who asks him:

"I hear that you are a great scholar, that you know the entire Talmud by heart. Is it true?"
"No, it is not."
"What? You are telling me what people say is not true?"
"Not really. I do not know the entire Talmud; I only know half of it."

"Half? Which half?"

"Any half," answers the visitor, lowering his head.

A peasant visits the big city and witnesses a grandiose funeral: the coffin is carried by horse and carriage draped in black; five cantors sing the appropriate chants; a crowd of hundreds accompanies the deceased to his resting place. "Who is he?" asks the peasant. Someone tells him: it is a very wealthy man who served as president of the community.

"Ah," exclaims the peasant. "*Dos heist gelebt*: that's called living!"

And another story: a cantor came home from his Shabbat luncheon, looking depressed. "What is the matter?" his wife asked. "Can you imagine?" said the cantor. "After all my hard work on today's service, as we left the synagogue, Yankel the shoemaker said to me: 'Well, Hazzen, today you were not *aie-aie-aie*: you could have been better.' How can I not be upset?" "What does a Yankel know about cantorial music? He repeats what everybody says . . ."

Still another anecdote, "*Eins foun di beide*."

An unhappy man tells his friend his troubles—more precisely, his son's troubles. He has been drafted to serve in the Czar's army, which is anti-Semitic, as everyone knows. "I am at a loss: what should I do?" says the man. "Don't worry," replies his friend. *Eins foun di beide*, it's either-or: either he passes the physical exam or he doesn't; if he fails, why worry? If he passes, *eins foun di beide*, either-or: either he is sent to the front or he isn't; if he isn't, then everything is OK; if he is, either-or: either he is wounded, or he isn't; if he isn't, why be upset? If he is, either-or: either he lives or he dies; if he lives, all is perfect; if he dies, *eins foun di beide*, either he goes to paradise or to hell; if he goes to hell, *eins foun di beide*: either he manages to bribe the guard or . . . Well, don't worry: knowing him, he will.

Naturally, laughter in the shtetl is a remedy for misfortune, fear, and despair. In a way, it is the best reflection of the shtetl's generosity of spirit.

In spite of the religious dissension, political splits, and social conflicts that can be found in every community, the shtetl's spirit of generosity cannot help but move the reader. Numerous groups, committees, and associations existed to cover well-defined sectors: the poor, the aged, the sick, the prisoners, the widows and orphans, the dead. Even the rich who were no longer rich. They were taken care of by a secret committee. *Matan be-seter,* the clandestine charity, had at its disposal special funds that were slipped under the doors of the recipients at night.

Even nobler was the way some communities dealt with *tzedaka*: every year, before Passover, people would line up at the entrance of the community offices. Inside, in an empty room, there was a table and on it a plate with money. A person would enter the room alone. If he or she was able, this person left money; if not, he or she took it. And no one ever knew how much was taken or given.

Another custom which reflects the shtetl's sensitivity to people's pain and sorrow:

At funerals, the beadle would precede or follow the coffin with a black charity-box in his hands, chanting: "*Tzedoko tatzil mimovess*: charity saves us from death." Question: is it true? If so, wouldn't the rich live to 120, if not longer? They could give charity every week, every day, every hour . . . But: it is not that simple. Listen to a superb commentary I heard from an American rabbi: "What is the meaning of charity?" he asked. "It is for the living to demonstrate that he or she is concerned with someone else's sadness or sickness. One who is not concerned, is in fact not sensitive; one who is not sensitive, is not really alive." And this is the meaning of the beadle's appeal: Charity saves one from dying while one is still alive . . .

In the shtetl people lived—well or badly—but they *lived* before dying. And that was so until the day when cruelest of our enemies reduced the shtetl to ashes.

In conclusion, I now speak of all that remains of the shtetl: its memory.

Long ago, I wrote a *Plea for the Dead*. Then I composed a *Plea for the Survivors*. And now, as we have entered the new century and millennium, I felt the need to write a new *Plea*: a plea for their right to be remembered.

I confess: in spite of my growing pessimism concerning the memory of Auschwitz and Treblinka, I did not anticipate the recent insults and attacks from various quarters that their survivors had to endure. Relentless and obscene, they reflect a total absence of sensitivity. It was as if they were to be hated for having suffered, for remembering, and above all, for surviving.

Their desire to bear witness is being questioned, as is the truth of their testimony. Unworthy motives are being attributed to them, their suffering is being transformed into farce and entertainment in films, plays, docudramas and musicals. At best, they are being used for pseudo-scientific tests so as to prove a thousand and one scholarly theories—and they, the survivors, are not allowed even to protest.

My friend and companion Primo Levi called these malevolent critics and commentators "Thieves of time . . . who insinuate themselves through keyholes and cracks and steal our memories without leaving a trace."

Was it better in the beginning when there were no such thieves, when few writers dared to approach the theme itself? When survivors themselves preferred to be mute since no one was willing to hear their tales which were considered "morbid"? Goodhearted people would interrupt them, giving them soothing counsel: "the past is past; forget it; better look tot he future . . ." Anyway, survivors forced themselves, or were forced, into silence, thinking: "What's the use? What we have to say, nobody would understand." Was Carlyle right in claiming that language belongs to time and silence to eternity? Must the ineffable remain outside the realm of words, simply because there are no words? Can Auschwitz be understood by anyone who wasn't there? Historians claim to be able to explain it, and in doing so only prove how far they are from understanding. Between facts and truth there is an abyss one may not cross with impunity. Only those who were there know what it meant to be there.

And yet. At one point, we all felt compelled to listen to Shimon Dubnov's last desperate plea and despairing appeal as he was led to his execution by a Gestapo chief, who was his former pupil: "*Yiden, shreibt ounfarshreibt*, Jews, write, write down everything." We decided to open up our memory and, within the framework of what is possible, to do the impossible. Is it because of the Holocaust deniers who now dominate so many websites with their repulsive stories and articles? No. They do not deserve such credit. We must never grant them the dignity of a debate. What they say is indecent and is to be ignored with disdain.

Lately, the attacks come from another directions—from Jews. Motivated by a senseless hatred of Israel, they try to de-legitimize its authority by depriving it from its memory. Then they slander those who defend it. One of them went so far as to write a preface to a book by the principal denier in Europe, Robert Faurisson. His disciple and ally published a frivolous pamphlet which became a bestseller in German-speaking countries because of its vicious attacks on Zionists and survivors; he calls them liars, profiteers, manipulators. In Germany, Martin Walser, seen as the Old Man of Letters, dared to declare publicly that he is sick of being reminded of Auschwitz. Ernest Nolte, who acquired notoriety by relativizing the Holocaust, received an important award that provoked shock on both sides of the Atlantic.

In many academic and literary circles, a taboo has been broken. Now everything goes. Nothing is off-limits. What used to be sacred is being commercialized, trivialized. Receiving a Tony award on a television show, watched by millions all over the world, a talented comedian found it permissible to say: "Thank you, Adolf Hitler" . . . then adding: "for being so funny on stage." Surely, to his victims, Hitler was many things, but never funny.

What then can the last survivors do but persevere? The task is getting harder and harder, more and more discouraging; we are all aware of that. But to abdicate, to abandon our memory, would be worse.

It would be treason.

About the Contributors

HENRY ABRAMSON is Dean for Academic Affairs and Student Services and Professor of Judaic Studies at Touro College South in Miami Beach. He is the author of *A Prayer for the Government: Ukrainians and Jews in Revolutionary Times, 1917–1920* (1999) and is currently working on a study of Hasidic life in the Warsaw Ghetto during the Holocaust.

ARNOLD J. BAND is Professor Emeritus of Hebrew and Comparative Literature at UCLA. He is the author of *Nostalgia and Nightmare: A Study in the Fiction of S. Y. Agnon* (1968); *The Tales of Nahman of Bratslav* (1978); and *Studies in Modern Jewish Literature* (2004).

ISRAEL BARTAL is Avraham Harman Professor of Jewish History, Director of the Center for Research on the History and Culture of Polish Jewry, and the academic chairman of the Project of Jewish Studies in Russian at the Hebrew University of Jerusalem. He also serves as the Co-Director of the Center for Jewish Studies and Civilization at Moscow State University. Since 1998 he has been the editor of *Vestnik*, a scholarly journal of Jewish studies in Russian. Among his publications are: *Exile in the Land* (1994); *From Corporation to Nation: The Jews of Eastern Europe, 1772–1881* (2002, 2005); *A Century of Israeli Culture* (editor, 2002); *Kehal Yisrael* Vol. 3 (editor, 2004); and *The Varieties of Haskalah* (editor, with Shmuel Feiner, 2005).

YEHUDA BAUER is Jonah M. Machover Professor Emeritus of Holocaust Studies at the Hebrew University of Jerusalem. For many years he was also the Director of the Institute of Contemporary Jewry at the Hebrew University. In 1998 he was awarded the Israel Prize, Israel's highest academic honor. He has also served as academic advisor to the International Task Force on the Holocaust that was created by the king of Sweden and is now sponsored by the European Union, and as Director of Research at Yad

Vashem. Among his many publications are: *Jews For Sale* (1994); *Rethinking the Holocaust* (2001); and *American Jewry and the Holocaust* (1981).

JEREMY DAUBER is the Atran Assistant Professor of Yiddish Language, Literature, and Culture at Columbia University. His first book, *Antonio's Devils: Writers of the Jewish Enlightenment and the Birth of Modern Hebrew and Yiddish Literature*, was published in 2004, and the anthology *Landmark Yiddish Plays*, co-translated and edited with Joel Berkowitz, will be published by SUNY Press in 2006.

IMMANUEL ETKES is Professor of Modern Jewish History at the Hebrew University of Jerusalem. He is also Director of the Dinur Center for Research in Jewish History at the Hebrew University and a member of the editorial board of *Zion*. He is the author of *Rabbi Israel Salanter and the Mussar Movement* (1993); *The Gaon of Vilna: The Man and His Image* (2002); and *The Besht: Magician, Mystic, and Leader* (2005).

GERSHON DAVID HUNDERT is Professor of History and Leanor Segal Professor of Jewish Studies at McGill University. His books include *Jews in Poland-Lithuania in the Eighteenth Century* (2004); *The Jews in a Polish Private Town* (1991); and *Essential Papers on Hasidism* (1991). He is Editor-in-Chief of the *YIVO Encyclopedia of Jews in Eastern Europe* to be published by Yale University Press in 2008.

SAMUEL KASSOW is Charles Northam Professor of History at Trinity College. He is the author of *Students, Professors and the State in Tsarist Russia: 1884–1917* (1989) and has co-edited *Between Tsar and People: The Search for Educated Society in Tsarist Russia* (1993). His study of the Polish-Jewish historian Emanuel Ringelblum will be published by Indiana University Press in 2007.

STEVEN T. KATZ, the editor of this volume, is Professor of Jewish Studies and Director of the Elie Wiesel Center for Judaic Studies at Boston University. Among his many publications are: *Post-Holocaust Dialogues* (1983), *Historicism, the Holocaust, and Zionism* (1992), and *The Holocaust in Historical Context*, Vol. 1 (1994), volumes 2-4 of this project are now in preparation and will be forthcoming from Oxford University Press. He is also the editor of *The Impact of the Holocaust on Jewish Thought* (2005), as well as the forthcoming anthology *Wrestling with God: Jewish Theological*

Responses to the Holocaust (2006). Among his other distinctions, he was awarded the Lucas Prize by the University of Tübingen in 1999.

MIKHAIL KRUTIKOV is Assistant Professor in Jewish-Slavic Cultural Relations at the University of Michigan. He is the author of *Yiddish Fiction and the Crisis of Modernity, 1905–1914* (2001) and co-editor of the three volumes of the *Proceedings of Mendel Friedman Annual Conference on Yiddish* (1999, 2000, and 2001). Krutikov also writes two weekly columns on European culture and politics for the Yiddish newspaper *Forverts*. Currently, he is editing the section on Modern Yiddish Literature for the forthcoming *YIVO Encyclopedia of Jews in Eastern Europe*.

NEHEMIA POLEN is Professor of Jewish Thought and director of the Hasidic Text Institute at Boston's Hebrew College. He is the author of *The Holy Fire: The Teachings of Rabbi Kalonymus Shapira, the Rebbe of the Warsaw Ghetto* (1994), and *The Rebbe's Daughter* (2002), which received the National Jewish Book Award. He is a contributing commentator to *My People's Prayer Book*, a multi-volume *Siddur* incorporating diverse perspectives on the liturgy. In 1994 he was a Daniel Jeremy Silver Fellow at Harvard University, and has also been a Visiting Scholar at the Hebrew University in Jerusalem. His most recent work (with Lawrence Kushner) is *Filling Words with Light: Hasidic and Mystical Reflections on Jewish Prayer* (2004).

NAOMI SEIDMAN is Koret Professor of Jewish Culture and Director of the Richard S. Dinner Center for Jewish Studies at the Graduate Theological Union in Berkeley. She is the author of *A Marriage Made In Heaven: The Sexual Politics of Hebrew and Yiddish* (1997) and of *Faithful Renderings: Jewish-Christian Difference and The Politics of Translation* (2006).

KATARZYNA WIĘCŁAWSKA was Teaching Assistant at the Centre for Jewish Studies of Maria Curie Sklodowska University in Lublin, Poland, where she designed educational programs to promote tolerance and introduce elements of Jewish history and culture into school syllabi. She wrote her doctoral dissertation on the shtetl motif in post-war Polish, Yiddish, and American literature. On August 14, 2004, at the age of 29, Katarzyna was killed together with her husband in a car accident. She is the author of "Shtetl Codes: Fantasy in the Fiction of Asch, Schulz, and I.B. Singer," *Polin: Studies in Polish Jewry*, Vol. 17 (2004); and "'The End of Reality is the

Beginning of Legend': Jewish Motifs in Contemporary Polish Fiction,"
East European Jewish Affairs, Vol. 34 (2004).

ELIE WIESEL is the Andrew W. Mellon Professor of the Humanities at
Boston University. He is the author of more than forty-five books, the
most recent being *The Time of the Uprooted*, a novel. He received the
Nobel Peace Prize in 1986 and the Presidential Medal of Freedom in 1985.
A new edition of his classic Holocaust memoir, *Night*, translated by Mar-
ion Wiesel, appeared in 2005.

KONRAD ZIELIŃSKI is Assistant Professor of Politics at the Center for
Ethnic Research at Maria Curie Sklodowski University in Lublin, Poland,
where he teaches modern Jewish history and culture. He is the author of
*In the Shadow of Synagogue: The Image of the Jewish Cultural Life in Lublin
during the Austrian-Hungarian Occupation* (1998); *The Jews of the Lublin
Region, 1914–1918* (1999); *Yeshivah Khakhme Lublin* (2003); and *Polish-Jewish Relationships in the Kingdom of Poland during World War I* (2005). He is
also co-editor of *Orthodoxy—Emancipation—Assimilation: Studies on the
History of the Jewish Population during the Partition of Poland* (2003).

Index

Aaron the Great of Karlin, Rabbi, 66, 297

Aaron the Second of Stolin, Rabbi, 66

Abramovitch, Sholem Yankev (aka Mendele), 140, 151, 163–73, 149, 193; author of *The Brief Travels of Benjamin the Third* (1878), 18, 196; author of *Fishke the Lame*, 163–73; author of *The Mare*, 163; death of, 213; author of *In the Days of the Earthquake* (1894), 196; and *Haskalah*, 163, 172; on Jews and nature, 178n. 43; Kabtsansk (fictional town), 213; Mendele novels, 213; parody in *Benjamin the Third*, 200–201

Abrams, M. H., and discussion of metaphor, 152

Adam, Rabbi, 143

Agnon, Shmuel Yosef, 24, 212, 229, 233–42; author of "Agunot" (1908), 203; author of "Bidemi Yameha" (1923), 238; author of "Bine'urenu uvizkenenu" (1920), 238; author of *Hakhnasat Kallah* (1929–30), 238; author of "Ma'ase Ha'ez," 241; author of *Oreah Hata Lalun* (1938–39), 238; author of *Sippur Pashut* (1935), 238; author of "Vehaya he'akov Lemishor," 235, 237, 239–40; Buczacz (birthplace), 24, 238; compared to S. Aleichem, 237; compared to Mendele, 237; compared to J. L. Peretz, 237; criticism of Mendele,

233–34; image of the shtetl, 24, 234–42; image of WWI, 238; theme of *agunah* as symbol, 203–4, 209n. 23; use of Hebrew language, 235, 240–41; use of Jewish history, 239–40

Agudat Yisroel, 128; cooperation with artisan groups, 130; percentage of vote, 255; in Poland in 1930s, 255

agunah, the, 21, 196; S. Y. Agnon on, 203–4; Dvora Baron on, 203–4; in *The Brief Travels of Benjamin the Third*, 200–202; as metaphor, 194–95; D. Miron on, 194–96; in shtetl, 194–95

Akhdes, 97

Akiva, Rabbi, 144

Aksenfeld, Yisroel, 7, 18, 20, 141–63; and Abramovitch, 172; author of *Dos Shterntikhl* (*The Headband*), 158; criticism of Hasidism, 162; on theme of *bes medresh*, 160; on theme of garden, 160; on theme of the ninth of Av, 161

Alcholic beverages, Jews and, 3

Aleichem, Sholom (Sholem, Sholam). *See* Sholom Aleichem

Alexander II, Tsar, 85

Algemayne Tzionisten (General Zionists), 93

Alter, Victor, 126

America, 87, 98; Mary Antin, 87–89, 90; immigration to, 87–88, 91; Jewish socialists in, 98